Captain Peter Hore retired from the Royal Navy in 2000, having served worldwide, mainly in frigates and destroyers, including exchange service in the United States Navy and two tours of duty in NATO's Standing Naval Force Atlantic. During the Falklands War he was the Joint Logistics Commander on Ascension Island. Uniquely, he has helped to direct the Royal Navy's applied research programme, and has headed its non-technical research programme. His last appointment in uniform was as Head of Defence Studies during the British government's Strategic Defence Review.

He is a trustee of the Naval Review and of the Royal Naval Museum Portsmouth, and chairman of the research, technical and programmes committee of the council of the Society of Nautical Research. He is the editor of author of numerous articles and books including Dimensions of Sea Power: Strategy in Change (1996), Maritime Aviation in the 21st Century (1999), Sea Power Ashore: 200 Years of Extraordinary Royal Navy Operations (2001), HMAS Sydney: The Cruiser and the Controversy (2001); and Patrick Blackett: Sailor, Scientist and Socialist (2002). Peter is also a writer of naval obituaries for the Daily Telegraph.

The National Maritime Museum is the largest of its type in the world. It aims to promote and illustrate the importance of the sea, ships, time and the stars and their relationship with people. Situated in Greenwich, London, and incorporating both the historic Queen's House and the Royal Observatory, Greenwich, the Museum contains nearly 2.5 million items. It attracts 1.2 million visitors a year and since 1997 has been part of the UNESCO Maritime Greenwich World Heritage Site.

# THE HABIT OF

# VICTORY

## *The Story of the Royal Navy*
## *1545 to 1945*

### CAPTAIN PETER HORE

PAN BOOKS

NATIONAL MARITIME MUSEUM

≋

First published 2005 by Sidgwick & Jackson

This paperback edition published 2006 by Pan Books
an imprint of Pan Macmillan Ltd
Pan Macmillan, 20 New Wharf Road, London N1 9RR
Basingstoke and Oxford
Associated companies throughout the world
www.panmacmillan.com

ISBN-13: 978-0-330-49171-6
ISBN-10: 0-330-49171-7

1 3 5 7 9 8 6 4 2

A CIP catalogue record for this book is available from
the British Library.

Typeset by SetSystems Ltd, Saffron Walden, Essex
Printed and bound in Great Britain by
Mackays of Chatham plc, Chatham, Kent

# Preface

History will surely judge the Royal Navy as a world-class institution, one which has affected the course of history itself. Over the five hundred years or so of its existence – the exact length is, as we shall see, debatable – the Royal Navy has played a prominent role at almost every level of British and international culture, strategy, discovery, and technology, and has amassed a rich heritage. It has built a heritage in which other navies are proud to participate and to which many more aspire. Large parts of the globe were colonized by English-speaking people, free trade developed, the Monroe doctrine flourished, slave traffic was stopped, and the oceans were charted and the knowledge gained was made readily available for the benefit of all. In breadth of achievement the Royal Navy compares to the Roman legions and its successes exceeded the grand armies of France. On these grounds alone any examination of such a successful organization must be worth study.

There are already many histories of the Royal Navy, such as William Laird Clowes' magisterial *The Royal Navy: a History from the Earliest Times to 1900*, and William James' six-volume *The Naval History of Great Britain*, which concentrates on the French Revolutionary and Napoleonic Wars, and both of these great works have been recently reprinted. The Royal Navy even publishes its own history on a website. There is also a three-volume naval history of Britain by Professor Nicholas Rodger, the first and second volumes of which, partly sponsored by the National Maritime Museum, have been published.

This book, however, is not a history, and does not attempt to replace any of the cited works. Nor is it an anthology, though I have tried to select some of the best extracts, nor an encyclopaedia, which would be a very much larger work. Rather it is an attempt to tell a story in which the Royal Navy itself is the hero, and to illuminate that story with words from documents in the rich archive of the National Maritime Museum, Greenwich. Here you will find the words of monarchs and masters, mariners and their mistresses. In some cases I have selected the words of admirals and captains who commanded events, in others I have focused on the eyewitness accounts of ordinary sailors. In transcribing various documents from manuscript to type-script I have tried as far as possible to preserve the original spelling (often highly original) and punctuation (accepted universal rules are a recent imposition), except where absolutely necessary to help the reader make sense of the words.

One of the aims of this telling of the story of the Royal Navy is to advertise the variety and wealth of the resources available at Greenwich and to provide a means of publishing some documents which on their own might otherwise never justify even a monograph. I have tried to write a broad-based story which moves away from the so-called 'quarterdeck' or admirals' view of history to one in which many, including seamen and marines, can help to tell the story of the Royal Navy. Generally the story has been told chronologically, even if this means some overlap. I have dealt at length with some individual topics, where the particular can be used to demonstrate the general, but space has not permitted every episode over four hundred years to be explored. The reader is asked to accept that in some cases one episode stands representative for many. For example, the problems of invading England from the sea which were set out by King Philip's advisers remained the same in subsequent centuries for Napoleon and for Hitler. Charles Middleton's innovatory approach to coppering sailing ships is an example of the Navy's ready acceptance of new technologies, which in this case gave it a tactical, operational and strategic advantage which helped win a war. The nearly contemporary but contrasting careers of Albert Markham and Walter Cowan must represent all those officers who served during the same period. There are of course plenty of tales of battles but many, including the great Battle of Trafalgar, are told through the words of ordinary seamen – though I hope that the reader will agree there was nothing ordinary about these men. If space had permitted I would have liked to have included a chapter about the wives and mistresses of these men, of which there are plenty of examples in the archives.

Nearly every quotation has been culled from the archives, but occasionally, I also have used the Society for Nautical Research's magazine *Mariner's Mirror* and the volumes of the Navy Records Society, of which there are full sets in the library, and in a few places I have taken in quotations from books, all of them, of course, in the library. The latter are acknowledged in the bibliography, which is also intended to be a succinct reading list for anyone wishing to delve further. The books are relevant, modern and, most of them, easily accessible.

The reader who wishes to know more should consult the Caird Library Catalogue of the National Maritime Museum, which is available online on the Web, and then visit the library, where there is a patient, cheerful, knowledgeable, expert team of people to help.

I wish to thank: Ruddock F. Mackay and Michael Duffy, who at the beginning and end of my uniformed career tried to teach me naval history; Alastair MacLeod, who proposed this project to me, Jane Ace and Rachel Giles, Brian Lavery, Daphne Knott and Jill Davies and their staffs, and everyone at the National Maritime Museum who assisted me; William Armstrong, Ingrid Connell and Nicholas Blake of Macmillan, who have encouraged me over many months; and very many others, friends and colleagues, too many to name individually, who have read and commented on parts of the manuscript and also answered, sometimes by late-night phone call or overnight e-mail, obscure questions and queries.

I am most grateful to family and friends who have tolerated my unusual hours during the preparation of this work.

PGH
*Rotherhithe*
*April 2004*

## Picture Acknowledgements

All images reproduced in this book are © National Maritime Museum, London.

Images and prints featured in this book may be ordered from the Picture Library, National Maritime Museum, Greenwich, London, SE10 9NF (tel: 020 8312 6600). Please quote the reference number listed next to the picture caption (e.g. BHC 2786). For further information, please contact the Picture Library's website at www.nmm.ac.uk/picturelibrary.

The following images come from special named collections in the National Maritime Museum, London:
BHC 2786 Greenwich Hospital Collection;
BHC 4227 Acquired with the assistance of the National Heritage Memorial Fund;
BHC 2957 Ministry of Defence Art Collection;
BHC 0498 Greenwich Hospital Collection;
BHC 0634 Greenwich Hospital Collection.

# Contents

# Chapter One

# Our owne Navie of Shippes

For an island like Britain the sea is pervasive, reaching, before metalled roads and wheeled transport, towns and villages which today would not be thought of as ports. The same sea connecting inland harbours was a highway for ships trading to Scandinavia, the Netherlands, France, Spain and Ireland, and through the Mediterranean to the Holy Lands. Ships needed crews for, as Richard Hakluyt wrote in his sixteenth-century *Principal Navigations, Voyages, Traffiques, and Discoveries of the English Nation*, 'ships are to little purpose without skilful seamen', and the British Isles provided generations of skilful seamen.

To turn ships and seamen into a navy there must be a distinct pattern of operations. In medieval times battle at sea was little different to fighting on land, and naval warfare meant ramming and boarding other ships, or transporting and landing invasion forces. There were a few exceptions: the Battle of South Foreland in 1217 was probably the first occasion on which a fleet sailed to gain the weather gage (to be between the wind and the enemy). At the Battle of Sluys in 1340 Edward III manoeuvred his ships to take advantage of the tide and sun, writing afterwards to his son, the Black Prince,

> Very dear son ... On the Saturday, St John's Day, soon after noon, in the name of God, we entered and attacked our enemies who had assembled their ships in strong array and offered noble defence. The number of the ships, galleys and barges of our enemies amounted to 190, all but 24 of which were taken. Their men-at-arms numbered 35,000 of which 5,000 escaped and the remainder are lying dead off the coast ...

This letter is probably the very earliest English naval despatch. Sluys may not have been decisive in the war but it helped to associate, as the historian Laird Clowes wrote, 'the image of national glory and military success with victory at sea'.

The first officer to be recognized as captain of the king's sailors and mariners, under Edward I, was Sir William de Leybourne, who in 1297 was styled Admiral of the Sea of the King of England. Admiral was originally an Arabic word; the officers were captains and lieutenants, their titles derived from Norman French, and the masters, boatswains, coxswains, cooks and pursers derived their names from Old English.

Integral to the possession and successful operation of a navy is some idea of its purpose, which Adam de Moleyns (or Molyneux), Bishop of Chichester, addressed in *The Libelle of Englyshe Polycye*, written in English sometime around 1436. He exhorted a policy to 'cheryshe marchandise, kepe thamyralte, that we be maysteres of the narowe sea' and to 'kepe the see environ and namely the narowe see shewynge whate worships, profite and salvacione commeth thereof'. These words were repeated down the centuries and have come to us in their latest form as a robust declaration in the preamble to the Royal Navy's *Articles of War*, that it is upon the navy whereon, under the good Providence of God, the wealth, safety and strength of the kingdom chiefly depend.

## THE TUDORS

During the Middle Ages English seafarers had fished off Iceland, and traded and raided there. The teeming fisheries of the North Atlantic seem to have been known and folk memories of islands and land further to the west may have circulated; the Azores were known about, and expeditions had sailed to find the rumoured island of Brazil. Then at the end of the fifteenth century came news of Christopher Columbus's fabulous discovery of, as it was thought, a westward route to China. A Genoese, John Cabot, who had settled in Bristol, persuaded Henry VII to sponsor the voyage of the *Matthew*, little larger than a modern-day Thames barge, and her crew of eighteen men in 1497. The place Cabot reached on St John's Day 1497 was not Asia, but part of America, forever to be known as New-found-land. There were no gold or jewels such as

Columbus and his followers were reputed to have found, but instead a larder of fish which would last five hundred years. The trade which developed in exporting dried fish from North America to Europe became a school for seamen and, in search of markets, English ships began trading to the Mediterranean. Such was the speed of the spread of information about these finds that by 1500 a Spanish map showed the flag of St George on the coast of North America, from Cape Breton to Cape Hatteras.

Henry VII had ventured just £10 on Cabot's first voyage, but he deserves the credit for laying the foundations of English naval power. Portsmouth was just one among many towns and cities, like the Cinque Ports and Southampton, in which to find sailors and ships and from which to mount naval expeditions, but by ordering in 1496 a dock to be built there, Henry ensured that it would eventually become the principal naval port of Britain. He also founded, in Bristol in 1505, 'The Mysterie and Company of Marchant Adventurers for the Discoverie of Regions, Dominions, Islands and Places Unknowen'.

## HENRY VIII

The small fleet which Henry VIII inherited from his father was distinctly medieval, the two largest vessels being the four-masted carracks *Regent* and the *Sovereign*, both completed between 1488 and 1490. Yet in the year before Henry VIII's death the Anthony Roll listed fifty-eight ships. The King's favourite ship was the *Red* or *English Galley*, though his most famous ship is the *Mary Rose*, which capsized in the King's view while repelling a French invasion attempt. The career of the *Jesus of Lubeck* was typical of the era: the four-masted *Jesus* measured 520 tons and was armed, in the 1530s, with guns of brass and iron as well as numerous 'bowes of yough' and smaller weapons, and carried '118 souldiours, 158 marrynars and 24 gonnars'. She had been hired from the Hanse town of Lübeck in 1544, the following year she was bought outright, and she then survived into the reign of his daughter Elizabeth I, when the Queen lent, or hired, the *Jesus* to John Hawkins, and she was seized by the Spanish at San Juan de Ulloa in 1568.

Henry paid some attention to the administration of his navy, and in about 1540 he set up an early Navy Board: 'in the said Kings latter times ye warrs and dooings growing great he established ye Treasurer ye Comptroller ye Surveyor and ye Clarke of ye Shipps ... these four officers are a Counsell which upon meeting do Consider what is needfull to be done for ye furtherance of ye Prince's ships', a system which survived more or less in similar form until recent times. Henry VIII also established, in 1513, 'The Guild of the Holy and Undivided Trinity and St Clement, at Deptford Strond' – in other words, Trinity House. At first Trinity House was used to examine the professional qualifications of officers and petty officers and to provide seamen for the navy, but soon it concentrated its duties on setting up beacons and daymarks and eventually lighthouses, buoyage, and pilotage.

## THE FIRST EXPLORERS

The journeys of exploration which were inspired by Cabot's transatlantic crossing soon became annual affairs: Bristol was pre-eminent, but these journeys were a national effort, with ships sailing from ports such as Dartmouth, London and Hull to explore the different routes. The North-East Passage via the coasts of Norway and Russia was tried and eventually abandoned. However, Richard Chancellor, who had sailed from Deptford to find a passage to China in 1553–56, returned overland from Archangel to Moscow, having greeted Ivan the Terrible with a message from Elizabeth I, and founded the Muscovy Company.

To the west, America inconveniently barred the route to China, but for generations men sought a route via the North-West Passage, a fabled ice-free route past the top of North America. Men like Sir Humphrey Gilbert, soldier, explorer, and in 1583 the founder of the first English colony in North America, argued that the discovery of this passage was the only way to become masters of the wealth of the East. Gilbert wrote the script for all who were to come after him: 'He is not worthy to live at all, that for feare, or danger of death, shunneth his countrie's service, and his own honour: seeing death is inevitable and fame of vertue imortall . . .' That archetypal

Elizabethan seadog, pirate, and patriot Martin Frobisher made three voyages to the north-west, in 1576–78. On his first voyage bad weather soon reduced his small squadron to the *Gabriel* (30 tons and a handful of men), in which he pressed on until he discovered a strait ten miles wide. He entered, thinking it was the northern version of the Magellan Straits, but 120 miles further to the north-west it shoaled into the shore. It was the first of many false leads. However, his discovery of ore, thought to be black gold, turned this voyage and the two subsequent ones into mining and colonizing ventures. The several hundred tons of worthless rock which he brought back are now incorporated into the old Dartford Priory.

John Davis, one of a remarkable group of Tudor seamen born on or near the River Dart in Devon, and a pioneering navigator and author of several treatises, made three more attempts to find the North-West Passage, in 1585–87. On his third voyage he reached 72° N; he proved Cumberland Sound to be another dead end, but he suspected the presence of another strait. In 1607–9 Henry Hudson made three voyages into the Barents Sea, still searching for the North-East Passage and reaching 80° 23′ N, a furthest north which was not bettered until 1773. Then, frustrated off Novaya Zemlya, he crossed the North Atlantic to explore a vast river, thinking that it might be the entrance to the North-West Passage, and named it after himself. Since he had sailed under Dutch colours, this gave the Dutch a claim to the New World and led to the founding of a colony called Nieuw Amsterdam, now New York. On a fourth voyage, in 1610, he found a new sea and wintered his ship, *Discovery*, there. His previous voyages had been marked by mutiny and this followed a predictable pattern: sometime in early 1611 he was cast adrift and abandoned by his crew. In the following year the sea he had discovered was shown by Thomas Button to be a large bay: Hudson's Bay.

Despite mutiny and murder, Hudson's second-in-command, Robert Bylot, was given command of expeditions to the north in 1615 and 1616 with William Baffin as his mate. In their first season they explored Hudson Strait, then in 1616 a temporary warming of the climate thinned the ice and allowed them to sail through the Davis Strait into Baffin Bay. Their orders were to sail to 80° N and then turn west for Japan: remarkably they reached 77° 45′ N and found a strait, which they named for one of their sponsors, Alderman Jones, but the cold defeated them. Sailing anti-clockwise round Baffin Bay, a path which subsequent explorers were to follow, they named several bays and sounds, including one after another sponsor, Sir Thomas Lancaster: unwittingly they had seen the start of the route to Japan. In subsequent years the climate grew colder and it was some two hundred years before British eyes saw the same headlands and frozen land and seascape. By the time Baffin died in 1622 on another voyage of trade and exploration, to the Straits of Hormuz, at the entrance of the Persian Gulf, English trade and exploration had become a global affair.

There were many other voyages on which men perished and others left their names in the Arctic, for example Luke Fox, who sailed from Hull in the *Charles* (80 tons, with a crew of twenty-two men and boys), and Thomas James of the *Henrietta Maria* in a similar vessel from Bristol. Their voyages in 1631–32 illustrate the continuing rivalry between the English ports, and the small size of the ships and crews who made these intrepid adventures into the unknown. Fox entered what is now Fox Basin and returned home in one season. James wintered on the south coast of Hudson's Bay and returned in 1632: James, at least, concluded that if the North-West Passage existed it would be narrow and choked with ice.

## THE QUEEN PAYS HER NAVY

Elizabeth I inherited an empty treasury, though one of the earliest surviving Elizabethan naval documents in the archives of the National Maritime Museum refers to shipbuilding and wages for the seamen of her navy, and was written by 'Elyzabeth by the grace of god Quene of England France and Ireland Defendor of the faythe etc' less than six weeks after the death of her half-sister Queen Mary in 1588. One can almost hear the Queen gritting her teeth as she instructed her 'tresysourer and Chamberlains of oure chequier' to release money for the navy. It was her

will and commaund yow . . . of our treasure remayning in your custody . . . paye or cause to be pajed to our servaunt Beniamin

Gonson treasourer of our marine affaires two thowsand pounds toward payment of suche charges as hathe bin susteyned as well in the narrow Seas with xiij [8] barkes and vjc [600] men servinge us there who be owinge wages from the first day of October last as also of diverse artificers and workemen now making two oure Shippes at Portesmouth and Woulwidge ... And thies our letteres shal be your sufficient waraunt ...

Two thousand pounds was huge amount of money in those days, and the navy was a cost which somehow the Queen had to avoid or defray, if she could.

Naval rivalry with Spain became a feature of her reign, and lasted for the next two and half centuries. A papal bull in 1493 had divided the New World between Portugal and Spain, who then negotiated the Treaty of Tordesillas in 1494 to exclude other nations from South America – and since the trade winds carried sailing ships to the New World, where they needed to victual and water before heading to the East Indies, effectively bar them from the rest of the world too. Despite official disapproval by the Spanish authorities at home, the Spanish colonists in South America needed the goods which Dutch, French, and, of course, English ships could bring from northern Europe or from West Africa. In 1562 John Hawkins made the first of a series of triangular voyages from England to Africa to the Americas and back, the sad cargo on the journey across the Atlantic being slaves to work in the Spanish and Portuguese colonies. Then in 1568 a storm forced Hawkins to take shelter in the port of San Juan de Ulloa, on the Mexican coast, under a flag of truce. Shortly afterwards the annual treasure fleet from Spain arrived and Hawkins, greatly outnumbered, was surprised and attacked. Many of his expedition were killed or taken prisoner but Hawkins and his young cousin Francis Drake escaped, abandoning the flagship, *Jesus of Lubeck*, in which Elizabeth I had a commercial interest. Elizabeth I accepted her part of the loss but would not risk war with Spain, despite the outcry for revenge.

## FRANCIS DRAKE

Francis Drake came from a fiercely Protestant West Country family whose poverty had driven him to sea, as apprentice to his cousin John Hawkins. He was a brilliant navigator, the first English seaman to circumnavigate the globe, the first commander to survive a circumnavigation, and quite simply one of history's greatest seamen. It is hard, however, to say which of his seagoing activities were trade, slaving, piracy, privateering, or regular service in the Queen's navy. He was in his mid-thirties, and had already spent more than half his life at sea, when in 1579 he captured a Spanish treasure ship in the Pacific, the *Cacafuego*, or *Spitfire* as her name is always politely translated. Then with his ship, *Golden Hind*, so heavily laden with treasure that she had gold and silver bullion for ballast, he turned northward, hoping to find the Pacific exit of the North-West Passage. His action turned what might have been a pirate adventure into the greatest maritime achievement of the century. He had already discovered Cape Horn; now he charted some five hundred miles of the California coast, ranging further north along the American seaboard than any European had before. He refitted his ship in June and July in northern California, probably a little to the northward of the present-day San Francisco, where he was crowned with feathers by the natives. He then started his sixteen-thousand-mile return voyage, first crossing the Pacific in two months without sight of land.

## THE CAMPAIGN OF THE ARMADA

During Elizabeth I's reign England and Spain drifted into war. While Philip II of Spain attempted to put down Protestantism in the Spanish Netherlands and to preserve his monopolies in the newly discovered lands, Elizabeth I waged war by proxy, helping the rebels in Flanders with men and money, and allowing her seamen to trade, as pirates or privateers, on voyages to the East and West Indies in which she often had a commercial share. Then when Philip seized the throne of Portugal in 1580, all the South Atlantic trade routes fell into the hands of a single monarch. The scene was set for open war.

A Spanish letter giving advice upon an invasion of England is quoted here at length because, with changes of causes and times, it is a template of all other invasion plans for the next four centuries, and one of the first essays in naval strategy.

In this case, it was 'very necessary for completing the pacification and reduction . . . of the States of Flanders and for safeguarding the Indies and their trade, apart from the service which would be rendered to Our Lord in extirpating the heresies of that Kingdom [England]'. There were several courses of action open to the King: he might 'form an alliance with the French [and] once the kingdom had been won . . . might then throw out the French and retain all the spoils'; he might make 'an alliance with the Pope, who should assist with men and money, and proclaim a crusade . . . and attempt to come to an understanding with the English Catholics, so that they would rebel against the Queen'; he might 'make an agreement with the King of Scotland, offering to place him in possession of England and to marry him to a member of the House of Austria'. In any case, 'the extirpation of the heresies of England and vengeance for the death of the Queen of Scots should be adopted as a war-cry; the same understanding with the English Catholics and the favour of the Pope should be obtained, and Monsieur de Guise [the King of France], being so closely related to the Queen of Scots, should give his support so that France would not interfere'.

However, the King's advisers urged him to make the expedition alone. He could get ready 'the whole of the equipment for the attack . . . with great secrecy, giving out that the preparations were being made for other reasons'. The expedition could even be directed first 'against Ireland [where] the Irish would rebel against the Queen on the slightest pretext as they have done at other times . . . and if His Majesty did not wish to continue the war, the Queen of England would exchange for Ireland all that she holds in Flanders, Holland and Zealand'.

Fifty thousand men would be needed, of whom 'twelve or fifteen thousand of them [would] remain at sea in order to be masters of it and to have safety for the ships'. The King's advisers' knowledge of geography was rather poor and they suggested 'the rest would disembark and land at Dover, which is the nearest stronghold to the Thames. This, being weak, could be taken in two days and in another two, the castles which are higher up at the mouth of the river, along which the Armada would be able to advance on London'. In order to keep a check on the rebels in Flanders and prevent 'the King of France ... making a diversion through Burgundy, Italy or Spain', the King should 'have a good number of German cavalry and infantry ... and a reasonable army in Flanders'. The expedition had international dimensions and friendly alliances would be needed 'with the King of Poland (so that he would allow wheat and other commodities to be sent from Dantzig for the provisioning of the Armada), with the King of Denmark (so that he would permit these goods to pass through his Sound) and with all the Baltic states, which would be able to help with many things'. However, the French were dismissed as unreliable allies 'because they have always been, and will be suspect as friends, and with their pride and arrogance, once the affair was finished they would want to keep everything ... [and] neither Flanders nor even the Indies would be secure, because the French would doubtless become masters of the sea'.

The Spaniards thought that Elizabeth would

> without any difficulty ... arm fifty to sixty or more large ships experienced in those waters, well provided with sailors servants and troops. The low countries will be able to fit out a similar number to make a bold attack and to maintain twenty or twenty five for a long time if necessary. Up to a certain point, France can also maintain as many as she wishes, as nearly all the naval forces she has are in those seas. Thus, with the ships belonging to the English and with those of their allies, there will be a large number fit for battle, because in all these parts they make a profession of seamanship and exercise it continually, and they will have the convenience of withdrawing into friendly ports of France, Holland or Zealand where they can provide themselves with everything they may need ... [So] having to land in England a sufficient number of soldiers to conquer it, and having to remain with forces to resist the above-mentioned quantity and quality of ships, [the Armada] cannot consist of less than a hundred and fifty large vessels which His Majesty

does not possess. New ones would have to be built, or ships taken at a very great cost of time and labour from those which navigate from many parts to the Indies, and this would not be convenient.

The King was bluntly warned that his ships

would not be of equal use with those of the enemy in that sea because in any case they would not have sailed so much in it and there would be a lack of good mariners who understood it. His Majesty's Armada would have to be subjected to every storm and tempest without having a shelter port or friend to turn to in time of need, for everything would be against it. Thus it would go in evident and grave danger of being lost.

Philip's advisers showed a clear understanding of the advantages of a sea-based, or maritime, strategy over a continental one, even if their advice to so mighty a monarch was couched in very cautious and polite terms. It would be better if the resources such as the Armada would require were applied to maintaining a fleet at sea. The King

should have some ships of the fleet in the ocean, to stop the English pirates. Experience has shewn that they did not dare to be so brazen and to cross the route to the Indies until His Majesty's galleons which sailed in it had been removed. If His Majesty had mastery of the sea and were to take away from Holland and Zealand the commerce of their States, making cruel war on them from Flanders, necessity would reduce them to his service by force, as they can neither live nor sustain themselves without the commerce and trade which they have freely in Spain and wherever they wish, for there is not a single ship in the sea belonging to His Majesty to curb and to stop them.

There was to be little change in this essay on sea power or the strategic and logistical difficulties of invading England, and although his advisers had told him bluntly of the risks, the King of Spain was determined upon war.

## SINGEING THE KING OF SPAIN'S BEARD

The English were aware of the King's preparations, and in April 1587 Francis Drake made a pre-emptive raid which became known as the singeing of the King of Spain's beard. With Spanish ships gathering in Mediterranean and Atlantic ports, Drake reported the raid on Cadiz in straightforward language:

> knowing that you, amongst many of my good friends, are desirous to hear of our proceedings in this action, I have thought good to satisfy your expectation with this short advertisement. You shall understand that ... we arrived at Cadiz, where, finding divers huge ships loaden and to be loaden with the King's provision for England ... we burnt 32, and sank a great argosy, and carried away four with us. We remained in the Road two days, in which time twelve of the King's galleys sundry times encountered us; in which fights we sank two of them, repulsing the residue with very little loss on our parts. Howbeit the ordnance from the shore vehemently thundered at us during our abode there, and the power of the whole country, being raised, resorted in great numbers to their succour, yet (thanked be God) we went thence, in despite of them all, with great honour, being at our departure courteously written unto by one Don Pedro, general of those galleys ...

The expedition had strategic objectives, and Drake added:

> Now being well furnished with necessary provision, our intent is (God willing) to impeach the fleet which is to come out of the Straits and divers other places before it join in with the King's forces, in the accomplishment whereof neither willing minds or industry shall be wanting. For want of time I leave the report at large of this good success unto this bearer, and thus in much haste do bid you heartily farewell. From aboard her Majesty's good ship the *Elizabeth Bonaventure*, the 27th of April, 1587.

He signed himself 'Yours, very willing to be commanded, Francis Drake', which coming from that inveterate rule-breaker must be seen as a rather heavy joke.

Like other Elizabethan expeditions, there was always hope that the capture of booty would make it self-financing, and in 1587 Drake had not only gained valuable intelligence about Spanish plans and set back the invasion of England by a year, but was able to victual his ships from his enemy's stores. There was so much captured provisions that he was able to send home nearly three thousand barrels of sack. This sack was probably sherry, strong, long-lasting and well suited for taking on long sea voyages: both Columbus and Magellan had drunk it on their voyages. Now, through celebratory drinking, it became fashionable in London.

Drake was determined to disrupt the reinforcements which were flowing from Spanish provinces and possessions in the Mediterranean, and attacked the forts defending Lagos road. Here for centuries ships leaving the Mediterranean had made the jutting promontory of Cape St Vincent their landfall and waited for a favourable wind. Drake took a convoy assembled there and as more ships arrived he captured these too. The dislocation was such that troops for the Armada had to land at Cartagena and take an overland route across Spain. Then, on the rumour of a treasure ship homeward-bound from the East Indies, Drake decided on a cruise to the Azores. The weather disrupted his run of luck, dispersing his fleet over the seas between St Vincent and the port of San Miguel, but when he made his landfall in June 1587, the treasure ship *San Felipe* seemed to have been set in the sea to wait for him. She was then the largest ship in the world, and she was about to become the richest prize. According to the historian Julian Corbett, 'in her hold were hundreds of tons of spices and precious gums; chests upon chests of costly china, bales of silks and velvets, and coffers of bullion and jewels'. She was eventually valued at £114,000: the Queen, who had a large commercial share in the expedition, had found a way to make her navy pay for itself.

Papers seized on board the *San Felipe* disclosed all the long-held secrets of the East Indies trade, and the capture was claimed to have inspired London merchants to found the East India Company, which eventually led to the foundation of the British Empire in India. So in 1591, James Lancaster sailed to explore and trade in the East Indies, returning in 1594. In 1600, the East India Company was given by royal charter a monopoly of trade with the

East Indies, and the company's first ships soon sailed for India. Meanwhile, in 1598 William Adams, who had sailed under Drake, was shipwrecked in a Dutch ship in Japan, where he intrigued the Japanese about ocean navigation and inspired the latter-day novelist James Clavell to write *Shogun*.

However, by the high summer of 1587, when the King's own orders and counter-orders and the simple fear of where Drake might appear next had paralysed the Spanish war effort, Drake was home in England.

## FOUR LETTERS OF PHILIP II OF SPAIN

The Spanish war effort continued nevertheless, and by the summer of 1588 the bulk of the Armada had reached Corunna in north-west Spain. No adequate logistic infrastructure existed for it there, and even before leaving its friendly harbours the fleet and the embarked troops had begun to suffer. The King was worried. By July it was already too late to make a difference, but Andrés de Alva, the King's secretary, was given a commission for the

> superintendence of the provision of supplies and of all persons concerned in it of whatever rank both on the coast and inland in Spain and Portugal. I command all such persons to carry out his instructions. I authorize him to take all necessary steps including requisitioning of goods, chartering of ships, appoint-ment of subordinate officers, etc. without further instructions. I charge the Marquis de Cerralvo, Governor of Galicia, and all local justices and officials and citizens to give Andrés de Alva all assistance that he requires.

The King had also learned that 'there has been much loss and damage to the provisions carried in the Armada, so that its success is endangered, and whereas such damage cannot have occurred without blame on the part of the persons responsible for provision-ing'. Alva was given a second commission: 'to enquire into the quantity and quality of the provisions taken on board in Andalusia, Biscay and Lisbon, and into the causes and extent of the damage and deterioration which have taken place'.

Most importantly, the King realized that the Armada would consume food, and stores, whether it was in harbour or at sea, and so Alva was made his personal emissary:

> You are to proceed as quickly as possible to Corunna, and to hand your letter of credentials to the Duke of Medina Sidonia and inform him of my solicitude for the proper provisioning of the fleet and of your appointment for this purpose. You are to convey to the Duke my wish that the fleet should set out as soon as possible. The Duke is to take on to his own ship persons well qualified in navigation and in fighting to advise him.

The King, who liked to deal personally in the minutiae of affairs, also realized the need to delegate:

> You are to visit all the ships and inspect their supplies; to see how much food is required to feed the men while in port; how much should be embarked and how much sent on after the fleet, and diligently to attend to its provision. Your experience in such matters makes detailed instructions unnecessary. 20,000 ducats will be placed at your disposal, and all persons concerned in the provision of victuals are to obey your orders. You are to stay in Corunna as long as the fleet is there and as long after as is necessary for the despatch of provisions, unless you find some other place more convenient for the purpose.

He could not help adding: 'You are to report fully and regularly on everything you do'.

## ENGLISH PREPARATIONS

In England preparations were as just as unsure. The Queen did at least send her 'Threasurers and Chamberlaynes of our Exchequeur greeting' and tell them that 'we have resolved for the Surety and defence of our Realme to have our owne Navie of Shippes and vesselles imployed on the Seaes'. It was November 1587, the sums of money she authorized to be spent were small enough, and, indeed, her navy of ships was small compared to the Armada which King Philip continued to prepare.

To augment the fleet the Queen needed men and ships to be taken from trade, and letters were sent to all ports. Typical of the replies was the letter from the Mayor of Exeter in April 1588, who had been asked 'for the setting forth of three ships and a pinnace, to attend on Sir Francis Drake'. The mayor

> caused a present view to be taken of all our shipping, but found none left fit for that service, saving two only bound for Newfoundland, which were gotten out of the haven, and being still upon the coast are now stayed for this purpose; which ships being of good burden, Sir Francis Drake, whom we have made it known unto accepteth, rather than three others of lesser portage.

However, he thought that other ports should be asked to assist the war effort:

> by reason your Honours' letters are directed only to Exeter and Topsham, all the rest of the places and creeks belonging to the Port of Exeter, whereunto the most number and best ships of the whole harbour doth belong, do allege that because they are not specially named in your Honours' letters, this service concerneth them not; whereas in truth, there is but one serviceable ship of the said harbour in all, belonging in part to some of the inhabitants of this city, namely the *Rose of Exeter*, of the burden of one hundred tons or more; which, being one of the two ships aforesaid, together with a fine pinnace, we mind, according to your Honours' direction, to cause to be thoroughly furnished and prepared by the appointed time, although the same will be to our very great charge.

The mayor asked 'most humbly beseeching your Honours to direct your honourable letters unto Topsham, Kenton, Exmouth, Lympstone, Sidmouth, Seaton, Colyton, Dawlish, Teignmouth, Tiverton and Collumpton, for the preparing of that other ship so stayed, or some other like, for the better furtherance of this her Majesty's service, which God prosper'. Some of the places named have changed little over the years, which serves to emphasize how dependent a county like Devon was on water transport, and how small were the ships which would guard England from the galleons of Spain. The names of the patriotic mayor and his colleagues deserve to be recorded: Jo. Peryam, Mayor, G. Peryam, Nicholas Martin, Geoffrey Thomas, and Richard Prouz (Prowse).

When *la felicissima* or the most fortunate Armada eventually sailed, under its new commander, the Duke of Medina Sidonia, there were thirty thousand Spanish and mercenary soldiers commanded by the Duke of Parma waiting in the Netherlands. (Contemporaries never knew it as the invincible Armada; this name seems to be a Victorian invention.) The English fleet, commanded by Lord Howard of Effingham, was more raggle-taggle, but the mood was more determined. The Queen herself rode among her troops at Tilbury, where she is reported to have said, 'I have the body of a weak and feeble woman, but I have the heart and stomach of a king, and a king of England too'. The news that the Armada had been sighted off Cornwall soon spread: in Plymouth Drake is said to have been playing bowls on Plymouth Hoe when the news arrived, but that clever sailor had time to finish his game before the tide served to carry him out of Sutton harbour.

Whether or not there were beacons which warned of the approach of the invasion fleet, this is how Howard reported the sighting of the Armada:

> on Friday last [19 July], Sir Francis Godolphin wrote unto my Lord Admiral, that the Thursday before, a bark of Mousehole in Cornwall, being bound for France to lade salt, encountered with nine sail of great ships between Scilly and Ushant, bearing in North-East with the coast of England. Coming near unto them, he, doubting [suspecting] they were Spaniards, kept the wind of them. They perceiving it, began to give him chase. So in the end, three of them followed him so near that the Englishman doubted hardly to escape them. At his first sight of them there were two flags spread which were suddenly taken in again, and being far off could not well discern the same. They were all great ships, and, as he might judge, the least of them from 200 tons to 5 and 800 tons. Their sails were all crossed over with a red cross. Each of the greater ships towed astern them either a great boat or pinnace without mast ... On

Saturday, there came another Englishman from the west part of Cornwall, who likewise had been chased with a fleet of ships, being shot at by them, but recovered the shore with little hurt ... On Sunday, one Simons of Exeter gave advertisement to my Lord Admiral that on Friday last he was chased with a fleet of great ships, having some of his men hurt with shot from them; escaping their hands, landed in Cornwall, and came post to Plymouth unto my Lord Admiral ...

## OTHERWISE OCCUPIED THAN WITH WRITING

Howard was busy and wrote again

from aboard the Ark, thwart of Plymouth, the 21st of July, 1588 ... I will not trouble you with any long letter; we are at this present otherwise occupied than with writing. Upon Friday, at Plymouth, I received intelligence that there were a great number of ships descried off of the Lizard; whereupon, although the wind was very scant, we first warped out of harbour that night, and upon Saturday ... the wind being at South-West; and about three of the clock in the afternoon, descried the Spanish fleet, and did what we could to work for the wind, which by this morning [Sunday] we had recovered, descrying their fleet to consist of 120 sail, whereof there are 4 galleasses and many ships of great burden. At nine of the clock we gave them fight, which continued until one. In this fight we made some of them to bear room to stop their leaks; notwithstanding we durst not adventure to put in among them, their fleet being so strong. But there shall be nothing either neglected or unhazarded, that may work their overthrow. Sir, the captains in her Majesty's ships have behaved themselves most bravely and like men hitherto, and I doubt not will continue, to their great commendation. And so, recommending our good success to your godly prayers ...

The English ships were smaller and fewer but more manoeuvrable than the Spanish ships, so Howard's tactic was to engage the enemy at long range and reduce the risk of being boarded by his larger opponents. Thus he fought a running battle as the Spanish ran up-Channel, while Medina Sidonia vacillated over whether to land on the Isle of Wight or at Margate and where he should rendezvous with the Duke of Parma. Several ships were taken, until the Armada took refuge in the road of the neutral port of Calais, where in the early hours of Monday 29 July Howard sent in fireships. The Spanish cut their cables and in the darkness many collided.

In the shallow, rough water off Gravelines many Spanish ships risked grounding, until the wind changed and blew the disorganized Armada far into the North Sea. There, though the English were in poor condition, Howard's council agreed:

> We whose names are hereunder written have determined and agreed in council to follow and pursue the Spanish fleet until we have cleared our own coast and brought the Firth [of Forth] west of us; and then to return back again, as well to revictual our ships, which stand in extreme scarcity, as also to guard and defend our own coast at home; with further protestation that, if our wants of victuals and munition were supplied, we would pursue them to the furthest that they durst have gone.

The heroes who signed this declaration were 'C. Howard, George Coumbreland, T. Howard, Edmonde Sheffeylde, Fra. Drake, Edw. Hoby, John Hawkyns, Thomas Fenner'. The threat of invasion was over, and the weather could be left to ravage the Spanish fleet as it straggled home round Scotland and Ireland.

## NOT A CORN OF ALL THAT WAS SET DOWN

It was convenient to suggest that God had taken sides by making the winds and waters to rise, but in truth the margin between success and failure had been narrow and it was seamanship which had made the difference. The logistics of maintaining a large fleet at sea had not yet been overcome, sickness had broken out in the English fleet, and food and ammunition were dangerously low. The whereabouts of the Spaniards were not known, but the danger seemed to have passed, and little thought seems to have been given to the seamen who had fought the battle. Howard gave up the chase 'having left the Spanish fleet for lack both of powder and meat, having not received a corn of all that was set down in paper by my Lord Treasurer', and it was claimed that the fleet was

> driven to such extremity for lack of meat, as it is reported (I wot not how truly) that my Lord Admiral was driven to eat beans, and some to drink their own water. Thus the Spaniards be gone whither it please them; to Scotland or Ireland, they may; or else home about both, they may, with this wind. These things would be timely considered on . . . And concerning new provisions of victual and munition to her Majesty's navy, which need be more substantially done than it hath been . . .

Howard's letter ought to have stung some consciences:

> Sickness and mortality begins wonderfully to grow amongst us; and it is a most pitiful sight to see, here at Margate, how the men, having no place to receive them into here, die in the streets. I am driven myself, of force, to come a-land, to see them bestowed in some lodging; and the best I can get is barns and such outhouses; and the relief is small that I can provide for them here. It would grieve any man's heart to see them that have served so valiantly to die so miserably . . . for they have been so long at sea and have so little shift of apparel, and so [few] places to provide them of such wants, and no money wherewith to buy it . . . I would think it a marvellous good way that there were a thousand pounds worth or two thousand marks worth of hose, doublets, shirts, shoes and such like, sent down . . . for else, in very short time I look to see most of the mariners go naked . . .

The fate of the victorious seamen was only partly due to deliberate neglect, and their plight was due as much to inexperience and incompetence. Only gradually over the next two centuries would the navy's administrators learn to overcome these difficulties.

# THE COLONIZATION OF NORTH AMERICA

Meanwhile trade across the North Atlantic had already been so well established that in 1536 one Richard Hore had organized the first transatlantic sightseeing trip, comprising 'six score persons whereof thirty were gentlemen', though it ended rather badly with the gentlemen tourists eating each other. In 1578 Humphrey Gilbert had obtained from Elizabeth I a charter to colonize remote heathen and barbarous lands, and he attempted to found the first English colony in Newfoundland, where some hardy fishermen from the West Country may have already been used to over wintering. However, Gilbert was drowned and Walter Ralegh, his half-brother, inheriting the charter, sent an expedition in 1584 to explore the North American coast. They landed near Roanoke Island, returning with two Indians, and Ralegh called the land Virginia. The next year he sent a second expedition to North America, seven ships commanded by Richard Greynville (as he spelled his name) in the flagship *Tyger*. The ships sailed south by way of Puerto Rico and Florida; the route was partly due to the uncertainty of the navigation and the desire to avoid bad weather, but more to give the opportunity to capture a Spanish prize, which helped to finance the expedition. Leaving the would-be colonists on Roanoke Island, Grenville sailed for home promising to return by Easter 1586.

The new expedition had not even left England when the settlers were found by Drake, returning from a raid on the Spanish in the West Indies. Drake offered supplies and a ship, but the colonists preferred to return with him to England. Another colony was left at Roanoke in 1587 but war intervened and when Ralegh searched for them in 1590 they had disappeared without a trace. It would be twenty years before the next English settlers arrived in North America and landed at Jamestown.

# THE FIGHT OF THE *REVENGE*

In 1591 Elizabeth I sent a small squadron under Lord Thomas Howard to the Azores to try to intercept a Spanish treasure fleet reputed to be on its way from the West Indies. When the Spanish learned of this they delayed its arrival beyond the normal season when the English fleet could stay at sea, and sent a second, powerful fleet from Spain to trap Howard, his second-in-command, Sir Richard Grenville, and the six ships which remained of the fleet sent from England. The end of August was longer than these ships had intended to stay out, and though victualling ships had brought out fresh provisions, there was sickness in the fleet, and some ships had already been sent home. The rendezvous for the fleet and the victuallers was Flores in the Azores, and there the most sick had been put ashore, while others were foraging for fresh food on their own account. Grenville, in the *Revenge*, had ninety men, or about half his crew, sick. So, the English might have been able to take on the odd treasure ship, but they were in no condition to take on Don Alonso de Bazan when he hove over the horizon with more than fifty ships including some galleys.

Bazan was well informed of Howard's predicament and hoped to surprise him at anchor. Before Howard could tell his ships to recover their men from shore and weigh, some ships cut their cables and ran, *Revenge* being the last to sail. Perhaps Grenville's sailing was more leisurely than it needed to be because he mistook the approaching sails for the treasure fleet rather than Bazan's fleet of war. However, it was too late and his enemy surrounded him: the fight which followed was epic. Over the next fifteen hours Grenville's *Revenge* fought with fifteen ships, sinking two. Only when there were forty dead and all the others wounded, including Grenville, with six feet of water in her hold and all her powder gone, did *Revenge* surrender. The dying Grenville wanted to sink the ship, but was carried on board the Spanish flagship, where he passed away some days later.

The expected treasure fleet began to arrive a few days later, in ones and twos and then in squadrons, just as Howard would have wished to find them, until Bazan had some hundred and forty sail under his command. Then in a storm a large number of these ships, and *Revenge*, were blown ashore on the island of Terceira and wrecked. Although the Spanish had taken other ships, most notably Sir John Hawkins' *Jesus of Lubeck* in 1568, *Revenge* was first ship lost while sailing under the Queen's commission.

## THE DEATH OF ELIZABETH

By the time of the death of Elizabeth I in 1603, the leaders of the nation had learned what sea power meant, and some of its limitations and advantages: as summed up by Julian Corbett, that 'the real importance of maritime power lay in its influence on military operations'. Corbett, whose papers are deposited at the National Maritime Museum, incorporated these thoughts into his influential work *Some Principles of Maritime Strategy* (1911) but he had foreshadowed these in the preface to *The Successors of Drake* written some two years before, and he was invited to lecture at the newly formed (1900) War Course at the Royal Naval College, Greenwich. He noted that the Tudors had learned 'that the fleet was an integral part of one great force, in a way that it had never probably been regarded before'. They had also learned that success in war lay, first, in closing the Channel to enemy shipping and then in mastering the enemy's trade routes.

All this had been achieved in scarcely one hundred years. In addition, the fleet which Elizabeth I left behind was, if not modern, then distinctly transitional, consisting mainly of race-built galleons, handy, speedy ships specialized for fighting at sea. The main features of the sailing line-of-battle ship, and of most smaller warships, had been determined for the next three hundred years: frame-built, ship-rigged, with continuous gundecks and broadside-firing guns. The scene was set for the birth of the Royal Navy.

# Chapter Two

# Under Crown and Commonwealth

By the time James VI of Scotland came to the throne of England as James I, in 1603, the lessons and rewards of being strong at sea had entered the folk memory, and a popular ballad of the time ran 'pilots ... take card and compass in hand ... And hye again to Neptune's seas, Where we'll have riches when we please', but this sentiment found its expression in privateering ventures rather than in the expansion of a state navy. James made peace with Spain, agreeing to end expeditions to the Spanish Main, and even tried to forbid piracy against Spanish ships and possessions.

In 1619 Charles Howard, who had led Elizabeth's navy against the Armada, was still Lord High Admiral. However, an inquiry found that while the costs of the navy were rising steadily the number of ships in service had fallen to about half of those which James had inherited from Elizabeth I. Howard was undoubtedly honest and straightforward, but his deputies had become more than usually corrupt and Howard was forced to resign aged eighty-two.

The choice of his successor fell upon George Villiers, who later became the Duke of Buckingham, and whose qualifications for office included his French-taught skills as a dancer and fencer and his naked ambition. The navy was no better run than before, and after nine years of office what was left of the navy detested him as much for his run of shameful disasters as for their lack of pay. Adam of Moleyns had been murdered in Portsmouth in 1450 by sailors rioting for their pay, and so following precedent Buckingham was assassinated there in 1628.

However, Buckingham left at least one lasting legacy to the navy, by organizing the fleet into separate squadrons of red, white, and blue, each flying the appropriate coloured flag bearing the new union flag, itself introduced for use at sea in 1606, in the upper canton of the hoist. Increasingly in the eighteenth century orders were given for ships to fly the same ensign in battle to prevent confusion with the enemy, and so the white ensign came to distinguish the Royal Navy. Coloured squadrons were abolished in 1864, though some British warships fought the Battle of Jutland in 1916 flying the red ensign, to distinguish themselves from Germans flying the imperial flag, which with a dark cross on a light background had been copied from the British white ensign.

## THE *SOVEREIGN OF THE SEAS*

Despite the overall decline of the fleet, the Pett family, shipbuilders since the time of Henry VIII, were active, ship design progressed, and the size of ships steadily increased. The most important development was the final disappearance of the medieval fore and after castles, though forecastle, pronounced and written fo'c'sle, has survived in the language to the present day. The Stuart kings appreciated the value of ships as instruments of diplomacy: they became more ornate, and in 1608 Phineas Pett's *Prince Royal*, first of the new design of warships, was described as 'the greatest and goodliest ship that was ever built in England'.

The change in design was not without some debate, William Monson writing that

There are two manner of built ships: the one with a flush deck, fore and aft, snug and low by water; the other lofty and high charged . . . The ship with a flush deck I hold good to fight in, if she be a fast ship by the wind and keep herself from boarding . . . [but if] it happen that she be boarded, and put to her defence, she lieth open to her enemy; for gaining her upper deck you win her, having neither forecastle nor other close-fight to retire unto; and in that case half the defensive part of the ship is the strength of the forecastle . . . A high built ship is the better for these reasons – majesty and terror to the enemy, more commodious for the harbouring of men. She will be able to carry more artillery, of greater strength, within-board, and make the better defence. She will overtop a lower and snug ship; her men cannot be so well discerned, for that the waist-cloths will take away the view and sight of them . . .

The design of warships was as much a question of seamanship and choice of tactics, and if actual boarding was not the intention then, as Monson noted in the same passage, 'The advantage of a ship with a flush deck, that [approaches] another to windward, is this: she may with her lee ordnance shoot the other under water, and herself in no hazard; the ship that is . . . to leeward of her is at the other's mercy, and becomes weak in comparison of the other to windward.'

Monson was already somewhat old fashioned, not least in his view that 'a ship with three decks [would be] very inconvenient, dangerous, and unserviceable; the number and weight of the ordnance wrings her sides and weakens her. It is seldom seen that you have a calm so many hours together as to keep out her lower tier, and when they are out, and forced to haul them in again, it is with great labour, travail and trouble to the gunners when they should be fighting.' He was in good company at the time, for according to Laird Clowes, Trinity House rubbished the idea of building three-decked ships, arguing not only that they were 'beyond the art and wit of man' to construct but that there were no docks large enough for such projects. This was an argument which would echo down the ages whenever new designs were mooted.

The most notable ship of the period was the *Sovereign of the Seas*, designed and built by Phineas Pett and launched at Woolwich in 1637. She was reckoned the finest ship of her day, and in the first Anglo-Dutch War the Dutch called her the *Golden Devil*, a reference both to her extensive gilding and to her guns. Not initially a success and much modified in mid-life, she was nevertheless so strongly built that her active service career lasted for almost sixty years, until she was destroyed by fire in an accident in 1696.


## PIRACY IN THE CHANNEL

In these years trade, and the piracy which went hand in hand, prospered and English ships sailed to Africa, India, China and the Spice Islands. The first successful colonies were established in Virginia and New England, and Barbados and Bermuda were settled. However, the navy at home was weak, and foreign pirates raided in the Channel. Dunkirk had been a pirates' nest for years, but now there were Barbary, or Sallee, pirates from North Africa who wanted not goods but slaves. In 1626 William Plumleighe, Mayor of Dartmouth, then still a major port in the West Country, wrote for help to London, reporting that Sallee men-of-war were taking men and ships.

At the low ebb which the navy had reached under the first Stuart kings, North African pirates also operated unchecked in the Thames as well as in the Irish Sea. Historically the king had raised a fleet by levying a tax called ship money on coastal towns, and when in 1634 Charles I issued a writ for ship money, specifically for the City of London to deliver a number of ships furnished for war to Portsmouth, he did so partly on the grounds that pirates were endangering commerce. Religion, the King's insistence upon his divine right and his friendship with Spain were all leading the nation into civil war, and the King's increasing difficulties in raising ship money were a measure of the proximity of civil war which broke out in 1642.

## THE COMMONWEALTH

The Civil War affected the fleet, though the mutiny at the Downs in 1646 and an attempt at control by the army, which became known as Pride's Purge, were less about politics than about pay. The royalist part of the fleet was commanded by Prince Rupert from 1648 a base at Kinsale, in southern Ireland, from where he continued the war. In 1649 the Council of State had appointed three generals-at-sea to command that part of the navy loyal to Parliament, one of the more successful being Robert Blake.

Though a soldier and a Member of Parliament, Blake had some nautical connections, having in his earlier years looked after his father's shipping business. His first objective was to destroy Rupert's fleet, and he chased him from Ireland to the Mediterranean where eventually he destroyed royalist power at sea, though Rupert himself escaped. Blake proved an exceptionally good administrator, and not only were many new ships laid down, he also reorganized the navy, its dockyards, victualling, and pay. He also regularized the payment of prize money, laying down that

all captains, seamen, and others that do or shall serve in any of
the State's own or merchants' ships employed in their service,
shall for time to come in lieu of all prizes have and receive from
the State, for every ship or prize they shall lawfully take, the
sum of 10 shillings for every ton the said ship shall measure,
and £6 13 shillings 4 pence for every piece of ordnance, to be
shared and divided amongst them proportionally, according to
the respective places and offices in the ship in which they served;
and for every man-of-war sunk or destroyed by firing or
otherwise, to have £10 a gun only.

Ships were also categorized into their various sizes or rates, initially
by the number of their complement, then by the number of their
guns, and the navy as a national force under the control of
Parliament dates from this time.

## THE DUTCH WARS

Commercial rivalry between England and Holland led to three
wars. In the first, between 1652 and 1654 Blake fought one battle
with the Dutch Admiral Martin Harpertzoon Tromp, and defeated
another Dutch admiral, de Witt, at the Battle of the Kentish
Knock. Until this war there had been few battles at sea between
two efficient fleets of sailing ships firing their guns broadside; tactics
had yet to be evolved, and these first fights were more like a series
of cavalry charges. Against Tromp, after the usual council of war,

We sailed towards them, and the Hollanders stood to us, being
well manned, and every ways very well fitted, and about our
number, each party being between 50 and 60 sail, and the
Hollanders had two Admirals.
First Major Bourne with the *Andrew* led on, and charged the
Hollanders stoutly, and got off again without much harm.
Captain Badiley with his ship . . . charged exceeding gallantly;
but was in very great danger to have lost his ship, for the
Hollanders were so close on both sides of him, charging against
him, that one might have flung biscuits out of his frigate into
the Dutch ships.

All his sails were so torn and shattered that he could not sail either to or fro, or any more but as the tide drove him, and there were about 60 men killed in that frigate, and she had near 100 shot in her hull, and was in danger of sinking or taking; but, blessed be God, they got her safe to harbour, the fight being not above 6 leagues from the shore.

The water being shallow upon the sands, we were in some danger of sustaining great loss, in so much that the *Sovereign*, and the ship in which General Blake was, with the admiral began to stick, but, blessed be God, were got off again without any great harm thereby . . .

The *Sovereign* referred to here was, of course, Charles I's *Sovereign of the Seas*, now cut down in name and in size to a two-decker: she was still a large ship and on this occasion, 'she sailed through and through the Holland fleet, and played hard upon them. And at one time there were about 20 Holland frigates upon her . . . [and she got] some shot in her, which her great bigness is not much prejudiced with'.

The war had opened with a refusal by Tromp to salute the flag, an ancient claim, which in the previous century Charles Howard had insisted upon from even the King of Spain in person when he arrived for his marriage to Mary. A clause in the Treaty of Westminster, which concluded the war in 1654, continued to insist that 'the ships and vessels of the said United Provinces [i.e. Holland], as well those of war as others, which shall meet any of the men-of-war of this Commonwealth in the British seas, shall strike their flag and lower the topsail, in such manner as the same hath ever been observed at any times heretofore, under any other form of government'.

Blake was a thinking officer, and consulting with his fellow generals-at-sea, Deane and Monck, set out the first orders for what would become the normal fighting formation at sea: the line of battle. These instructions were one more stage in the development of a professional navy, and in the next half-century the distinction between warships which were powerful enough to fight in the line or line-of-battle ships, and those which were fit only to serve as cruisers also grew, as did the number of guns a ship had to carry in order to stand in the line of battle. Blake's instructions established the line of battle 'upon pain of the severest punishment' as the normal fighting formation of the fleet, a tactic which would not change until the end of the eighteenth century when Howe, Rodney, and Nelson developed the tactic of breaking the line:

> No one presume to go to windward of the chief of his squadron in sailing at any time unless in chase or fight . . . in tacking or sailing at any time everyone keep good order, and not strive for the wind, or place, one of another, whereby prejudice or damage may come to any ship or ships of the fleet . . .

On the same day he issued a set of fighting instructions:

> At sight of the [enemy] fleet the vice-admiral . . . as also the rear-admiral . . . are to make what sail they can to come up with the admiral on each wing, the vice-admiral on the right wing, and the rear-admiral on the left wing, leaving a competent distance for the admiral's squadron if the wind will permit and there be sea-room enough.
>
> As soon as they shall see the general [i.e. admiral] engage . . . then each squadron shall take the best advantage they can to engage with the enemy next unto them; and in order thereunto all the ships of every squadron shall endeavour to keep in a line with their chief . . . every ship of the said squadron shall endeavour to keep in a line with the admiral, or he that commands in chief next unto him, and nearest the enemy . . . the ships of the fleet or of the respective squadron are to endeavour to keep up in a line as close as they can . . .
>
> In case the admiral should have the wind of the enemy, and that other ships of the fleet are to windward of the admiral, then upon hoisting up a blue flag at the mizen-yard, or the mizen-topmast, every such ship is then to bear up into his wake or grain . . . In case the admiral be to leeward of the enemy, and his fleet or any part thereof to leeward of him, to the end such ships to leeward may come up into the line with their admiral, if he shall put abroad a flag as before and bear up, none that are to leeward are to bear up, but to keep his or their luff to gain his wake.

After the First Dutch War the fleet was kept busy in the Mediterranean, where Blake took up the war on the Barbary pirates. England also intervened in a war between France and Spain, which gave Blake the opportunity to capture a large Spanish fleet in the harbour of Santa Cruz, Tenerife, though he did not enjoy the spoils of victory but died as his ship was entering Plymouth Sound. Nevertheless General-at-sea Robert Blake, with his genius for administration, his ordered methods of fighting, and above all his leadership, had restored the navy's self-confidence and its reputation.

## THE RESTORATION OF THE MONARCHY

The Commonwealth was no better than the King in repeatedly failing to raise adequate revenue from taxes, and one consequence was that seamen's pay was often months or years adrift. Cromwell seized upon the idea that the navy could be made to pay for itself, and toyed with both France and Spain for a subsidy to use the Commonwealth's navy to attack the other. Eventually he fixed upon a 'Western Design', which was for war on Spain, ostensibly for the long-claimed right to trade freely in the Americas, and he gave command of an expedition to capture Hispaniola to William Penn. Robert Venables commanded the army and the expedition was under the command of three commissioners: Penn, Venables, and Edward Winslow, a man who had sailed with the Pilgrim Fathers, and whose role in the 'Western Design' was that of political commissar. The expedition went awry when the army was defeated at Hispaniola, but on his own initiative Penn diverted the expedition to Kingston and captured Jamaica. Returning home in 1655 Penn was imprisoned in the Tower of London for dis- obedience to his orders, but any victory over Spain was greeted by the populace with acclaim and Cromwell found he had locked up a national hero. On Penn's grudging and half-hearted apology Crom- well let him go, but Penn, otherwise a pious Protestant, had had his loyalty tilted towards the monarchy and its restoration.

Meanwhile there was continuing disaffection in the navy, leading to another mutiny in 1653. After the death of Oliver Cromwell a military junta staged a coup d'état and closed Parliament but they in turn were brought down by a third mutiny in the fleet. As General Monck marched slowly south from Scotland declaring he was going to restore laws and liberties, but all the time sniffing the political wind, the fleet at Portsmouth, under Admiral John Lawson, declared itself for Parliament. There the matter might have ended, but the seamen learned that the wages intended for them had been diverted to pay the troops of the junta which was occupying London. The military junta which had so far outfaced Monck and overcome the revolt of troops in the provinces and riots in London was stunned when, in mid-December 1659, Lawson arrived off Greenwich and closed the Thames to traffic. This blockade soon decided matters, Parliament was recalled before the end of the month, and there was little doubt that it would declare for King Charles.

Penn's loyalties were shifting and complex, and following the restoration of the monarchy in 1660, he served as a commissioner of the Navy Board until 1663, helping the Duke of York (who was to become James II) to revise earlier sailing and fighting instructions, and during the Second Dutch War (1665–67) serving in the *Royal Charles*, as captain of the fleet to the future monarch. Despite the unreasoned jealousy of Pepys and the religious animosity of most of the court, Penn earned the patronage of Charles II, partly through the professional performance of his duties to the King's brother, and partly by the large sum, estimated to be some £12,000, which was owed to him by the King. Notably, Charles II granted land in what was to become Pennsylvania to William's son, also called William, in recognition of the father's service to the crown.

## THE SECOND AND THIRD DUTCH WARS

At the restoration of the monarchy, Charles II adopted Blake's reforms of the navy and made his brother, James, Duke of York, Lord High Admiral; Prince Rupert returned and George Monck became the Duke of Albemarle. When Edward Montagu was made Earl of Sandwich, his clever private secretary, Samuel Pepys, was rewarded by being by being made Clerk of Acts in the Navy Office. The survival of Pepys' diary, and the books and official papers which found their way into his private library, means that the age is largely known through these sources. Pepys' administration, often held up as a model of virtue, was not perfect as this short note in 1665 from Albemarle, who wanted seamen, to Pepys, who was at Greenwich, shows:

> Understanding that divers Seamen who are recover'd of their sicknesse and fitt to goe to Sea, but want Shoes & other conveniencies to goe on board, what monies shall bee necessary to goe to Sea & doe service agen I desire you to lay itt out, and the Treasurer of his Ma'ties Navy shall repay itt you againe . . .

In the Second Dutch War, 1665–67, Holland and France were allies, and while the European powers captured each other's colonies, at home the fleet commanded by Albemarle and Prince Rupert was generally successful. Even when outnumbered, as in the Four Days' Fight against the Dutch (1666), there seems to have been a moral victory. This is how Albemarle and Rupert, the joint commanders, reported it to Charles II in a letter which they both signed:

> Wee have had no tyme since we began the fight with the Hollander to give yor Majtie an Acct: till now . . . [and] we shall now only further acquaint yor Majtie that our masts and sayles and rigging are very much prejudiced and our ammunition spent very low especially in that part of yo. fleet that began the fight first, and we have many men hurt and killed, wherefore we desire yor Majtie that there be speedy order for the pressing of more Seamen and that care be taken in providing of fresh supplyes of masts and sayles and ammunition.
>
> The dutch are gone backe for Holland very glad as we suppose they are quitt of us, and we believe yor Majtie will heare that they have susteyned great losse in theyre Seamen there being many slayne sunke and Burnt. Seven ships were Burnt and two Sunke that we know of and from 83 Ships which was the number they brought to ye first engagm't we could not number above 40 sayle last night when they left us; But we were also our-selves so lamed in our masts sayles and

rigging that neyther the *R. James* nor the *R. Charles* were able to follow them, nor to tacke without repairing . . .

Yet the war ended with the astonishing sight of the Dutch in the Medway. While peace negotiations were underway in Breda, de Ruyter slipped across the Channel with a small squadron and caught the fleet badly off guard. What happened next was so traumatic that two hundred years later it inspired the normally staid Laird Clowes to write:

> The river was full of moving craft and burning wreckage; the roar of guns was almost continuous; the shrieks of the wounded could be heard even above the noise of battle, the clangour of trumpets, the roll of drums, and the cheers of the Dutch as success after success was won; and above all hung a pall of smoke, illumined only, as night closed in, by the gleam of flames on all sides and the flashes of guns and muskets . . .

De Ruyter took with him to Holland the flagship, the 100-gun *Royal Charles*, and her stern carving now hangs in the Rijksmuseum in Amsterdam.

The Treaty of Breda returned various West Indies islands to England and confirmed English possession of New York and New Jersey, while the Dutch were allowed to carry Germany's and the Spanish Netherlands' produce to England.

The peace was short lived, and when France and Holland fell out, England's entry into a new war against Holland was motivated by a bribe from Louis XIV to Charles II. There were two significant battles, Southwold or Sole Bay (1672) and the Texel (1673), when, possibly due to the difficulties of language or signals, the French fleet took no part in the action, and the Dutch concentrated their attacks on the English fleet, which suffered heavily and was forced to withdraw. The peace which was signed marked the ascendancy of English commercial interests over Dutch, but it was accompanied by a growing realization the real enemy now was not the Dutch but Louis XIV's France.

# THE GLORIOUS REVOLUTION

In 1685 Charles II died and was succeeded by his brother James II, an overt Roman Catholic. As a person he was popular with the fleet, but the fleet was Protestant and was antagonized when James sent them a Catholic commander-in-chief and priests to say mass. As the threat of an invasion from Holland grew the fleet absented itself from its proper station in the Channel and went to Gunfleet, leaving the way open for William of Orange, and his English wife Mary, who landed at Torbay in November 1688. James II fled to France.

Following the Glorious Revolution, King Louis XIV of France abetted the exiled James II with money and men in an effort to restore him to his throne. One invasion attempt was thwarted in 1690 at the Battle of the Boyne, in Ireland, but the French were encouraged by a temporary success over an Anglo-Dutch fleet off Beachy Head. Louis had planned a major assault on England and prepared a large army while his navy was to seize control of the Channel. When the fleets met off Cape Barfleur, the French squadrons separated and were pursued separately; and a few days later the fireships and boats of Vice Admiral George Rooke's division destroyed twelve French ships at La Hogue, where they had run themselves into shallow water. Watching from the shore was James II, who saw his hopes of restoration go up in flames with the burning French warships. He is reputed to have turned to his French hosts and asked, 'Who but my brave English tars could do such a thing?'

The Battle of Barfleur in May 1692, which ranged for six days east and west along the Cherbourg peninsula in fog, light airs, and strong tides, was almost the last set-piece naval battle of the seventeenth century. John Lloyd, surgeon of the *Stirling Castle*, a 70-gun ship of the rear or blue squadron, witnessed the battle with the French by an Anglo-Dutch fleet commanded by Admiral Sir Edward Russell. Lloyd, however, overestimates the strength and losses of the French, and does not mention the fog which confused operations as the fleets drifted, kedged, and were towed along the coast. The poor visibility may have deceived the French admiral, the Comte de Tourville, into engaging a fleet almost twice as strong as his. The closing engagement which Lloyd describes was remarkable because when the boats of Rooke's squadron burned six three-deckers, the tide was so low that French cavalry of the would-be invasion army rode into the water to use their sabres and were pulled from their chargers by English seamen using boathooks.

Lloyd's mention of bribes and bravadoes below is a reference to Jacobite expectations that the fleet would desert to the Stuart cause. The battle was in part a test of the navy's loyalty to William and Mary, but Admiral Carter, one of the principal suspects, put his loyalty to the throne beyond doubt when he was mortally wounded with his dying words: 'Fight the ship as long as she will swim.' This was a sentiment which Grenville in the *Revenge* would have recognized and Lawrence in the *Chesapeake* would repeat.

Lloyd wrote from 'Saint Ellins' (St Helen's) near Portsmouth:

Thursday the 19th of May (92) early in the morning we found Monsieur Tourvell with about 70 sayle of french men of war to windward of us many of them being three deck ships of great force being then about mid-channel between the Isle of Wight and Cape de Hague in france; they very bravely bore down upon us and between tenn and eleven in the forenoon fell in furiously with our Red division ... they fired smartly and behaved themselves very courageously fighting in a very good line. But then they found the brave Russell was neither bribed nor fearfull but he and all other commanders entertained them otherwise than they expected ... notwithstanding all the brava-does of the Jacobites or the french valor though they made a running fight of it till almost tenn at night at which time we were forced to come to an anchor; we burned two of their capital ships this day and some were sunk but know not certainly the number of them, they took the advantage of the night to make their escape in so confused a manner that the next morning their fleet was wholly divided, in this action not above one third of our fleet ingaged I think the Red division only with about seven or eight sayle of the Dutch (the rest not having an opportunity to come in) and put the terrible fleet of the french Tirant to flight.

fryday the 20th we perceived their fleet standing into their own shore and chased them so close that some stood one way and some another endeavouring to get into some of their harbours to secure themselves, but still we gave them chase and having little wind and the tide being done we came to an anchor as they were forced to doe for fear of driving towards us.

on Saturday the 21 some of the French cutt for their most speedy escape and we likewise cutt and chased them so close that four of them run ashore at Cherborough about 2 leagues to the eastward of Cape De Hague where Sir Ralph Delavall Vice Admiral of the Red in the Royall Sovereign stayed with about half a score of small frigatts till he might have an opportunity burning them which he happily effected the next day (one of them being Tourvielle the Admiral's ship) whilst we stood after the rest our headmost shipps still keeping sight of them till they got into a Bay between Cape barfloor and Sion head . . .

on Sunday ye 22 and before we could up with them they runn into shore under a couple of forts, but on Munday ye 23rd we standing in towards them they hawled so close under the forts that several of them went aground so that that afternoon Sir Clousely [Cloudesley] Shovel went in with his boat to observe the place and about four o'clock we had orders to send our barges and longboats on board the Eagle whose vice admirall Rook had hoisted his flagg and about six a clock we weighed and stood in as near as we could, then all our boats manned and armed went in close under one of their forts and burnt six of [their] three Deck men of war.

Tuesday the 24 about 4 a clock in the morning we took all our boats in again well manned and armed and two or three fire shipps where they burnt several saile more of men of war besides several small vessell that lay up the head of a river notwithstanding the fort at mouth of river played their great guns coutinuly on them and all the shore on both sides was lined with small shott their being an army of 14 or 15000 soldiers encamped hard by and it is credibly reported that the late King James dined a board on one of their shipps yesterday and that the army was to be landed in England But I hope we have disapointed him and all the rest that designed such a thing. We reckon that we have burnt 21 sayle of their shipps of war most of them being capitall shipps; Sr I doubt not, that you may have had an account of this before; yett I made bold to trouble you with this being I was an eye witness of most of the transactions if not all . . .

Russell's victory was tactically and strategically decisive, though, in view of his superiority, commentators rated it as workmanlike rather than brilliant. The French army, which elsewhere was all-conquering, was frustrated, and, symbolically, the 106-gun *Soleil Royal*, pride of King Louis and of the French navy, was run ashore by the French and burnt by the English. The fighting off Barfleur and La Hogue ended a period of French domination in the Channel and marked the start of a century of British success at sea.

## DISCOURSE ON PIRATES, 1696

At the beginning of the century piracy had been a problem in English waters: the Dunkirkers continued for many years, but the Barbary pirates were stopped once England was able to impress with her sea power and the North African pirates turned to easier victims in the Mediterranean. However, other forms of piracy spread to North America. Daniel Defoe's *General History of Pyrates* (1724) deals with piracy in the first quarter of the eighteenth century, but a document in the archives of the National Maritime Museum shows how piracy, based in the British colonies of North America, was a much earlier problem. Edward Randolph, English agent in Boston, wrote a 'Discours about Pyrates, with proper Remedies to Suppress them' dated 1696. 'About 20 years ago King Charles the Second was pleasd to send me to New England, to Enquire into their Trade & Commerce. I observed that they fitted out vessels of 60: or 70: Tons a peece, very well mand whom they calld privateers & sail them without commission to the Spanish West Indies . . .' Privateers were licensed by the state to wage war on the state's enemies and were thus legitimate, while pirates had no licence or letters of marque and thus placed themselves outside the law. It was a fine distinction, often lost as well on the casual reader as on the simple sailor, and nearly always on the victim.

Piracy was clearly a profitable business in the colonies, where expeditions brought home great quantities of silver in coins and bullion, much of it church plate from raids on the Spanish Main. The Spanish Ambassador in London complained to the King, who eventually agreed to send ships to suppress piracy in the West Indies, at the same declaring an amnesty for those who would give up their vicious trade. Meanwhile North America became the centre for new piratical voyages to the Red Sea and the Indian Ocean. As Randolph tells us,

> I have heard of no Pyracies done these severall years in those places [the West Indies] for the Pyrates have found out a more profitable & less hazardous ways to the Red sea, where they take from the Moors [actually Arabs and Indians] all they have without Resistances & bring it to some one of the Plantations on the Continent of America or Islands adjacent, where they are receivd and harbourd and from whence allso they fit out their vessels to the same places . . .

One such case was William Kidd, who in 1689 commanded a privateer named the *Blessed William*. Kidd made himself rich enough to marry well in New York and to become a merchant, but his next privateering adventure, in 1695, was less fortunate. He sailed from the Thames in command of another privateer, the *Adventure Galley*, with the backing of Richard Coote, the Earl of Bellamont and Governor of New York, and other nobles, including, allegedly, the King himself. Kidd claimed that the Royal Navy had pressed many of his best men and that when he recruited more men in New York he had been forced to take some unreliable seamen. Nevertheless, he sailed for the Indian Ocean, with a commission to clear the sea of pirates.

Some of the prizes he took were doubtful, and there were no great rewards until in 1698 he captured an Indian-owned ship, the *Quedah Merchant*, whose French papers clearly showed her to be a legitimate and valuable prize. However, Kidd was betrayed by his political friends; he was arrested when he returned to New York, and was sent to London for trial, where his privateering was adjudged in retrospect to have become piracy and he was hanged at Execution Dock in 1701.

Whether it was privateering or piracy, it was a semi-respectable trade in the colonies, and Randolph recommended measures 'for suppressing those Pyrates, and the preventing the like mischeif for the future'. The first was for better government of the colonies and in particular 'that no person be made Govr: in any of the proprieties, untill he be first approvd of by his majesties own council'. The second was that 'his Majesty be pleasd to send a sixth rate friggott, under the comand of a sober person well acquainted with the Bahama Islands, & other places where the pyrates usually resort, with a comission to grant pardons to all such who will . . . settle quietly in the plantations'. The third was forfeiture of the proceeds of crime and 'That all encouragement be given to discover what mony or jewells has at any time bin given to any of the Govrs: or their confidents in the plantations, either by pyrates or by their agents, and that all such money be forfeited to his majesty'. Much of Randolph's advice was eventually acted upon.

After the notorious pirate Woodes Rogers had imitated Drake with a privateering venture into the Pacific and brought home fabulous wealth, he too became respectable and was sent in 1718 as Governor of the Bahamas. His new capital, Nassau, was home allegedly to some two thousand pirates who dominated the town with their permanently drunken revelry. However, Woodes proved himself a good poacher turned gamekeeper and eventually reduced the islands to order.

One of the few men who did not accept an amnesty was Edward Thatch or Teach, better known as Blackbeard. He fled the Bahamas and cruised successfully, but by defying and beating the *Scarborough* frigate he made a remorseless enemy of the navy. He was hunted and chased into Pamlico Sound, where Lieutenant Robert Maynard followed him in the boats of the 40-gun *Pearl*. Maynard fought Blackbeard hand to hand and killed him, returning with Blackbeard's head hanging from his bowsprit. The suppression of piracy became one of the Royal Navy's permanent duties.

## SIR CLOUDESLEY SHOVELL

The career of Cloudesley Shovell spanned the turn of the century. Strong measures were necessary to contain the Barbary pirates within the Mediterranean, and they were not finally overcome until the wars between the European powers ended in the early nineteenth century. Shovell, however, played a major role in a typical measure against these pirates in 1676. Charles II had sent a fleet under Rear Admiral Sir John Narbrough, Commander-in-Chief of the Mediterranean Fleet, to Tripoli with the usual demands, for compensation for past depredations, the release of slaves, and a guarantee of good behaviour in the future. Narbrough trusted the negotiations to the twenty-six-year-old Shovell, who was convinced that the Dey would not concede any points and, having used his calls on the Dey to survey the harbour, persuaded Narbrough to burn the pirates' ships in their harbour. By night, Shovell crept in under the guns of the fortress with boats filled with combustible material, and destroyed four large pirate galleys.

Like Nelson after him, Shovell came from humble origins in Norfolk and was known for his outstanding qualities as a leader. He fought in the Second and Third Dutch Wars, served in the Mediterranean and the West Indies, was a tacit supporter of William of Orange in 1688, commanded a ship at the Battle of Bantry Bay in 1689, in 1690 took part in the Battle of Beachy Head, and at the Battle of Barfleur helped burn the beached French ships at La Hogue. Shovell went on to serve under Rooke, bringing home Rooke's silver from Vigo, and was at the capture of Gibraltar in 1704 and of Barcelona in 1705.

Without knowing the time reliably, it was impossible to measure longitude accurately (longitude is displacement east or west from a given line running north to south on Earth's surface). So, returning from an abortive attack on Toulon in 1707, Shovell and many men were lost when his ship, the *Association*, with the *Eagle*, *Romney* and *Firebrand*, struck on the Scillies in poor weather. According to legend Shovell had the curious habit of taking his considerable wealth to sea with him and, though he reached the shore alive, was murdered by an island woman for the emerald ring he wore. Shovell was a popular hero, and was one of the first naval officers to be buried in Westminster Abbey. The drama of his death overshadowed his achievements in life, but it also helped to trigger the search for a means of accurate timekeeping, a story which is brilliantly told at the Greenwich Royal Observatory, part of the National Maritime Museum at Greenwich.

# Chapter Three

# The Wonderful Year

With the death of the King of Spain in 1700, Europe was threatened by the potential unification of France and Spain under one Bourbon ruler, Louis XIV's grandson, and there could be few neutrals in what became the War of the Spanish Succession, 1702–14. The naval story of this war, and the rest of the eighteenth century, can be told through brief lives of the British admirals.

## GEORGE ROOKE

In 1702 Admiral George Rooke commanded an Anglo-Dutch fleet tasked to capture Cadiz, an English objective since the sixteenth century, and cripple the Spanish war effort by stopping the import of treasure from America. Rooke proceeded in a desultory fashion, his councils of war turning into councils of inaction. The allied fleet invested Cadiz, but after burning stores at the ports of Rota and Santa Maria the troops re-embarked to return home at the end of the campaign season. By chance Rooke learned of a treasure fleet, guarded by Spanish ships and their French allies, lying at Vigo in Galicia, and this, at last, inspired him to action. Although the enemy was anchored behind booms and protected by forts, far into Vigo Bay, Rooke took or burned a score of French and Spanish ships, set seventeen galleys alight and captured some of the richest galleons that had ever reached Europe from the Spanish Main. Some of the cargo had been landed, but the immense treasure brought to London was estimated at between thirteen and twenty million pieces of eight, and Rooke was forgiven for his previous indecisiveness.

The following year was marked by the Great Storm, which raged across southern England on the night of 17/18 November. There was immense destruction on land, and the effect at sea was disastrous: the navy lost fifteen hundred men and twelve ships, five of them on the Goodwin Sands.

In 1704 Rooke again commanded an Anglo-Dutch fleet, this time in the Mediterranean, but it was just as half-hearted and bedevilled by councils of war as his previous expeditions. However, at one of these councils, called to discuss the pursuit of a French fleet, it was decided to make an assault upon Gibraltar, which then was held for Felipe V, the French candidate for the throne of Spain. The small garrison defended gallantly but after four days surrendered not to Rooke but to the representative of the rival claimant in Spain's civil war, Carlos III. However, it was English marines who took occupation of the Rock of Gibraltar, which has been British ever since, and is the only battle honour worn by the Royal Marines. Curiously, if Carlos had won the war of succession Gibraltar would no doubt have been handed over to him as an ally of England, but by the Treaty of Utrecht in 1713 the price of peace which was extorted from the otherwise victorious Felipe was the cession of Gibraltar to Britain. Meanwhile the British had also taken and occupied in 1708 Minorca with its important harbour at Port Mahon.

By the terms that ended the War of the Spanish Succession, the Protestant succession through the house of Hanover was assured, the Pretender was expelled from France, the crowns of France and Spain were permanently severed, and as well as Gibraltar, Newfoundland, Nova Scotia, the Hudson Bay territories, and Minorca were ceded to Britain. There had been no great successes in the war at sea, but rather a steady accumulation of trade and improvements in the organization and management of the navy.

## THE WAR OF JENKINS'S EAR

Spain still endeavoured to close the Caribbean and her South American possessions to free trade and to exclude Britain and her colonies in North America from markets there, and the next war again grew out of a commercial struggle, leading, seamlessly, to the larger War of the Austrian Succession. The incident which gave its name to the war occurred when Robert Jenkins, master of the ship *Rebecca*, had his ear cut off by Spanish coast guards. When Jenkins's carefully preserved ear was held up in a bottle in the House of Commons, a reluctant Robert Walpole was forced to recognize the inevitability of war, thus beginning a period of conflict which continued with short intervals for more than seventy years.

## EDWARD VERNON

Edward Vernon entered the navy in 1700, and during the War of the Spanish Succession saw action during the attack on Cadiz, when he was made lieutenant. He saw service in the Mediterranean, the West Indies, and the Baltic, and at the outbreak of war with Spain in 1739, as Vice Admiral of the Blue, was appointed Commander-in-Chief in the West Indies, where he captured Portobello. Vernon's fleet of six ships, reinforced by four battalions of troops raised in Virginia, bombarded the fortifications at close range and stormed the walls. As one sailor wrote to his wife:

> We have taken Porto Belo with such coridge and bravery that I never saw before; for my own Part my hart was rasd to the clouds and would have scaled the moon had a Spaniard been there to come at him, as we did the battry. Jack Cox is my messmate; you know he was always a heavy arsed dog and sleepy headed, but had you seen him climb the Wals of the battery, you would never forget him, for a cat could not exceed him in nimbleness, and so in short it was with all of us . . .

Vernon did not sack the town after its surrender, but some ten thousand pesos intended for the pay of the garrison was distributed amongst the fleet, a welcome bonus for the sailor, who wrote,

> My Dere I have got some token of Suces to show you. I wish I could have sent some of them to you. Our dear Admiral ordered every man some Spanish dollars to be immediately given, which is like a Man of Honor, for I had rather have 10 dollars in hand than to have 100 for seven years together . . .

When news of this victory reached London, Vernon was hailed as a hero: his reputation was enhanced by a new song:

> When Britain first at Heaven's command
> Arose from out the azure main,
> This was the charter of the land,
> And guardian angels sung this strain:
> Rule, Britannia, rule the waves
> Britons never will be slaves.

He was not so fortunate in his next attack on Cartagena in 1741: though he commanded the largest fleet yet seen in the West Indies, 124 sail, 15,000 sailors and marines, and 8,000 soldiers, the expedition was marred by a failure of communication between the fleet and the army. The Spanish defence, led by the very determined Blas de Lezo, was stubborn, while disease and dissension took their toll in the British forces. Some Spanish ships were destroyed, and outlying fortifications guarding the entrance to the harbour were captured, but after heavy losses Vernon withdrew. He refused to admit he had been repulsed by a much smaller force, and the version of events that he wrote to his wife afterwards was presumably intended to be spread in her social circle:

After the glorious success it has pleased Almighty God so wonderfully to favour us with, Whose manifold mercies I hope I shall never be unmindful of, I cannot omit laying hold of the opportunity of an express I am sending home to acquaint you of the joyful news, though in my present hurries I have no leisure to enter into many particulars ... I have only time to add, it has pleased Almighty God to preserve me in good health, to go through all these glorious fatigues, and in a full disposition to push this beginning with all possible vigour, to humble the proud Spaniards, and bring them to repentance for all the injuries and long-practised depredations on us. I have only time to send you my sincerest love and affection for you and blessing to our dear boys ...

His attack on Santiago de Cuba that July was also repulsed, and an attempt to cross the isthmus to the city of Panama was made in the rainy season when sickness prevented the expedition from achieving much. Eventually London recalled him, and though he arrived home a popular hero, he was out of favour with the government. Then in 1745, at the height of the invasion scare, he was appointed Commander-in-Chief in the Downs, but he promptly fell out with the Admiralty and was soon dismissed.

Vernon has other claims to fame, one concerning the issue of rum. Rum had been introduced into the navy in the middle of the seventeenth century, its chief advantage being its good keeping qualities compared to beer. It was issued neat, that is without water, but Vernon changed this by his order to captains no. 349 on 21 August 1740. He noted that 'the pernicious custom of the seaman drinking their allowance of rum in drams, and often at once, is attended with many fatal effects to their morals as well as their health' and ordered his captains that the sailors' daily allowance should be

> every day mixed with the proportion of a quart of water to a half pint of rum, to be mixed in a scuttle butt kept for that purpose, and to be done upon the deck, and in the presence of the Lieutenant of the Watch who is to take particular care to see that the men are not defrauded in having their full allowance of rum.

Vernon, who habitually wore a grogram cloak, was known as 'Old Grog' and the watered rum become known as grog.

Generous measures of rum, understandable when life at sea was tough and battles fought at short range, did indeed have a stupefying effect, even when watered down, but the custom lasted into the twentieth century. Finally the Admiralty braced itself for the decision that there was no place for the daily issue of rum in a modern navy, and the ration was abolished on 31 July 1970.

Another of Vernon's claims to fame concerns the American volunteers who fought under him in the West Indies. Three thousand marines were raised in Virginia, where they were commanded by the state governor, William Gooch, and known as Gooch's Marines. A captain in this force was Lawrence Washington, who inherited an estate which had been in his family's possession since 1674, Little Hunting Creek Plantation, on the banks of the Potomac. In 1761 Lawrence Washington's widow bequeathed the property to her husband's younger half-brother, George, who came to live there for forty-five years on an estate and in a house which had been renamed Mount Vernon in honour of the admiral.

## EDWARD BOSCAWEN

The Cornishman Edward Boscawen entered the navy in 1726 aged fifteen, and was sent in the 60-gun *Superbe* to the Caribbean, where he survived three years of disease and bad diet. In 1739 he distinguished himself at Porto Bello as a volunteer, and at Cartagena in 1741 he led a brigade of 500 seamen and marines which attacked and took two Spanish forts, whereupon Vernon gave him command of the 70-gun *Prince Frederick*. Once returned to England, Boscawen was elected MP for the family seat of Truro, married Frances, the great-great-niece of John Evelyn the diarist, and was given another command. From the 60-gun *Dreadnought* he got his nickname 'Old Dreadnought', and in 1744, after a sixty-hour chase, he captured the 26-gun *Médée*, commanded by the Frenchman de Hocquart, who subsequently made a habit of surrendering to him. Boscawen was relied upon to command at the Nore during the rebellion of 1745, and he became one of William Pitt's more trusted admirals.

In 1747, France prepared two convoys, one for India and the other for America. They sailed in April, but Sir George Anson, Vice Admiral of the Blue, intercepted them off Finisterre. The French commodore, the Marquis de la Jonquière, bravely formed a line of battle with his best ships while the merchant ships and troop transports tried to make their escape, but, after a little hesitation, Anson ordered a general chase. In the running fight which developed he captured two French line-of-battle ships and four frigates, and before nightfall two French East Indiamen, a privateer, and six of the convoy. Hocquart in the 30-gun *Diamant* surrendered to Boscawen in the 74-gun *Namur*.

Next Boscawen, who was now one of the youngest admirals in the navy, was given command of a joint force in India and a commission as a major-general in the army. Boscawen's campaign there was not notable for its success, but a young officer called

Robert Clive was blooded, and Madras, under the terms of the
peace treaty between Britain and France, was handed over to
Boscawen in 1749, and French fortunes in India began their
decline.

There followed four years of relative peace, which the French
used to strengthen their position in North America, ejecting British
colonists from posts west of the Allegheny Mountains. Not all the
colonies took the threat seriously, but the Governor of Virginia
appointed a young officer to his militia, and sent him to face the
French. That officer was George Washington. Meanwhile intelligence reached London of French reinforcements for North America,
and when an officer with sound political judgement and resolute
fighting ability was needed, the choice naturally fell on Boscawen.
Over four foggy days in June 1755 Boscawen, now Rear Admiral
of the Blue, sighted and chased a squadron of four French warships
and captured two. In this engagement the 60-gun *Dunkirk* was
commanded by Richard Howe, who captured the 64-gun *Alcide*,
commanded by none other than Hocquart, who once more became
Boscawen's prisoner. In Paris news of these captures caused an
outcry, and although there was no formal declaration until May
1756, the Seven Years War had begun.

## JOHN BYNG

The Seven Years War, 1756–63, which is usually reckoned to have
been the first true world war, was complex in origin, involving the
colonial rivalry between France and England and the struggle for
supremacy in Germany between Austria and the rising kingdom of
Prussia. In America it was preceded by the outbreak of the last of
the French and Indian Wars, and in India there was fighting among
native factions and between the French Governor, Dupleix, and the
British, led by Robert Clive. Many of the most important battles
were fought at sea to win control of overseas colonies. Britain
emerged from the war as the dominant imperial power in Europe,
having made large territorial gains in North America, the Caribbean, and India, but the war started badly.

John Byng, Admiral of the Blue, was sent to the Mediterranean to relieve Minorca, and at Gibraltar he learned that the French were already in occupation of the island and that only a small British garrison at Port Mahon still held out against the enemy. Pressing on, he met the French and was outmanoeuvred, the French concentrating their fire on masts and rigging before withdrawing, leaving him unable to chase and bring the enemy to decisive action. Minorca was lost, and, worse for Byng, the news reached London via Paris. No one doubted his courage in battle, but he became a political scapegoat. Boscawen's views are revealed in letters between him and his wife, Frances: 'the President [of the court martial] is not, to my mind, stern enough', she wrote, but she anticipated correctly, some months before the question arose, that the King 'will not exert his prerogative of mercy'. Frances herself would not be satisfied until Byng 'was hanged or shot'.

If anything, Byng's real offence seems to have been that he was middle-aged, unmarried, and of the wrong political persuasion. He was duly executed, on the quarterdeck of a captured French man of war, *Monarch*, by a firing squad of British marines. To the last the admiral maintained his innocence, even as he knelt in the pile of sawdust and tied his own blindfold. Whatever the quality of Byng's actions, the episode was a blot on Boscawen's reputation: he had been a member since 1751 of the Board of Admiralty, which had published an edited and thus prejudicial version of Byng's despatch, as Commander in Chief at Portsmouth he had convened the court, which was packed with his protégés, and neither he nor any of his political friends made any sincere effort to appeal to the King for mercy. According to Byng's epitaph, which he wrote himself, he died 'To the Perpetual Disgrace of Public Justice [and] Fell a martyr to Political Persecution, March 14, 1757, when Bravery and Loyalty were insufficient Securities for the Life and Honour of a Naval Officer'. In France Voltaire jibed: 'Il est bon de tuer de temps en temps un amiral, pour encourager les autres'. Byng's ghost walks the corridors of the naval college at Greenwich today.

## THIS WONDERFUL YEAR

French plans for an attack on Britain, which hardly changed over the decades, were to sail a fleet from Toulon, unite with ships at the French Atlantic ports, and land an invasion force in Ireland or England. British plans for war with France hardly changed either: pay a Continental ally to fight a land war, usually on France's eastern borders, and use the navy to attack French colonies and trade. These ideas were strongly advocated by, for example, Edward Vernon in Parliament and taken up by politicians and by businessmen, and they worked because after each new cycle of war in the eighteenth century British trade and commerce emerged stronger than before.

When David Garrick, actor and dramatist, included 'Hearts of Oak' in an operetta, the topical words ran, 'Come cheer up, my lads, 'tis to glory we steer, to add something new to this wonderful year . . .' The wonderful year was 1759 and it is generally reckoned that Garrick was referring to the capture of Quebec by Admiral Charles Saunders and General James Wolfe, and Admiral Edward Hawke's victory in Quiberon Bay. However, other victories included the capture of Louisbourg, the key to the St Lawrence River and to Quebec, and the defeat of the French invasion plan, both by Edward Boscawen.

In 1758 Boscawen, now Admiral of the Blue, again commanded a joint expedition to North America (in his fleet were Samuel Wallis, George Rodney, Edward Hughes, and James Wolfe). There the turning point in the struggle for North America was the siege of Louisbourg and its capture by Boscawen's sailors and marines, and its permanent result was the end of French expansion in North America. Next year, while Hawke watched the French Atlantic coast, Boscawen was sent to the Mediterranean to reinforce Gibraltar and to blockade Toulon. The French fleet escaped from Toulon (just as they would half a century later when Nelson was watching) and Boscawen, as Nelson would likewise do, sailed in pursuit. He found the French off the coast which runs from Gibraltar via Cadiz to Lagos in Portugal, a frequent meeting ground for the French and British fleets. After a general chase, the Frenchmen either ran into

the surf and were later captured or burned by the British, or
blockaded in Cadiz. Unfortunately for Boscawen's place in history,
this, his last victory, was overshadowed by Hawke's great triumph
in Quiberon Bay.

## THE CAPTURE OF QUEBEC

Pitt followed up Boscawen's success at Louisbourg by sending
Charles Saunders, Vice Admiral of the Blue and a survivor of
Anson's circumnavigation, to Canada with an army commanded
by Major General James Wolfe: their target was the French capital
of Canada, Quebec. The French commander had removed all the
buoys and marks on the river and, not for the first or last time, the
French believed they were protected by waters in which the British
could not sail. Saunders brought twenty line-of-battle ships and
numerous frigates and smaller ships, carrying Wolfe's small army of
ten thousand men to the basin below Quebec. Amongst his expert
navigators was one James Cook. On 12 September the British in
boats made upriver as if to land and attack from the west, a French
corps marching laboriously through the dark along the bank trying
to keep pace. In another diversion marines landed on the Beauport
shore, east of the citadel, under a noisy barrage of gunfire from
Saunders' ships. Then Wolfe returned downstream at great speed
rowing with the current and his soldiers scrambled up the cliffs of
the Heights of Abraham. There, with their backs to the river and
secured by Saunders' fleet, they formed up ready to face the French,
who were advancing from the city: meanwhile seamen hauled their
guns up the cliffs. Wolfe died early in the battle, but when their
general, Montcalm, was wounded the French broke before more
disciplined British troops and fled back inside the city. They did
not immediately capitulate and the British army occupied the plains
for two days between two theoretically superior forces. The stalemate was ended when Saunders 'sent up all the Boats in the Fleet
with Artillery and Ammunition; and on the 17th [September 1759]
went up with the Men of War, in a Disposition to attack the Lower
Town, but in the evening they sent out . . . and offered terms of
Capitulation'.

The whole expedition had been characterized by that essential ingredient to any amphibious campaign: harmony between the army and the navy. Saunders wrote: 'during this tedious campaign there has been perfect good Understanding between the Army and Navy', and Brigadier General George Townshend, who had succeeded to command of the army on Wolfe's death, added: 'I should not do Justice to the Admirals and the Naval Service if I neglected this Occasion of acknowledging how much we are indebted for our Success to the constant Assistance and support received from them, and the perfect Harmony and Correspondence which has prevailed throughout all our Operations'. He did not forget to mention 'the drawing up [of] our Artillery by the Seamen, even in the Heat of Action' and ended by acknowledging 'how great a Share the Navy has had in this successful Campaign'.

## EDWARD HAWKE

Edward Hawke, another Cornishman, entered the navy in 1720 and was promoted to lieutenant in 1729. He served in the Mediterranean, the West Indies, and off the West African coast between periods on half-pay, becoming a captain in 1734. So far his career had been one of monotonous cruises or uninteresting passages, and even his command of the decrepit *Portland* in the West Indies, 1737–42, was years of 'tedious duty'. However, given command of the new 70-gun *Berwick*, he distinguished himself in the Mediterranean and in 1746 was appointed second-in-command of the Channel Fleet and later to full command. A decisive victory off Finisterre in 1747 won him a knighthood and he was elected a Member of Parliament, holding his Portsmouth seat for thirty years. For the next ten years, with some breaks, he was Commander-in-Chief of the Channel Fleet, and in 1759, as Admiral of the Blue in the *Royal George*, he was blockading Brest.

In November the weather forced him to withdraw to Torbay. The enemy sailed and, as the weather worsened, Hawke gave chase. The French ships sought refuge again, this time in Quiberon Bay. In the battle that followed, two of Hawke's ships were wrecked, but he shattered the French fleet and with it all hope of invasion.

Hawke tells the story in a direct, seamanlike style: in his letter, Penvins Point, the Four Shoal, the Cardinals, Dumet island, Croisic church are all dangers or features on the French shore. As the letter reveals, he did not have pilots to navigate 'on a part of the coast among islands and shoals of which we were totally ignorant', but he knew the coast sufficiently well to name its features and, more significantly, he wrote knowing his readers in London also understood enough not to require explanation:

In my letter of the 17th by express, I desired you would acquaint their Lordships with my having received intelligence of eighteen sail-of-the-line and three frigates of the Brest squadron being discovered about twenty-four leagues to the N.W. of Belle Isle, steering to the eastward ... their squadron consisted, according to the accompanying list, of four ships of 80, six of 74, three of 70, eight of 64, one frigate of 36, one of 34 and one of 16 guns, with a small vessel to look out. They sailed from Brest the 14th instant, the same day I sailed from Torbay. Concluding that their first rendezvous would be Quiberon, the instant I received the intelligence I directed my course thither with a pressed sail. At first the wind, blowing hard at S. by E. and S., drove us considerably to the westward; but on the 18th and 19th, though variable, it proved more favourable. In the meantime having been joined by the *Maidstone* and *Coventry* frigates, I directed their commanders to keep ahead of the squadron, one on the starboard and the other on the larboard bow. At ½ past 8 o'clock in the morning of the 20th ... the *Maidstone* made the signal for seeing a fleet.

I immediately spread abroad the signal for a line abreast in order to draw all the ships of the squadron up with me. I had before sent the *Magnanime* [Howe's ship] ahead to make the land. At ¾ past 9 she made the signal for an enemy. Observing, on my discovering them, that they made off, I threw out the signal for the seven ships nearest to them to chase and draw into a line of battle ahead of me and endeavour to stop them till the rest of the squadron should come up, who were also to form as they chased, that no time might be lost in the pursuit.

That morning they were in chase of the *Rochester*, *Chatham*, *Portland*, *Falkland*, *Minerva*, *Vengeance* and *Venus*, all of which joined me about 11 o'clock (and the evening the *Sapphire*) from Quiberon Bay. All the day we had very fresh gales at N.W. and W.N.W., with heavy squalls. Monsieur Conflans kept going off under such sail as all his squadron could carry and at the same time keep together, while we crowded after him with every sail our ships could bear. At ½ past 2 p.m., the fire beginning ahead, I made the signal for engaging.

We were then to the southward of Belle Isle and the French admiral, headmost, soon after led round the Cardinals while his rear was in action. About 4 o'clock the *Formidable* struck; and a little after the *Thésée* and *Superbe* were sunk. About 5, the *Héros* struck [her colours] and came to an anchor; but, it blowing hard, no boat could be sent on board her. Night was now come and, being on a part of the coast among islands and shoals of which we were totally ignorant, without a pilot, as was the greatest part of the squadron, and blowing hard upon a lee shore, I made the signal to anchor and came to in fifteen fathom water, the Island of Dumet bearing E. by N. between two and three miles, the Cardinals W½S, and the steeples of Croisic S.E., as we found next morning.

In the night we heard many guns of distress fired; but blowing hard, want of knowledge of the coast, and whether they were fired by a friend or an enemy, prevented all means of relief.

By daybreak of the 21st we discovered one of our ships dismasted ashore on the Four, the French *Héros* also, and the *Soleil Royal*, flagship of Marshal Conflans, which under cover of the night had anchored among us, cut and run ashore to the westward of Croisic. On the latter's moving, I made the *Essex's* signal to slip and pursue her; but she unfortunately got upon the Four and both she and the *Resolution* are irrecoverably lost, notwithstanding we sent them all the assistance that the weather would permit. About fourscore of the *Resolution's* company, in spite of the strongest remonstrances of their captain, made rafts and, with some French prisoners belonging to the *Formidable*, put off and I am afraid drove out to sea. All the *Essex's* are saved with as many of the stores as possible, except one lieutenant and a boat's crew, who were drove on the French shore and have not since been heard of. The remains of both ships are set on fire.

We found the *Dorsetshire*, *Revenge*, and *Defiance*, in the night of the 20th, [had] put out to sea – as I hope the *Swiftsure* did, for she is still missing. The *Dorsetshire* and *Defiance* returned the next day and the latter saw the *Revenge* without. Thus what loss we have sustained has been owing to the weather, not the enemy, seven or eight of whose line of battle ships got to sea, I believe, the night of the action.

As soon as it was broad daylight in the morning of the 21st I discovered seven or eight of the enemy's line of battle ships at anchor between Point Penvins and the River Vilaine, on which I made the signal to weigh in order to work up and attack them. But it blowed so hard from the N.W. that, instead of daring to cast the squadron loose, I was obliged to strike topgallant masts. Most of those ships appeared to be aground at low water. But on the flood, by lightening them and the advantage of the wind under the land, all except two got that night into the River Vilaine.

The weather being moderate on the 22nd, I sent the *Portland*, *Chatham* and *Vengeance* to destroy the *Soleil Royal* and *Héros*. The French on the approach of our ships set the first on fire and soon after the latter met the same fate from our people. In the meantime, I got under way and worked up within Penvins Point, as well for the sake of its being a safer road as to destroy, if possible, the two ships of the enemy which still lay without the Vilaine. But before the ships I sent ahead for that purpose could get near them, being quite light and with the tide of flood they got in.

All the 23rd, we were employed in reconnoitring the entrance of that river which is very narrow and only twelve foot of water on the bar at low water. We discovered at least seven, if not eight, line of battle ships about half a mile within quite light, and two large frigates moored across to defend the mouth of the river. Only the frigates appear to have guns in. By the evening I had twelve longboats fitted as fireships, ready to attempt burning them under cover of the *Sapphire* and *Coventry*. But the weather being bad and the wind contrary obliged me to defer it till at least the latter should be favourable. If they can by any means be destroyed, it shall be done.

In attacking a flying enemy it was impossible, in the space of

a short winter's day, that all our ships should be able to get into
action or all those of the enemy brought into it. The commanders and companies of such as did come up with the rear of the
French on the 20th behaved with the greatest intrepidity and
gave the strongest proofs of a true British spirit. In the same
manner I am satisfied would those have acquitted themselves
whose bad going ships, or the distance they were at in the
morning, prevented from getting up.

Our loss by the enemy is not considerable for, in the ships
which are now with me, I find only one lieutenant and thirty-
nine seamen and marines killed and about two hundred and
two wounded. When I consider the season of the year, the hard
gales on the day of action, a flying enemy, the shortness of the
day, and the coast we are on, I can boldly affirm that all that
could possibly be done has been done. As to the loss we have
sustained, let it be placed to the account of the necessity I was
under of running all risks to break this strong force of the
enemy. Had we had but two hours more daylight, the whole
had been totally destroyed or taken, for we were almost up with
their van when night overtook us.

In 1760, Boscawen took over from Hawke the watch on the
French coast. He captured several prizes, but the French fleet did
not, indeed could not, sail. It was Boscawen's last service, and he
returned home to die. His epitaph reads that he 'died . . . in the
50th year of his age, at Hatchlands Park in Surrey, a seat he had
just finished at the expense of the enemies of his country and
amidst the groans and tears of his beloved Cornishmen was here
deposited.' He had indeed served his country with 'ardent zeal
[and] successful valour' but his deeds and career, which have been
sketched here, anticipating the great Nelson's, were overshadowed
by those of Anson and Hawke.

Something more was added to this wonderful year. In 1762,
Sir George Pocock, Vice Admiral of the Red, commanded an
expedition to capture Havana, where he made a fortune from prize
money and ransoming the city. After Charles Saunders was preferred over him to be First Lord of the Admiralty, Pocock retired
to live on the fortune he made there and during his years of service
in the East Indies. Also in 1762 a British expedition mounted from

India, consisting of regular and East India Company troops under Samuel Cornish, Vice Admiral of the Blue, captured Manila: a remarkable achievement, not least because the route from Madras to Manila was uncharted. Both expeditions were triumphant and resulted in huge wealth for individuals; moreover they demonstrated the proficiency which British arms had reached in amphibious warfare. However, the news of the capture of Manila reached Europe too late to affect the Peace of Paris which ended the Seven Years War. Under this treaty Canada was acknowledged to be British, and by acquiring eastern Louisiana, then pretty much all the lower basin of the Mississippi River, and the right of passage on that great river, the road was opened for the westwards expansion of the original thirteen states. The growing effectiveness and the global influence of the Royal Navy were clear for all to see.

# Chapter Four

# Exploration in the Age of Sail

The long eighteenth century was a remarkable age of exploration, endeavour, and expectation. Often the advantage which men deployed over the unknown and the rages of the weather was little more than personal bravery. In slow cumbersome vessels, rarely larger than modern pleasure yachts, without charts, knowing little about the cures for unfamiliar illnesses but in the assurance that many would die, and absent for so long that others thought they had died, they set off on voyages to the unknown and attempted tasks which men today with their modern knowledge and modern tools would not. A voyage to the South Sea or the Arctic was still the equivalent of a journey to the moon, but without the benefit of mission control back on Earth.

## THE CHAIN OF SUCCESSION

The men who hazarded their lives on these perilous voyages were a thoroughbred race. In at least two cases they built new ships on foreign beaches from the wrecks of their hopes, and in another a boat only eight feet long. They followed each other in unbroken chains of succession, the father of them all, connecting the Tudor buccaneers with the scientific expeditions of discovery, being William Dampier, an orphan farmer's son from Somerset who was sent to sea at the age of sixteen in 1668. He sailed with John Stradling, who abandoned Alexander Selkirk on Juan Fernandez Island. Also of their crew were John Clipperton and Simon Hatley, who also sailed with Woodes Rogers. Rogers' pirated wealth made him acquainted with Admiral Sir Charles Wager, and Wager, when First Lord of the Admiralty, sent Anson to the Pacific and Middleton to the Arctic. In Anson's squadron were Charles Saunders and John Byron. Saunders was among the first to recognize James Cook's brilliance and sent him on the first of his famous voyages, so launching a plethora of officers who mapped the world, including William Bligh, George Vancouver, William Broughton, and Peter Puget. Cook's faithful lieutenant Charles Clerke first learned his trade under Byron, and another of Byron's officers was Samuel Wallis. Richard Pickersgill sailed under both Wallis and Cook then commanded his own expedition, and Matthew Flinders had sailed with Bligh.

By the end of the century, Alexander Selkirk had been transformed into Robinson Crusoe and it was boyhood reading of Defoe's great story which inspired Flinders. There were still heroic voyages to be undertaken under sail and steam, but with Flinders' death in 1810, with five more years of world war to run, the age of exploration stuttered, temporarily, to a halt. A young cousin, John Franklin, sailed under Flinders, and he carried the torch into the nineteenth century and was responsible, posthumously, for opening up another continent.

## THE HEART OF MAN

Richard Pickersgill's journal, written as he sailed on Cook's second voyage, stands as an epitaph for all these brave men. Quoting 'my favourite author', he wrote:

> The Heart of Man is naturally inclined to attempt things the advantage of which appear to increase in proportion to the difficulties which attend them; it spares no pains, it fears no danger, in attaining them, and instead of being diverted from its purpose is animated by fresh vigour from opposition. The Glory inseparable from arduous enterprises is a powerful incentive which raises the mind above itself; the hope of advantages determines the will, diminishes dangers, alleviates hardships and levels obstacles which otherwise would appear insurmountable; how far desire and resolution has been crowned by success I leave to be judged of from the sequel which follows . . .

At the end of the seventeenth century, English knowledge of the Pacific Ocean was kept alive by pirates and privateers, foremost amongst them being William Dampier, whose career spanned forty years: prudish historians are silent as to why one of his ships was called *Batchelor's Delight*. His book, *A New Voyage Round the World*, first published in 1697, ran to many editions, and he was given command in 1698–1701 of the navy's *Roebuck*, in which he charted the west coast of Australia, sailed the northern coast of New Guinea and discovered Dampier's Passage. *Roebuck* sank at her moorings off Ascension Island in 1701: in fact Dampier seems to have made a habit of choosing leaky and rotten ships, and on the last expedition he commanded, the *St George* had to be abandoned. Heroically he made it home across the Pacific in a much smaller craft – a task made easier after desertions reduced his crew, including his mate John Clipperton. It was on this expedition that Alexander Selkirk preferred to be left on the island of Juan Fernandez rather than endure the appalling conditions on board John Stradling's *Cinque Ports*.

One of the most successful pirates was Woodes Rogers, who circumnavigated the world in 1708–11. Badly manned with raw recruits, one third of whom were foreigners, the expedition, in two ships (*Duke* and *Dutchess*), was financed from Bristol. William Dampier was making his last voyage, as master of the *Duke*, and the rest of the crew was somewhat eclectic, including a Dr Dover, who represented the owners' interests and doubled as 'chief surgeon and captain of marines', and Carleton Vanbrugh, older brother of the playwright and architect John Vanbrugh. Rogers was not the commander of the expedition, which was run by a series of piratical councils, but he does seem to have got his way on most occasions. He dealt ruthlessly with a mutinous crew who wanted to sack an innocent Swedish merchant ship early in the voyage, and thereafter showed strong leadership and good powers of organization. The expedition seems to have enjoyed relatively good health, which can perhaps be explained if Rogers's enthusiasm for careening his ships extended to cleaning the tween decks too. The expedition rescued Selkirk from Juan Fernandez, giving Defoe his model for Robinson Crusoe, and placed him in command of a prize, the *Increase*. Together they sacked Guayaquil and captured a Spanish treasure ship off the coast of Mexico – the first to be taken by an Englishman since Thomas Cavendish in the Elizabethan days.

Rogers' *A Cruising Voyage Round the World* was published in 1712, thus ensuring that his version of events entered the public consciousness. *A Cruising Voyage* became compulsory reading for any South Seas explorer for the next century, is compulsive reading today, and has been plagiarized many times by authors of pirate stories. With his new-found wealth Rogers became a member of the establishment and ended his life as Governor of the Bahama Islands.

When another expedition was mounted in 1717, it too was commanded by pirates. Strangely, it was originally planned from Vienna but organized in London: John Clipperton, who had once deserted Dampier and who also had sailed with Woodes Rogers, commanded the 36-gun *Success* and George Shelvocke commanded the 24-gun *Speedwell*. Little is known about Shelvocke, but his mate, Simon Hatley, had also sailed with Rogers. Shelvocke resented having been demoted from the chief command of the expedition and as soon as he could he deserted with his ship. Passing though the Straits of Magellan, both ships were driven far to the south where, in 60° 30' S, Hatley shot an albatross, believing it to be an omen of bad luck. When they made landfall, *Speedwell* was duly wrecked on the beach at Juan Fernandez. There, displaying the resourcefulness for which sailors the world over are known, Shelvocke build a new ship of twenty tons from the wreckage, which he christened *Recovery*, but was forced to abandon fourteen of his crew to an uncertain fate. Shelvocke and Clipperton raided the coast and made small captures but achieved limited success; crossing the Pacific to Macao they sold their ships and returned home as passengers with their booty. Clipperton returned in 1720 and Shelvocke in 1721, when he was tried for piracy but acquitted for lack of evidence.

## ANSON'S VOYAGE

The first properly naval expedition to the Pacific was Commodore George Anson's in 1740 – though it retained some of the characteristics of a privateering voyage. His orders, from the First Lord of the Admiralty, Sir Charles Wager, were to 'to take, burn, sink, or otherwise destroy the ships and vessels belonging to [the] Crown of Spain', words echoed by Admiral Somerville two hundred years later in the Mediterranean. Anson's squadron took a year to be readied and was manned with great difficulty, including five hundred out-pensioners of Chelsea Hospital (all those who did not desert on the march to Portsmouth died on the voyage). East of Cape Horn, as they left the Strait of le Maire, the squadron met furious weather, two ships deserted, and the rest of the squadron was dispersed in about 60° S. There was mutiny amongst the crew of the *Wager* after she was wrecked, the men arguing that once their pay had been stopped they were no longer subject to naval discipline; some deserted but the captain and a few followers, including Midshipman John Byron, grandfather of the poet, were rescued by Indians and handed over to the Spaniards. Three months later the 60-gun *Centurion*, Anson's flagship, reached Juan Fernandez with 130 sick on board, having buried 200 men at sea.

Lawrence Millechamp was purser of the *Tryal* but as ships rotted and were lost he transferred to the *Tryal Prize*, to the *Gloucester*, and finally to the *Centurion*. Again, killing an albatross seems to have been the cause of bad luck. Millechamp could be writing about almost any passage of Cape Horn in the age of sail:

> the Straits Le Maire lie in latitude 55° 01′ S. There are a great many different currents in these Straits, which causes great rippling of the water and would incline a stranger to believe they were all shoals. We saw abundance of strange sea fowl as albatrosses which is a prodigious large sea fowl whose wings when extended will measure fourteen or sixteen feet. They are shaped and coloured much like the different colours of geese, but vastly larger; they eat [taste] something fishy, but we were always rejoiced when we could catch any, and for want of fresh meat always esteemed them excellent eating. I remember one caught with a hook and line, the hook being baited with a piece of salt pork and buoyed up with cork so as to make it swim on the water, which the bird took eagerly, and was caught. And notwithstanding he measured fourteen foot on the wing, and weighed twenty-eight or thirty pounds, the captain, lieutenant, surgeon and myself ate him all up for dinner ... We got well through the Straits, but met with most intolerable weather

immediately after, the climate being very cold, and the continual rain, snow or sleet with a constant head wind and a monstrous deep sea made it quite insupportable ... The weather was still stormy with huge deep, hollow seas that frequently broke quite over us, with constant rain, frost or snow. Our decks were always full of water, and our men continually falling ill with the scurvy; and the allowance of water being but small reduced us to a most deplorable condition. We are now in latitude 60° S., sometimes lying to, at others plying to windward under our courses, pinched with cold, having no refreshments even for our sick men but salt meat, which in some of the ships could not be boiled for many days together, but a purser's quart of water (which is seven-eighths of a wine quart [i.e. 828 ml or 33 floz]) for one man a day, our men almost all sick and those that were dying as well as many of the rest almost devoured by vermin, insomuch that I have frequently seen by a modest computation above a peck of lice on a man even after he was dead. This afforded but a melancholy spectacle, but this was no time for reflection, nor were these all the miseries we were to undergo.

On the twenty-sixth [of March] 'twas observed that the *Severn* lagged astern, whereupon the Commodore sent the *Tryal* to see what was the matter with her; which she did, and found that she had split her courses. Next, on the thirty-first, the *Gloucester* made a signal of distress, having carried away her main yard. About the same time the *Tryal's* pumps proved very bad, and the sloop leaky, which reduced them to great difficulties, being obliged to bale her constantly with buckets for several days together. The next misfortune that attended us (except the loss of numbers of our men who were dying every hour) was on the eighth of April, when the *Wager* lost her mizen mast and maintopsail yard. On the eleventh we lost company with the *Severn* and *Pearl*, and never saw them after. And now completely to ruin us, on the thirteenth when we imagined we had weathered Cape Horn, and had some distant hopes of heading out to Juan Fernandez Island, we fell in with the land in the night, which convinced us of our error, and obliged us to stand again from latitude 54° 36' S., which is the latitude of the land we saw, and run into once more. Our seamen now almost all despairing of ever getting on shore voluntarily gave themselves up to their fatal distemper, and only used to envy those whose good fortune it was to die first. Nothing was more frequent than to bury eight or ten men from each ship every morning.

On the twenty-fourth of April 1741 we all parted company in a hard gale of wind . . . Our misfortunes continually increase upon us: nay sometimes we had no more than the captain, lieutenant, surgeon, myself and two boys, with now and then one marine, to work the sloop, mend the sails, bury the dead, and do the more servile offices. In this situation our food was generally bread toasted over burning brandy to kill the numerous insects it abounded with. We frequently had our sails blown away for want of strength to take them in. We lost several of our yards, and I think all the topsails we had. On the ninth of May being in latitude 45° 28′ S., we saw a sail to the eastward which we spoke with, and found her to be the *Anna* pink, who separated from the rest of the squadron the same day we did. She gave us but a melancholy account of her condition, but spared us a small quantity of wine and sour cider which proved of great service to us. On the thirteenth we parted company with her again, and met with most intolerable weather soon after. On the eighteenth we made the land, but were in too bad a condition to cruise there for the rest of the squadron; we therefore resolved to make the best of our way to the island of Juan Fernandez.

The weather now began to be more favourable than it had been for above two months past and the air more serene, and our men who had long languished almost all died, and the officers and boys who had been serviceable hitherto now began to be too much harassed and fatigued to hold out much longer. But very providentially the alteration of climate that hurried off a great number of those who had been long ill, helped to recover others.

On the eleventh day of June at break of day we had the joyful sight of the long wished for island of Juan Fernandez, bearing due north of us, and some time after we discovered a great ship in the large bay. This ship proved to be the *Centurion*, which much increased our transports. We got well into the bay, and came to an anchor with the assistance of some of the *Centurion's* people; but not having sufficient strength to moor, even with their assistance, we were obliged to lie at a single anchor . . .

As soon as we anchored we went to work on shore to raise tents and make some conveniences for our sick, a great many of whom died in getting on shore. And before we had removed them all the sloop drove to sea again by a violent squall from off the mountains, and was four days before we got in again, which proved fatal to many of the sick men who had the misfortune to be then on board . . . but with the greens and other refreshments we met with together with the smell of the earth recovered them to a miracle.

On Juan Fernandez, Anson's men caught goats which had been raised by Alexander Selkirk some thirty years earlier. Having recovered something of their strength, Anson's squadron went on to raid Payta, which Shelvocke had raided twenty years before, and to take several prizes, but they missed the Spanish treasure ship bound for Manila. Sailing on across the Pacific, Anson's squadron suffered more sickness and he was forced to burn the last of his consorts, the *Gloucester*, in order to be able to man the *Centurion*. They reached Macao in 1742 where they recruited and refreshed themselves. Then in the spring of 1743 Anson cruised off Luzon where, after a three years' voyage and an hour and a half's fight, he took one of the richest prizes in naval history. It took his crew two days to carry all the treasure they found in *Nuestra Señora de Cavadonga* into the *Centurion*. This is how Millechamp describes events:

On the twenty-first of May we arrived on our station off of Cape Espiritu Santo, on the island of Luzon, one of the Philippines, where we cruised for the Acapulco galleon, and saw the land from masthead bearing SE. ten leagues distance.

We continued here cruising until the twentieth of June without meeting with anything, and were much dejected, fearing the galleon had escaped, when about daybreak a young gentleman from the masthead called out that he saw a sail on the SE. quarter, and that he imagined that she bore directly down upon us. This first report was soon confirmed by numbers who then immediately discovered her, and we all well knew it must be the Acapulco ship we had been so long in search of. Our ship immediately grew into a ferment; the people, quite overjoyed, knew not how to express it. They ardently longed for a close engagement, and used their utmost endeavours to obtain it, for on setting the least sail, or making the least disposition towards coming up with the chase, every man was ready to assist, and everyone thought the thing could not be well done without his having a hand in it. For my part I thought they would all have run mad with joy. The ship was cleared and the guns unlashed in an instant, anything standing in the way, let it belong to who, or be of what value it would, the sailors immediately threw it overboard to clear the ship for the engagement. But after all this trouble we should have made nothing of it had not the other ship been kind enough to come to us, for she was (when we first saw her) at a prodigious distance, and right to leeward, that it would have been almost impossible for us to come up with her, had she not bore down with an intent to engage with and take us. What led the commander of her into so gross an error was the information he received from Guam by means of some prisoners we released at Tinian, and who afterwards got to Guam. These people informed him that our complement could not exceed 120 or 130 men, which seemed to correspond exactly with the accounts he had before heard, and he having upwards of 600 to oppose us was thereby encouraged to bear down on us and give battle, which he might easily have avoided had he kept his wind and used his endeavours to escape us. The particulars of the engagement that ensued are hardly worth mentioning excepting only that Mr. Anson took great care to get nigh enough his antagonist to be sure of even a pistol ball doing execution. Before he began his general fire the galleon had before that brought to in form, with her headsails to the mast, had clewed up her courses, hoisted her jack and ensign and a flag (the standard of Spain) on her main topmast head. We exchanged several shot before we got so nigh as we intended without much damage on either side. At last, being at a convenient distance (no more than twenty or thirty yards off), we began an excessive hot fire on them, both with great guns and small arms, for notwithstanding we were so weakly manned as to have hardly men enough to manage the

great guns, Mr. Anson made so good a disposition of the small
arms that the want of men to be quartered to them was not felt.
He ordered all the small arms in the ship to be loaded and laid
along on the gratings for such people as were quartered at the
great guns to use when they had leisure, which often happens,
for when the great gun is loading there cannot well be more
than two men employed. The rest then discharge the small
arms, and lay them down again for others (who were appointed
for that purpose) to load. I must also do justice to the gentlemen
who were quartered in our tops. They certainly behaved exceeding well, for on our first engaging they did not fire on the decks,
where were numbers of people quite open and exposed to them,
but prudently considered that the people on our deck must be
exposed in like manner to their tops; and therefore resolved to
fire only on the enemy's tops, till they had cleared them, and
then fire on the decks. This they did with such success that they
drove the Spaniards from their tops in about ten minutes, which
greatly contributed to the preservation of our men, who otherwise must have been greatly annoyed by them. We continued
the fire without any intermission; nothing was to be seen but
fire and smoke, nor heard but the thunder of the cannon, which
was fired so quick that it made one continued sound. We soon
shot away their ensign staff, on which some people imagined
she had struck, left off firing, till they were convinced of their
mistake. She maintained a brisk fire for the first hour, and
afterward flagged much. The engagement lasted about an hour
and a half, when she struck her flag and became our prize . . .

We were kept continually employed, whenever the weather
would permit, in transporting the money out of the prize into
the *Centurion*, until the ninth of July when we discovered a
large sail, which put us into a great hurry, as our crew were so
divided, and we had such a number of prisoners to secure. We
took as many of our people out of the prize as we possibly
could, leaving not above nine or ten to manage her, and having
put the *Centurion* into a tolerable fighting posture we chased
the sail, but to little purpose, for they took great care to get
away from us, and we were in no extraordinary condition to
pursue. We saw her again the next morning, but our inclination
to chase being then something abated, we left off, and pursued

our voyage towards Macao, off of which to our great joy we arrived on the twelfth . . .

[We] came to an anchor about four miles below Whampoa. We now began to make a thorough search of the prize, and found a great deal of concealed treasure, some cast into large lumps like cheeses, and so artfully covered in the rind of cheese, that 'twas by the weight only we could discover them. Some parcels of money we found hid between the beams and timbers of the ship, and in all places where there was any possibility of concealment we were sure to find money. Thus were many employed while the rest were purchasing rigging, sails etc., and refitting the ship, and procuring provisions to carry us to England . . .

Anson's triumph was nearly ruined in the last days of his three-year voyage, when he met a French squadron in the English Channel, but he sailed through undetected. However, only 188 men of the *Centurion*'s complement of over 600 had survived the voyage and en route he had had to recruit the men of a score of nations, Europeans as well as Asians. The death rate on board spurred James Lind to a scientific study of scurvy, though there is no evidence that the results of the first ever clinical trials, published in 1753, had any influence on Cook in his voyages of discovery. There were other consequences: though every survivor became rich from this voyage, a lengthy court case ensued over the exact share of prize money, and an amendment to the Navy Discipline Act in 1749 extended naval discipline to the crews of shipwrecks.

The major consequence was that many of the officers who sailed with Anson rose not only to fortune but also to fame. They were helped by Anson, who was First Lord of the Admiralty twice between 1751 and 1762 and a noted reforming administrator, and who never forgot to exercise his patronage in favour of the officers who had sailed with him. Nine officers were promoted to captain, and all of these, bar Philip de Saumarez, who was killed at the Second Battle of Finisterre (1747), reached flag rank. One, Charles Saunders, in turn became First Lord of the Admiralty in 1766, and it was Saunders who noted the promising young navigator James Cook, when he helped bring the British fleet up the St Lawrence to capture Quebec in 1759.

Charles Proby, whose young eyes had been the first to sight the
*Cavadonga*, became captain after the war, and the fourteen-year-
old Richard Howe, whose ship had turned back in the Strait of le
Maire, rose to become one of the Royal Navy's most famous
fighting admirals and victor at the Glorious First of June in 1794.


## A MOST DIFFICULT FEAT

In the meantime Commodore John Byron, who was to earn the
nickname Foul-Weather Jack, made the fastest circumnavigation
of the world to date, 1764–66. In the South Atlantic he took
possession of the Falklands, but in the Pacific, where he had been
sent to explore the west coast of North America, he disobeyed his
instructions and sailed westwards across the vast and unknown
ocean just below the Equator. Considering that the Pacific and the
East Indies were one vast theme park for explorers and just how
much was unknown, that Byron managed to discover nothing new
was, as the historian Laird Clowes remarked, 'a most difficult feat
on his part'.

Part of the reason for Byron's fast passage was that his ships were
copper-bottomed, the Admiralty having decided 'to make some
farther Experiments of the efficacy of Copper Sheathing'. Copper
sheathing protected a ship by slowing the growth of barnacles and
weed on its bottom and preventing the attack of shipworm. The
*Dolphin* and her consort the 16-gun *Tamar* were coppered at
Woolwich and Deptford respectively in 1764, and Byron declared,
'Copper Bottoms . . . is the finest invention in the World'. The
Admiralty already knew empirically about the effect of mixing
copper and iron on a ship's hull, though no one understood the
reasons. The *Dolphin* was the first ship to have copper rudder braces
and pintles as well as copper sheathing, and although they wore
away faster than iron, they lasted another two years; the *Tamar's*
mountings were of iron, and electrolysis wore them away so badly
that she had to mount a spare while beached in Antigua, while the
iron prevented the copper from dissolving, so that she was very
dirty and barnacled.

In fact *Dolphin's* hull was in such good condition that less than three months after her first circumnavigation one of Byron's officers, Captain Samuel Wallis, was able to sail her in another, 1766–68. Unfortunately he was another half-hearted explorer, who shared Byron's distaste for discovering anything new. He did find Tahiti, which inconveniently obstructed his westwards passage, but hardly stopped to explore. In the Magellan Strait, taking with him all the principal stores, he also abandoned his consort, Philip Carteret, in the *Swallow*. Carteret had accompanied Byron in the *Dolphin* as a lieutenant, and on his return he was immediately given the tiny *Swallow* and ordered to sail, despite his complaints that she was totally unfit for the voyage. Leaving the Magellan Strait, Carteret pressed on in his ill-found ship to Juan Fernandez Island, discovering Pitcairn Island en route, which was soon to play its own part in British naval history. He also named several other Pacific Ocean islands, and discovered that New Britain was in fact two islands, the northern of which he named New Ireland, with a sound in between, which he named St George's. Despite poor health and an even poorer ship, Carteret achieved more than his commanders during his two voyages. All told, however, these were meagre enough achievements for Byron's and Wallis's expeditions, and in truth both men probably had been hoping for war and booty rather than discovery.

## JAMES COOK, PEERLESS NAVIGATOR

The origins of Cook's voyages to the Pacific are in 1716, when Edmund Halley pointed out to the Royal Society the significance of two transits of the planet Venus across the face of the Sun, due in 1761 and 1769. He showed that the scale of the universe and the distance of Earth from the Sun, then both unknown to man, could be calculated if the time taken for the transit could be measured at widely separated points on the Earth. Halley had done important work while in command of the quaintly named *Paramore*, researching magnetic variation in the North Atlantic and tidal streams in the Channel, and as Astronomer Royal he had started to tabulate the movement of the stars across the skies, but attempts to observe the transit of Venus in 1761 failed for various reasons, while Cook served in obscurity on a survey of the coast of Newfoundland. However, in 1766 Cook observed the eclipse of the Sun, and his paper was read to the Royal Society just when plans were being laid for mounting new expeditions, to the north and to the south, to catch the next transit of Venus. The Royal Society wanted a scientific man to go to the South Pacific, but long memories at the Admiralty wanted no more philosophers like Halley to command its expeditions: Cook seemed like the ideal candidate.

In 1768 Cook sailed on his first Pacific voyage, in a shallow-draft Whitby collier, the 370-ton *Endeavour*, and using only the slow and laborious method of determining his longitude by measuring lunar distances: that is, comparing the angular distances between the Moon and ten selected stars against tables prepared by Nevil Maskelyne, the Astronomer Royal at Greenwich. The method was slow, laborious, and prone to error, and, of course, it was only available when the Moon was up and was not obscured, but Cook produced charts of such high quality and accuracy that they were still in use a hundred years later. Unlike his predecessors, on entering the Pacific from the east Cook avoided both the Magellan and le Maire Straits and sailed far to the south before shaping course for Tahiti. The ostensible purpose of his voyage was to observe the transit of Venus, which task he performed on 4 June 1769 at Tahiti, having learned about these islands from Wallis just before sailing from Plymouth.

Admiral Hawke, the First Lord, thought that Wallis's expedition might have sighted the southern continent and gave Cook secret orders to survey part of New Zealand and the east coast of Australia. Although he missed the natural harbour of Sydney, Cook did find Botany Bay, which in consequence became the destination of the First Fleet when Britain started to export convicts to Australia in HM Ships *Supply* and *Sirius* in 1787.

One of Cook's greatest achievements was his contribution to the health of seamen, and to the defeat of scurvy, a debilitating and fatal disease brought on by the lack of vitamins derived from fresh meat and vegetables. He achieved this by strictly enforcing a health regime on board his ships, which included taking assorted antiscorbutics, eating plentiful green vegetables which were taken onboard as often as possible, cold-water bathing, ventilating and heating the tween decks to keep them dry, and supplying warm clothing for the men. It was not a complete cure, as Richard Pickersgill's journal tells us, but 'we found our scorbutic patients much relieved by the use of the wort & sower krout [pickled cabbage] etc but yet had many visibly bad of that disorder . . .' Some basic mother–child psychology was necessary in persuading the men to eat unusual food:

> We got on Board a quantity of wild celery and scurvey grass . . . I wish this article was more attended to by Commanders of Ships, for its by their example it might be brought into use in general, for common Seamen, seeing their Commanders collect and eat these things; they immediately conclude that what will do him good will do them good and as they naturally suppose, his knowledge greater than theirs, they fall into it with their consent; which they would never heartily do by orders without example, for in the later case they would either evade finding of such things or when found would by some means or other evade eating them as they did not see their superiors do the same . . .

Cook's precautions could not prevent dysentery and malaria when his ship arrived in Batavia: nevertheless over half of his crew returned to England.

For his second voyage, 1772–75, Cook chose the *Resolution* (461 tons), and *Adventure* (336 tons), whose master and commander, Tobias Furneaux, had once sailed with Wallis. On his first voyage Cook had established his longitude by measuring lunar distances; on the second he carried four chronometers (one of them 'Kendal's first watch made in exact imitation of Mr Harrison's'), and one of his objects, besides completing the discovery of the southern hemisphere, was to check the error and the rate of these new-fangled clocks. Sailing east-about this time, he surveyed the high latitudes from the Cape of Good Hope, where the Dutch governor 'had orders to supply us with every thing we possibly might want . . . as we were bound on an universal cause' and on to New Zealand, the Friendly Islands, and South Georgia (which he discovered), searching for a southern continent. After running under bare poles in the biggest seas that anyone on board had ever seen,

they saw their first iceberg: 'three large lumps of ice floating in
the sea, which had a blue cold & wintery appearance . . . the snow
and sleet prevented our seeing above half a mile & rendered it
very dangerous running in an unknown sea amongst large Ice
Islands . . .' By now it was 'very cold and the thermometer stood
at 34° & the masts sails & ropes were all caked with Ice and it
constantly snow'd which froze as fast as it fell . . . most of the live
stock which we had brought from the Cape died thro' the severity
of the Cold'. On 17 January 1773 his crew became the first to cross
the Antarctic Circle, his furthest south being 71° 10′ S. Finally,
having followed the edge of the ice, 'we were regaled with the
pleasing sight of the Mountains of New Zealand after an absence
from land of 17 Weeks and 3 Days being the most of this time
immersed in ice and snow'. Sailing north, he rediscovered the
Marquesas, which had not been seen by European eyes for two
hundred years, charted the New Hebrides and New Caledonia, and
revisited New Zealand. Cook returned after three years and eighteen
days having lost only four men, 'without claiming any merit but
that of attention to my duty'.

Cook's third voyage was in the *Resolution*, with William Bligh as
his master, and with Clerke in command of the *Discovery*. The
proposed voyage was even more ambitious, with orders to try to
find the exit from the North-West Passage into the Pacific. Again
he sailed east-about: Cook was a driven man, and this is how
William Bligh described their arrival at Cape Town:

I am happy to tell you we are thus far arrived safe and well,
after a fourteen Weeks tolerable Passage . . . our stay here will
be a Month, from thence to N. Zealand where we wood and
water, this will take us ab't a week when we proceed for
Otaehite [Tahiti]. The *Discovery* is not yet arrived, And whether
she comes or not will be of no consequence, as C. Cooke seems
anxious to get away. Perhaps about May we may leave Otaheite
and stretch to the Northward. I think we shall bundle through
some how other, the very thought of having so many hundred
leagues to run over if we come back is sufficient spur. I can give
you no more intelligence as we must be governed principally by
circumstances, but that Siberia is separated from America is
certain, whether we can get through Baffins Bay is not . . .

After waiting at the Cape for Clerke to rendezvous, Cook wrote to his patron, the Earl of Sandwich, with more news of Omai, a native of the Society Islands who had been taken to England, where he had been feted. Cook, who seems to have been an archetypal, dour north-countryman, wrote in an uncharacteristically humorous style:

> we are at length ready to put to sea ... having onboard provisions for two years and upwards. Nothing is wanting but a few females of our own species to make the *Resolution* a compleat ark, for I have taken the liberty to add considerably to the number of animals your Lordship was pleased to order to be put onboard in England ... The taking onboard some horses has made Omai completely happy, he consented with rapture to give up his Cabbin to make room for them, his only concern now is that we shall not have food for all the stock ...

Omai was returning laden with presents and his newly acquired social skills, and continued to

> enjoy a good state of health and great flow of spirits ... he has obtained during his stay in England a far greater knowledge of things than any one could expect or will perhaps believe ... and the people here are surprised at his genteel behaviour and deportment.

Sadly, he died two years later.

As for the proposed voyage, knowledge of the northern Pacific had not advanced since Drake had visited the west coast of America two hundred years before. Cook proceeded to chart more of Tahiti, discovered Christmas Island and the Sandwich Islands (the Hawaiian Islands), and then charted North America from Drake's New Albion northward, entered the Bering Straits, and turned eastwards hoping to find the North-West Passage. He pressed on until reaching shoal water on a lee shore with ice to windward in 70° 6' N and 160° E, naming his furthest east Icy Point. Returning to the Sandwich Islands, Cook became involved in a squabble over a stolen boat and was murdered by the natives. All that remained of the great navigator were his head and hands, which were buried at sea.

Charles Clerke, also known as Clark, who had sailed with Byron, had accompanied Cook on all his voyages and now succeeded to his command. Clerke continued Cook's work for a few months before he too died and the expedition was brought home by his lieutenants. Like others before, as well as its discoveries and new charts, Cook's third voyage proved to be excellent training for naval officers, including fighting officers like Edward Riou, who fell at the Battle of Copenhagen in 1801, and a promising midshipman, George Vancouver, after whom Cook had named an island off the North American coast.

## MUTINY ON THE *BOUNTY*

Another of Cook's officers, William Bligh, has already been quoted and it was Bligh's own expedition, 1787–89, to transport breadfruit seedlings from the Pacific to feed slaves on the sugar plantations of the West Indies, which went so disastrously wrong and has entered history as the mutiny on the *Bounty*. In brief, mutineers, led by Fletcher Christian, took the *Bounty* with their native wives to Pitcairn, while Bligh was set adrift in a twenty-three-foot-long open boat with eighteen other men and sailed 3,600 miles across the ocean to Timor.

Whatever the relations between Bligh and his crew, the mutiny seems to have broken out without warning, and the previous evening Fletcher Christian had been planning to escape the *Bounty* on a makeshift raft. John Fryer was the master of the *Bounty*, and a man with whom Bligh found relatively little fault. Christian had the morning watch, from 4 a.m. to 8 a.m., and on 28 April, 'just at the break of day', Fryer was woken by a noise. 'When I jumped up,' he later wrote,

> A man laid his hand upon my breast and told me to lay down again Sir you are a prisoner Sir I wanted to expostulate with them but they told me to hold my tongue or else I was a dead man but if you make yourself quiet Sir there is no one on board will hurt a hair of your head. I then . . . saw Mr Bligh on the ladder when I asked what they was going to do their Captain

they shut my cabin door and said make yourself easy only put
him into a boat Mr Christian is Captain of the Ship I said for
God sake my lads consider what you are about . . .

The impromptu nature of the mutiny was evident from the chaos
and uncertainty which followed, men not knowing who was on
whose side, Bligh's or Christian's. The first plan to put Bligh and
three others into the jolly boat was abandoned when it began to
sink. In any case the number of men determined to stand by Bligh,
about twenty, was far larger than the mutineers had expected.

Once cast adrift in the launch, and apparently at the suggestion
of William Peckover, the gunner, who had also sailed with Cook,
Bligh sailed for the Dutch settlements on Timor, through the Fiji
Islands to make landfall in Queensland, and then on through the
Endeavour Strait. In the tradition of the greatest explorers and
navigators Bligh kept up his log, including descriptions of the
islands and the coasts he saw with sketches which are recognizable
today. Only the drama of the mutiny and the mystery of the fate of
the *Bounty* can detract from Bligh's achievement in reaching Cou-
pang on 14 June 1789, his force of personality, which had precipi-
tated the mutiny, being the greatest single factor in preserving his
people. The voyage ended prosaically: once in a Dutch harbour, the
launch's crew were refreshed by 'a soldier' who 'came down to the
boat with a kettle of tea and some small cakes'.

That Bligh had an evil temper is beyond doubt, but whether he
deserved the calumny which history has generally bestowed upon
him must be doubted. John Barrow, the Secretary of the Admiralty,
started the slander, his principal gripe seeming to be that Bligh had
come to the quarterdeck through the hawsehole and that he was
absent from England when ten of the mutineers were brought home
to trial by court martial. Whatever his personal faults, Bligh was a
peerless navigator, and certainly not all his contemporaries shared
Barrow's views: he was entrusted with a second breadfruit
expedition in 1791–93 in the *Providence*. This is how Francis Bond,
whose mother, Catherine, was a half-sister of Bligh, described him
in a letter to his brother:

Let me enjoin the strictest secersy [sic] . . . Yes, Tom, our
relation has the credit of being a tyrant in his last expedition,

where his misfortunes and good fortune have elevated him to a situation he is incapable of supporting with decent modesty. The very high opinion which he has of himself makes him hold every one of our profession with contempt, perhaps envy. Nay, the Navy is but a sphere for fops and lubbers to swarm in, without one gem to vie in brilliancy with himself. I don't means to depreciate his extensive knowledge as a seaman and nautical astronomer, but condemn that want of modesty, in self-estimation. To be less prolix I will inform you that he has treated me (nay, all on board) with the insolence and arrogance of a Jacob; and not-withstanding his passion is partly to be attributed to a nervous fever, with which he has been attacked most of the voyage, the chief part of his conduct must have arisen from the fury of an ungovernable temper . . .

The mutiny on the *Bounty* was one of several in which Bligh was involved. In the fleet mutinies of 1797 he was one of many officers who were turned out of their ships. He subsequently served with distinction, commanding the 64-gun *Director* at the Battle of Camperdown in 1797, and at Copenhagen in 1801 he anchored the 54-gun *Glatton* next astern of Nelson's own *Elephant*. Nevertheless as Captain-General and Governor of New South Wales from 1805 onwards he ruled the colony so badly that a force of the New South Wales Corps were driven to depose and imprison him.


## COOK'S OTHER PROTÉGÉS

Erasmus Gower, a Welshman, was master's mate of the *Dolphin* under Byron, lieutenant of the *Swallow* with Carteret, and also, as a protégé of George Rodney, first lieutenant of Rodney's flagship, *Sandwich*, in 1780. So when Rodney captured a Spanish squadron off Cape Finisterre, Gower was promoted to command the *Guipuscoana* prize, commissioned as the 64-gun *Prince William*. Three years later he commanded the 28-gun frigate *Medea* in the Indian Ocean, where he recaptured the sloop *Chaser* carrying despatches to Suffren and a few days later captured the 50-gun Dutch East Indiaman *Vryheid*. In 1792 he was chosen for his knowledge of Chinese waters and his fighting prowess to command the 64-gun *Lion* and take Lord Macartney, the new ambassador, to China.

Another of Cook's midshipmen was George Vancouver, who though he had sailed twice with Cook was more in the mould of Bligh. Nevertheless he held his squadron, the *Discovery* and the *Chatham*, together for nearly five years, 1791–95, while he completed some of Cook's work and thoroughly explored and charted the north-west coast of America. He ousted the Spanish from their settlement in the Nootka Sound, and, mostly in open boats and against strong currents, surveyed the intricate inlets and channels of the north-west, including San Francisco before it was settled by any other Europeans, the Columbia River, and California. Puget Sound was named after one of his midshipmen. Vancouver displayed the worst side of his character when, despite all his precautions, scurvy broke out in his ships. He found that slush had been sold to his crew to flavour their dried peas and make them more palatable. (Slush is the fat which floats to the surface of the coppers when salt meat is boiled, and enterprising cooks sold this either to grease the blocks or to make rather smoky candles or, illegally, as a comestible, to spread on hard biscuit or bread or for frying. Ever since, cooks in the Royal Navy have been known as slushies.)

Once of the remarkable characters in Vancouver's crews was William Broughton, who commanded the *Chatham*. After surveying the Columbia River, he was sent home from San Blas in the North Pacific to Vera Cruz with Vancouver's despatches: his reward was in October 1793 to be made commander of the *Providence* sloop (a veteran of Bligh's second breadfruit expedition) and sent to the north-west coast of America again. Missing Vancouver, he then decided to survey the Chinese and Japanese coasts, which took a further four years. After the *Providence* was wrecked off the coast of Formosa (Taiwan) in 1797, Broughton continued the survey for a further year in a small schooner he purchased until he returned to England in an East Indiaman from Trincomalee.

## MATTHEW FLINDERS AND THE *TOM THUMB*

There was a last chapter to be written in the southern hemisphere.
As a boy Matthew Flinders had been inspired by reading Defoe's
*Robinson Crusoe*, and in 1790 at the age of sixteen he joined the
navy. He sailed on Bligh's second breadfruit voyage in the *Providence* from 1791 to 1793 and saw action in the *Bellerophon* at the
Battle of the Glorious First of June in 1794, but he soon found
himself as a master's mate in the 10-gun storeship *Reliance*, taking
the new governor to New South Wales, and on the outward journey
he kept convoy with Broughton's *Providence*.

Once in New South Wales, Flinders determined to fill in the
blanks in Cook's general chart of the coast, and with his friend the
surgeon George Bass he set out in 1795. Their first boat, *Tom
Thumb*, was a skiff eight feet long with a crew of one, a boy whose
duty it was to keep bailing. A later boat in which Bass undertook
his own survey was the *Francis* with a crew of five convicts. At first
Flinders and Bass received little official support, but then they were
given a sloop, the *Norfolk*, and a crew of eight regular seamen, and
in her they charted the coast of Van Diemen's Land, as Tasmania
was then known, in 1798–99. On his return home, Flinders,
having convinced the influential Joseph Banks of the need to chart
the whole of Australia, was promoted to commander in 1801 and
sent out in the *Investigator* sloop with a team of scientists. He sailed
northward along the coast of Australia, amplifying and sometimes
correcting the work of Cook, but had to abandon his voyage in
1803 when the *Investigator* began to deteriorate. However, when he
attempted to return home the spirit of the international truce which
ruled between explorers was broken by the French on Mauritius
and he was imprisoned for six and a half years. Released in 1810,
he survived only long enough to complete and publish his *Voyage
to Terra Australis* (1814). His wife's letters to French residents
in Mauritius about her husband's captivity make heart-rending
reading.

## BACK TO THE ARCTIC

No European had visited Hudson's Bay for years, but when the ice opened in the Davis Straits in 1668, one Captain Gillam in the *Nonsuch* had sailed as far as 75° N, entered the Hudson Strait, and wintered on the southern shore of the bay. The Hudson's Bay Company, now familiar in our high streets as a clothes store, was founded the next year by royal charter as a company to trade in furs and skins. The French, who had reached the western shore of the bay, traded there too from 1697 onwards but gave up their posts under the Treaty of Utrecht in 1713. The Hudson's Bay Company sent home valuable annual cargoes, but while a belief continued in a north-west passage from the Atlantic into the Pacific via Hudson's Bay the company defended its monopoly by discouraging voyages of discovery. An expedition was mounted from London in 1719 but both ships, *Albany* and *Discovery*, were lost without trace. In 1722 a rescue attempt sailing from Fort Churchill, the company's base on the western shore, entered the sound known as Sir Thomas Roe's Welcome and reached a point at 64° 15′ N which was named for the expedition's ship, *Whalebone*.

The first truly naval expedition of the century was not until 1741. While Anson was about to become fabulously rich in the Pacific, Christopher Middleton had drawn a short straw and was sent to discover the North-West Passage in the converted bomb vessel *Furnace*, with William Moor in the *Discovery*. Wintering at Fort Churchill, Middleton sailed up Roe's Welcome in 1742 as far as 65° 10′ N, naming various landmarks after his sponsors in London and then for the progress of his expedition, Cape Hope, Repulse Bay, and Frozen Strait. Armchair geographers still believed in a north-west passage out of Hudson's Bay and in 1745 an act was passed offering a reward of £20,000 to anyone who discovered it. In 1746, Middleton's former second-in-command, Moor, took another expedition in the 110-ton *Dobbs*, with Francis White in the 160-ton *California*: perhaps this name was optimistic, but contemporary charts did show California extending much further north along the west coast of North America than its present-day limits. Moor took with him a dedicated surveyor, Henry Ellis, whose task it was to make charts, and to record bearings, distances, soundings, and variations of the magnetic compass. The expedition, however, did little more than confirm Middleton's findings and that Frozen Strait was just that: frozen and impassable to sailing ships. Both Middleton and Moor lost men to scurvy.

Two more expeditions to find a western exit from Baffin's Bay were unsuccessful. In 1776 Richard Pickersgill, whose journal of Cook's second voyage has already been quoted, got to 68° 14' N in the Davis Strait and returned home; the next year a Lieutenant Young took the same ship, *Lion*, north, but his voyage was even less successful.

Meanwhile the Royal Society had persuaded the Admiralty that there was value in reaching the North Pole, and Captain Constantine Mulgrave was despatched in 1773 with two bomb vessels, *Racehorse* and *Carcass*. Mulgrave also explored the possibility of a north-east passage, and reached 80° 48' N, above Spitzbergen, higher than his two Greenland pilots had themselves ever been. He named some newly discovered islands, but at every attempt over some 20° of longitude his northward passage was blocked by pack ice. For some weeks both ships were surrounded by ice and eventually Mulgrave prepared to abandon ships and take to the boats amongst the shifting ice. They did make their escape, but it had been a foolhardy, unnecessary, and unscientific expedition and Mulgrave, who had repeatedly tried to barge the ice in his specially strengthened ships, was lucky not to have been trapped. If his expedition had been lost, history would be different, for one of the boys in the *Carcass* was the fourteen-year-old Horatio Nelson. The expedition is now best known for Nelson's attempt to kill a polar bear so he could take the skin home to his father.

When the Great War came to an end in 1815, it would be one of Flinders' midshipmen, his cousin John Franklin, who among others, would lead a return to Arctic exploration.

# Chapter Five

# War with America

## THE AMERICAN WAR OF INDEPENDENCE

Nowhere is the special relationship between the USA and the United Kingdom more distinctive than in the friendship between the two navies, yet they fought fierce wars two hundred years ago and remained rivals for some time afterwards.

The cost of the Seven Years War, known in the USA as the French and Indian War, had nearly bankrupted Britain, but taxes which London imposed in order to recoup the expenses of the war and the cost of stationing troops flared into a civil war which quickly became the War of American Independence. The Royal Navy had already been involved in police work and made petty expeditions against disaffected colonists, and when disaffection turned to rebellion the navy became deeply involved. In May 1775 the little armed schooner *Diana* of six guns had to be abandoned and burned by her crew near Boston, and marines, from ships in Boston harbour, were part of the force which marched on Lexington and Concord. In Boston itself, a young midshipman, Cuthbert Collingwood, was sent ashore to command a party of British seamen fighting at Bunker Hill in June 1775. Then the 20-gun ships *Glasgow* and *Lively* cannonaded the rebel positions and used red-hot shot to burn the village of Charlestown.

That year George Washington besieged Boston and chartered ships to raid the British supply lines, and, when other states began to follow suit, Congress set up a Naval Committee which began to purchase and arm ships. Neither the navies of the individual states nor the Continental Navy itself was particularly successful and the first purpose-built ships were all captured, or burnt to prevent their capture, in the next five years.

## ELPHINSTONE PREPARES *ROMNEY*

The first naval action of the American War of Independence was the capture of the *Hunter* by two American privateers on 23 November 1775. She was almost immediately afterwards retaken, but American privateers were soon operating far afield, off Ireland and Cornwall, in the Channel and the Mediterranean, against British merchant shipping. Clearly reinforcements were needed, and one of those sent for was George Elphinstone, who would serve throughout the War of Independence and the Great War with France. Having entered the navy aged fifteen, Elphinstone commanded first the 50-gun *Romney* and then the 20-gun *Perseus*; at the beginning of the Great War he commanded the 74-gun *Robust* during the occupation and evacuation of Toulon; by 1799 he was second-in-command to St Vincent in the Mediterranean Fleet, and then Commander-in-Chief himself until 1802; and in 1803, Lord Keith, as he had become, was made Commander-in-Chief in the North Sea where for four years his prime concern was the protection of the English coasts against invasion. From 1812 to 1814 and again in 1815, when Napoleon escaped from Elba, he commanded the Channel Fleet, and after the war he organized Napoleon's passage to prison on St Helena.

On 11 March 1775 plain George Elphinstone was sent down to Deptford to get the *Romney* ready for sea. Although she was a 50-gun ship, *Romney* was of the old two-decker type, and while the Admiralty gave Elphinstone fifty seamen less than her regulation complement, they were mindful of her future role and he was given the marine complement of a larger ship. His orders, signed by the Board of Admiralty, including Lord Sandwich, the First Lord, read: 'Having appointed you Captain of His Majesty's Ship *Romney* at Deptford which we have ordered to be fitted out at that place for a Voyage to Newfoundland mann'd with Three Hundred Men Victualled to Eight Months with all Species except beer of which she is to have as much as she can conveniently store; you are hereby required and directed to use the utmost despatch in getting her ready for the Sea accordingly, and then falling down to Long Reach take in her Guns and Gunners Stores and proceed to the Nore for further Orders'. Four days later the Victualling Office acknowledged having received their orders to victual the *Romney* 'for a voyage to Newfoundland for her Complement of Three Hundred Men, to Eight Months of all Species of Provisions'.

What happened next gives some idea of what it was like to prepare warships for sea in the late eighteenth century. Keith had some followers in Portsmouth who were volunteers for his ship and he asked the Admiralty to take them into the receiving ship there, which meant they would be put on pay, 'until a proper opportunity should offer to bring them round to the Thames'. A week later the Admiralty agreed that the 'many Seamen at Portsmouth who are willing to enter for the Ship you Command . . . [should] be borne as Supernumeraries on board the [receiving ship] *Barfleur*', adding, since they did not want the extra expense of paying their passage to the Thames, 'till you arrive at Spithead'. Still Keith wanted more men, so he sought permission on 5 April 'to send a Lieutenant and Two Petty Officers to Town to open a Rendezvous' where volunteers could be recruited. The Admiralty agreed, but only allowed a month before they 'order'd Lieut Frederick to break up his rendezvous and repair to his duty on board'.

Keith also needed additional officers. On 21 March the Office of Ordnance was 'pleased to appoint William Smith to be Armourer and Robert Wilson Armourer's Mate'; on 30 March he requested that Mr David Conway be appointed schoolmaster. On 7 April the Navy Office ordered 'Four Months Supply of Surgeon's Necessaries to be hasten'd on board' for the use of the newly appointed surgeon. On 5 May it agreed, after the dockyard officers at Deptford had provided a certificate of his qualifications, that John Brown should be appointed Master Sailmaker, and on the same day the Admiralty advised that a captain of marines would join her at Portsmouth and, when he got to Plymouth, '1 Subaltern, 2 Serjeants, 2 Corporals, 1 Drummer and 50 Privates'. Evidently his recruitment of seamen was going well because the Admiralty felt it necessary to advise Keith to 'leave room for [the marines] in her Complement'. Once at Spithead, which he did not reach until the end of May, Keith's carpenter, James Eagle, exchanged duties with a James Carter and so he asked the port admiral to 'order a Survey to be taken on Carpenter's Stores, that they may be regularly delivered'.

The *Romney* herself had to be got ready. Keith asked for larger ship's boats, and gave some clue as to how these boats would used when he told the dockyard officers: 'a launch is better adapted . . . the Cutter employed in fishing for the Ship's Company was found to be too small . . . and dangerous for her to go to the Fishing Grounds'. (Ships were supplied with fishing and turtling lines and nets, and fish could be a very valuable source of fresh food.) The entrance to St John's Newfoundland is narrow and the winds fluky so Keith also wanted 'an Additional Stream Anchor and Cable for the purpose of warping in and out of the harbour of St Johns'. The boatswain complained that the spare ropes which he had been supplied were too large, so Keith had to ask the dockyard for 'a proper quantity . . . [of] sundry Ropes . . . being of 4 and 4½ Inches [circumference] to be supplied with the Sea Stores'. And as soon he was clear of the malign influence of the dockyard, Keith, like generations of officers before and since, found causes to complain about the dockyard officers, for example: 'upon receiving the Boats . . . I found that none of the oars were made for them, nor were they long enough . . . also the Iron work on board turns out but indifferently'.

On 21 April Keith had received the unwelcome news that he was to carry an admiral and his staff to Newfoundland, and so asked the dockyard for more stores including an accommodation ladder, which the yard would have to make. By mid-May he was dropping down the Thames to the Nore and by 27 May he was at Spithead. Once he was on board, the admiral began to make a nuisance of himself, one of his first orders to Keith being that 'you have on board Fourteen Seamen over and above your Established Complement . . . [and] are required and directed to Discharge the said Men into Her Majesty's Ship *Barfleur*'.

*Romney* had been readied for sea with 'utmost despatch' in less than two months, but now she needed her marines. Whether the cause was a sense of the growing crisis in North America, or the prospect of war and prize money, or merely that he was being needled by the admiral, the urbane flow of Keith's correspondence with the several offices of state, departments of the navy, and the Admiralty itself was interrupted by his letter from Plymouth Sound on 3 June 1775. He wrote to the Port Admiral there asking where his marines were, in language which for him was almost peremptory: '[I] beg you will be pleased to cause them to embark as soon as possible being much in want thereof'. Even when they arrived, Keith had cause to complain to Colonel Bell, the commanding marine officer at Plymouth, that 'Abraham Finimore of the 52nd Company is troubled with a hernia and I therefore beg you will be pleased to exchange him for another man, and cause him to be sent on board as soon as possible; if he should be a Taylor, it would be advantageous'.

Having been ordered to carry as much beer as he could, Keith could not now stow any more last-minute provisions and was embarrassed by having a store ship alongside with 'a quantity of wine equivalent to a months allowance for the Ship's Company ... by reason of the Ship being so full of other Provisions, and the smallness of the hold, we cannot stow that quantity in safety'. He therefore asked for the wine to be replaced by spirits, which, the ration being smaller, would take less room.

*Romney* made a fast passage to St John's, Newfoundland, where the complex process of keeping the ship at sea and caring for her people continued. On 10 July the surgeon was granted 2d per man for three months' supply of 'surgeon's necessaries'. Cash was needed to pay for stores and so bills of exchange had to be negotiated with merchants in St John's. The butter and cheese, which had been supplied in barrels by contractors in England and should have lasted six months, were much 'complained of' and, as disease was associated with bad smells, were surveyed and condemned. In August, Keith's purser was ordered to purchase on behalf of the squadron in Halifax sufficient fresh meat to make an issue on two days each week, and in October, as the *Romney* completed her sea stores for the return to England, he was given approval 'to complete the Provisions of [the ship] to three months ... Pork – 885 pieces, Flour – 5720 pounds, Suet – 779 pounds, Pease – 30 bushels, Oatmeal – 30 bushels'.

In the Atlantic thirteen men had been found to be unfit 'from old age, sickness, and other infirmities' and Keith asked the admiral if he could send these men home as invalids: he had been right to recruit some extra hands because by October not just the *Romney* but all the ships at Halifax were 'much distressed for want of Men' and Keith was given permission 'to raise in this Island [Nova Scotia] some Seamen, Seafaring Men, or stout able-bodied Landmen, as soon as possible for the said Squadron'.

## PRIZE MONEY AND MEN

The American station was popular with the navy, and the logbook of the 32-gun *Emerald* tells why: prize money. Among other captures the logbook shows: 12 February 'set up steering sails, at 10 came up with the Chase, which proved to be a Ship, the *Two Friends*, from Boston bound to Williamsburgh, in ballast, sent a Petty Officer & 10 Men on board her, and received the People from Her'; 14 February 'Lynn Haven Bay . . . came up with the chace, which proved to be the *Phoenix* schooner loaded with salt and Guns from St Thomas's belonging to St Anns in New England . . . all the People had left her but One Man sent a Mate and 5 men to take charge of her'; and, on the same day, 'fired to bring the chace too [sic] she proved to be the *Betsy* Sloop from Sta Criuz [?] bound to Petersburg loaded with salt, Josh Frith Master, sent a Mid and 4 Men to take charge of her'.

Ships on detached duties often worked in cooperatives, usually within closely defined geographical areas, and captures inside agreed areas were shared. Keith kept careful records of his prize agreements and the value of his prizes, and had already appointed a prize agent, who warned him 'the Circumstances of this country render the re-establishment of civil Government impracticable, which necessarily creates difficulties and delays in the Prize Business. The chief difficulty is the securing of the Cargoes from Embezzlement; arising principally from the want of trustworthy persons'.

Nevertheless Keith was pleased when, newly arrived from Portsmouth, he was sent on detached duty by Commodore William Hotham: 'You are hereby directed to compleat His Majesty's Ship under your Command to three Months Provisions . . . when you are immediately to proceed to Sea and range along the Coasts of the Carolina's, Georgia and East Florida, as far as St Augustine occasionally, for the purpose of cutting off the Trade of the Rebellious Colonies, and taking or destroying the Armed Vessels especially, by every means in your power. You are to continue upon this Service so long as your Water and Provisions will last with a due sufficiency to carry you back to New York or Rhode Island'.

Not every prize was riches, so that on 15 February when Keith 'came up with ye chace, found her to be ye *Hope* Schooner from Plymouth bound to Virginia, in ballast and a little rum, thought her not worth carrying, set her on fire'. Everyone in the *Perseus'* crew had an interest in prize money, however, so that when Keith found his prizes at the rendezvous he had set, he also found that they had taken a 'Brigg . . . from Providence bound to Baltimore Jno Gordon Master, with Eight Casks of sugar and a few Cheeses'. This war and the next made Keith wealthy, and he earned more in prize money than any other officer except perhaps Edward Pellew, later Lord Exmouth. For Keith there was no Spanish treasure ship, but there was a steady accumulation of wealth. A typical example of the many small prizes he took was a small schooner called the *Betsy*, a popular name amongst the rebels. She was taken off Florida, and outside any of his cooperative sharing agreements, and her cargo of tobacco, shingles, turpentine, and lard, together with her hull, was worth £571 8s 8½d. Elphinstone's share was two-eighths, or £142 17s 2d before expenses; his basic pay as a captain of a Fourth Rate was £182 a year.


## WAR IN NEW ENGLAND

The journal of Commodore Sir George Collier, then in command of a squadron of ships at Halifax, reveals much about British opinion of their opponents and the divided loyalties of the colonists. According to Collier,

> Commodore Manley sailed from Boston the 21st of May having his broad Pendant hoisted on board the *Hancock* . . . 34 Guns & 290 Men, He had with Him the *Boston* of 30 Guns The *Miflin* & *Tartar* of 22 Guns; Brig *Hawk* of 18 Guns, & four schooners each of 14 Guns . . .
>
> The Squadron cruised for a short time together upon St George's Bank in expectation of meeting some of the Kings

Ships, who were often stationed there singly; a hard Gale of wind however dispersed the Rebel Fleet & Manley having omitted one part of a commanding Officers Duty, i.e. giving out Rendezvous! The scattered Ships knew not where to rejoin him, but each one proceeded wherever the Caprice of the Commander led him: the *Boston* was the only one that remaind with the *Hancock*, & finding they were not likely to meet the rest of their Squadron, proceeded together towards Newfoundland with the Intention of putting their destructive schemes of destroying the Fishery into Execution . . . These two commanders accordingly got upon the Banks of Newfoundland without any accident, & soon after, met with many of the small Fishing Vessels industriously at work procuring a cargo; Manley without Remorse took the Crews out & burnt them all without Mercy when their numbers grew too alarming he generally gave them some old rotten vessel in which they might attempt getting ashore; this Practice he pursued, to the infinite Distress of the poor People and Great Prejudice to the Fishery.

Not satisfied however with these savage acts of Cruelty & revenge, he determind to pursue it still further, by going into the small Harbours & destroying the Fishing Stages: he was on his way to put this intention in Practice, when early in the Morning of the 8th June a large ship was discovered to leeward with a Tier of Guns, which Manley believed to be a Frigate belonging to the King; He immediately harangued his people to encourage them, at the same time bearing down upon the Stranger: this Ship provd to be the *Fox* Man of War of twenty eight Guns, who seeing the *Hancock* approaching, took her for one of the King's Frigates as there had been no account of any ships so large being fitted out by Congress, nor of their cruising on that Station. The *Fox*, however was soon convinced what she was by Manley hoisting Rebel Colours & ordering her to 'strike instantly' the Reprisal was accompanied with a Broadside, which was soon returned by the *Fox* tho her Decks were not sufficiently cleared for Action.

A running fight now commenced, The *Fox* endeavoured to get off in order to be better prepard for battle, She set her Sails at New York & it was near one in the Afternoon before Manley could bring the *Hancock* again alongside of her, after which a warm Action commenced – During the contest several of the rebel Crew Shewd strong signs of fear & Dismay; Manley sensible of this ran continuously from one end of the Ship to tother, in his waistcoat, his shirt tucked up to his shoulders, flourishing and swinging a great Cutlass round his head & with the most horrid Imprecations swearing he would 'cut down' the first man who should attempt to leave his Quarters!

These threats had the intended effect & the Action continued with Spirit, till the *Fox* a good deal disabled, thought proper to strike her Colors; which she had scarcely done before the *Boston* who had hitherto kept at a Distance, came under her stern & gave her a Broadside, to the Great Displeasure of Manley who inveighed loudly against a proceeding so unfair and unnecessary . . .

The fight had lasted two hours and the *Fox* had two dead and ten injured, but *Hancock* was also badly damaged and it took some days to make repairs: Manley wanted to return in triumph to Boston, but hubris was waiting in the wings, or rather in St John's.

Collier, having recently careened and refitted the 44-gun frigate *Rainbow*, sailed from St John's on the same day that Manley and his small squadron had passed, and in the afternoon Manley was seen by lookouts from *Rainbow*'s masthead 'at an immense distance'. *Rainbow* 'immediately gave chase with every sail that could be set & before Night ascertained they were ships of force'. The chase continued all night with Collier's ship cleared for action and the men at their quarters. Then with the *Rainbow* gaining on her chase, about 9 a.m. another ship crossed her bows and 'fetch[ed] into the wake of the Rebel Ships Tackd & seemd to make a fourth in the Line of Battle'. Knowing that Manley's squadron consisted of many ships, he was surprised that they allowed him to pursue them, instead of them attacking him.

However, when Manley changed course about 10 a.m. several shots were exchanged between the stranger and the sternmost of the Americans: only then did Collier realize the stranger was the British 32-gun frigate *Flora*. Collier left the *Flora* in pursuit of the *Fox*, which was now manned by the Americans, and concentrated on the largest of the enemy ships, which one of his midshipmen, who had been prisoner in Boston, identified as *Hancock*. *Hancock* outsailed the *Rainbow* but Manley, endeavouring to make his ship sail even faster, emptied the water in his hold and upset her trim so that by dark Collier was so close that he could keep sight of her all night, despite Manley altering course and practising 'all the doublings and finesse usual on such occasions'. Manley's luck had run out; at dawn a small brig was discovered lying in his path, and as she passed fired several shots at the *Hancock*, one of which killed her helmsman. The brig was the *Victor* (10) and she was soon left behind, but about four hours later Collier fired his bow guns at the *Hancock*, and hailed Manley that if he 'expected any Quarter he must surrender immediately', but without reply. Then, as the breeze sprang up, *Rainbow* ranged alongside and opened her broadside armament. After about thirty minutes 'they struck the Rebel colors and surrendered to His Majesty's Arms'.

Meanwhile *Flora* recaptured *Fox* but *Boston* escaped. Manley was not in the best of moods when he was brought on board *Rainbow*: 'a Macneal, whom Manley execrated with many Oaths, for his Cowardice in not assisting Him', had commanded the *Boston*. In Collier's opinion 'all three deserved the Name of errant Poltroons for not attacking the *Rainbow* the Night they first saw her, as their Force was so infinitely superior, for they had between Three and Four hundred Men more than the *Rainbow*, & as the Water was perfectly smooth, they might have boarded her, and if they had behavd as brave Men, ought to have carried her'. The commodore's pendant from the *Hancock* was sent to England and presented to the King.

Two years later Collier was ill, 'but the Advice & Entreaties of the Physicians could not divert Him from his purpose of going in Person, & He saild from New York . . . attended by 3 able surgeons' and was soon again in the thick of action, when he chased an American squadron up the Penobscot River in Maine until he ran out of water. On 3 August 1779 Collier sailed from New York to relieve Loyalist Americans and British troops on the Penobscot. His force consisted of the flagship, the 64-gun ship-of-the-line *Raisonable*, the 32-gun frigates *Blonde* and *Virginia*, and several smaller warships, *Greyhound*, *Camilla*, *Galatea*, and *Otter*. After ten days of thick weather, his squadron met off the mouth of Penobscot Bay and next morning, 14 August, they found a rebel force of forty-one ships, headed by the 32-gun *Warren*, with fourteen smaller frigates and brigs of between twenty-two and twelve guns each, transports, and merchant ships, drawn up in a crescent formation besieging Fort George. What happened next has been described as the largest fleet loss, over forty ships, and a defeat the magnitude of which would not be seen again until Pearl Harbor.

> The voyage was not long but the whole of it was made through black & thick Fogs, which obscurd the Face of Day ... the Commodore immediately led them into Penobscot Bay; the light airs of wind, currents & innumerable dangerous shoals, obligd them to anchor for that Night; but at dawn of Day next morning, they weighed, & proceeded up the Bay with a light, but favorable Wind; about Ten o'Clock an advanced Frigate made a signal for seeing the Enemy's fleet ... they were all under sail, & seemd forming into the shape of a crescent their Commanding Officer in the Center ... the whole seemd rather in confusion & not decided how they should act, notwithstanding their force appeard to be seventeen or eighteen ships of war; the wind still continued very faint, tho it blew directly into the Bay; the Enemy therefore had no other alternative than bravely to try the Fortune of the Day, or to be destroyd ... The Prospect that then must have presented itself to the British Troops on the shore, was certainly highly interesting & pleasing; the Rebel Army had received Intimation of the Approach of the Kings Squadron the Night before; they had labor'd ever since without ceasing, to reimbark some of their heavy Cannon & Mortars, together with their Baggage, & men; and they had succeeded so well, that the whole Rebel armament of Land and Sea forces presented itself at that time afloat to the sight of the King's ships ...

Collier believed that the rebels, with so many extra troops on board, would try to close with him and take him by boarding, and was amazed when he saw the transports

> flying towards the mouth of Penobscot River; their men of war caught the panic, & followd; the broad Pendant of Commodore Saltonstall was no longer to be discovered, & it was thought that Officer was one of the first to abandon his Squadron: the

scene was highly Picturesque; the Enemy spread all their Sails to assist their Flights, & lookd like a moving Forrest skimming over the Waters; a universal shout from the British Fleet was heard, & Echoed from Ship to Ship; Joy was lit up in every countenance, & the highest Satisfaction appeard at the inevitable Defeat & Destruction of so considerable a part of the Rebel forces . . .

Collier gave orders for a general chase. While the body of the rebel fleet went up the Penobscot River, two men of war, the privateers *Hunter* and *Defence*, made an attempt to get round Long Island, but *Raisonable* captured one and blew up the other. The excitement was sufficient to rouse Collier from his sickbed to conduct the chase from a chair on deck, until the *Raisonable* 'was forced to Anchor for want of depth of Water' and Collier fainted through fatigue. Next day he had recovered and he recorded that:

The course of the Night afforded many distant Views of blazing Ships, accompanied with frequent explosions caused by kegs blowing up: the pursuit & destruction continued part of the next Day; the scene was awful, & the Service dangerous; the channel grew narrower & shoaler in advancing, the Branches of Trees on different sides the River were often brushed at the same time by the Yards of the pursuing Ships, whilst those of the rebels lay on each side aground & blazing! Besides the *Hunter* there was only the *Hampdon* [sic] of Twenty Two Guns taken, the rest were all blown up & destroyd: amongst the former was a beautiful Frigate called the *Warren* of Thirty two Guns (10 pounders) on board which, the Rebel Commodore had his broad pendants hoisted: The remainder of His armaments blew themselves up to prevent falling into their Enemy's possession & for the same reason they burnt their Transports, not a single one of any kind escaping!

Three years after the start of the War of Independence the revolution was not universal, and many ports in New England remained open to Collier's ships. Tension arose, however, when one party of Americans allowed Collier's men to land, and another group arrested his watering party. Collier solved this problem by patient diplomacy, but when he heard about a cargo of masts in the

Sheepscut River waiting for shipment to France, he took more drastic action:

> Understanding from Intelligence . . . that a large ship laden with Masts for France was ready to sail from the River Sheepscut . . . [he] cruized off the mouth of it for many Days, in hopes of intercepting Her, keeping at such a Distance by Day from the Shore as not to be discovered, & in the Night causing a small armed Schooner with a Detachment of Seamen & Marines to keep near the River that she might not Escape in the Dark; after waiting for about a Week, every body's Patience was almost exhausted, & Sir George began to imagine his Object had by some Means escaped Him: He took the Resolution therefore to send Eighty determined Men under Command of Lieutenant Haynes . . . up the River . . .

Collier followed in the *Rainbow* but when he was

> within a Mile of the Mouth of it & entangled amongst breakers & Shoals, a thick Fog came on & occasioned great Danger of her being lost; it continued the remainder of that Day & Night, & with very little Wind: Providence, however, was again gracious in protecting the *Rainbow* from the Perils that surrounded Her, for She got at a great Distance from the Land without having struck upon any of the sunken Rocks. The following Morning being clear & bright the *Rainbow* again steered towards Sheepscut River, to support & protect the little Tender; as She proceeded, a very pleasing sight presented itself; a lofty Ship with Top Gallant Sails appeard coming out, & the little Schooner close by, escorting Her!

The prize was a large French ship called *Marquisse de la Fayette* (sic), laden with masts, spars, and planks. Haynes described what had happened: 'soon after the Schooner had got into the River the thick Fog had obliged him to Anchor . . . a small Boat approached, hailing the Schooner, & asking where they came from? Mr Haynes with great Presence of Mind told them He was a Privateer called the *True Blue*, from Boston'. Learning where the Frenchman was at anchor, Haynes steered towards her through the fog and was not discovered until too late. In a minute he brought the schooner alongside: his marines appearing out of the fog with bayonets fixed presented a terrible sight to the French. While a line of marines presented their loaded weapons, Haynes's seamen swarmed on board with pistols and pole axes and the *Marquisse de la Fayette* was taken without a loss on either side.

## FRANCE DECLARES WAR

If the Royal Navy ruled the waves as far as there was water to carry its ships, Britain was not impervious to attack, and American privateers ranged as far as the Mediterranean and the North Sea. Meanwhile France, neutral but biased against Britain, allowed American privateers to use French ports, and supplied arms and volunteers to the rebels across the Atlantic. The most serious challenge to British sea power arose when John Paul Jones purchased an old French East Indiaman, rechristened *Bonne Homme Richard*. Jones was in command of a Franco-American squadron, comprising also the *Alliance* (36), *Pallas* (32), a French corvette and a brig, and two privateers, when on 23 September 1779 off Flamborough Head he met a British convoy from the Baltic under escort of the 44-gun frigate *Serapis*. Captain Richard Pearson of the *Serapis* was outwitted and allowed an enemy inferior in guns but superior in men and leadership to close: the French and American crew of the *Bonne Homme Richard*, which was sinking, swept the upper deck of the *Serapis* with their small arms, then threw hand grenades and took *Serapis* by boarding. The convoy escaped and Pearson, for his bravery, was knighted and forgotten, but Jones entered the folk memory of the US Navy and is now interred at Annapolis.

The American army's victory at Saratoga convinced France that the war in North America was rather more than a minor rebellion and she declared war on Britain in July 1778, Spain following suit, after a secret treaty, in 1779. France sent large convoys to the colonies in the West Indies and to North America, and Spain besieged Gibraltar.

## SAVANNAH AND CHARLESTON

Arriving from the West Indies in 1779, the French admiral, the Comte d'Estaing, hoped to reinforce Charleston, but the weather drove him on to Savannah. D'Estaing's fleet comprised twenty sail-of-the-line, many smaller craft, and over 3,000 troops who had been withdrawn from French islands in the West Indies. So on 9 September he commenced a blockade of the Savannah River and occupied the island of Tybee, landing his troops at Beaulieu ('Bowley' in Captain Henry's report). Under the command of Captain John Henry in the *Fowey*, a much smaller squadron of British ships and seven galleys, some of which were manned by loyalists, landed guns and men and prepared to defend the town. The British army also brought up reinforcements while d'Estaing dithered. When the French and Americans did attack on the night of 3/4 October they suffered heavily.

Captain Henry's report is a fine example of naval warfare of the period and of how the army and the navy could cooperate. In his account, written in the Savannah River on 8 November 1779, he was as keen to justify sinking one of the King's ships as a blockship as he was to report his victory:

the French fleet, under the Count d'Estaing, consisting of 20 sail-of-the-line, 2 of 50 Guns, and eleven frigates, arrived on this coast the 1st of September ... On the 8th, forty-one sail were discovered to the southward of Tybee, plying to windward, the wind being northerly, as it had been for some days past, drove them to the southward of this port. Major Gen. Prevost at Savannah was immediately acquainted with their appearance, who went to work with every exertion, to increase the fortifications of the town. Dispatches were sent to the Hon. Col. Maitland, who was posted with part of the army on Port Royal Island, and to Capt. Christian of the Majesty's ship *Vigilant*, to repair to Savannah as soon as possible with the troops, Ships and gallies there. The *Fowey*, *Rose*, *Keppel* armed brig, and *Germain* provincial armed ship, were so placed, that if the French ships came in superior, we might run up the river; & the leading marks for the bar were cut down. On the 9th the whole French fleet anchored off the bar, and next day four frigates weighed and came to Tybee anchorage. It was determined on their approach to run up the river with the King's ships, and join our force with the General for the defence of the town; at this time the French were sending troops from their ships . . . from whence they were landed in launches at Bowley, thirteen miles from Savannah, under cover of four gallies and their frigates were preparing to advance up the river.

From the 10th to the 13th we were very busy in sending to town part of the *Fowey* and *Rose's* guns and ammunition, in vessels sent by the General for that purpose. On the 13th, the *Fowey* and *Rose* being much lightened, sailed over the Mud flat to Five Fathom Hole, three miles below the town, from whence were sent up the remainder of the guns and ammunition. The *Comet* galley, and *Keppel* armed brig, were directed to place themselves so below the Mud flat, as to cover the passage of Col. Maitland, with the King's troops from Port Royal, through Wall's cutt, from whom we had not heard since our dispatches to them were sent, the communication with boats being cut off.

The 14th and 15th the seamen were employed landing the cannon and ammunition of the Ships, from the small vessels, which having done, the seamen were appointed to the different batteries, and the marines incorporated with the grenadiers of the 60th regt. On the 16th the Count d'Estaing summoned the General to surrender the town to the arms of his most Christian Majesty . . .

D'Estaing accompanied his summons with the direst threats, which the British took time to consider while reinforcements were arriving by boat, then resolved to fight. Seamen and marines worked with the army, regular and colonial, to fortify the place, working

indefatigably night and day, raising new works and batteries which astonished our enemies; and every officer, soldier and sailor, worked with the utmost chearfulness: and I have the pleasure to inform their lordships, the General had been pleased to express his particular satisfaction with the services of the officers and seamen of the King's ships & transports during the whole siege.

Fearing an outflanking movement, Henry sank the 20-gun *Rose* as a blockship. Her condition makes interesting reading:

> it being apprehended the enemy's ships might come too near the town, and annoy the rear of our lines, it was judged expedient to sink a number of vessels to stop the passage; his Majesty's ship *Rose*, making at this time seventeen inches water an hour ... her bottom worm eaten quite through, and her stern rotten, as appears by a survey of shipwrights held on her a short time before, wherein it is declared she could not swim above two months, her men, guns and ammunition being on shore, I thought her the most eligible to sink, as her weight could keep her across the channel, when lighter vessels could not, owing to the rapidity of the current, and hard sandy bottom, which prevented them sticking fast where they were sunk.

Henry anticipated well and his precautions were sound, so that when two French frigates and some rebel galleys did try to attack from the rear, they could not get within effective range. Had the French attacked as soon as they arrived they might have been successful, but d'Estaing was overcautious and now the attempt

> proved most fatal to them, for they met with so severe a repulse from only 300 men, assisted by the grape shot from the batteries, that from this day they worked with indefatigable labour to carry off their cannon & Mortars, & descended to a degree of civility we had hitherto been strangers to. Their loss was very great, most of their best officers & soldiers being killed or wounded; the Count d'Estaing among the latter.

When Henry's report reached New York, which was still held by the British, Admiral Arbuthnot and General Clinton despatched a large force against Charleston, the capital of South Carolina. Arbuthnot's ships of the line could not cross the bar and had to be sent back to New York but he lightened his smaller frigates, transferring his flag to the 44-gun *Roebuck*. Port Royal and James Island were quickly occupied and as the Franco-American fleet retreated upriver, so the British followed, passing Fort Moultrie with little damage.

Clinton asked, as the army often did in such circumstances, for heavy cannon and a detachment of seamen from the fleet, and these were put under the command of Captain Elphinstone, who opened this chapter. As d'Estaing's attack at Savannah had been hesitant, Arbuthnot's and Clinton's was just the opposite:

Every thing being in readiness for crossing the army over the Ashley river [forming the south side of the promontory on which Charleston was built], the boats of the fleet, with the flat boats, under the command of Capt. Elphinstone and Capt. Evans of the *Raisonable*, the whole army, with the artillery and stores necessary for the siege, were landed under cover of the galleys on the town side with astonishing expedition. As soon as the army began to erect their batteries against the town, I took the first favourable opportunity to pass Sullivans's island [which Clinton had failed to take in June 1776], upon which there is a strong fort and batteries the chief defence of the harbour; accordingly I weighed at one o'clock on the 9th ult. . . . and, passing through a severe fire, anchored in about two hours under James island, with the loss of 27 Seamen killed and wounded. The *Richmond's* fore top mast was shot away, and the ships in general sustained damage in their rigging, however not materially in their hulls . . . Having stationed ships and armed vessels off the different inlets upon the coast, and the town being now nearly invested, attempts were made to pass a naval force into Cooper river [to the north of Charleston] by Hog's island, the main channel being rendered impracticable, and small vessels to carry heavy guns were fitted for that service; but it being found the enemy had also sunk vessels in that channel, and its entrance was defended by the works on Sullivans's island and Mount Pleasant, it was resolved to dispossess them of the latter by the Seamen of the fleet; and in the mean time, to arm the small vessels that had been taken by Lord Cornwallis in the Wando river. For this purpose a brigade of 500 Seamen and Marines was formed from the squadron, and under the command of the Capts. Hudson, Orde, and Gambier, landed at day break on the 29th at Mount Pleasant; where . . . by their sudden appearance [they] prevented the rebels from carrying off their cannon and stores, or from destroying their works . . .

Evidently loyalties on the American side were still not fixed, because deserters came in daily with useful information about the state of the garrison, and Arbuthnot took the initiative.

> I therefore formed a plan to attack it, which should not interfere with important operations the army were carrying on ... The attention of the rebels I found had been chiefly directed to the south & east sides of the fort, which were most open to attack; but the west face, and north west bastion, I discovered, had been neglected. I therefore determined to attempt the fort by Storm, under cover of the fire from the Ships of the squadron. The Capts. Hudson and Gambier, and Capt. Knowles agent for transports, with 200 seamen & marines, embarked in the boats of the squadron in the night of the 4th inst. & passing by the fort unobserved, landed before day light and took possession of a redoubt on the east end of the island; whilst other boats were preparing to carry over the same number of seamen and marines from Mount Pleasant, under the command of Capt. Orde. On the whole being ready, and the ships only waiting for the tide to begin the attack, the fort was summoned by Capt. Hudson, when, after a little consideration, the garrison surrendered themselves prisoners of war ...

Charleston surrendered four days later. Arbuthnot's report began: 'I have the satisfaction to acquaint you, for the information of my lords commissioners of the Admiralty, that Charlestown, with all its dependencies, the shipping in the harbour, and the army under Gen. Lincoln; has surrendered to his Majesty's arms ...' He commissioned various rebel and French frigates into the navy, including the frigate *Boston*, sunk as a blockship, as the *Charleston*, and gave the commands of them 'to officers of long Service and acknowledged merit'.

In his report Arbuthnot particularly praised the officers who distinguished themselves on shore. Further, he was pleased to tell the Admiralty, 'The fleet has endeavoured most heartily and effectually to co-operate with the army in every possible instance; and the most perfect harmony has subsisted between us'. To ice the cake of this very successful, short, sharp campaign, he was able to add 'that rebel privateering has recently received a severe check; the

*Iris* and *Galatea* having lately, in the space of ten days, taken nine
privateers, two of which were ships of 20 guns, and none less than
16, and 800 Seamen'.


## ADMIRAL RODNEY IN NORTH AMERICA

Meanwhile, a large French convoy had sailed from the West Indies
for France. Admiral Rodney who was chasing it thought it might
have gone to North America to assist the rebels, and this idea was
reinforced when he heard of a French squadron and troops at
Rhode Island. This, however, was a fresh squadron under the
French admiral de Ternay, intended to help Washington, but it was
more than offset by the arrival in New York of a British squadron
under Thomas Graves, so when Rodney arrived there the British
had overwhelming numbers of ships on the American coast. However, Rodney's arrival was 'unexpected and unwelcome to friend
and foe alike.' Arbuthnot, who had returned from Charleston, was
junior to Rodney but was unwilling to surrender his command, or
to share the prize money which was available on this lucrative
station, while Rodney, having displayed considerable initiative in
coming north, now remained inactive. One reason for this may
have been his poor health, and after a short period ashore to
recover, Rodney sailed again for the West Indies leaving a few
reinforcements for Arbuthnot.

The following letter, which Rodney wrote from New York on
1 October, illustrates his state of mind, some of the workings of
patronage in the navy of the time, and the speed of the mail:

> . . . yesterday by one of my Frigates from the West Indies I was
> made happy by the receipt of your most obliging letters [of]
> July as before this time I did not know my letters concerning
> the junction of the French and Spanish fleets and their retreat,
> without daring to attack His Majesty's Fleet under my com-
> mand or any of the Leeward Islands . . . have reached the hands
> of the Kings Ministers. When by certain and secret intelligence
> I found that Jamaica was in perfect security, and that the
> Spaniards were gone to the Havannah, and in no manner of

condition to undertake any expedition of consequence that the
French fleet under Mons Guichen were in such a condition as
to oblige them to return to France with their Convoy, except
a Squadron which I concluded may have at all events joyn'd
Monsieur Ternay at Rhode Island. This being the state of
affairs, when I reflected in my mind on the critical situation of
HM Fleet and Army, I am sure you will applaud my Motives
for the step I have taken, that I shall have the approbation of
my most Gracious Sovereign, and his Ministers, I have not a
doubt . . .

Rodney had been in self-exile in France at the start of the war,
in order to escape his creditors, so the next artifice of his letter may
have raised a few eyebrows in London. Of course his 'Happyness'
or his health may have overriding motives, but he protests too
much about foregoing his 'Princely Fortune':

had lucrative motives biased my mind, I had kept within the
strict letter of my instructions and gone with the Squadron I
command to Cruize during the hurricane months upon the
Spanish Main, where in all probability a Princely Fortune would
have been the consequence . . . That the hand of adversity had
learnt me the value of Money, I acknowledge, but it has not,
nor ever shall, make such an impression on my mind as to
eradicate from it the Duty I owe my King and country or make
me prefer riches to honour. I therefore did not hesitate one
moment in the choice, riches to myself with the loss of America,
or a mediocrity of Fortune with the Happyness of having saved
so large a portion of the British Empire being rent forever
from it.

In any case by leaving his subordinate behind in the West Indies,
Rodney probably hoped the secure his flag officer's share of any
prize money:

I therefore left a sufficient force with Commodore Hotham for
the protection of the Islands and without any person knowing
my intentions, flew with the wings of national enthusiasm to
disappoint the ambitious designs of France, and to cut off all
Hopes from the Rebellious and deluded Americans. Thank
God, my most sanguine wishes are . . . answered but ill will it

become me to dwell longer on this subject, I will leave it, to the Army, Navy, Loyal and Disloyal Americans, to point out its consequences, and if my conduct can but meet with the approbation of my Gracious Sovereign and his administration I shall feel more true satisfaction than riches would have given me.

Rodney's strategic sense was admirable:

Since my arrival I have strengthened Mr Arbuthnot's Squadron in such a manner to enable him effectually to block up Mon Ternay ... and should a superior squadron attempt to joyn Ternay, in the meantime I have lined the coast of America with my frigates, who have allready taken six of their privateers, and have likewise settled with [Sir] Henry Clinton an expedition against the rebels which will take place in a very few days, and I hope the little space of time the season [of] the year will allow for action will be spent in convincing the Americans tis their Duty and Interest to return to their allegiance.

He did, however, fail to take direct action against Ternay, who now occupied that 'best and noblest harbour in America', Narangansett Bay.

Rodney could not refrain from some toadying, promising a fast ship and a private cruise to the nephew of the Secretary of the Admiralty: 'Your Nephew is a gallant good officer, whenever a copper bottom Frigate becomes vacant he shall certainly be removed into her and have the best cruise I can give him ...' And he begged a favour in return:

I must now my Dear Sir, return my sincere thanks for your very kind attention to Lady Rodney, and your friendly concern for me and mine, the very great obligations I, and my family, owe to Lord North must ever be remembered by my Posterity. I have wrote to him upon a subject that is dearest my heart, and if not thought improper, beg'd his very kind assistance in my obtaining the desire. I have a Son, dearer to me than life. His character is such as merits all my Attention, and if the poor Services I have been enabled to do my Country merits any reward, similar to what Lord Hawk [sic] had conferr'd upon his family, I could wish and it would make me completely happy, if my Son could participate of some part of them after my Death. Pardon a father, few have a Son like mine . . .

And the 'Princely Fortune' waiting in the West Indies could not be forgotten even for the length of time it took to write one letter: 'In all probability by the time this letter reaches your hand I shall be on my way to the West Indies where I hope before Christmass to congratulate Lord North on some event of consequence which shall put it out of the power of his enemy's to insult him'.

## THE LOSS OF THE *SAVAGE*

The British remained confident, so confident that Captain Charles Stirling in the 16-gun sloop *Savage* felt capable of taking on a 20-gun privateer, but the ship he chased turned out to be an even larger privateer, the 24-gun *Congress*. The action which resulted might have been an augury for the frigate actions of the War of 1812, in which the American ships, which tended to be more heavily armed, had more men and made effective use of musketry at close quarters. This then is Stirling's report to his admiral, Graves, dated 23 September 1781, written with 'most poignant grief':

Early in the morning of the 6th instant, 10 leagues east off Charlestown, we espied a ship bearing down on us, who, about four miles distant, hauled her wind to the eastward, shewing, by her appearance, she was an American cruiser; her force could not be so easily distinguished: I therefore gave way to the pleasing idea that she was a privateer, carrying 20 nine pounders whom I had intelligence was cruising off here, & resolved either to bring her to action, or oblige her to quit the coast; for which purpose we gave chace, but were prevented continuing it long, by her edging down, seemingly determined to engage us. Conscious of her superiority in sailing & force, this manauvre coincided with my wishes. I caused the *Savage* to lay by, till we perceived, on her nearer approach, she was far superior to what we imagined, and that it was necessary to attempt making our escape, without some fortunate Shot, in the course of a running fight we saw inevitable, admitted our taking advantages, & bringing on a more equal conflict . . .

The British should have taken more notice of the tactics which the *Congress* used in 1781, as they would be repeated in the many single-ship actions of the War of 1812:

At half past ten she began firing her bow chases, & at eleven, being close on our quarter, the action commenced with musquetry, which, after a good deal of execution, was followed by a heavy cannonade on both sides. In an hour's time I had the mortification to see our braces & bowlings shot away, & not a rope left to trim the Sails with, notwithstanding every precaution had been taken: however, our fire was so constant & well directed, that the enemy did not see our Situation, but keep along side of us, till accident obliged him to drop astern. The *Savage* was now almost a wreck; her sails, rigging, & yards, so much cut, that it was with the utmost difficulty we could alter our position time enough to avoid being raked, the enemy lying directly athwart our Stern for some minutes. This was the only intermission of great guns, but musquetry & pistols still did execution, & continued till they opened again, which was not till both ships were almost on board each other, when the battle became more furious than before. Our quarter-deck & forecastle were soon now nearly cleared, scarce a man belonging to either not being killed or wounded, with three guns on our main-deck rendered useless. In this Situation we fought near an hour, with only 5 six pounders, the fire from each ship's guns scorching the men who opposed them, shot & other implements of war thrown by hand doing execution; when our mizen-mast being shot away by the board; our main-mast tottering, with only three shrouds standing; the ship on fire dangerously; only 40 men on duty to oppose the foe, who was attempting to board us in three places; no Succour in Sight, or possibility of making further resistance; I was necessitated, at a quarter before three, P.M. to surrender to the *Congress*, a private ship of war, belonging to Philadelphia, who carried 215 men, & mounted 20 twelve pounders on her main deck, & four sixes above, fourteen of which were fought on one side. She lost during the action eleven men, & had near thirty wounded, several of them mortally; her masts, her sails, & rigging, were so much damaged, that she was obliged to return to port, which partly answered my wishes prior to the action, as great part of the Carolina trade was daily expected on the coast, & this privateer we saw Sailed remarkably fast. Three days were employed putting her in a condition to make Sail, & five for the *Savage*, who was extremely shattered. Indeed it is astonishing more damage was not done, as the weather was fine, the water remarkably smooth, & the ships never thirty yards asunder ... the men fought with a cool determined valour, that will ever redound to their credit. I cannot conclude without observing, that Captain Geddis, & the officers of the *Congress*, after fighting us bravely, treated us when prisoners with great humanity ...

## THE BATTLE OF CHESAPEAKE BAY, 5 SEPTEMBER 1781

Meanwhile Rodney, having beaten the French in the West Indies, sent Hood to chase the remnants of the French fleet north. Hood overtook the French, looked into the Chesapeake, and, finding it empty, sailed on to New York, where he came under command of Sir Thomas Graves, Rear Admiral of the Red, who, now with nineteen ships of the line, sailed back to the Chesapeake. There he found a French fleet of twenty-six sail-of-the-line and eight smaller ships under Admiral the Comte de Grasse, who had arrived from the West Indies having taken Tobago and declined an action with Rodney, and was cooperating with Lafayette and Washington in the siege of Cornwallis' forces at Yorktown. The Battle of Chesapeake Bay, or as it is known in America the Battle of the Capes, is held to be one of the most significant in American history.

The French were at anchor and extended across the entrance of the Chesapeake from Cape Henry to Middle Ground, when at about 9.30 a.m. de Grasse was warned of the approach of the British from the north. De Grasse had to wait three hours for the incoming tide to slacken, and when he could sail, his leading ships bunched around Cape Henry and the rearmost ships straggled: it took several more hours for all his ships to clear the cape. Graves had the weather gage and plenty of sea room; he was a brave officer, and seemed to have every intention of attacking, but he allowed the French to form their line of battle unmolested. He should have attacked the French ships in isolation as they rounded Cape Henry, or, steering eastwards away from the Chesapeake as they were, fallen on the French centre and rear. Instead he allowed his van to attack the leading French ships, and these ships actually passed through the French line and were badly mauled – particularly in their rigging. The battle had not become general before dark, and though the fleets remained in sight of each other for five days, de Grasse avoided further battle. Meanwhile a French convoy with reinforcements for Lafayette reached the Chesapeake, thus sealing Cornwallis' fate.

There is little evidence in contemporary accounts that anyone realized the significance of the Battle of the Chesapeake. This is how Graves described it, writing from Sandyhook, off New York.

I beg you will be pleased to acquaint my Lords Commissioners of the Admiralty, that the moment the wind served to carry the ships over the bar, which was buoyed for the purpose, the squadron came out; and Sir Samuel Hood getting under sail at the same time, the fleet proceeded together, on the 31st of August, to the southward . . .

The cruisers which I had placed before the Delaware could give me no certain information, and the cruisers off the Chesapeak had not joined. The wind being rather favourable, we approached the Chesapeak the morning of the 5th of September, when the advanced ship made the signal of a fleet. We soon discovered a number of great ships at anchor, which seemed to be extended across the entrance of the Chesapeak, from Cape Henry to the middle ground: They had a frigate cruising off the Cape, which stood in and joined them; and, as we approached, the whole fleet got under sail, and stretched out to sea, with the wind at N.N.E. As we drew nearer, I formed the line first a-head, and then in such a manner as to bring his Majesty's fleet nearly parallel to the line of approach of the enemy; and, when I found that our van was advanced as far as the shoal of the middle ground would admit of, I wore the fleet and brought them upon the same tack with the enemy, and nearly parallel to them, though we were by no means extended with their rear. So soon as I judged that our van would be able to operate, I made the signal to bear away and approach and soon after, to engage the enemy close. Somewhat after four, the action began amongst the headmost ships, pretty close and soon became general, as far as the second ship from the center, towards the rear. The van of the enemy bore away, to enable the center to support them, or they would have been cut up. The action did not entirely cease till a little after sun-set though at a considerable distance; for the center of the enemy continued to bear up as it advanced; and, at that moment ... seemed to have little more in view than to shelter their own van, as it went away before the wind.

His Majesty's fleet consisted of nineteen sail of the line; that of the French formed twenty-four sail in their line. After night, I sent the frigates to the van and rear, to push forward the line, and keep it extended with the enemy, with a full intention to renew the engagement in the morning; but, when the frigate *Fortune* returned from the van, I was informed, that several of the ships had suffered so much, that they were in no condition to renew the action until they had secured their sails; we, however, kept well extended with the enemy all night.

We continued all day, the 6th, in sight of each other, repairing our damage. Rear-Admiral Drake shifted his flag into the *Alcide*, until the *Princess* had got up another main-top mast. The *Shrewsberry*, whose Captain lost a leg, and had the first Lieutenant killed, was obliged to reef both top-masts, shifted her top-sail yards, and had sustained very great damage. I ordered Captain Colpoys of the *Orpheus* to take command of her, and put her into a state for action.

The *Intrepid* had both top-sail yards shot down, her top-masts in great damage [sic] of falling, and her lower sails and yards very much damaged, her Captain having behaved with the greatest gallantry to cover, the *Shrewsberry*. The *Montague* was in great danger of losing her masts; the *Terrible* so leaky as to keep all her pumps going; and the *Ajax* also very leaky.

In the present state of the fleet, and being five sail of the line less in number than the enemy, and they having advanced very much in the wind upon us during the day, I determined to tack after eight, to prevent being drawn too far from the Chesapeak, and to stand to the Northward . . .

Battle was never renewed. The French reinforcements were sufficient to persuade Cornwallis to surrender, and, though there were plenty more small skirmishes by land and sea, with his submission the Americans had effectively won their independence.

# Chapter Six

# Revolution, Mutiny, and War at Sea

France watched the American War of Independence closely and when she was ready declared war on Britain. One of the first actions of this new war was an indecisive battle off Ushant, in July 1778, which resulted in the courts martial of both British admirals, Keppel and Palliser.

Hugh Palliser, born in 1723, was a skilful seaman and an able officer, whose friends and patrons included the greatest admirals of his age, Anson, Boscawen, and Saunders. Having entered the navy aged eleven, by twenty-four he commanded the 70-gun *Captain*. In the Seven Years War he served under his near-contemporary Augustus Keppel, sailing up the Potomac to Alexandria, where no ships of such size had ever been seen before. Keppel and Palliser returned home together in the *Seahorse*, and the two men struck up a friendship despite being political opposites.

In 1759 Palliser was at the capture of Quebec, when he commanded the seamen whose landing in Lower Town persuaded the French of the hopelessness of their cause. After the war he became Governor of Newfoundland, where he strictly enforced British rights over the French, and he is still known there for Palliser's Law.

Augustus Keppel, a survivor of Anson's circumnavigation (1740–44), was born in 1725 and had been appointed in command of the frigate *Greyhound* when he was still nineteen. After service in the Mediterranean and on the North American station, in 1759 he fought under Hawke in Quiberon Bay, captured Goree in 1758 and Belle Isle in 1761, and in 1762 was second-in-command on the expedition to Havana under Admiral Sir George Pocock. He sat on Admiral John Byng's court martial in 1755, and served briefly on the Board of Admiralty in the 1760s.

When France declared war, Palliser, who had spent the 1770s as

Controller of the Navy and then a Lord of the Admiralty, helped to secure for Keppel the command of a fleet, and, while keeping his place on the Board of Admiralty, also agreed to serve under him. It was a recipe for trouble.

The British and French met off Ushant in July 1778, and after several days of manoeuvring the two fleets exchanged broadsides briefly and drifted apart. Whigs and Tories took sides and when the rumours turned to talk of failure to obey orders, if not actual cowardice, Palliser asked for a court martial of Keppel, and when he was acquitted, Palliser asked for a court martial on himself. He was acquitted in turn, but it was symptomatic of a temporary decline of the Royal Navy that both trials were highly politicized. Palliser never served at sea nor in the Admiralty again, while Keppel was First Lord of the Admiralty in the 1780s.

## RODNEY'S CAMPAIGN

On the declaration of war, George Rodney, who in 1759 had raided and burned a French invasion fleet in Le Havre, was in voluntary exile in Paris taking refuge from his debtors. It says much for the civility of the age that a Frenchman paid his debts, enabling him to return home to take up a major command against the French.

Rodney's personal relations with his peers were always difficult and he was often critical of his junior officers, though he also enjoyed a reputation for his care of his people on the lower deck. He was a devoted family man, as is shown by one of those curious survivals, a letter to his wife which is a mixture of public news and private thoughts before he sailed from Spithead:

> My Dear Henny ... to learn you and the Girls are well is always the greatest pleasure I can possibly receive, may you ever continue is my most sincere wishes, for Gods sake don't be uneasy but keep up your spirits ... as to the Boy you mention from Lady Robert Manners, tis certainly too late, and she should be told, that none can be taken under 13 years old and whose parents can allow them at least thirty pounds a year as

the king allows no pay to Boys. People imagine that Admirals and Captains are Schoolmasters and that they have nothing to do but send the Boys to Sea and they are provided for without giving themselves further trouble, however ... if the contents can be comply'd with I will receive the Boy, but I now received my Sailing Orders and sail the moment the Wind comes fair, when that will be, God knows, for at present it blows hard at South West ... Jennys account of Loup, knowing my purse when she dropt it, shews what a sensible Dog he is, and must as she says, endear him more to me, but he must pardon me, if I say non credo ... Every thing here is all noise and hurry, the Wind continuing Westerly ever more time, for the fleet to get ready, I wish I was once at Sea you know then an Admiral has not a tenth part of the trouble and fatigue as when in Port. Ministers and Merchants are eager to have me gone, but I cannot command the Seasons. With my love to my Dear Girls, I am Yours most affectionately ...

Rodney sailed in late December 1779 with orders to escort an outbound convoy, relieve Gibraltar and Minorca, and then reinforce the West Indies. On 8 January he ran down a Spanish convoy and captured a 64-gun ship and six smaller warships to the British flag, and sent twelve captured provision ships into Gibraltar. Rodney reported:

> Yesterday at daylight, the squadron of his Majesty's ships under my command descried twenty-two sail in the north east quarter; we immediately gave chace, and in a few hours the whole were taken. They proved to be a Spanish convoy ... under the protection of seven ships and vessels of war ... the convoy was loaded with naval stores & provisions, for the Spanish ships of war at Cadiz; the rest with bale goods ... Those loaded with naval stores and bale goods I shall immediately dispatch for England, under the convoy of his Majesty's ships the *America* & *Pearl*; those loaded with provisions I shall carry to Gibraltar ...

The Spanish flagship was an exceptionally fine ship, *Guipuscoana*, which was added to the Royal Navy as the *Prince William* and sent as escort to the captured ships, as Rodney told the Admiralty:

You will likewise please to acquaint their lordships, that as I thought it highly necessary to send a 64 gun ship to protect so valuable a convoy, I have commissioned, officered, & manned the Spanish ship of war of the same rate, & named her the *Prince William*, in respect to his Royal Highness, in whose presence she had the honour to be taken. She has been launched only six months, is in every respect completely fitted for war, and much larger than the *Bienfaisant*, Capt. Macbride to whom she struck. I beg leave to congratulate their lordships on this event, which must greatly distress the enemy, who, I am well informed are in much want of provisions and naval stores . . .

## THE MOONLIGHT BATTLE

Then on 16 January Rodney met a Spanish squadron of thirteen warships: Rodney had no great tactical insight but in the fading light, on a lee shore, and with the wind rising he did what seemed expedient and urgent: he ordered 'general chase'. In the Moonlight Battle that ensued, he captured six out of eleven line-of-battle ships and a seventh blew up. Significantly, though the British officers reckoned the Spanish ships were better built and more beautiful, the British ships were copper-bottomed and this gave them an advantage in speed. Rodney's despatch, within three weeks of his earlier victory, must have given him some satisfaction, though there was little triumphalism in his words:

It is with the highest satisfaction I can congratulate their lordships on a signal victory obtained by his Majesty's ships under my command, over the Spanish squadron commanded by Don Juan Langara, wherein the Spanish Admiral and the greatest part of his squadron were either taken or destroyed . . . at one P.M. the Cape [St Vincent] then bearing north four leagues, the *Bedford* made the signal for seeing a fleet in the S.E. quarter; I immediately made a signal for the line of battle a-breast, and bore down upon them; but before that could be well effected, I perceived the enemy were endeavouring to form a line of battle a-head upon the starboard tack; and as the day was far advanced, and unwilling to delay the action, at two

P.M. I hailed down the signal for the line of battle a-breast, and made the signal for a general chace, to engage as the ships came up by rotation, and to take the lee-gage in order to prevent the enemy's retreat into their own ports . . . At four P.M. perceiving the headmost ships very near the enemy, I made the general signal to engage and close . . . [when] the four headmost ships began the action which was returned with great briskness by the enemy. At forty minutes past four, one of the enemy's line of battle ships blew up with a dreadful explosion; every person perished. At Six P.M. one of the Spanish ships struck. The action and pursuit continued with a constant fire 'till two o'clock in the morning, at which time the *Monarca*, the headmost of all the enemy's ships, having stuck to the *Sandwich*, after receiving one broadside, and all firing having ceased, I made the signal and brought to . . .

The gallant behaviour of the admirals, captains, officers, & men, I had the honour to command, was remarkably conspicuous: – they seemed actuated with the same spirit, and were anxiously eager to exert themselves with the utmost zeal to serve his Majesty, and to humble the pride of his enemies. I may venture to affirm, though the enemy made a gallant defence, that had the weather proved but even moderate, or had the action happened in the day, not one of their squadron had escaped.

In a few days Rodney had taken more enemy warships than were taken in both the previous wars, and he had done so despite the presence of a superior Franco-Spanish fleet which was wind-bound in Cadiz.

## IN THE WEST INDIES

Under cover of more bad weather Rodney also relieved the garrison in Minorca and then sailed for the West Indies, where he took command of the ships already there. He was soon in action, with the first of two indecisive actions against the French admiral the Comte de Guichen. In the first action, the Battle of Martinique, which opened on 16 April 1780, Rodney tried to avoid the stalemate of fighting in line by reducing the interval between his ships and by concentrating on the rear portion of the enemy, but not having shared these ideas with his captains before the battle, he was handicapped by the existing signal book, which was an inadequate means to communicate his ideas. So too, when his officers misunderstood him, Rodney had no means to recall them.

He was soon ready for a return match, and

As soon as the fleet could possibly be got ready, I . . . offered the enemy battle; the fleet being near enough to count all their guns, and at times within random shot of some of their Forts. Monsieur Guichen, notwithstanding his superior number, chose to remain in port. I thought it most proper for his Majesty's service to leave a squadron of copper bottomed ships to watch the motions of the enemy, and to give me timely notice should they attempt to sail. With the other I anchored in Gross Islet Bay, ready at a moments warning to cut, or slip, in order to pursue or engage the enemy, should they leave Fort Royal Bay . . .

There followed prolonged manoeuvring, until

the enemy with their whole force put to sea in the middle of the night; immediate notice of which being given me, I followed them, and having looked into Fort Royal Bay, and the road of St. Pierre's on the 16th we got sight of them about eight leagues to leeward of the Pearl Rock. A general chace to the north-west followed; and at five in the evening we plainly discovered that they consisted of twenty three sail of the line, one fifty gun ship, three frigates a lugger and cutter. When night came on, I formed the fleet in a line of battle a-head, and ordered the *Venus* & *Greyhound* frigates to keep between his Majesty's and the enemy's fleets, to watch their motions, which was admirably well attended to by that good and veteran officer Capt. Ferguson. The manoeuvres the enemy made during the night indicated a wish to avoid battle, which I was determined they should not, and therefore counteracted all their motions. At day light in the morning of the 17th we saw the enemy distinctly beginning to form the line a head . . .

Rodney began to signal.

I made the signal for the line a-head at two cable's length distance. At forty five minutes after six I gave notice by public signal, that my intention was to attack the enemy's rear with my whole force; which signal was answered by every ship in the fleet. At seven A.M. perceiving the fleet too much extended, I made the signal for the line of battle, at one cable's length asunder only. At thirty minutes after eight, A.M. I made a signal for a line of battle abreast, each ship bearing from the other N. by W. & S. by E. and bore down upon the enemy . . . who discovered my intention, wore, & formed a line of battle on the other tack: I immediately made the signal to haul the wind, and form the line of battle a-head at two cables length on the larboard tack. The different movements of the enemy obliged me to be very attentive, and watch every opportunity that offered of attacking them to advantage . . . The manoeuvres made by his Majesty's fleet will appear to their lordships by the minutes of the signals made before and during the action. At eleven A.M. I made the signal to prepare for battle, to convince the whole fleet I was determined to bring the enemy to an engagement. At 50 minutes after eleven A.M. I made the signal for every ship to bear down and steer for her opposite in the enemy's line, agreeable to the 21st article of the additional fighting instructions. At 55 minutes past eleven A.M. I made the signal for battle. A few minutes after, the signal that it was my intention to engage close, and, of course, the Admiral's ship to be the example . . .

Eventually the British fleet did get within range of the French, and

A few minutes before one P.M. one of the headmost ships began the action. At one P.M. the *Sandwich* in the center, after having perceived several of our ships engaging at a distance, I repeated the signal for a close action. The action in the center continued till 15 minutes after four P.M. when Mons. Guichen in the *Couronne*, in which they had mounted 90 guns . . . after engaging the *Sandwich* for an hour and a half, bore away. The superiority of the fire from the *Sandwich*; and the gallant behaviour of her officers and men, enabled her to sustain so unequal a combat; though before attacked by them, she had beat 3 ships out of their line of battle, had entirely broke it, and was to leeward of the wake of the French Admiral . . .

Rodney claimed a moral victory:

At the conclusion of the battle, the enemy might be said to be completely beat; but such was the distance of the van and rear from the center, and the crippled condition of several ships, particularly the *Sandwich*, who for twenty four hours was with difficulty kept above water, that it was impossible to pursue them . . .

Next, on 6 May, Rodney 'having received intelligence of the enemy's approach to the windward of Martinique . . . put to sea with 19 sail-of-the-line, two 50 gun ships, and frigates'. In this meeting with de Guichen, despite five days of manoeuvring and skirmishes, Rodney thwarted French plans to invade St Lucia, while the French kept the weather gage and avoided battle. Rodney reported thus:

From the 6th to the 10th of May . . . Nothing could induce them to risk a general action, though it was in their power daily: they made at different times, motions which indicated a desire of engaging, but their resolution failed them . . . As I watched every opportunity of gaining the wind, and forcing them to battle, the enemy, in my ordering the fleet to make a great deal of sail on the 15th upon a wind, had the vanity to think we were retiring, and with a press of sail approach'd us much nearer than usual. I suffered them to enjoy the deception, and their van ship to approach a-breast of my center, when, by a lucky change of wind, perceiving I could weather the enemy, I made a signal for the third in command (who then led the van,) to tack with his squadron and gain the wind of the enemy. The enemy's fleet instantly wore and fled with a crowd of sail. His Majesty's fleet, by this manoeuvre, had gained the wind, and would have forced the enemy to battle, had it not at once changed six points when near the enemy, & enabled them to recover that advantage . . .

Despite his manoeuvring and signalling in the baffling winds, the ensuing battle was desultory rather than decisive:

... their rear could not escape, being closely attacked by the ships of the van, then led by Commodore Hotham; & with pleasure I can say, that the fire of his Majesty's ships was far superior to that of the enemy, who must have received great damage by the rencounter ... several other ships received considerable damage ... The pursuit of the enemy had led us 40 leagues directly to windward of Martinico; and as the enemy had stood to the northward with all the sail they could possibly press, and were out of sight the 21st instant, the condition of his Majesty's ships being such as not to allow a longer pursuit, I sent the *Conqueror, Cornwall* & *Boyne* to St. Lucia, & stood with the remainder of his Majesty's ships towards Barbadoes, in order to put the sick and wounded on shore, and repair the squadron ...

At Barbados other news awaited Rodney which stimulated his getting his ships ready for sea quickly:

We anchored in Carlisle Bay on the 22nd instant, where every dispatch possible has been used both night & day in refitting, watering, and victualling the fleet; and I hope that every thing will be in readiness to proceed to sea tomorrow, in quest of the Spanish fleet which sailed from Cadiz the 28th of last month; intelligence of which has been brought me by the *Ceberus*, Capt. Man, who parted company with them on the 4th instant in latitude 31 & a half, steering W.S.W ...

The Spanish fleet, which was carrying reinforcements to Havana, avoided Rodney, but refused to delay in order to cooperate with de Guichen. In turn, de Guichen refused entreaties to go north to support French forces operating with the American rebels and instead sailed for France.

## THE GREAT HURRICANE, WEST INDIES, 1780

The story of Rodney's own absence in New York has been told in a previous chapter. While in the north, he missed a series of particularly violent hurricanes which swept the West Indies. Only Antigua was spared, but Barbados, St Lucia, and Jamaica were all badly affected. All supplies for the islands were destroyed including precious naval stores, and with no docks anywhere in the islands, even those ships which survived could not be repaired or remasted. The British lost more ships to the weather than from any action: two ships-of-the-line and eleven frigates and smaller warships. In St Lucia, this is how William Hotham experienced the storm on 10 October 1780:

there arose a hurricane at N.E. which encreased by the morning to a degree of violence not to be described. The *Ajax, Montagu, & Egmont,* which had been anchored before the entrance of the harbour, were before day light, all forced to Sea, as was the *Amazon* soon after; and the *Deal-castle* and *Camelion,* which had been Stationed in Gross Islet bay for the protection of the hospitals, shared the same fate. The *Vengeance,* with the *Etna & Vesuvius* bombs, and the *San Vincente* snow, were moored within the Carenage, & prepared with every caution that could be taken to withstand the tempest, which had already put several of the transports on shore, & by this time blew with an irresistible fury, attended with an incessant flood of rain. A little after twelve o'clock the *Vengeance* parted her cable, and tailed upon the rocks. It now became absolutely requisite to cut away her masts, the loss of which, with the help of a number of guns that were got forward, eased considerably the force with which she struck; and by the wind fortunately shifting two or three points further to the eastward, the stern swung off the rocks, and she was, beyond every expectation, saved; for it now blew, if possible, with redoubled violence, & nothing was to be seen or expected but ruin, desolation, and destruction in every part. The *San Vincente* snow, with many of the transports, victuallers, and traders, were dismasted, and mostly all on shore; in short, no representation can equal the scene of distress that appeared before us. The Storm continued with incredible vehemence during the whole day; but the weather about midnight became more moderate, & by the next morning the wind was totally abated. The direction of it was from N.N.E. to E.S.E. of twenty nine hours duration. On the 13th the *Montague* anchored before the harbour, without a mast or bowsprit standing, eight feet water in her hold, & all her powder damaged: every assistance was given to get her into the Carenage, where she is now secured in safety. The *Ajax* returned to this anchorage on the 21st, with the loss of her main yard, main top mast, & mizen mast. The *Beaver's* prize being on her passage to Barbados, was unfortunately wrecked on the back of this Island near Nieux Fort; and it gives me pain to add, that all her officers and crew, except 17 men, perished. The preservation of the *Amazon* is so singular & extraordinary, that I herewith transmit a copy of the account given of it by Captain Finch . . .

And this is how Clement Finch, captain of the *Amazon*, described his experiences:

I am at a loss whether to express in the strongest terms my regret for the misfortunes that have happened to his Majesty's ship under my command, or my satisfaction, of having got her in safely to this port. I flatter myself you saw the necessity we were under of putting to Sea the morning after the commencement of the gale. We then stood under our storm stay sails W. by N. from the Carenage; it was but for a short time the canvass held; after that the ship behaved perfectly well, & appeared to every person on board as capable of standing the gale that ensued, as was possible for any ship. About Seven o'clock at night the gale encreased to a degree that can better be conceived from the consequences . . . a sudden gust overset the ship; most of the officers, myself, & a number of the ship's company, got upon the side of the ship; the wheel on the quarter deck was then under water. In that situation I could perceive the ship settle bodily some feet, until the water was up to the after part of the slides of the caronades on the weather side. Notwithstanding the ship was so far gone, upon the masts, bow sprit, &c. going away, she righted as far as to bring the lee gunwale even with the water's edge. By the exertions of all the officers & men we soon got the lee quarter deck guns and caronades overboard, and soon after one of the forecastle guns, & a sheet anchor cut away, which had so good an effect, that we were enabled to get [to] the pumps, and lee guns on the main deck; the throwing them overboard was in our situation a work of great difficulty . . .

The *Amazon* had gone over so far that the stump of the main mast had come out of its housing:

> The water was above the cables on the orlop-deck, with a vast quantity between decks; & the stump of the main mast falling out of the step occasioned one of the chain pumps to be rendered useless, as was the other soon after; by the great activity of the two carpenters mates they were alternately cleared . . . Besides the loss of our masts, &c. the ship has suffered considerable damages; the particulars of which I cannot send until a Survey has been held upon the ship. The books & papers are totally destroyed, so that it is not in my power particularly to ascertain the loss we have suffered in men; I believe twenty drowned, besides a number wounded . . .

The foregoing accounts were written by experienced seamen. To the landmen on board, the hurricane seemed, if possible, even more terrible, and this is how it appeared to John Stradley:

> we was greatly alarmed with the swelling of the sea and the birds which had been blown from the land came hovering round about the Ship as if they wanted to rest and the Skyes gathered black all around Everything lookd very alarming but as yet there was no wind, but at last Our fearfull aperhentions broke in upon Us in a most tremendous manner the wind came on in a seeding gust and blowed the see into the air and tore our sails from the yards it was with the Utermost difficulty that we could stand or hold Our selves from being washed from one side of the Ship to the other . . . several of the upper deck guns broke loose and one 18 pounder gun and Carriage came through the mane hatchway and pitchd into the middle deck and had very near stove the ships side out but by the blessing off God and the activity of the seamen they secured it between decks, but . . . the hatchway was laid Open which exposed us to great danger for we Shiped a great Quantity of water before we cold secure it again by this accident and the great quantity of water we had shipt therefore our bread was wet with Salt water and the Chain pumps rendered quit Usless so that we was obliged to bail the water Out with buckets . . . I was calld on for that Painful task to cut the guns luce to Through them Over

bord to lighten the Ship . . . while the Carpenters was cuting away the mane mast a suden gust of wind came and carried it away about 10 feet above whare they were cuting and as it was dark we cold not se to cutaway the back stays theirfore they brought the hed of the mast under the counter of the Ship which greatly alarmd us for the ship lay roleing up on it all night and we expected her bottom wold have been stove in before morning at this time the tiller broke so that we were left destitute of all means of help and Ever being saved, Our livestock all perished and washed overboard, our Provisions all Damaged Our strength quite exhausted with Extrem fatuge and want of refreshment our flesh worn from of our bones Our eyes sunk into our heds for want of sleep . . . thus we spent maney Days and Maney knights without the light of sun moon or stars I do not know how maney for I was almost spent with fatuge I remember tying myself to a Gun Carriage to prevent the water washing me from one side of the Ship to the other In this miserable State I layed down to endever to get a little rest I also recollect that I was in the Gun Room when the mainmast went Over board and the tiller Broke at the same time when instantly I heard a Cry from an Officer Lord have mercy on us for we are all lost . . .

. . . at Length it pleased the Lord to Speak to the Wind and Changed the almighty Command so that we now began to open the Ports and discover the sad hassock the long continued motion of the Ship had made with our Cloths and beds and hammocks and everything that was movable and found them all knockt to peces in such a manner that we cold scarcely tell what they had been for they were like Dung mixt together . . . we then began to clear the ship and to rig out a Jurey Mast as well we war able and cleard the rudder and endevered to steer for Jamaica again which we accomplished in a few weeks after the wind abated . . . now we heard of the *Thunderer* of 74 guns that went out with from Jamaica was totally Lost and every Soul Lost and that nothing cold be found of her but a spare top mast with her name stamped on the heel of it, and also of the *Sterling Castle* of 74 guns endevering to git into Jamaica had struck on the Rock called the Silver Keys . . . when they struck one part was left on the rock and the oather part drifted out to sea with the greater part of the men and were never heard of anay more . . .

The state of those left on Silver Keys without provisions was not much better:

> . . . at last they came to this conclusion that they wold tak the first that died before he was cold and cut him and it what blood out of him thay cold and Drink it as a means of subsistence . . . one of them came on board of Our Ship and gave me this Information that I am now writing he also Informed me that he drank Once and only Once of human blood and found it very refreshing but cold never drink anay more . . .

The voyage home to Britain was also a trial of endurance:

> we got refitted again with Jurey Mast and was Ordered home with a fleet of Merchant Ships which war ready to Sale from Jamaica to England . . . we had a long and suffering Voige for we was more than three months between Land and Land and six men on four mens Alowance and very short of water we were Obliged to com through the North Seas for the French fleet was crossing the English Channel theirfor we came North about and anchored in Leath Harbor whar we left our sick people . . . we were ordered from Leath around to Portsmouth to be repaired, Here the Ship was ordered out of commission and my Poor fellow suffers turned over to other Ships We cold muster only One hundred men that sailed out of this Port . . . we lost four hundred men in the space of about three years and a half, Here I was ordered on Shore with the Arms to repair them and return them into Store . . .

## THE BATTLE OF THE SAINTS

When Rodney returned to the West Indies in the autumn of 1782, he at last obtained the decisive battle he had so strived to bring about: '. . . and had the happiness at day light to find my most sanguine desire was near being accomplished, by my having it in my power to force the enemy to battle . . .'

The Battle of the Saints, a group of small islands between

Guadeloupe and Dominica, took place between 9 and 12 April. The battle revolved around an attempt by de Grasse to rendezvous with a Spanish squadron for an attack on Jamaica. It started along lines familiar from other engagements Rodney had fought with de Guichen, and in the perplexing winds Rodney ran the risk of seeing his van cut off while he was becalmed:

> before day light of the 9th, came up with the enemy under Dominique where both fleets were becalmed, and continued so for some time. The enemy first got the wind and stood towards Guadeloupe; my van division under that gallant officer Sir Samuel Hood, received it next and stood after them. At nine the enemy began to cannonade my van, which was returned with the greatest briskness. The baffling winds under Dominique did not permit part of the center division to get into action with the enemy's rear till half past eleven, and then only the ship next to me in the line of battle. – Their lordships may easily imagine the mortification it must have been to the fifteen gallant officers commanding the ships of the war, who could only be spectators of an action in which it was not in their power to join, being detained by the calms under Dominique ... but such was the steady behaviour of Sir Samuel Hood and the ships of the van, that the enemy received more damage than they occasioned ...

On the fourth day of manoeuvring, the two fleets passed each other on opposite tacks and the British broke through the French line of battle. The British retained the cohesion of their formation while the French lost theirs, and suffered more damage, losing their flagship, the 104-gun *Ville de Paris*. As Rodney reported from the *Formidable*:

> It has pleased God, out of his divine Providence, to grant to his Majesty's arms a most complete victory over the fleet of his enemy, commanded by the Count de Grasse, who is himself captured with the *Ville de Paris*, and four other ships of the fleet, besides one sunk in the action. This important victory was obtained the 12 inst. after a battle which lasted with unremitting fury from seven in the morning till half past six in the evening, when the setting sun put an end to the contest. Both fleets have greatly suffered; but it is with the highest satisfaction I can

assure their lordships, that though the masts, sails, rigging, and hulls of the British fleet are damaged, yet the loss of men has been but small, considering the length of the battle, and the close action they so long sustained . . .

Rodney was free with his praise:

The gallant behaviour of the officers and men of the fleet I had the honour to command, has been such as must for ever endear them to all lovers of their King and country. The noble behaviour of my second in command Sir Samuel Hood, who in both actions most conspicuously executed himself, demands my warmest encomiums; my third in command, Rear Admiral Drake, who, with his division led the battle on the 12th instant, deserves the highest praise; nor less can be given to Commodore Affleck, for his gallant behaviour in leading the center division. My own Captain, Sir Charles Douglas, merits every thing I can possibly say; his unremitted diligence & activity greatly eased me in the unavoidable fatigue of the day . . . In short, I want words to express how sensible I am of the meritorious conduct of all the Captains, officers, and men, who had a share in this glorious victory, obtained by their gallant exertions. The enemy's whole army, consisting of 5500 men, were on board their ships of war: the destruction among them must be prodigious, as for the greatest part of the action every gun told; and their lordships may judge what havock must have been made, when the *Formidable* fired near eighty broadsides . . .

## THE GLORIOUS FIRST OF JUNE, 1794

After Admiral Graves' failure at the Battle of Chesapeake, the surrender of the British army at Yorktown and the consequent loss of the American colonies, told in a previous chapter, any French satisfaction at Britain's discomfiture was short-lived. Revolution and regicide broke out in France and the Royal Navy found itself fighting not American revolutionaries, but French. Briefly in 1793 the Royal Navy supported the French royalist cause by occupying Toulon. In the winter of 1793/94 the French navy was reorganized and a large number of officers who were considered unreliable were purged: after this, warfare at sea between Britain and France reverted to a more traditional pattern. The Battle of the Glorious First of June, so named because it was fought far out to sea without landmarks to give it any other name, was a convoy battle: Admiral Howe's task was to escort a large convoy on its way to the East Indies and several smaller convoys into the Atlantic.

There were three Howe brothers: George, who was killed at Ticonderoga in 1758; William, who fought at Quebec under Wolfe and at the Battle of Bunker Hill in 1775; and Richard, who joined the navy aged fourteen in 1740. Richard Howe saw service on the Guinea coast, in the West Indies, the Mediterranean, and on the North American station, and in the Channel during the Seven Years War. At the Battle of Quiberon Bay in 1759, it was Howe in the *Magnanime* who led Hawke's fleet into the bay on that darkening November afternoon. As well as being a superb seaman, Howe was a superlative, if cautious, tactician, with a habit of winning his battles, and he introduced the navy to many changes in signalling. Nelson described him, and it may have been a little more than just outrageous flattery, as 'the first and greatest Sea-officer the world has produced'.

While Howe escorted the merchant ships into the Atlantic in May 1794, a small squadron sailed along the French coast. Edward Baker, an officer in the *Orion*, tells us, on 5 May 'At ½ past 1 stood in for Brest. The grand fleet [under Lord Howe] were then out of sight. The *Latona* went pretty far in & discovered 24 sail (but of what force, the captain of her could not tell) lying in Brest Roads . . .'

The French sailed to meet them on 14 May, and the action which followed took place over several days at the end of the month, culminating on 1 June. On 28 May, Baker noted:

cleared the decks for action. Stowed our hammocks in the tops, & got up a sufficiency of powder, & shot of all sorts & sizes . . . the signal was made to tack in succession, but we missed stays on account of the heavy seas . . . The whole fleet kept together for the night, & carried as much sail as so stormy a night would permit us, & every man remained at his quarters . . .

Howe nearly succeeded on 29 May, but appears to have mis-judged the timing of a tack:

> At daylight saw the enemy's fleet to windward, & much nearer to us than the day before ... The French pointed their guns very high which did a good deal of execution about our rigging, but we fired chiefly at their hulls, as we thought it best ... On breaking their line, we gave 3 cheers, & were exposed to a smart and quick carronading from the whole of the French line which we kept up with uncommon spirit, & our men behaved uncommonly well, nor did any accident happen from powder, but everything onboard went on with great regularity. We kept up a fine fire upon them till 3 oclock when having passed the whole of their line & received the fire of almost all their ships, with very few on our side to assist us, we hawled off ...

In this manoeuvre, however, Howe had gained the all-important weather gage. So far the battle had been fought in very lumpy seas, which made every movement difficult, but still *Orion*'s damage had to be repaired:

> ... we knotted our shrouds together which had been shot away, & cut away the mainsail which was so shot in pieces that it hung down on the booms ... besides this all our sails were full of shot holes, braces lifts main and mizen stays and mizen yard shot almost in two, several shot lodged in the lowerdeck's side, starboard main top sail yard arm shot away, & main top sail hanging in rags, only two of the main top mast shrouds left standing; main top mast wounded, main mast mizen mast and mizen top mast wounded, & 3 killed and 20 wounded ...

However, *Orion* was soon in action again:

> having repaired our rigging a little, and seeing very near us one of the French line of battle ships [the *Indomptable*] ... bore down upon her, & running close under her weather quarter poured a severe fire of great guns and small arms into her ...

On the 30th it was too foggy to renew the action:

> the Admiral made the signal to know if the ships were in readiness for action ... and we gave the *Queen* three cheers

which she returned ... [but it was] so foggy now that we lost entirely sight of the enemy ... At 2 [p.m.] it cleared up, & became pleasant sunshiny weather, & we saw the French fleet about 7 miles to leeward ... At 20 minutes past 7, the *Southampton* hailed us, & told us that the Admiral meant to carry the same sail all night, & that we were to keep a little to wind-ward of his wake ... The men stayed all night at their quarters ...

On 1 June Howe brought the French fleet to close action. The French commander was Rear Admiral Louis Thomas Villaret-Joyeuse, one of the few nobles in the French fleet who had not been executed or fled the Terror in revolutionary France. His officers were inexperienced but determined to pass their convoy through with wheat from America needed to feed the Paris mob: they were perhaps inspired by rumours that they were under threat of the guillotine if they failed. On the other hand, Howe's fleet was one of the strongest with which the British had entered any war, and was studded with famous names, including Thomas Duckworth, James Gambier, Cuthbert Collingwood, Thomas Graves, Alexander Hood, and Thomas Packenham.

Shortly before four o'clock in the morning, Howe made his first signal, forming his line carefully. Again he wanted his ships to pass independently through the enemy's line and to engage them from leeward, but only six ships managed this. In the fighting that became general, the British captured seven ships, of which one sank: it was not the annihilating victory Howe wanted but it was victory. The approach was very similar to that which Nelson was to use eleven years later, running down on his enemy before the wind, and holding his fire until he was at close range:

we bore down upon them before the wind ... At ½ past 9 the 2 fleets got within gunshot, & the action began, each ship engaging as he came up; a most beautiful sight to see 2 such large fleets meeting and keeping up a fire on each other. The fire from the enemy's ships was very smart & fierce before we got close. Our fleet did not fire much at first, as we thought the shot would not reach or do any execution. But the French were very smart at firing with long balls ... But as soon as we came to close quarters, we began a most extraordinary fire upon the enemy's ships which was kept up with remarkable spirit . . . about an hour and half after we had been engaged in close action, we looked round, & saw 6 or 7 of the French ships with all their masts gone; it was then that victory seemed ours . . . unfortunately our fleet was too disabled to pursue their victory . . .

Howe was criticized for not pursuing a defeated opponent, though it's likely that he was suffering from mental and physical exhaustion: after all, the sixty-eight-year-old admiral had fought the battle for five days from a chair on the quarterdeck of his flagship. The convoy, which was desperately needed in Paris, arrived unmolested, giving, perhaps, a strategic win to the French, though most of the grain was ruined on the long road from the west-coast ports to Paris.

Two letters describe the Glorious First of June from slightly different aspects, conveying a sense of how the news reached Britain. James Maxwell, a marine officer in the *Leviathan*, one of the ships which had succeeded in Howe's breaking-the-line manoeuvre on 29 May, wrote on 2 June:

Thank God Almighty my dear Mother I am in the greatest of good Health and Spirits after the most Glorious action that was ever fought – we were closely engaged with the enemy three different days and during every one my conduct gave Lord Hugh [Seymour] so much satisfaction that he has told me I shall ever find in him a very warm and sincere friend. I have not time to give you any particulars only that we engaged the *America* of 74 Guns (one of our Prizes) 3 hours and a half and totally dismasted her and on the 28 ulto the day on which we first took sight of them a ship [of] 120 guns for above 1 hour and a half I have not time to say any more Lord Howe is in so great a hurry to dispatch a ship with the agreeable account to England. On receipt of this tell Miss Ann to be so good as write me at Portsmouth where I hope we shall be soon after the arrival of the dispatches with 6 sail of the Enemy's Line of Battle ships, what number of Ships are gone to the bottom we know not yet in the *Leviathan* but think two. Thank God this

is the Second Glorious action I have been in and had the good
fortune to escape. I beg my kind Compliments to all Friends
and acquaintances and Believe me My Dear Mother to remain
Your most Affectionate son, J Maxwell Written in the greatest
haste . . .

PS. Be so good as send to Alexr Smith's wife who formerly
sailed with Tom and James Douglases wife who lives in Capn L
Browns house and assure them that their husbands are both
well, J M.

Francis Aimée, presumably an émigré officer in British service,
wrote a slightly different letter and for another purpose, from the
frigate *Pegasus* to a Mrs Jones in London:

Lord Howe with the Fleet has been on a cruise these 6 weeks &
has had a very severe action with the French fleet, which were
much of Equal Force, about 25 Ships of the line and 10 Frigates
each they had a small engagement on the 29th day of May but
could not form their Line of Battle properly before the First of
June on Sunday morning they began forming the line about
7 o'clock as soon as they had light to see each other on account
of a Fog that had continued for 3 days before, about 10 o'clock
they began firing at each other which continued for 4½ hours
the severest engagement that any person in the fleet saw, or they
believe ever was fought before, we have brought in here [to
Spithead] 6 of their first rates & sunk three of them & disabled
6 or 7 others which they got home to Brest with the ships that
were not disabled, I saw them make their escape in the midst
of the battle we have 6 or 7 thousand of them prisoners & I
believe there were 3 or 4 thousand killed beside three thousand
drowned in the three vessels sunk, for any other Information
I refer you to Lord Howe's account sent home to England by
a Frigate from the fleet we anchored here this day. I hope when
I receive my prize money to have the pleasure of seeing you in
London and all the rest of your good Family, please to let me
know if the Count De Voux went to Canada, if he has not I
request you will apply to him for money to get me some clothes
or to send me some Blue cloth to make them. Madam I hope
the Countess Mr Charles Jones & all the rest of the family are
in good health and please to remember me to them. We are to

remain here some time to have the ships repaired. Please to write to me as soon as possible as I would be sorry to go to sea again without hearing from you . . .

## TWO FRIGATE ACTIONS

As Comptroller of the Navy for fifteen years until 1831, Thomas Byam Martin was one of the most influential officers to emerge from the navy during the Great War, but he was no mere peacetime bureaucrat. He served with distinction in the Baltic and on the north coast of Spain during the Peninsular War. Nor was there any doubt of his personal bravery, and he was highly commended for his action in capturing the Russian line-of-battle ship *Vsevolod* in 1808. In this frigate action, however, the account reads more like a yacht race.

In June 1796, Captain Martin's *Santa Margarita* and Captain Thomas Williams' *Unicorn* were off the Scillies when Martin

discovered, at Two o'Clock in the Morning, Three Sail of Ships about a Mile on our Lee Beam; as the Day opened we perceived them to be Frigates belonging to the French Nation . . . each Ship steered for her Opponent; but the Enemy, determined to evade an Action, steered away large under a Press of Sail, the smallest Ship at the same Time making off to Windward: At Half past Eleven o'Clock, by our superior Sailing, we arrived within Gun-Shot of the Enemy; but as they appeared to close, for the mutual Support of each other, and the *Unicorn* being some Distance astern, I judged it prudent to postpone our Attack till she was sufficiently advanced to occupy the Attention of the French Commodore. At this Time the Enemy commenced a Fire from their Stern-Chace Guns. At One o'Clock, having approached them within Three Quarters of a Mile, we fired our Bow Guns, whenever a favourable Opportunity presented itself, the Enemy at the same Time yawing to discharge their Broadsides. At Two o'Clock, the *Unicorn* being on our Weather Beam, we made Sail, keeping up a running Fight till a Quarter past Four o'Clock, when the sternmost Ship finding it impossible to escape, put his Helm a-port, &

endeavoured to rake us; but being fortunately baffled in this Effort afforded us an Opportunity of placing ourselves abreast of him within Pistol Shot, when a quick and well directed Fire compelled him to Surrender to His Majesty's Ship in less than Twenty Minutes. She proved to be the *Thames*, commanded by Citoyen Fraden [Fradin], mounting 36 Guns and 306 Men . . .

The *Thames*, or rather *Tamise* as she had been christened by the French, was promptly restored to the British flag.

Meanwhile,

The Ship which the *Unicorn* continued in Chace of, is *La Tribune*, of 40 Guns & 320 Men, bearing the Broad Penant [sic], Citoyen Moulson, Commander of a Division; the other, which made off to Windward, is *La Legre* [actually *Légère*] of 24 Guns and 180 Men . . .

Williams in the *Unicorn* had a rather longer chase.

we discovered Three Ships of War on our Lee Beam, distant Two or Three Miles, to which we immediately gave Chace . . . At Nine A.M. they formed themselves in a close Bow & Quarter Line, and continued to run from us . . . the largest Ship under easy Sail, for the Support of his Squadron. In this Situation we approached them very fast, and must have speedily brought them to Action. I therefore made the Signal to form for Battle, the *Margaritta* being at the Time a-head of the *Unicorn* . . . On our nearer Approach, the Corvette, which detained the other Ships, gradually hauled out to Windward, & passed our Weather Beam in long Gun-Shot, steering afterwards the same Course as the other Ships, and with the Intention, I then imagined, to be in Readiness to give Support to either of her Friends eventually most needing it . . . At One P.M. the Two Frigates hoisted French Colours, the largest Ship a Commodore's Pendant, and at the same Moment commenced a quick and well-directed Fire on us with their stern Chaces the Corvette [the *Légère*] at this Time hauled more up, and, to my great Astonishment, brought to, to board a Sloop passing us on the contrary Tack. As the Commodore continued to wait for the *Thames* we thereby approached them both, but were considerably retarded by the Effects of their Shot. At Four P.M. the *Thames* being the sternmost Ship, bore round up, to avoid the Fire from the *Unicorn*, and to pour a Broadside into the *Margaritta's* Bow, when I had the pleasure to see Captain Martin manauvre his Ship with the greatest Judgment, and with the utmost Gallantry he laid himself close alongside his Opponent. The superior & well-directed Fire from the *Santa Margaritta* marked the Discipline of his Ship, and Soon put the *Thames* into his Possession . . .

So far the largest of the French ships had been under easy sail, but now:

The Commodore on seeing his Companion fall, made all Sail, and by a sudden & judicious though unsuccessful Manauvre, endeavoured to gain the Wind of the *Unicorn*. We were at this Time chacing him toward the Entrance of the Irish Channel, & soon after passed close to the Tusker Rock.

The ships were evenly matched, and the race was on:

The Parity of Sailing in the Two Ships, aided by the Judgment of the Enemy's Commander, kept us at running Fight for Ten Hours; during which Period we were much annoyed in our Sails and Rigging, & were for some Time unluckily deprived of the Use of our Main-Topsail; but on it's falling less Wind [sic] after Dark we were enabled to use our Supernumerary Flying Sails, Royal Steering [studdding] Sails, &c. which by slow Degrees, brought us so near his Weather Quarter as to take the Wind from his Sails; when, at Half past Ten at Night, after having pursued Two Hundred and Ten Miles, we shot up alongside of our Antagonist, gave him Three Cheers, and commenced close Action, which had continued in that Position with great Impetuosity on both Sides for Thirty-five Minutes; when, on clearing up of the Smoke, I observed that the Enemy had dropt on our Quarter, was close hauled, attempting, by a masterly Manauvre, to cross our Stern, and gain the Wind. This was happily prevented by our instantly throwing all aback, and giving the Ship strong Sternway, by which we passed his Bow, regained our Situation, & renewed the Attack. The Effects of our Fire soon put an End to all Manauvre, for the Enemy's

*Right.* A Spanish carrack before the wind, by Brueghel: the sight every English pirate or privateer longed for. [BHC 0707]

*Below, left.* Charles Howard, Earl of Effingham, commanded Elizabeth I's fleet in the defeat of the Spanish Armada. The Howards made the navy a family business, and descendants were still serving in the navy in the late twentieth century. [BHC 2786]

*Below, right.* Francis Drake, apprentice to his cousin John Hawkins, became a brilliant navigator and the most renowned sailor of the Elizabethan age. He was the first English seaman to circumnavigate the globe, the first commander to survive a circumnavigation and, quite simply, one of history's greatest seamen. [BHC 2669]

This order from Elizabeth I to pay £2,000 to her 'treasurer of marine affairs' is one of the earliest Elizabethan naval documents, and possibly the earliest known English naval document mentioning naval shipbuilding and the wages of the Royal Navy's seamen. It dates from less than six weeks after the death of Queen Mary. [F3559/F3559-2]

Eight fireships, 'burning fiercely . . . with sails set and wind and tide behind them', caused havoc amongst the Armada. The Spanish panicked and cut their cables, which led to the decisive Battle of Gravelines that finally destroyed the cohesion of the Spanish invasion force in 1588. [BHC0263]

Peter Pett, one of a famous family of shipbuilders, is seen here with *Sovereign of the Seas*, a radical design for the first three-decker, built in 1637. About a sixth of the ship's cost was for carving and gilding, a fact which helped to precipitate a crisis over ship money and led to the Civil War. [BHC 2949]

Perhaps the first written reference to a flag that is recognizably the White Ensign, 'to be borne as the flagg of those ships that are in the service of the state'. [F 3557]

GEORGIUS,

Dei Gratia, *MAGNÆ BRITANIÆ, FRANCIÆ & HIBERNIÆ* Rex, Fidei Defenſor : *BRUNSWICK* & *LUNENBURGH* Dux, SRI Arch-Theſaurarius & Elector & Inauguratus, 20. *Octobris*, 1714.

His MAJESTY's Royal Navy.

A. A. Is the Seven Firſt Rates, and Fourteen Second Rates Unrigg'd, and Lying in a Harbour.

B. Is Five and Forty Third Rates Fore-ſhortned, with the Heads toward, Under-ſail.

C. Is Three and Sixty Fourth Rates Fore-ſhortned, and with the Sterns toward.

D. Is Forty Fifth Rates, Under-ſail.

E. Is Thirty Fire Ships, Under-ſail.

F. Is Four and Twenty Sixth Rates.

G. Is Nine Bomb Veſſels.

H. Is Fifteen Yatchs, or Pleaſure Boats.

I. Is Ten Advice Boats.

*Above.* Taking advantage of unseasonable easterly winds, William of Orange's fleet, under the protection of the Dutch flag, passed down the Channel to land at Torbay on 5 November 1688: the Glorious Revolution followed. [BHC0326]

*Left.* This engraving by van der Gucht, dated 1714, shows George I surrounded by ships of the fleet and is one of the earliest uses in print of the title 'Royal Navy'. [PW3325]

*Above*. The Battle of Quiberon Bay: the bay is enclosed and encumbered with rocks and the battle that took place there in November 1759 was one of the greatest in naval history. In Admiral Hawke's victory seamanship counted as much as the fighting quality of his fleet. [BHC 0402]

*Below, left. The Honble Augustus Hervey Captn in His Majesty's Navy, Colonel of Marines and Commander in Chief of His Majesty's Ships in the Mediterranean 1763. Third Earl of Bristol* by Joshua Reynolds. The caption is straightforward, but Hervey was the naval Casanova, hence the painter's trick of showing him in this unusual pose with a sword of priapic extension. [PW 3442]

*Below, right*. Men had many motives to go to sea: the chance of earning riches from prize money was one, but rumours of South Seas beauties whose sexual mores were not the same as European women's was another, and persuaded seamen to volunteer for dangerous voyages into the Pacific. [BHC 2957]

Capt: James Cook
of the Endeavour.

*Above, left.* James Clark Ross, nephew and fellow explorer of John Ross, who was shipwrecked in the ice and spent four winters in the Arctic, where his leadership in bringing his men home was unequalled even by Scott and Shackleton a century later. [BHC 2982]

*Above, right.* James Cook, the foremost navigator of his and perhaps all time: information from his charts was extraordinarily accurate and some are still in use today. Most portraits of him are more romantic, but this portrait of the careworn Yorkshireman is probably truer. [BHC 4227]

*Below.* The destruction of the American fleet at Penobscot: George Collier's pursuit in 1779 of American forces until he was 'forced to Anchor for want of depth of Water' ended the rebellion in northern New England for the time being and led to bitter recriminations amongst the revolutionaries. [BHC 0425]

Weather frequently intervened in naval operations, and in 1703, 1780 and 1806, for example, caused as much damage as the enemy; but more often British ships and seamen triumphed by surviving when the enemy did not. Here the East Indiaman *Essex* on the morning after the great storm of 1780 signals her distress. [B4550]

The *Ville de Paris*, shown being captured by Admiral George Rodney as he breaks the French line at the Battle of the Saintes in 1781, in the West Indies. She foundered that September on the Banks of Newfoundland, but the name was kept when a 110-gun ship was launched at Chatham in 1795. She was one of the largest ships afloat for many years and served as a comfortable, and powerful, flagship in the Royal Navy. [BHC0446]

Very many officers' logbooks and journals were liberally and well illustrated. Here an episode from the Battle of the Glorious First of June, 1794 is shown: 'Le Vengeur being very much mawled between wind and water . . . filled with water and lay upon her beam ends; numbers of unfortunate wretches were seen clinging to her side; some were floating in the water and crying for assistance; in a minute's time she heeled right over, and went to the bottom . . . the *Rattler* cutter picked up several, but much the greater part of her crew which consisted of over 800 men were lost . . .' [F3560]

A rare example of the 'convoy book' of Charles Middleton (later Lord Barham), showing how he kept this vital document and how merchants made their bids for the Royal Navy's protection of their ships into and out of the Channel. [F5361]

Ship was compleatly dismantled, her Fire ceased, & all further Resistance appeared to be ineffectual; they called to us they had surrendered . . .

Williams concluded his report:

The Ship proves to be *La Tribune*, commanded by Commodore John Moulston, mounting 44 Guns, though pierced for 48; on the Main Deck 26 Twelves, on the Quarter-Deck and Forecastle 16 long Sixes, and 42 lb. Carronades; had on Board at the Commencement of the Action 337 Men, 37 of whom are killed, 13 badly & 2 slightly wounded. The Ship is quite new, launched since the Commencement of the War, Sails extremely fast, is of large Dimensions, being on the Gun-Deck Two Feet broader and Thirteen Feet longer than the *Unicorn*. Commodore Moulston, who I am sorry to add is among the Wounded, is by Birth an American, but has served Sixteen Years in the French Navy, and during the present War has always had the Command of a Division . . .

## THE BATTLE OF CAPE ST VINCENT, 1797

John Jervis's naval career spanned nearly sixty years: he had already been in the navy eleven years when he took part in the storming of Quebec. His influence reached every corner of the navy, from the close blockade of Brest which strangled French naval operations to giving the marines their Royal title. Jervis, Old Jarvie to his men, was a stern, dour disciplinarian but also 'one of the foremost seamen and fleet organisers of his day', noted for his care of his people. One of his biographers observed that 'although his attitude to his seamen was often harsh, his discipline savage, his humour occasionally curt and language sometimes unbridled and rough, his letters are full of warm and generous praise for officers and men, and his kindness to individuals was considerable and frequently secret . . . Civil administrators suffered from his over-enthusiastic zeal . . .' Jervis became one of the father figures of the Royal Navy; he was also one of the first to recognize Nelson's talent and to give him his opportunities.

On the grey misty dawn of 14 February 1797, Jervis, with fifteen sail-of-the-line and five frigates, sighted a Spanish fleet of twenty-five sail-of-the-line escorting a valuable cargo towards Cadiz. The numerical superiority of the enemy seemed even greater, as Jervis mistook the convoy for more warships. Jervis's fleet had kept its close order during the night, but as the Spanish commander, Vice Admiral José de Córdoba y Ramos, manoeuvred his ships, they broke into two bunches, the main body of about eighteen line-of-battle ships, and, slightly astern and to the south-east, the convoy and its immediate escort.

By noon the battle had already taken an unconventional course: Troubridge in the *Culloden*, leading the British column on a south-westerly heading, cut the Spanish line and divided their fleet, and tacked in the wake of the Spanish main body. Vice Admiral Moreno, commanding what was now the Spanish rear, attacked the British as they turned ahead of him, but was soon beaten off, leaving Jervis free to concentrate on Córdoba's portion of the fleet. However, Moreno's counter-attack had caused a delay, and when a wind shift headed Jervis's ships on to a more southerly course, it seemed that the Spanish might escape to the north-west.

Then Jervis ordered an unusual manoeuvre. With the van of the British fleet ranging up along one side of the Spaniards, he planned to lead the ships of his centre up the other, and he ordered the rear division to tack to attack the leading Spanish ships. He had devised this complicated and original order of battle while splattered with the blood and brains of one of his seamen, pausing in his thinking only long enough to ask the captain of the flagship, 'Do, George, try if you can get me an orange' to rinse his mouth out. However, tacking in succession meant they had to sail south until they reached the point at which the leading ship had tacked; it was by disobeying this order that Nelson seized his opportunity.

According to Nelson,

At 1pm the *Captain* having passed the sternmost of the Enemy's ships, which formed their Van and part of their centre, consisting of 17 sail of the line they on the Larboard, we on the Starboard Tack, the admiral made the signal to Tack in succession.

He saw that Córdoba was altering course to the east and that he might escape and join up again with his convoy: but

> perceiving the Spanish ships all to Bear up before the wind or nearly so, evidently with an intention of forming their line going large, joining their separated division at that time engaged with some of our centre ships, or flying from us, to prevent either of their schemes from taking effect, I ordered the ship to be wore . . .

In other words he turned the stern of his ship through the wind, a quicker manoeuvre than tacking which would have meant putting her head or bows through the wind. Nelson then passed

> between the *Diadem* and *Excellent* at ¼ past one o'clock was engaged with the headmost and of course leewardmost of the Spanish Division, the ships which I know, were the *Santissima Trinidada*, *San Joseph*, *Salvador dell Mundo*, *San Nicholas*, another first rate and [a] 74, names not known, I was immediately joined and most nobly supported by the *Culloden* Captain Troubridge, the Spanish fleet from not wishing (I suppose) to have a decisive battle hauled to the wind in the Larboard tack . . .

– that is, they resumed their original course to the north-west.

Nelson subsequently claimed he and the *Culloden* had fought the Spaniards alone, but in reality he simply could not see the other ships as they sailed into the smoke of battle, and he was obliged to alter the next sentence:

> and for near an hour I believe (but do not pretend to be correct as to time) did the *Culloden* and *Captain* support this apparently but not really unequal contest, when the *Blenheim*, passing between us and the enemy, gave us a respite and sickened the Dons, at this time the *Salvador dell Mundo* and *San Isidro* dropt a stern and were fired into a masterly stile by the *Excellent*, Captain Collingwood, who compelled the *San Isidro* to hoist English Colours . . .

Both Nelson and Collingwood thought that the *Salvador del Mundo* had surrendered, but Collingwood, disclaiming the parade of taking possession of beaten Enemys, most gallantly pushed up with every sail set to save his old friend and Messmate who was to appearance in a critical state, the *Blenheim* being a head and the *Culloden* crippled and astern . . .

Collingwood in the *Excellent* had passed through the Spanish fleet and now sailed between Nelson's *Captain* and the *San Nicolas*, ranging up

within 10 feet of the *San Nicholas* [and] giving a most tremendous fire, the *San Nicholas* luffing up the *San Joseph* fell on board her and the *Excellent* passing on for the *Santissima Trinidada*. The *Captain* resumed her situation abreast of them and close alongside at this time the *Captain* having lost her Foretopmast, not a Sail, Shroud, or Rope left, her wheel shot away and incapable of farther service in the line or in chase, I directed Captain Miller to put the Helm a starboard and calling for the boarders ordered them to board . . .

What happened next can be told in Nelson's own words:

The soldiers of the 69th regiment with an alacrity which will ever do them credit and Lieutenant Pearson [Peirson] of the same regiment were amongst the foremost on this service, the first man who jumped into the Enemys Mizzen chains was Captain Berry late my first Lieutenant (Captain Miller was in the very act of going also but I directed him to remain) he was supported from our spritsail yard which hooked in the mizzen rigging, a soldier of the 69th regiment having broke the Upper Quarter Galley window jumped in followed by myself and others as fast as possible, I found the Cabbin doors fastened, and some Spanish officers fired their pistols, but having broke open the doors the soldiers fired and the Spanish Brigadier . . . fell as retreating to the Quarter deck on the Larboard side near the wheel, having pushed on[to] the Quarter deck I found Captain Berry in possession of the Poop and the Spanish Ensign hauling down, I passed with my people & Lieutenant Pearson on the Larboard gangway to the Forecastle, where I met two or three Spanish officers prisoners to my seamen and they delivered me their Swords, at this moment a fire of pistols or musquets opened from the admirals stern Gallery of the *San Joseph*, I directed the Soldiers to fire into her stern and calling to Captain Miller ordered him to send more Men into the *San Nicholas* and directed my people to board the first Rate which was done in an instant. Captain Berry assisting me into the Main Chains, at this moment a Spanish officer looked over the Quarter deck rail and said they surrendered, from this most welcome intelligence it was not long before I was on the Quarter deck where the Spanish Captain with a Bow presented me his sword, and said the admiral was dying of his wounds below, I asked him on his honor if the ship was surrendered, he declared she was, on which I gave him my hand and desired him to call to his officers and ships company and tell them of it which he did and on the Quarter deck of a Spanish first rate extravagant as the story may seem did I receive the swords of Vanquished Spaniards, which as I received I gave to William Fearney one of my Barge men who put them with the greatest sang froid under his arm, I was surrounded by Captain Berry, Lieutenant Pearson of the 69th Regiment, John Sykes, John Thompson, Francis Cook all old *Agamemnon's* and several other brave men, seamen and soldiers, thus fell these ships.

Boarding two Spanish ships in this fashion became known as 'Nelson's patent bridge for boarding first rates', and clearly it was a unique and very bold deed. Somewhat ungenerously, however, Nelson tried to claim all the credit for these two large ships having surrendered, whereas the *Prince George* was also pounding both ships, and did not stop firing until she was hailed from the *San Josef* by Captain Berry. Nelson also circulated, somewhat vaingloriously, his own description of the battle to amplify Jervis's official despatch. However, his reputation as a fighting officer was made.

## THE GREAT MUTINIES, 1797

Within a few weeks of the Battle of Cape St Vincent, one of the most dreaded events broke out at home – mutiny. 'Mutiny' signifies both a failure by officers to lead their men and to manage events, and the disappointment of their men's attempts to communicate their ideas and wants. However, although some of the revolutionary spirit that was abroad in America and France had spread to Britain, the mutiny in the fleet at Spithead in 1797 was primarily about pay, which had not been increased since 1653. The mutineers reckoned that pay 'was intended as a Comfortable Support' but that the cost of the 'Necessaries of Life . . . is now almost double'. Other complaints, some about individual officers, were later larded into the mutiny, or inferred by subsequent historians, but many officers sympathized with the mutineers. Even if the subsequent mutiny at the Nore was more political. Nelson wrote: 'I am entirely with the Seamen in their first Complaint. We are a neglected set, and, when peace comes, are shamefully treated; but, for the Nore scoundrels, I should be happy to command a ship against them . . .'

Admiral Howe, the respected victor of the Glorious First of June, and nominally in command of the fleet at Spithead, was sick on shore when he received a number of anonymous petitions, 'all exact copies of each other'. It took more than six weeks for the Admiralty to react, when on 17 April the First Lord and two commissioners, thus making the board quorate, went personally to Portsmouth 'to take such measures as may appear the most advisable . . . for redressing the grievance complained of without suffering the dissatisfaction . . . to proceed any further.'

So far the mutiny had been a very British affair: there had been no violence, the seamen said 'that they would go to sea if the enemy was on the coast', the internal routine on board continued, and frigates on convoy escort duty had been allowed to sail, but otherwise the men adamantly refused to sail to join the fleet until their demands were answered. The delegates of the fleet summarized all their grievances into a single petition, a printed version of which reads:

WE, the Seamen of His Majesty's Navy, take the Liberty of Addressing your Lordships, in an Humble Petition, – shewing the many Hardships and Oppressions we have laboured under for many Years, and which we hope your Lordships will Redress as soon as possible, we flatter ourselves that your Lordships, together with the Nation in General, will acknowledge our Worth and great services both in the American War as well as the present for which good Service your Lordships Petitioners do unanimously agree in Opinion that their Worth to the Nation and laborious Industry in Defence of their Country, deserve some better Encouragement than that we meet with at Present; or from any we have experienced. We, your Petitioners do not boast of our good Services for any other Purpose than that of putting you and the Nation in mind of the Respect due to us, nor do we ever intend to deviate from our former Character so far from any thing of that kind, or that an Englishman or Men should turn their Coats, we likewise agree in Opinion, that we should suffer double the Hardship we have hitherto experienced before we would suffer the Crown of England to be in the least imposed upon by that of any other Power in the World; we therefore beg Leave to inform your Lordships of the Grievances which we at present labour under.

We, your humble Petitioners relying, that your Lordships will take into early Consideration the Grievances of which we complain, and do not in the least doubt but your Lordships will comply with our Desires, which are every way reasonable.

The first Grievance which we have to complain of is, that our Wages are too low & ought to be raised, that we might be the better able to support our Wives and Families in a Manner comfortable, and whom we are in duty bound to support as far as our Wages will allow, which we trust will be looked into by your Lordships and the Honorable House of Commons in Parliament assembled.

We, your Petitioners beg that your Lordships will take into consideration the Grievances of which we complain, and now lay before you,

First – That our provisions be raised to the weight of Sixteen Ounces to the Pound, and of a better Quality, and that our Measures may be the same as those used in the Commercial Trade of this Country.

Secondly – That your Petitioners request your Honours will be pleased to observe there should be no Flour served while we are in Harbour, in any Port whatever, under the Command of the British Flag; and also that there might be granted a sufficient Quantity of Vegetables of such kind as may be the most plentiful in the Ports to which we go; which we grievously complain and lay under the Want of.

   Thirdly – That your Lordships will be pleased seriously to look into the State of the Sick on shore and with your accustomed Goodness and Liberality comply with the Prayer of this Petition, – and your Petitioners as in Duty Bound will ever Pray, &c.

   We, the Delegates of the Fleet, hereunto sign our Names for the Ships Companies . . .

Two brave men from each ship signed their names.

   The Board of Admiralty assembled at Portsmouth acceded to the mutineers' requests, but the delegates insisted on their demands being agreed to in writing – 'signed with their proper signature, not what they intend to do, but what they done'. The members of the board and the senior officers were exasperated by this and after part of the fleet had been persuaded to drop down from Spithead to St Helen's Roads minor scuffles broke out and two of the delegates of the fleet were killed. Only on 14 May when Lord Howe arrived with plenary powers and an Act of Parliament did the mutineers agree, and on 16 May the fleet put to sea.

   Now a more serious mutiny broke out at the Nore, and ships hoisted the red flag. The demands were more extensive and less reasonable, and the mutineers, led by one Richard Parker, demanded that they too should be visited by the same members of the Board of Admiralty. After three months of indiscipline, the Admiralty, and the government, seemed to have learned. A pardon was offered, and the militia called out to prevent the mutineers meeting ashore, but this could not prevent Admiral Duncan's squadron from deserting him, or the protesting seamen (not for the first time in history) attempting to blockade the Thames. Neverthe-less on 4 June 1797 they did remember to fire off a salute to mark the King's birthday. The mutiny collapsed of its own accord in mid-June, not before the sad spectacle of British warships firing upon each other, without further concessions and no pardons for the ringleaders. Parker was court-martialled and hanged, others were flogged or imprisoned, and only after the Battle of Camperdown, when the victorious Admiral Duncan interceded, were they released.

## MUTINY IN THE *ST GEORGE*, 1797

The first mutiny, at Spithead, had been about pay, and despite some violence ended with a pardon for all concerned. The mutineers at the Nore had added other minor, but similar, grievances, and the mutiny ended with the execution of the ringleaders. As news of the mutiny, but not its remedy, spread to individual ships new grievances were piled on and there were more outbreaks of indiscipline. However, having agreed to pay rises and the abolition of short measures, the navy was not prepared to tolerate further indiscipline and courts martial sat throughout 1797: those found guilty were hanged or flogged.

Despite an appeal from St Vincent saying that he trusted in 'the loyalty, fidelity and subordination of the rest of the fleet', a particularly determined mutiny broke out in the *St George* in July 1797, which St Vincent reported thus:

> We have had some awkward sensations in this squadron [off Cadiz]: One on board the *Irresistible*, I am assured by the Rear Admiral Nelson, is finally settled. The *Diadem*, spiritedly commanded, has a dirty blackguard Crew, who have gone lengths, but are kept down with a tight hand. A Plan laid on board the *St George* on Sunday last, to wrest the Command of the Ship from the Officers; the pretext, a determination that two men condemned to death for sodomy, should not be executed on board that Ship, has been happily frustrated by the timely precautions and manly courage of Captain Peard, ably supported by his Officers, and more particularly by Captain Hinde at the head of a detachment of the 25th Regiment doing duty on board that Ship as marines, who ought to be promoted to a majority immediately: Three ringleaders are confined on the Poops at the *Ville de Paris* and *Prince George*, and I think there is Evidence to convict them of the conspiracy . . .

Actually there were four ringleaders, who were found guilty and hanged next day, despite its being the Sabbath. While quelling incipient mutiny, it was also business, or rather war, as usual: 'in the mean time, we are carrying on the most active, desultory war, against the Port & Town of Cadiz, to divert the Animal, from these damnable doctrines and positions, which letters from England have produced'.

## MUTINY IN THE *HERMIONE*, 1797

There had been mutinies in the navy, large and small, since it began, the principal cause usually being mistreatment and cruelty by officers. The mutiny in the *Hermione* was one of the bloodiest in its history. The cause was the tyrannical character of her commander, Captain Hugh Pigot. Pigot's behaviour was cruel and unpredictable: quite why has not been examined, but, like Bligh before him, he found the loneliness of command too much to bear, and picked on and alienated individuals in his ship: one of his victims was Midshipman David O'Brien Casey. Casey himself seems to have been something of a Jonah, his ships always running aground or into other trouble. Nevertheless, this does not seem to be justification for the brutal murder and mutilation of the *Hermione*'s officers.

The *Hermione* was a small frigate of an obsolete class on a distant station, where her commander was expected to exercise considerable independence and initiative. Pigot had been promoted to command at the early age of twenty-five, yet does not seem to have possessed any real talent, which suggests that some family interest had been at work. He had been in the West Indies for three years and in command of the *Hermione* since July 1797, and the record shows that he was a flogger. According to Casey, a midshipman, who had been given a dozen lashes for insolence and banished from the gunroom mess,

A few days after my punishment a melancholy circumstance occurred in reefing topsails, which greatly increased the previous dislike of the Captain and no doubt, hasten'd, if not entirely decided, the Mutiny; three Boys fell from the Mizen Topsail yard on the quarter Deck, and were kill'd – the melancholy accident caused a painful sensation where it was observed, and a momentary relaxation in the duties aloft, particularly in the

Main Top, to which place two Boatswains Mates were instantly sent, to start the entire Topmen, which was accordingly and indiscriminately done ...

Edward Southcott, the master, had been hurt by one of the boys falling on him: and Pigot is alleged to have said of the corpses, 'Throw the lubbers overboard.' Then there was

on the following morning a very severe punishment of several men, I believe twelve or fourteen, took place in the usual way, at the public place of punishment – That evening, or the following, I am not certain which, but on the 21st of September 1797, the Mutiny took place – It commenced about Eleven o'clock at Night, in three separate parties, against the Quarter Deck, Captain's Cabin, and Gunroom, with a wild indescribable noise, and shouting; no resistance being made in any quarter, the Ship was instantly in possession of the Mutineers when the Captain, second, and third Lieutenants, and one Midshipman, were at once murder'd, in the most savage, and cruel manner. The party that attack'd the Cabin, knocked down the sentinal at the door, and attack'd the Captain as he jumped out of his Bed, all taking a cut or stab at him, according to the weapons they were arm'd with (which were various) accompanied with horrible language, & reminding him of his own severity, and cruelty; they then left him in a dying state, and join'd those on the Quarter Deck, when they insisted on the third Lieutenant's being put to Death; he was at once cut, and stabb'd, and thrown overboard (he was officer of the Watch, and a humane good young man, and was spared by the first party) ...

The third lieutenant landed in the chains, but when he attempted to climb back over the side, one of the leading mutineers pushed him into the sea. Meanwhile, the mutineers

return'd to the Captain, put him to Death, and threw him out of his Cabin Window – The Gunroom party put the Second Lieutenant and one Midshipman to Death in the most savage manner, and as they dragged them up the Hatchway, apparently Dead, they continued cutting and stabbing them with various weapons, till they reach'd the Main Deck, when they threw them overboard; the conduct of some of the Crew was truly savage, and brutal, and cannot be described. It was then warmly debated how the remaining officers should be disposed of, and there appear'd every hope of their lives being spar'd, till a great part of the crew (many of whom were not concern'd in the commencement, but now much worse than the original Mutineers) got access to the spirit room, and got drunk; not more than three hours had then elaps'd from the first massacre, when there was a general cry to put every officer, young and old, to Death – The scene now became dreadful, and the greatest confusion prevailed, all were more or less, inflam'd, and excited by spirits, except about 40 or 50 of the principal Mutineers who kept sober and steady, and opposed to taking any more lives; but the majority of the crew prevailed against them, and the remaining unfortunate officers were brought on Deck, and disposed of as their fate was decided; some were wounded and thrown overboard, and others thrown over unhurt; the language, noise and scene altogether, was horrible . . .

The fate of the few remaining officers was debated the next morning: and, according to Casey,

I was subsequently told by my friends, that I was twice or thrice condemn'd, and on the point of suffering, and that it was with the greatest difficulty I was saved; two or three of them always kept near me during the Night, as a protecting guard and removed me occasionally from place to place, for more certain safety. The Master was principally sav'd by two of the principal Mutineers placing themselves as sentinals at his Cabin Door, and by his servant boy, (quite a youth, and who died in prison) going through the ship crying, and begging of the crew, most pitiously, that his Masters life might be spared . . . The Gunner, and Carpenter, who had not been very long promoted, were also saved; the latter had been some years in the ship, as Carpenter's Mate . . .

Some of the petty officers joined the mutiny, including William Turner, the master's mate, whom Casey described as a clever but disappointed midshipman, and Laurence Cronin, the surgeon's mate, 'a treacherous, drunken infamous character . . . in many instances worse that the worst of the Mutineers . . .' Cronin took no part in the murders with knives and tomahawks, but he seems to have been a 'lower-deck lawyer' and his words certainly seem to have inflamed the mutineers as much as any rum.

Four men were murdered in the actual mutiny and six more killed in cold blood:

> Those who suffer'd were the Captain, three Lieutenants, Lieut. Marines, Surgeon, Purser, one Midshipman, Boatswain & Captains Clerk, ten in all – It was then decided to run for La Guira, on the Spanish main, where we arrived on the 27th following – The ship was in the greatest possible confusion during the passage, many of the crew continually in a state of drunkenness, and frequently fighting; those officers saved, as well as myself, were consequently in continued dread of being put to Death; on one or two occasions, our death appear'd almost certain, and but for the steady good conduct of some of the principal Mutineers . . .

At La Guaira the mutineers gave up the ship to the Spanish, who were at war with Britain. The remaining officers and the men who had been loyal became prisoners of war and were soon exchanged, bringing with them the terrible story of the mutiny. The Spaniards rewarded the mutineers, who had already helped themselves to the officers' possessions, and some of them took Spanish service while others found their way into merchant ships and privateers. They were not, however, forgotten by the navy, who hunted the mutineers for nearly ten years. Some were found in neutral merchantmen, one was found in a French privateer's crew, one in a Dutch frigate, one of the ringleaders was found under an assumed name in an American schooner and extradited to Jamaica, one even found his way back into the Royal Navy but was recognized in the streets of Portsmouth. The last of the mutineers was hanged in 1806.

The *Hermione* spent two years under the Spanish flag until she too was hunted down by the *Surprise* and, in a famous boat action, cut out and taken to Port Royal. With *Hermione* renamed the *Retaliation*, and then the *Retribution*, the stain of this particular mutiny had been wiped out. There were lesser mutinies in the fleet up to the time of the Peace of Amiens in 1802: when war was renewed in 1803 the incidence of mutiny seems to have dropped off – the officers had learned a lesson as well as the men. Significantly, however, the fleet had been held together as a fighting force.

## THE BATTLE OF CAMPERDOWN, 1797

In early 1797 a Scottish admiral, Adam Duncan, was off the island of Texel blockading the French-controlled Dutch fleet. When news of the mutiny reached Duncan's fleet many ships sailed for the Nore to join with the mutineers and by May he found himself with just two ships, the *Adamant* and the *Venerable*. Keeping close off the Texel, Duncan stationed his meagre force so that they could signal to (non-existent) ships over the horizon, and reply to their (non-existent) messages. By the time the Dutch fleet came out the Nore mutiny was over, the ringleaders had been hanged, and Duncan's disaffected ships had rejoined him.

By the end of June his fleet was more or less back to strength and he was able to reimpose his blockade in reality. Then in October the Dutch sailed, apparently intending to join the French fleet in Brest. Duncan was refitting and revictualling in Yarmouth when a lugger called the *Black Joke* brought him the news that the enemy were at sea. Duncan soon found them and attacked in two divisions, breaking the Dutch line in two places. Battles with the Dutch were usually bloody stand-up affairs and this was no exception: the Dutch had fired low and several ships were badly mauled suffering some ten per cent casualties, but more than half the Dutch fleet, eleven line-of-battle ships and frigates, surrendered. The twin victories off Cape St Vincent earlier in the year and now Camperdown had prevented the merger of enemy fleets; but it might well have been a different story if Duncan's bluff had not been so successful.

Joseph Samain, a seaman of HMS *Venerable*, flagship of Admiral Duncan, wrote to his parents at the sign of the White Horse, Hare Street, Bethnal Green, London:

Dear Father & Mother i send this with my love to you hoping it will find you all are in good health as I are at present thanckes be to god for it considering the hard engagement we had for three hours and ten minutes and we had 4 ships of the line and one friget at us for all most three hours ... we took two admirals but you will see the list the first broad side we give the Dutch admiral we laid 100 men on there decks total kiled and wounded 250 on board the frigit killed 36 wounded 90 and we had one hundred killed and 3 killed and wounded and very much shattered our ship is we are at an anchor in the swin [the Swynne, a channel through the sandbanks in the mouth of the Thames] but we shall be at the nore in two days so pray remember my love to my Brothers and sisters we had the bloody battle in the eleventh day of Oct. Our admiral says it was the hardest battle that was ever fought by two fleets but three of our ships did not come in to the action not anything to speek of which did look cowardly wich was 74 and two 64 ...

Samain was clearly writing for the neighbours and for posterity because he concluded his letter:

I beg you will tack care of this letter if you want to tack it to the hailehouse do not take this but copy it off and mind and keep it clean.

## THE BATTLE OF THE NILE, 1798

In 1797 St Vincent, while maintaining a blockade of Spanish ports and islands, sent Nelson to look for a Spanish treasure ship thought to be at Santa Cruz in Tenerife. In a night attack he lost his right arm, and suffered one of his few personal and military defeats. Meanwhile, within just a few years of the start of the revolution, the French were masters of Europe on land, and now in 1798 planned to capture Egypt and use this as a base to attack British interests in India. The British government was suspicious but knew little of these plans, though when St Vincent heard that a fleet was being got ready in Toulon, he selected Nelson – recovered from his wound – to investigate. The first information Nelson had was that the French had been sighted off Sicily; on arrival there he learnt that they had reached Malta (Sir William Hamilton, the envoy plenipotentiary in Naples, had learned that the French had told the Neapolitan government they were sailing for Alexandria, but he thought this was a ruse and did not pass it on to Nelson); then on 22 June he learned from a Ragusan brig that the French had sailed from Malta on the 16th, destination unknown: it was Nelson's genius and seamanship that led him to conclude the destination was Egypt – but he thought the conclusion so unexpected that he asked his favourite captains' advice before committing the squadron. Nelson overtook the French fleet without realizing, passing within a few miles of them: one can only speculate on the course of history had he met Bonaparte and his army at sea.

Nelson found Alexandria empty and sailed back to Sicily, where he revictualled. Meanwhile Bonaparte had landed in Egypt. Returning to Alexandria, on 1 August 1798, Nelson learned that there were thirteen French sail-of-the-line and several smaller vessels in Aboukir Bay, a few miles to the east. The French commander, Vice Admiral Brueys, had anchored his ships in a curved formation close inshore. With night falling, Nelson attacked at once, and, realizing that where there was room for a French ship to swing at anchor there was room for a British warship to float, Captain Foley in the *Goliath* led a division of British ships inshore, and Nelson in the *Vanguard* attacked from seaward. The attack, by doubling upon their line, devastated the French and only two of the French ships of the line and two frigates escaped destruction or capture. This account of the battle is given by John Jup, a seaman in the 74-gun *Orion*, in a letter to his parents:

> On the 1st of August Came in Sight of Alexandria and the french fleet lying at Anchor at the head of the River Nile . . . But Now my Brave Boys for Old England Glory our Adml. made a Signal to Come to an Anchor Close along Side of them and hammar a way so now at 6 oclock at Night began the bloody fray we continued a most thundering and tremendous Noise till near half past ten during which time we sett the *LeOrient* of 120 Guns on fire and Burnt her to the Magazine and then She blue up . . .

For several minutes there was a shocked silence, while burning debris showered the ships around, setting other ships on fire:

... the Explotion made the Whole Element Shake and was a most Glorious Seean ... the fireing tho not so hot lasted till 10 Oclock [a.m.] next day when we found our selves totaly master of the french fleet as I will State altho they where Superior to us Considerable Such a defeat as never was known in the world before as for the Number of their killed and wounded I Cannot account for them that was not killed where most of them wounded I suppose 500 Blue up in the *Le Orion* – as She had 1100 on Board and about 600 where Saved from Death by Swimming ... I was on board *Le Dourin* and She had about 50 out of 550 left free from Death and wounds ...

Jup had an exhortation for his countrymen:

it is the Supream that fighteth the Battle and whilst we have his help we will Defy the World before us my good lads drink your tea in quiet and let no false alarmes frighten you think on the wooden walls and the Brave fellows that are in them Remember they are your Safety therefore when you see poor Jack tar in distress Relieve him as one good turn deserves another ...

He also recorded the British seaman's customary humanity in battle:

the french Come Swimming from their Ships that was on fire and our Brave Spirited Englishmen threw them Roap and took them in and stript of there own Cloths and gave them to Cover their Nakedness and went without themselves as our Bags where stowed a way and we could not get them for a day or two afterwards ...

Victory at Aboukir Bay gave the British command of the Mediterranean and isolated Bonaparte's army in Egypt, though he himself managed to escape in a frigate and resume the war in Europe in 1799. The Battle of the Nile or Aboukir Bay was also Nelson's first action in command of a detached squadron, and by nearly annihilating his enemy, he had set a new standard of decisive battle. For this he was created Baron Nelson of the Nile and of Burnham Thorpe in Norfolk.

## THE SIEGE OF ACRE

The loss of his fleet left Napoleon stranded in Egypt and he resolved to march home along the seaboard of the Holy Land and through Asia Minor, no doubt seeing himself as a latter-day Alexander. However, he reckoned without the Royal Navy and Sidney Smith. Learning of Bonaparte's march, Smith took his small squadron to St Jean d'Acre and there reinforced the Turkish garrison with his seamen and marines and guns from his ships, the *Tigre* and *Theseus*. Smith captured the heavy guns of the French siege train, which were being brought up by coastal craft, and added them to the guns on the ramparts of Acre. Then for two months he defied the French, who could not leave Acre in their rear, and without taking the place could not advance into Turkey. Smith on one side and Bonaparte on the other took personal charge of the siege operations and of the defence, Smith occasionally fighting in hand-to-hand combat. When, after several bloody assaults, and having ravaged the countryside and the coastal districts for many miles about, Bonaparte abandoned the siege, Smith could claim the honour of being the first to defeat the Frenchman in a land battle.

Bonaparte slunk back to Egypt, where he left his wrecked army and chanced a voyage to France in a frigate. The remnant of his army was roundly defeated by General Abercromby, who had been sent out for the purpose in 1801. Smith could not resist being present at the new Battle of Aboukir. When a prisoner on St Helena and reflecting on his past life, Bonaparte said of Smith, not Nelson and not Wellington, 'That man made me miss my destiny.'

## COPENHAGEN, 1801

When Napoleon attempted to create an economic blockade against Britain in which he tried to stop the Baltic trade upon which she depended for vital naval supplies, a strong fleet commanded by Admiral Sir Hyde Parker, with Nelson as second-in-command, was sent north. The aims of the expedition were to require Denmark to withdraw from the League of Armed Neutrality, then to destroy the

Russian squadron at Kronstadt before the ships at Reval could join it. However, Copenhagen was defended by a line of ships and floating batteries, and two forts:

> The Enemy's line extended for nearly four miles, & consisted of 25 of these formidable vessels of defence, besides the two fortified islands called the Crowns . . . to attempt therefore an attack upon Such a chain of defence thro' a channel not broader than a large river, with Shoals on every Side, set the history of Aboukir at nought, & even strikes us all with astonishment, now the Affair is over.

When, however, it was clear that the Danes intended to resist, Hyde Parker sent Nelson's squadron into the attack. Two ships ran aground and Hyde Parker, who when the wind dropped could not fulfil his part of the plan, signalled Nelson to break off the action. When this was received aboard the *Elephant*, Nelson, sensing that victory was near, moved his fin – the stump of his right arm – in a manner which he did when agitated and putting the telescope to his blind eye remarked that he had a right to be blind sometimes. The battle was described by Alexander Nairne of the *Polyphemus* in a letter to his brother in Edinburgh:

> Admiral Nelsons division anchored about six miles from [Copenhagen] . . . we found it to be very strong, the north passage being defended by the crown Battery and some ships of the line and the south by a smaller one and two Ships of the Line. On the afternoon of the 1st the whole of Lord Nelsons division weighed and stood up to the south passage or Kings Channel . . .
>
> On the morning of the 2nd we got all clear for action and to weigh . . .

Nelson summoned his officers:

> about ten all the Captains went on board of the Admiral when they got a plan of the attack and every one of them to know their opponents, we then found we had to take one of the northernmost ships, which was by far the hottest part of the action – at half past ten we weighed and just as we were coming into the fire of the enemy our signal was made to take the

*Agamemnons* station, she being aground, we then found there
was two seventy fours aground just outside of us . . .

During the battle Nairne and the other young officers were each
given a gun to command, although, he told his brother,

> their [sic] is a Captain to every gun a steady and good man and
> I had for the Captain of the Gun Jas Lumsdaine.

Nelson was only the second in command at the battle, and there
were both suggestions that the main body of the fleet, commanded
by Sir Hyde Parker, had not supported his squadron adequately
and counter-suggestions that Parker did not praise Nelson sufficiently for his part in the victory. As before, however, Nelson took
care to provide himself with a sympathetic witness to his actions,
and one with powerful connections with the court. Colonel William
Stewart was serving as a marine in the *London* and had, like others
before him, fallen under the great hero's spell. He endorsed his
letter 'if Nelson is commander in chief I care not how long I am a
Marine if he do not, I may again look for land service'. Stewart's
letter, with its implied criticism of Parker, and apparent knowledge
of Parker's despatch, was addressed to 'Colonel Clinton Aide de
Camp to H.R.H. the Commander in Chief' and there is evidence
that when it was read in London it changed perceptions of what
had happened at Copenhagen. 'How the whole affair may appear
to you all in England we know not here, but to us here the conduct
of our fleet on the day of the 2nd strikes as something the most
hazardous, enterprising, & intrepid which ever was attempted by
our British navy'. Nelson had lived up to his reputation:

> When I first proceeded upon Service with Such an officer as Ld.
> Nelson I predicted that our campaign would not be exactly
> similar to the *cautious* conduct which some of our great generals
> observed during last year in diverse quarters of Europe, nor have
> I been deceived in my expectations, for successful as has been
> our battle of the 2nd & in my opinion well worthy of the
> damage which has ensued, yet there are many people in this
> fleet, about headquarters too, who think our victory brought
> infinitely too dearly – our damage in ships is certainly great, so
> much so that we fear four of them must be sent home, but even

if that be the case I maintain that the panic we have struck into our Enemy, the confidence which our tars now have of overcoming any thing after the difficulties which we Surmounted on this last action, well recompenses these & still more severe losses . . .

Stewart was unstinting in his praise of Nelson:

The conduct of Ld. Nelson, to whom alone is due all praise both for the attempt & execution of the contest, has been most *grand* – he is the admiration of our whole fleet, & as I was scarcely once from his side for three days proceeding, & during the Action I can positively say that too much praise cannot be given him. The multitude of anecdotes & traits of the hero, which I shall give you of him when we meet, will raise him in your mind, as they have done in mine, beyond any officer now alive . . .

In fact Nelson had secured an armistice from the Danes by addressing a letter to the Crown Prince of Denmark addressed 'To the Brothers of Englishmen, the Brave Danes'. Modern Danes think this was a ruse, and they are almost certainly right, as Stewart describes:

The armistice which has been observed ever since the close of battle until this moment, & which he has been employed in negotiation (with or without effect will be seen in two hours time for it then ceases unless our terms are acceded to) was a masterpiece of policy of the little hero's, for victorious as we were, the narrowness of the Channel in which our Ships were engaged & the commanding Batteries on shore had left our ships, six of which were aground, in a most perilous situation, L. N. then *commanded* a cessation of hostilities, & by prolonging it under one pretext or another, in four & twenty hours after got our crippled ships off the shoals, & from under the guns of the enemies' batteries, & also took possession of all our prizes – which otherwise we should have found some difficulty in doing . . .

Stewart, and others too, compared the recent battle with the Battle of Aboukir, and applied yet more praise:

The nature of the battle of the 2d is I believe unparalleled in history, & for enterprise, & difficulties, as well as the length of the contest (for we were *five* hours in one incessant roar of cannon) infinitely Superior to the famous action of Aboukir – I was during the whole of the action, excepting whilst employed in working my carronade on the Poop or carrying Capt. Foley's orders to the different Decks, on the quarter Deck of the *Elephant* with Ld Nelson, & never passed so interesting a day in the course of my life, or one which so much called for my Admiration of *any officer* – After the Action had lasted about three hours, & that we had fired about forty broadsides, (we fired *above* 60 in all) he said to me 'Well Stewart, these fellows hold us a better Tug than I expected, however we are keeping up a noble fire, & I'll be answerable that we shall bole [sic] them out in four if we cannot do it in three hours, at least I'll give it them till they are sick of it.'

Parker was criticized for not supporting Nelson's squadron yet was understandably nervous about the time Nelson was taking to subdue the Danish forces:

Our grand fleet was under Sail all this time, about two leagues on our Starboard beam, & as there are a number of Croakers, or what you may call cautious Men, in it, (names I shall not mention,) the Signal was made for us to leave off Action – this is a fact, & is a Source of much conversation in our fleet now. L.N. however never answered it, & expressing his astonishment to me at the circumstance, turned & said what I have written above, in a most animated manner . . .

Given this eyewitness account from someone who was close to Nelson throughout the battle, the story about Nelson putting a telescope to his blind eye appears to be a later embellishment. However, 'the only signal which the hero kept flying was the very reverse, viz "for close Action" . . .'

Nairne gives a good account of the relief felt in the British ships when the firing ceased:

we then had you may be sure three good cheers – after you met any one who had not seen you during the action you had a cordial shake of the hands as if you had not seen one another for twenty years before – the only midshipman that was killed on board was a messmate of mine and a particular friend we had about an hour before the action been playing the flute together and I was running along the Main deck with some orders to deliver what should I hear but the poor Bell [his messmate] was killed never did anything affect me so much since I was born but upon going a little further it was no use to lament for him alone as their was many who was wounded most cruelly without it ever being probable they would recover – but our ship came off well by what some of them did, owing I believe to keeping up a smart fire – about quarter of an hour after the action, I was sent out in one of the boats to assist one of the ships that was aground until ten oclock, when I came on board I found all our place in the cockpit was taken up with the wounded . . .

Nairne rested where he could because action was expected next morning:

we expected to be at some of the batterys in the morning we did not get our hammocks down that night and I slept so sound, until three oclock I was sent for to go on board one of the Danish ships, as there was orders to get them all ready for burning . . .

The British ships were mauled, some so badly that they had to be sent home. As Nairne reported, he

was on board several of them but it is impossible to describe in what a condition they were in, cut to pieces you would have thought it impossible for any one to have been saved from immediate destruction.

Operations in the Baltic continued after Copenhagen, and there were other campaigns including Nelson's raids on the invasion fleet at Boulogne. However, the murder of Tsar Paul in March and a change in policy by his successor meant the end of the alliance against Britain. By October there was a weary and uneasy cessation of hostilities between Britain and France, and from the spring of 1802 to the following spring a temporary peace, which both sides used to prepare for more war. The Peace of Amiens lasted barely thirteen months, and what happened next is described in next chapter.


## DANCE'S ACTION, 1804

The last incident in this chapter might be considered not to hang in any story of the Royal Navy, except that it was made possible by the moral advantage the navy had gained over its opponents. It was as a consequence of this that merchant ships mimicking the manoeuvres of the navy were able to frighten a French admiral out of what should have been an easy victory.

The end of the Peace of Amiens saw an immediate resumption of the colonial wars, in the West Indies, the Mediterranean, off Africa, South America, and India, and in the East Indies. A French rear admiral, Durand Linois, had actually sailed during the peace, taking a small squadron and a military force to Pondicherry. He was met at his destination by a strong British squadron and rumour of fresh war, and he escaped by using the simple ruse of inviting the British admiral to breakfast next day – and sailing at midnight. Formal notice of declaration of war in May did not reach India until August and September, but by then the British and French ships were already jockeying for advantage. The British admiral, Rainier, defended India and provided convoy escorts, while Linois sailed to Réunion to land troops and refit his ships. Linois then sailed for Batavia, as the Dutch East Indies were known, and en route found some rich prizes.

Linois's object was the annual East India Company convoy, which was waiting in Canton for its escort. The convoy consisted of sixteen East Indiamen and perhaps nearly as many smaller ships. The East Indiamen were painted to look like line-of-battle ships, but this was generally superficial: each ship had a crew of not more than 150, half of whom would have been locally recruited, compared to 500 or 600 in a regular warship of the same size. The East Indiamen were armed, but only with thirty to thirty-six guns, half the number of one of the navy's 64-gun line-of-battle ships, and these were not cannon but short-range light-weight cannonades. Nevertheless the convoy was worth some

£8 million, and therefore of vital importance to the British national economy.

The convoy was commanded by Nathaniel Dance, 'Commander of the *Earl Camden*, in the service of the Honourable East India Company, and Commodore of the China Fleet, in the year 1804'. Of the escort which was supposed to be on its way there was no sign, so after a conference in Canton the convoy sailed, hoping by its appearance to overcome any opposition. For Linois the problem was easy; he had a 74-gun ship, two frigates, a corvette, and a brig, and no shortage of men; all he had to do was wait in the Straits of Malacca until the convoy showed. The outcome was rather unusual.

Archibald Hamilton of the Honourable East India Company was commander of the *Bombay Castle*:

> The China Fleet of Indiamen, consisting of sixteen sail, none of which were under 1200 tons, and all the country ships then in China, I believe eleven, which had previously resolved to avail themselves of the convoy of the Indiamen, sailed from Macao on the 6th of February . . . on the 14th of February at day light; and at 9 A.M. the *Royal George* made the signal for strangers in the S.W; shortly afterwards the signal was made by Commodore Dance for the *Royal George*, *Alfred*, *Bombay Castle*, and *Hope* to chase. Their manoeuvres soon made us suspicious of the Strangers, their weathermost ships bearing down to join their ships to leeward and then heaving to; the *Royal George* first made the signal for an Enemy, when the chasing ships hove to on the same tack with the Enemy to windward of them and reconnoitred their force. I very soon perceived them to be a line of battle ship, two frigates, a Corvette, and a brig; and shortly afterwards was convinced that it was Admiral Linois and his squadron such as I had heard Captain Craig describe them at Bombay . . .

While John Timmins, a former naval lieutenant, in the *Royal George* was reconnoitring Linois's squadron, Dance was forming a pretend line of battle with the other East Indiamen:

> As soon as the chasing ships made sail to windward to join the Commodore, the Enemy made all sail towards the Fleet working to windward; at 6 P.M. the chasing ships fell into their stations

in the line of battle a head, which had been formed at 2 P.M. laying to on the starboard tack. The enemy before sun-set were directly in the wake of our line of battle, and tacked to gain the wind. From this period until day-light they kept us in constant expectation of an attack; as they bore down three times towards our rear, and as often hauled their wind again . . .

By dawn on the next day, the French had gained the weather gage and were in an ideal position to attack: 'At day-light on the 15th the Enemy were laying to on our weather quarter in a close line a head and about 4 miles distant: we could perceive them communicating but they shewed no decided intention of attacking us'. Some of the survivors of Matthew Flinders' *Investigator* were passengers in Hamilton's *Bombay Castle*, including the young John Franklin, who transferred to the *Earl Camden* to act as Dance's signal midshipman:

at 8 o clock we made sail by signal and kept in a close order of sailing, hoisting our colours: the Enemy then hoisted French colours, except the Brig which shewed Dutch colours, and made all possible sail, the *Marengo* carrying Admiral Linois flag at the mizen, leading the attack in a very close line of battle a head and edging down towards us, our fleet being now under such sail as to accommodate our worst sailors. We did not perceive what would be the Enemy's mode of attack until a little after noon, when he clearly bore up to attack our rear. The situation of the ships in the rear now became very critical, and they must have been cut off from the van and centre, which would have lost us the day . . .

According to Hamilton,

Captain Timmins of the *Royal George*, by the most masterly and daring manoeuvre, saved the rear, and perhaps the fleet. He hailed Dance, our Commodore, and told him the Enemy were going to attack our Rear; Dance then asked him, what he thought should be done, Timmins reply'd, that the Van should immediately tack under all possible sail and engage the Enemy. This was put in execution and the *Royal George* led the attack, followed by the *Ganges*, *Camden*, *Alfred* and *Warley*, the other ships all tacking and following in succession. This seemed to throw quite a new face on the business . . .

If Linois had already delayed his attack inordinately, he was now thrown into confusion, especially as the *Royal George* bore down on him withholding her fire. In reality, of course, Dance had to close in order to bring his guns within range: but now Linois

> seemed wavering and undetermined, and by the time the *Royal George* was abreast of him he had wore and brought his starboard broadside to bear: in this situation the *Royal George* for some time sustained alone the united fire of the Enemy's squadron; but the animated fire of this ship, and the spirit of the manoeuvre, so astonished Linois, that he soon made all possible sail on the Larboard tack, running away as fast as possible . . .

What happened next has the air of the ludicrous about it, the East Indiamen chasing French warships, like so many geese chasing a fox, and golden geese at that:

> The whole fleet now chased until 5 P.M. when we certainly were gaining on the Enemy. But the Commodore very prudently made the signal to tack, when they were allowed to make the best of their way to Batavia, as we suppose, from whence they had last come.

When Dance met the two 74-gun ships *Albion* and *Sceptre* off Penang, their escort across the India Ocean might have seemed unnecessary. As Hamilton concluded his letter:

> when the Van ships had put about, and were leading the attack, the ships in the rear cheered them as they passed to go into action, and thus pledged themselves to stick by each other; never was the genuine spirit of British tars more manifest. Whilst our fleets are manned with such seamen, and they are led by enterprising officers, the British Empire has nothing to apprehend . . .

# Chapter Seven

# The Campaign of Trafalgar

If the experience and the achievements of the British navy were to be distilled into one episode, that would be the Battle of Trafalgar, because victory on 21 October 1805 was the culmination of over two centuries of British efforts at sea, and helped set the world stage for the next hundred years and more. The battle was part of a campaign which has been well told many times over, not least in *The Campaign of Trafalgar* from the National Maritime Museum's collection.

In brief, the Peace of Amiens lasted from March 1802 to May 1803, giving the European powers a short respite in a near quarter-century of warfare. The peace signed by the British Prime Minister, Henry Addington, infuriated many interests in Britain as it gave back to France, Spain, and Holland all the conquests of the war except Trinidad and Ceylon. France, however, refused to withdraw from occupied Holland and Britain refused to withdraw from Malta, both sides using the temporary suspension of hostilities to re-arm. In the first six months of 1803 the British fleet increased from thirty-two to sixty line-of-battle ships, and by the end of the year there were seventy-five line-of-battle ships in commission. New ships were started on the stocks too, and in the following year, on 17 November 1804, in further demonstration of Britain's industrial and financial might, two line-of-battle ships and two frigates, *Hibernia*, *St George*, *Circe*, and *Pallas*, were launched or undocked on the same tide at Plymouth. The French used the truce to prepare for the invasion of England, and Bonaparte, who had placed orders for over three thousand invasion craft, began to mass troops on the Channel coast, and paraded at his headquarters at Boulogne.

At the Admiralty the Earl of St Vincent, born plain John Jervis, was not a success as First Lord, where, perhaps believing that the Peace of Amiens was rather more permanent, he commenced a period of retrenchment and tried to reform the dockyards, directing his efforts at profiteering contractors, corrupt dockyard officers, and striking, or 'combining', workmen. When Addington was forced to resign, St Vincent, whose changes had made him many enemies at home, was driven from office too, only to return later to his proper element, the sea, where he continued to trouble the enemy for a few years yet. The Commission of Enquiry into Irregularities, Frauds and Abuses in the Naval Departments and Business of the Prize Agency, which had been turned against St Vincent, now caused the downfall of his successor, Henry Dundas, 1st Viscount Melville, Treasurer of the Navy until 1800 and First Lord of the Admiralty in 1804–5, and his impeachment in 1806 – a unique event in the annals of the Royal Navy. The reports of the parliamentary commission of inquiry into the royal dockyards give considerable insight into the running of what was already the largest and most sophisticated military–industrial complex in the world: Melville was acquitted and his son, Robert, inherited not only his father's office but also many of his schemes for the reform of the navy, and was inspired to become one of its greatest peacetime administrators.

Melville's impeachment brought to office Charles Middleton, who took the title of Lord Barham. Like St Vincent, Barham had spent over fifty years in the navy, first going to sea in 1741 in the First Rate line-of-battle ship *Sandwich*: the ship's name was appropriate as Middleton's subsequent career was intertwined with that of John Montagu, 4th Earl of Sandwich and First Lord of the Admiralty 1771–82 during the American War of Independence. Barham's principal appointments in London were Comptroller of the Navy 1778–90, and First Lord of the Admiralty 1805–6: though his career has been ignored by historians of blood and guts, it has recently been reappraised. While others were closely blockading the French, Barham was pulling together the logistical system which made the Royal Navy such a formidable fighting machine. Unlike St Vincent, who had no patience at all with bureaucrats, Barham, though not easy to work with, was a brilliant administrator. One of his principal claims to fame is the coppering of the fleet. Various methods had been tried to stop ships' hulls from becoming fouled with weed and eaten by worm. In 1759 the navy had coppered the keels of two ships and in 1761 the underwater hull of the frigate *Alarm*. However, science knew little about electrolysis and the effect in salt water of copper on the iron bolts which held ships together, and eroded bolts were alarming. Barham deserves much praise for the analytical way in which he approached this problem and his determination to copper the entire fleet: copper alloy fittings, liberal use of lead paint, and watertight seals made of cartridge paper and tar were found to serve. In two years from 1779 to 1782, over 300 ships were fully coppered, effectively increasing the size of the fleet, since coppered ships sailed faster, required fewer dockings to clean their bottoms, and so freed docks for repairs and more new construction. When his hour came, Barham masterminded the closing phases of the campaign of Trafalgar, showing himself to be no mean strategist, with a thorough command of detail too.

The Peace of Amiens was not a halt to all hostilities at sea. The large merchant fleet of the new American republic, trading into the Mediterranean, had lost the protection of the Royal Navy and was preyed upon by the Barbary states of North Africa. In America's Barbary Wars (1801–5) William Bainbridge lost the USS *Philadelphia* in the harbour of Tripoli, but Stephen Decatur avenged the insult by boarding and setting fire to her under the walls of the city. It was an action which drew Nelson's admiration and was a hint of the force which the United States Navy was to become.

The campaign of Trafalgar lasted from the recommencement of the war in May 1803 to the end of 1805. The British fought to prevent a French invasion: though the details of the French plan changed over time, in general the strategy was to unite the Mediterranean and Atlantic fleets by making a rendezvous in the West Indies. The French squadrons would sail independently to attack or reinforce colonies in West Africa, South America, and the West Indies, thus forcing the Royal Navy to lift its blockade of France, whereupon the Brest squadron would land an army in Ireland. Then all French ships would return to western France, sail up the Channel in overwhelming force, and, seizing temporary sea control, guard the invasion force while it crossed to England.

True, the French fleet was dispersed in penny packets at several ports, but so too were the British ships on blockade and convoy duties. In some cases the British were potentially outnumbered, as at Toulon where the French, under the command of Vice Admiral Villeneuve, had the same number of line-of-battle ships as the British, nine (with five more under construction), and numerous smaller ships. Fundamental to the course of the ensuing campaign was St Vincent's decision to send to Toulon an officer who by his force of personality alone might intimidate the French: Vice Admiral Nelson. On 17 May 1803 letters of marque and reprisal were issued against French ships and on 23 May Nelson sailed in the *Victory* for the Mediterranean, narrowly missing Napoleon's brother Jerome at the end of the month – when he learned this, Nelson wrote that he regretted 'not having laid a little salt on his tail'. Outnumbered and short of men, Nelson nevertheless maintained a distant blockade, hoping to entice the enemy to come out and fight. He kept a small squadron of six or so ships together, often refitting at sea, while the remainder of his ships were employed ferrying and scouting. After having been at sea for over a year, he was able to write to St Vincent, 'I have the pleasure to acquaint you that the squadron under my command is all collected . . . and in perfect state of readiness to act as the exigency of the moment may determine'.

In January 1805, Nelson was at Agincourt Sound off north-east Sardinia when the frigates *Active* and *Seahorse* brought news that the French had broken out of Toulon. In a coordinated operation, Rear Admiral Burgues Missiessy also broke the blockade of Rochefort, in a snowstorm: the weather was so bad that the gale sank one of the watching frigates. Missiessy's whereabouts were unknown for several weeks, giving him time to cross the Atlantic with his storm-damaged ships under jury rig and make for the rendezvous in the West Indies, where, having escaped Admiral Graves' squadron, he now evaded Commodore Hood and wreaked havoc on the rich British islands. Once he realized that no more French ships would join him, Missiessy returned to France and slipped into Aix Roads on 20 May. The ungrateful and landlubberly Napoleon failed to appreciate Missiessy's achievements, and for his pains he was dismissed.

Meanwhile, in the Mediterranean, Nelson's frantic search for the French reached as far as Alexandria: 'I am in a fever. God send that

I may find them! ... I have neither ate, drank or slept with any comfort since last Sunday'. It was not until 19 February off Malta that he learned that the French had been driven back into Toulon by storm damage. Relieved, he went to Sardinia and Palma Bay to victual his ships and was back on station again by 9 March. By this time Nelson was thoroughly exhausted, and he scribbled this all too human love letter, which has recently been rediscovered in the archive of the National Maritime Museum, to his mistress, Lady Hamilton:

> Victory March 16th 1805
> The Ship is just parting and I take the last moment to renew my assurances to My Dearest beloved Emma of My eternal love affection and adoration, you are ever with me in my Soul, your resemblance is never absent from my mind, and my own dearest Emma I hope very soon that I shall embrace the substantial part of you instead of the Ideal, that will I am sure give us both *real pleasure* and *exquisite happiness*, longing as I do to be with you yet I am sure under the circumstances in which I am placed, you would be the first to say My Nelson try & get at those french fellows and come home with Glory to your own Emma, or if they will not come out then come home for a short time and arrange your *affairs* which have long been neglected, don't I say my own love what you would say. Only continue to love me as affectionately as I do you and we must then be the happiest couple in the World May God bless you Ever prays yours and only your faithful Nelson & Bronte ...

On 30 March Nelson was again at Palma Bay when Villeneuve once more left Toulon with a north-easterly gale behind him. Once more Nelson sent his cruisers in search and on 9 April he learned the French had passed westwards through the Straits of Gibraltar: Nelson followed. It was still not clear where the French had gone, and uncertainty even reached the lower deck of Nelson's flagship. On 7 May Thomas Mackinrey wrote to his mother:

> We ancored at the Rock of Gibraltar yester Day About four a clock in the After Noon & the Wind Drawing fair We got Under Way & Shaped our Course Down the Streat in Great

> Expectation to Come to ingland but I greatly fear We Shall go
> to the West Indies has The french fleet are gone that Way.

Like his admiral, Mackinrey was obviously homesick, and he added:
'I Long to See my Neative land once more'.

On 11 May Nelson sailed from Lagos Bay, nearly a month
behind Villeneuve. Yet by early June he was only two days behind:
Villeneuve had wasted time and opportunity by reducing Diamond
Rock and his only other achievement was the capture of a British
convoy. In 1804 Commodore Samuel Hood had commissioned a
600-foot pinnacle of rock off the French port of Port Royale,
Martinique as a sloop of war. The French had regarded this rock as
unclimbable, but Hood's seamen, under the command of Lieutenant James Maurice, thought otherwise. They swayed heavy guns to
the summit, established living quarters and a hospital in caves, built
a cistern to catch water, and set up batteries to observe and to
annoy French shipping, and for a year and a half British sailors and
marines held HMS *Diamond Rock* against the French. Bonaparte
himself called this a 'symbol of insolence at Martinique's doorstep'.
It took two French ships of the line, three smaller warships, eleven
gunboats, 1,500 troops, and finally an earthquake – which cracked
open the recently built cistern – to force Maurice's surrender. The
capture of Diamond Rock was one of the few French successes in
the campaign of Trafalgar. Of French reinforcements from the
Atlantic ports there was no sign, and the very news that Nelson was
close was sufficient to startle Villeneuve into recrossing the Atlantic.

Nelson's search of the West Indies included a cast to the south
as far as Trinidad, where his advancing sails caused the British
garrison to burn and abandon its positions thinking he was the
French, and Nelson, thinking the smoke a sign of the French
having landed, to enter the Gulf of Paria under all sail. Once he
knew that Trinidad was safe he returned to the north.

Though inferior in number of ships, Nelson was prepared to
fight the combined Franco-Spanish fleet, and he told his officers:
'we won't part without a battle. I think they will be glad to let me
alone, if I will let them alone, which I will do until we approach
the shores of Europe or they give me an advantage too tempting to
be resisted'. He would, presumably, have been furious to know that

not everyone in his fleet shared his aggressive spirit. William Pringle Green was master's mate in the *Conqueror*, under Captain Israel Pellew, and his account of the chase of the French fleet to the West Indies is not so sanguine:

> during this cruise we completed with provisions from the transports, and cleared ship for action ... made all sail for the West Indies, Barbadoes on the 18 [May] ... distance 729 leagues ... Nothing remarkable all the Passage. On the 4 of June made Barbadoes, anchored Bridge Town ... The *Northumberland* Adm Cochran and three sloops of War a schooner and a Brig in harbour ... [after a search of the islands] ... sailed again not finding the Enemy at any of the Islands proceeded to the North ... doing our best to return again with the available wind ... It was a good thing for England that he [Nelson] did not meet the Enemy as they were so much superior and we had a great number ill with the Scurvy. We disembarked the troops at Antigua ... nothing remarkable ...

However, Nelson, in a paroxysm of anxiety and uncertainty, renewed the pursuit. On 16 June, Dempsey Wade, master of an American schooner, *Sally*, out of New Burn, North Carolina, and laden with timber for Antigua, saw the French fleet in mid-Atlantic. The next day he gave the vital intelligence to the British frigate *Amazon* that the British were only 200 miles behind. Nelson was able to report that after over two years since sailing from Spithead, having blockaded the French in Toulon for eighteen months and chased them to the West Indies and back, 'the whole of the Ships are complete to bear for months and in perfect health'. Despite Green's observations, there appears to have been very little sickness in Nelson's ships, whereas the French had landed over a thousand men sick during their brief stay in Martinique and buried another thousand dead at sea.

As the combined fleet approached Europe with the British fleet in hot pursuit, Nelson guessed again and again guessed wrong. He headed for the Mediterranean, but Villeneuve had orders to rendezvous with the French fleet at Brest. Meanwhile, the French squadron at Rochefort had escaped again, this time under Allemand, while Admiral Ganteaume in Brest had orders to unite the squadrons of Rochefort, Toulon, and Cadiz off Ushant. Fast-sailing frigates brought Barham, in London, intelligence, where his genius lay in piecing together these fragmentary reports and sending orders and reinforcements to Admiral Cornwallis, who was blockading Brest. He instructed him to detach Vice Admiral Sir Robert Calder, who, risking an escape by the enemy ships there, was ordered to cruise further out into the Atlantic to block Villeneuve's route to the west coast of France or into the Channel. Ganteaume never seized his opportunity but in London, with Nelson's whereabouts in the Atlantic unknown, it must have looked very much like Napoleon's grand design was coming to fruition.

However, on 22 July 1805, in one of the decisive events of the whole war, Villeneuve's combined fleet emerged from the fog very much where Barham's orders had put Calder. The ensuing two-day battle, fought in poor visibility and baffling winds, was desultory. Calder's Action has never been graced with the name of a battle, but he attacked a superior fleet, captured two of the enemy, and prevented Villeneuve from uniting with other French forces, thus putting an end to Napoleon's grand strategy. Napoleon was furious when he learned that Villeneuve was not in a French port. Calder proclaimed a victory and asked Barham, in a letter received in London on 2 August, for the usual share of patronage after a victory. Writing from the *Prince of Wales* on 23 July 1805, he reported:

> I have had the good fortune to have fallen in with the Combined Squadrons of Toulon and Cadiz upon their return from the West Indies. The action has been unique having been fought in a fog at night. I hope Your Lordship and my Royal Master will think I have done all that was possible to have been done. If so, and you should think me deserving of any mark of his Royal Bounty, I beg leave to observe I have no children but I have a nephew, the son of an old faithful servant of the Crown who died in the Service as a General and Lieutenant-Governor of Gibraltar to whom I hope his Majesty's Royal Bounty may extend, if my services should be thought worthy of any mark from his Majesty. I shall as soon as I have secured the prizes and put my Squadron to rights do everything I shall judge prudent at these critical times well knowing the consequences

of missing this Squadron at this moment, when the Ferrol and Rochefort squadrons are upon the move. If I find things are as I apprehend I shall make the best of my way to Ushant. I shall look about me for a few days in the hope of falling in with Lord Nelson who may be close at the heels of those gentry. Let what will happen, rest assured My Lord, I shall be upon my guard and at the same time do all in my power for his Majesty's service and the good of my country as far as my abilities will enable me to act . . .

Barham seems initially to have agreed that Calder had done well, and Calder 'received the Board's approbation, with the Commander-in-Chief's . . . in obtaining the Victory over the Combined Squadrons on the 22nd July'. However, the tide of public opinion was against him, and when he read what the newspapers were saying Calder realized that 'John Bull thought I might have done more'. It did not help that a Spanish report of the battle in which victory was claimed for the Combined Fleet had reached London about the same time as his despatches. Admiral Gravina's account of the battle, which despite losing two ships alleged a Franco-Spanish victory, was published in Madrid on 6 August and reported in London only a few days later:

The action began at ¾ past 4pm . . . The enemy came up with us and then a rigorous fight commenced at the distance of half cannon shot, between our van and the whole of the enemy's line. The fog was so thick although we were very near the enemy yet at times they were concealed from our vision. The fire was well kept up and directed we perceived a 3 decker without a foremast and one of ours lost a main and mizzen masts [sic]. The action continued between the van and centre of our line till 9 o'clock when the enemy bore up withdrawing themselves from the combat and we kept our station. The fog still continuing and in counting our squadron two ships were missing the *Firme* and *St Rafael*. We discovered the enemy on the other tack. We immediately tacked and reformed our line giving them chace. We observed they had three dismasted ships in tow and that the line of battle was composed of thirteen ships including one that had lost her main topmast. We continued all that day in chace but the enemy avoided a second encounter. The same happened on the 24th still in chace. At break of day the enemy were far to windward but by dint of sailing we neared them with a light breeze from the NE on the larboard tack. At break of day on the 25th the wind NE and blowing fresh with a heavy sea we found we lost sight of the enemy and that day we made Cape Finisterre bearing east. In this situation with a contrary wind to reach Ferrol, several of the French having only six days water onboard and having more than 1300 sick and wounded in the squadron without means of relieving them, we determined to put into Vigo for refreshments and necessaries. As soon as I can collect the particulars of the action I shall inform your Excellency in which the six ships under my immediate command fought with the greatest obstinacy and resolution and I think that the English having avoided a second attack was occasioned by their having suffered so much in the action since our forces were equal as to the number of guns as we had no 3-deckers [sic: the flagship was the three-decked *Argonauta*] and two small 64 gun ships . . .

In the aftermath of Trafalgar, when Nelson had indeed won a victory on the hoped-for scale, Calder requested a court martial and was found guilty of failing to renew the battle, but really his offence lay in not having lived up to the public's expectations. What John Bull did not appreciate was that Calder had been instrumental in preventing the juncture of the French fleets. With Calder's Action, the campaign of Trafalgar, a game of chess played out on the vast board of the Mediterranean and Caribbean Seas and the Atlantic Ocean, had entered the end game.

Nelson had arrived off Gibraltar and set foot ashore on 20 July for the first time in twenty-five months: he was physically and mentally exhausted, and soon took passage in the *Victory* to Portsmouth. Meanwhile other fleets and squadrons blockaded French and Spanish ports, and this is Lieutenant William Clarke's account of blockade duty.

After doing duty at Head Quarters about three months I was ordered in April 1805 to embark on board HMS *Achilles* (74) Captn Sir Richard King [as second in command of the marines].

We proceeded to join a Squadron off Cadiz under Admiral Collingwood, where though employed in blockade, the superior climate and an occasional detached cruise rendered the service far preferable to that in the Channel . . .

Cruises, with their attendant opportunity to enrich the crew, the captain, and their admiral, were the usual reward given to successful ships, and even in times of tension there was hope of such riches. Clarke continues, with some humour:

The *Achilles* was several times detached, once to Tangier on the African coast, once to Lagos (in Portugal) and on one occasion on a Cruize where we had a flattering vision of a Golden Harvest, but . . . we were reckoning our chickens before they were hatched. It was understood that a Spanish ship of the line (the *Glorioso*) was expected from South America, with treasure, and the *Achilles* was detached off Cape St Marys (the point of land usually first made by Spanish Ships when returning from their American possessions) to endeavour to intercept her (and much were we envied by the rest of the squadron) after cruising some time, a sail was discovered one morning at day light in a direction calculated to excite suspicion and sanguine hopes, we soon made her out to be a Sail of the line and evidently not British, her snow white Sails and weather beaten Hull proclaimed her at once (in our imaginations) the identical object on which we had fixed our affections, and Dollars and Doubloons glittered before our eyes as we speedily prepared to greet with a warm reception. Sail was made, Decks cleared, Guns primed and all ready, we were coming up with her hand over hand, the amount of each Mans Prize Money was settled, some fifteen or twenty minutes or half an hour at the most allowed for taking her, in short little doubt was entertained but that all our fortunes were made, we had shewn our colours and fired one or two Guns, but she took no notice, but stood on under all her canvas, another Gun! when! Uprose the Sun in the Horizon. Bang! Went a Gun from the chace and – upwent – the Portugese Ensign!!! and all looked blank on board HMS *Achille* [we] could fancy something like . . . a Stock Exchange Panic. She was a Portugese 74 from the Rio Janeiro, bound to Lisbon and the broad Pendant of Commodore Campbell a

Scotchman. She had not hoisted her Colours sooner from a rule
in their service of not doing so until sunrise . . .

However, there was some lesser prize money:

We made prizes of some American Ships for break of Blockade
and spoke many others from Cadiz, and on board one of them
I saw the famous French General Moreau who was on his way
to America . . .

*Achilles* was part of Collingwood's small force watching Cadiz
and the Straits of Gibraltar. Collingwood had met Nelson as he
returned from his chase of the French to the West Indies and back,
and was able to reassure him that the French had not gone into the
Mediterranean. Clarke continues:

In the month of July Lord Nelsons fleet passed us on their
return from the West Indies in chase of the French fleet, but I
think we only communicated by signals. We were however kept
on the qui vive knowing the French fleet was at sea, and
uncertain where they might make for on their return to Europe.

News of Calder's Action reached Collingwood's squadron off
Cadiz, and when Villeneuve did sail south for the Mediterranean,
rather than north as Napoleon wanted, Collingwood risked being
trapped and overwhelmed, if only the Combined Fleet had had
greater heart for a fight.

Early in August we heard of the action between them and Sir
Robert Calder, and events seemed thickening and a great and
decisive engagement appeared probable in some quarter; our
Squadron was weak only four or five sail of the line, and if the
Enemy intended to rendezvous at Cadiz we could not prevent
them, and this proved eventually the case. The morning of the
20th of August was very foggy, we were pretty close to Cadiz
with four or five, I think four Sail of the line, a small Frigate
and the *Thunder* bark . . . on a partial clearance of the fog, a
sail or two was discovered to the Westward, and on our standing
towards them their number appeared to be increasing, but still
the fog for some time prevented our making out what they were
and we were disposed to think them a convoy bound through

the Straits, at last the Man at the Mast Head pronounced one to be a Line of Battle Ship, this did not alter the opinion, but, as the fog continued to clear away, another Line of Battle Ship, another and another, a Fleet!!! were the progressive proclamations from aloft, and at last the Tricoloured Flag was plainly discovered floating in the wind, the wind was Southerly, and had they when they first discovered [us] shaped their course for the mouth of the Straits they must have reached there before us, and cut us off from all retreat unless that of fighting our way through. I suppose the Spectre of Nelson and his fleet followed in their wake, and made their own safety their first consideration. When doubt no longer existed as to what they were, we tacked and stood in direct for the Straits as the wind would allow, but it was very doubtful whether we could fetch them. The headmost Ships of the Enemy made Sail as if intending to follow and on a slight change of wind taking place which would enable us to lay our heads for the Straits, we brought to, to see whether they would or not, but, they rejoined their main body and stood for Cadiz, I think seven and twenty Sail-of-the-line. The frigate and especially the old *Thunder*, had a narrow escape, several of them passing within half a gun shot of her, but she having hoisted Danish colours, and being Merchantmanlike in appearance, passed unsuspected. The next morning saw us again at our old grounds, I suppose I must not say Blockading but watching the united squadrons of France and Spain. Our little squadron was well on the increase and the juncture of Sir Robert Calder with the ships under his command constituted us a powerful fleet, which was perfected on the 29th September by the arrival of our Gallant Commander in Chief the immortal Nelson . . .

Clarke, however, was not destined to see the battle. Calder, stung by the criticisms in the newspapers, some of it, he believed, inspired by the government, now committed further offence in the eyes of the officers of the fleet, by insisting that the allegations made against him be investigated, and he compounded this by asking to go home in his flagship, the 90-gun *Prince of Wales*, one of the largest ships in the British fleet off Cadiz. There was a shortage of marines in other parts of the navy and as part of Barham's redistribution of forces to counter any French invasion, Clarke went home too.

Then, though the *Prince of Wales* sailed eight days before the battle took place, she did not arrive in Portsmouth until after the reports of the battle were in the newspapers. Clarke, clearly aggrieved, wrote:

> the cause was . . . the increased number of Ships in Commission requiring Marines. There was an insufficiency of Officers and it was determined to take one Subaltern from each two deck Ship of the Line . . . and an order arrived to send home a Senior Sub from each Ship having her full complement and in consequence of this with several others [I] was ordered home in the first ship, and Sir Robert Calder being ordered to England to be subjected to a Court of Inquiry relative to his late action, Lord Nelson with great reluctance permitted him to proceed in his own ship the *Prince of Wales* (90) in which ship I left the fleet on the 13th October. We had a tedious passage not reaching Portsmouth until the 13th November and the gazette containing the official account of the great Battle of Trafalgar was put on board as we anchored at Spithead: our exultation on the glorious event was mingled with great individual mortification at having lost our share in the conflict which was crowned by matchless victory . . .

The campaign of Trafalgar is, of course, not just about Nelson. While Nelson chased Villeneuve to the West Indies and back, Barham deployed nearly six hundred warships, under a dozen other commanders-in-chief, ranging from the Channel ports, to Cornwallis off Ushant, Admirals Gardner and Gower off North America, and Edward Pellew and Thomas Troubridge in the East Indies.

Lord Keith, for example, commanded a fleet responsible for the area between Shetland and Selsey Bill comprising ten line-of-battle ships, fifteen frigates, and over a hundred and fifty sloops and smaller vessels; off Ushant, Admiral Sir William Cornwallis commanded twenty-six battleships and as many frigates and smaller vessels. The smallest deployed force was four frigates off Newfoundland under Admiral Sir Erasmus Gower, a contemporary of Cornwallis. Furthest afield, Admiral Edward Pellew commanded several ships in the Indian Ocean. Pellew was 'longstop' and, with his flag in the *Culloden*, served as Commander-in-Chief, East Indies for five years.

The Admiralty had its own spy network on the Continent, and Barham was kept informed of what was happening there. So he learned that 'Bonaparte has left Paris with all his Staff on Saturday last the 21st inst [September 1805] for Strasburg [with] the French Troops on the Rhine . . . making about 150,000 men . . . Superintended by Bonaparte himself'. It was too late to stop Nelson, even if that had been desirable. After a respite in England of only, in his words, 'twenty five dinners', he had sailed from Portsmouth on 15 September and joined the fleet off Cadiz on 28 September, the day before his forty-seventh birthday. While Collingwood had commanded the blockade of the Combined Fleet he had stationed his fleet fifteen to twenty miles offshore. Now Nelson, anxious to tempt the enemy out, withdrew to about fifty miles, leaving frigates to maintain a close watch on Cadiz and a chain of ships to repeat any signals.

He then told his officers of his plan of attack. When they 'came onboard to welcome my return, [they] forgot my rank as commander-in-chief in the enthusiasm with which they greeted me' and, for a birthday treat, Nelson, 'as soon as these emotions were passed', 'laid before [them] the plan I had previously arranged for attacking the enemy'. Or, as he wrote to Emma, 'I believe my arrival was most welcome . . . and when I came to explain to them the Nelson touch, it was like an electric shock. Some shed tears, all approved, it was new, it was singular, it was simple . . .'

Nelson had invited his captains on board to dinner in two groups on successive afternoons and a few days later wrote his famous memorandum, several copies of which survive in the National Maritime Museum. The memorandum is significant for the delegation of authority which it gave to the second in command and to individual ship's captains, and few further tactical orders were necessary. He wrote:

*Victory* Off Cadiz, 9th October 1805 . . .
    Thinking it almost impossible to bring a Fleet of forty sail of the line into a Line of Battle in variable winds, thick weather,

and other circumstances which must occur, without such a loss of time that the opportunity would probably be lost of bringing the Enemy to Battle in such a manner as to make the business decisive, I have therefore made up my mind to keep the Fleet in that position of sailing (with the exception of the First and Second in Command) that the order of Sailing is to be the Order of Battle, placing the Fleet in two Lines of sixteen Ships each, with an Advanced Squadron of eight of the fastest sailing Two-decked Ships which will always make, if wanted, a Line of twenty-four sail, on which ever Line the Commander-in-Chief may direct . . .

On the day of battle Nelson had only twenty-seven ships, but this did not alter the principles upon which he planned. Nelson intended not a battle in parallel lines, but to break the enemy's line and to defeat him piecemeal:

If the Enemy's Fleet should be seen to windward in Line of Battle, and that the Two Lines and the Advanced Squadron can fetch them, they will probably be so extended that their Van could not succour their Rear. I should therefore make the Second in Command's signal to lead through, about their twelfth Ship from their Rear . . . The Second in Command will, after my intentions are made known to him, have the entire direction of his Line to make the attack upon the Enemy, and to follow up the blow until they are captured or destroyed.

This delegation was repeated twice in Nelson's memorandum: 'The Second in Command will in all possible things direct movements of his Line' and unless

otherwise directed from the Commander in Chief, which is scarcely to be expected, . . . the entire management of the Lee Line, after the intentions of the Commander in Chief, are signified, is intended to be left to the judgment of the Admiral commanding that Line.

Nelson had orders for his individual captains too:

Something must be left to chance, nothing is sure in a Sea Fight beyond all others. Shot will carry away the masts and yards of friends as well as Foes, but I look with confidence to a Victory

. . . But in case Signals can neither be seen or perfectly understood, no Captain can do very wrong if he places his Ship alongside that of an Enemy.

Nelson's memorandum is well known and many copies of it were made throughout the fleet, but there was a flurry of other orders regarding the management and maintenance of a fleet at sea, which show just how much attention to detail and care for his people was possible for the little lovesick admiral. The first set of orders refers to the management of the fleet: 'It is my Instructions that the Captains and Commanders of His Majesty's Ships and Vessels under my Command do send me a Copy of their Log when they Join'; 'The Ships and Vessels of the Fleet under my Command are desired not to shew their Colours on Joining unless the Commander in Chief should shew his'; and, as had been practice since the Battle of St Vincent to distinguish British warships in the smoke of battle, 'When in presence of an Enemy all the Ships under my Command are to Wear White Colours and a Union Jack is to be suspended from the Fore Top Gallant Stay'.

Other orders concerned the order of sailing, and as might be expected in Nelson's fleet, it was disciplined, but a great deal of initiative was given to individual captains: 'it is expected in fine weather that Ships in order of sailing do not keep more than Two Cables Length from each Other'; and 'As gales of Wind increase suddenly in this Country [sic], the Ships of the Fleet are directed particularly in the Night to shorten Sail and get Top Gallant Yards and Masts down and take such other precautions as the Captains may judge necessary without waiting for the Admirals Motions'.

Concerned for the economy of the fleet, Nelson ordered:

that the Captains and Commanders under my Command . . . have their Muster Books in Readiness when the Naval Officers at Gibraltar and Malta go onboard to muster their Ships Companies [and] do not purchase any article of Stores whatsoever in Lisbon unless such purchase should be absolutely necessary but apply . . . to the Naval Officer at Gibraltar or Malta for a supply of such stores as they may be in want of and can be furnished by the said officer.

Many orders concerned the purchase of fresh meat, vegetables, and fruit to counter scurvy:

> Captains and Commanders ... who may purchase ... Fresh Beef, Lemmons Onions or any other spicies of Provisions as Refreshment for their Respective Companies whether such purchase for a particular ship or for the Fleet in general and whether it is made by my Order or otherwise that a Voucher of the Fresh Beef, Bullocks so purchased for the individual Ship or Fleet is transmitted to me, immediately when the ship making such purchase shall join the Fleet

and

> When in port ... It is therefore my positive directions that Pursers are obliged to purchase Vegetables for the Ships Soup when it is possible to procure them ... Ships absent for any length of time from me are at liberty to purchase the gratuitous Onions of Government for Recruiting the Health of their Ships Companies whom may have been fed long upon Salt Provisions.

Nor did Nelson overlook the frailties of human nature and the endless possibilities of fraud:

> As frequent and very serious mistakes happen on Receiving Provisions ... the Masters take a Regular account of each spicies and which they are to compare with the Bills of Lading sent with such Provisions from the Agent Victualler or Contractor previous to their entering them in the Log Book which is to be done immediately ... that Government may not either from the mistake or neglect of Individuals be defrauded or the Ships Companies in want of these spicies ... It is also my particular direction that every Pound of Fresh Beef whether received from Agent Victuallers or Contractors is weighed

and

> The weekly returns of the remains of Provisions etc are in future to be signed by the Captains Masters and Pursers of the Respective Ships.

Nor, of course, did Nelson forget the individual seamen in his fleet:

It is my directions that whenever Men are sent to the Hospital a Statement of the Case is sent with them that the Medical Gentlemen belonging to the Hospital may know what has been ... the Disease ... [and that] the very important service of invaliding Seamen and Marines of the different Ships of the Fleet under my command ... be most strictly and duly attended to ... the Captains order the Surgeons of their Ships to deliver to them a List containing the Names etc of such Seamen and Marines as may be considered fit objects for Invaliding ... which List the Captains of such Ship is to transmit to me in his Letter of application for the Survey [on the invalid].

Finally, Nelson remembered the families at home, ordering that

the home and family of every officer, Seaman, and Marine who may be killed or wounded in action with the enemy on board any of His Majesty's Ships under my Command is returned to me as soon after as circumstances [shall permit] ... that I may Transmit it to the Chairman of the Patriotic Fund at Lloyds Coffee House that the Case of the Relations of those who may fall in the Cause of their Country may be taken into consideration.

The outline of the ensuing battle on 21 October 1805, especially events on board *Victory*, is well known. The opposing fleets were not as large as Nelson had anticipated but in other respects the battle developed much he had planned. The Combined Fleet was spied preparing for sea and began to leave Cadiz on 19 October. For two days the fleets manoeuvred off Cadiz, both fleets wearing (reversing course) several times, the French and Spanish fleets trying to take up their formation and enter the Mediterranean, and Nelson intent on bringing about a battle. Eventually, at dawn on 21 October and in light airs, the two fleets sighted each other about eleven miles apart and about twenty miles off Cape Trafalgar.

The 74-gun *Minotaur* was the second to last ship in the windward line, ninth behind the *Victory*, and so light was the wind that she did not come into action until about 3.30 p.m., some hours after the *Victory*. On board the *Minotaur* William Thorpe, a volunteer from Coventry, had a grandstand view of the action as it developed:

21st at 6.30 Turned the hands up. Up all Hammocks. Saw the French & Spanish Fleets bearing East. Bore up. Answered the signal to prepare for Battle. Observed 33 sail of the Enemy in line of Battle, with [7] Frigates, & Brigs. Our fleet consisting of 27 Sail of the line, 3 of which where of 64 guns. At 8 all clear for action. The hands turned up, & assembled on the Quarter Deck. Capt. Mansfield addressed the officers and ships company to the following effect. Men whe are now in sight of the enemy, (the men at this moment was going to chier, but the Capt prevented & proceeded) wich, there is every probability of engaging, & I trust that this Day or to morrow will prove the most Glorious our country ever saw. I shall say nothing to you of courage, our country never produced a coward, for my own part I pledge myself to the Officers, & Ships Company, never to quit the ship I may get alongside of, till either she strikes, or sinks, or I sink. I have only to recommend silence, & a strict attention to the order of your officers, be carefull to take good aim for it is to no purpose throw shot away, you will now every man repair to your respective stations, & Depend, I will bring the ship into action as soon as possable, God Save the King. At ½ past 10 the headmost ships coming up with the Enemy. At noon, light winds and fine weather. The *Victory* made general telligraph, the purport of wich was, I hope every man will do his duty like an English man. Fleet in chase, Enemy on a wind, on the Larboard tack in line of Battle. P.m. Light breezes and fine weather at 12–18 The *Royal Sovereign* commences action with the Enemys rear . . .

The British fleet bore down from the west in two columns, though even with studding sails set their speed of advance was very slow. The Combined Fleet was not in the tight formation that it should have been, but was spread out in a shallow crescent heading north. This how the battle was seen by Hampshire-born William Rivers, 'late Midshipman and aid du Camp to his Lordship', writing from Greenwich Hospital many years later (the order of words has been changed slightly to make more sense of Rivers' reminiscence):

Lord Nelson was standing on the starboard gangway [and said] to Captain Hardy 'See how nobly that gallant fellow Colling-wood is taking his ship into action' . . . it was his Lordships intention to pass through the enemys line between the 11th and 12th Ships so to cut off their van ships, the Master said it was impossible to get through, and recommended his Lordship to alter the course a point or two to starboard and run between the 13th and 14th Ships. We did so and brought the light air of wind right aft consequently we passed between the *Bucentaure* and the *Redoubtable* and hawled up to port . . . in passing under the *Bucentaure's* stern the fly of her ensign touch[ed] the *Victory's* mizzen rigging; the raking fire of the enemy cut away the studdingsail before we opened our fire . . . The *Redoubtable* . . . came along side the *Victory* with her mizen mast between the *Victory's* main and mizen mast. A rifleman shot Lord Nelson from her mizentop he fell near the centre of the Quarter Deck . . .

The first British ship into action had indeed been Vice Admiral Cuthbert Collingwood's *Royal Sovereign*, leading the leeward column, which, at a few minutes past noon on 21 October 1805, crashed through the enemy line about twelve ships from the rear. Standard time was not kept in the British fleet, but this is what Thorpe in the *Minotaur* saw ahead of him, with his timings: 'At 12.50 General signal for close action. At 1 observed one of the Enemys ships on fire. At 1.5 *Victory's* mizzen top mast shot away by a Spanish 3 decker ship, she not having fired one shot'. And looking to the south at Collingwood's lee column:

At 1.6 *Tonnants* fore top mast shot away. At 1.25 a Spanish 3 decker lost her mizzen mast, engaging the *Royal Sovereign*, three fireing constantly at her same time. At 1.30 *Tonnants* main top mast shot away. At 1.56 two Spanish ships struck to the *Victory* & *Temeraire*. A Spanish 3 Decker totally dismasted. At 2.6 a Spanish 3 decker struck. At 2.15 a Spanish Admirals ship dismasted. The Spanish 4 decker [*Santísima Trinidad* – taken by the *Prince*] fore top mast shot away, a Spanish 2 decker dismasted . . .

There were many others who recorded the battle, including the Irishman James Bayley on board the *Victory* (nearly a quarter of Nelson's fleet were Irish), who wrote to his family:

[this] Comes with my kind love to you hoping that you are in good health thank God I am: for [it is] very certain that it is by his mercy that me and my country is and you and your religion is kept up for it had pleased Almighty God for to give us a complete victory and the combined fleets of France and Spain for there was a signal for them being out of Cadiz 19th October but we did not see them till the 21st in the morning and about 12 o'clock we gave 3 cheers and then the engagement began very hot on both sides, but about 5 o'clock the victory was ours and 20 sail of the line struck to us, they had 34 sail of the line and we had 27 of the line, but the worst of it the flower of our country Lord Nelson got wounded at ten minutes past one o'clock and closed his eyes in midst of victory dear sister it pleased the Lord to spare my life and my brother Thomas his . . . it was very sharp for us I assure you, for you had not a moments time till it was over, and the 23rd. of the same instant . . . a most shocking gale of wind, and we expected to go to the bottom but thanks be to God he had mercy on us, for every ship of ours got safe into harbour and all the French but 4 got knocked to pieces on the rocks . . . we had 125 killed and wounded, and 15 hundred in the English fleet killed and wounded and the enemy twelve thousand so I shall leave you to judge how your country fights for the religion you enjoy and the lands you possess and on the other hand how Bonaparte has trampt them causes down . . . Lord Nelson['s] . . . last words . . . [were] never haul down your colors to France . . . they wanted to take Lord Nelson from us but we told them as we brought him out we would bring him home so it was so and he was put into a cask of spirits . . .

The 64-gun *Africa*, one of the last reinforcements to join Nelson's fleet off Cadiz, and one of the smallest line-of-battle ships, had got lost during the night prior to the battle and at dawn found herself to the north of both the British fleet and the Combined Fleet. At one stage the entire Combined Fleet, steering north, would have appeared to have been heading for her, but from her isolated position those on board also had a clear view of the battle as it developed and the signals hoisted from *Victory*. Captain Henry Digby took the *Africa* on a reverse course along the enemy's line, much of the time under fire, and joined the fight before the rear ships of Nelson's division came into battle. This account, written a few months after the battle, is by John Mason from Stepney in London, an experienced seaman who, though recently recruited, was already a quartermaster on board her. Various versions of Nelson's famous signal circulated during and after the battle, and in this account John Mason gives another to his brother and sister:

This comes with my kind love to you hoping to find you in good health as I am at present. If agreeable will give a few particulars of the Glorious Action with the French & Spanish combined Fleets ... On the 3rd October sailed from Torbay under sealed orders. Oct 13th 1805 fell in with his H.M.S. *Amiable* she had on the 11th fell in with the Rochefort Squadron consisting of 5 Sail 2 Frigates and Brig which took the whole of the Oporto Ships under convoy on the 14 joined Lord Nelson's Fleet off Cadiz consisting of 29 Sails of the Line 2 Frigates and a Brig on 19 his Lordship received Information by Signal from the Frigates in Shore that the Enemy where preparing for sea and that some of them where in the Outer Roads of Cadiz his Lordship made the signal to prepare for Battle and General Chace every ship was immediately under a crowd of sail. On 20th during the Night observed the Enemy setting off Rocketts blue lights etc firing guns, on 21 in the Morning the whole of the Enemy's Fleet bearing South about 3 leagues consisting of 33 Sail of the line 5 Frigates and 2 Brigs at 9 the Enemy formed the line of Battle in one line on the Starboard Tack the English then bearing down upon them lead by Vice Admiral Collingwood in the *Royal Sovereign* in a most seaman like manner at Ten the Enemy wore round on the Larboard Tack our Ship (viz) the *Africa* then between the Two Fleets at 10.53 his Lordship made our signal to make all Sail possible at 11 our Gallant Hero communicated by Telegraph to the Captains of the Fleet requiring them to make it known to their perspective ships Company's that England depends on Victory and that England expects every man will do his duty when the perspective crews answered that there country should not be deceived, at 11.30 his Lordship made a General Signal to anchor with springs on the cable [the actual signal was

'prepare to anchor', after the battle] at 11.34 Vice Ad Collingwood in the *Royal Sovereign* commenced the Action in a most
gallant & daring manner on the Enemy's Rear at 11.40 the
*Africa* commenced her fire on the Enemy's Van with a Spanish
84 bearing the Flag of a Rear Admiral nearly about the same
time our Gallant Hero in the *Victory* engaged the Enemy's
Centre, and the *Brittania* [sic] bearing the Flag of Rear Ad. the
Earl of Northesk our three Admirals now most warmly engaged
when they in a most gallant & desperate and skillful manner
broke the Enemy's line in 3 places & cut off 11 of there van
ships. Our ship engaged from Van to Centre till we came under
the stern of the *Victory* & pass'd the Enemy's Line when the
signal was made to haul to the Wind on the Starboard Tack
then engaged with the Enemy's Centre at 1 bore down under
the stern of the Spanish 4 Decker mounting 140 guns bearing
the flag of a Rear Ad. when our ship was laid alongside of her
and raked her from stem to stern at the same time the *Neptune*
& *Conqueror* where engaging her at 1.15 the whole of her masts
went by the board and she struck her Colours & the *Neptune*
cheer'd us which was returned. Sent Lieut. Smith a Marine
Officer & a Midshipman with a party of men to take charge of
her. Nearly about the same Time observed the Enemy's van
bearing down to the assistance of the Spanish 4 decker at 2.30
observed one of the French 2 Deckers bearing away made all
sail after her at 3.13 brought her to an action. At 4.30 her
Mizen and main Topmast went by the board 4.38 the *Orion*
came up and cheer'd us immediately her Main mast went by
the board at 5.8 she struck her Colours. Observ'd 19 Sail of the
Enemy's Ships standing away (viz) 12 Sail of the line 5 Frigates
& 2 Brigs. Nearly at the same time observed the *Temeraire*
lashed between two 2 Deckers a Frenchman & a Spaniard and
boarding them both in a most Gallant Manner. The Ship that
struck to us last prov'd to be *L'Intrepide* a Ship of 74 guns but
mounted 88 . . .

Few sailors' letters home seem to end without some reference to
love or money or both. Mason, who had apparently gone to sea
after quarrelling with his brother, ends his letter hoping 'we shall
meet Friends again', sending his kind love to a Sarah Cobham, and

asking for a loan since 'being so little time on board here and receiving no Wages as yet neither shall we at present And if it lays in your power to assist me at this time with a little and it would be highly acceptable'.

The *Belleisle* was one of the more heavily engaged ships in Collingwood's lee column, as Lieutenant Nicholas of the marines noted, and 'after having been engaged by three ships and having sent a party to take possession of the 80-gun Spanish ship *Argonauta*' she needed a tow. Nicholas' letter to his brother also gives the first hint of the effort which was necessary in the storm after the battle: 'The *Naiad* had . . . got us in tow, we parted from the Fleet during the night and after 8 days of Fatigue, Anxiety, and extreme bad weather we arrived at Gibraltar'.

By the time *Minotaur* came up with the battle it had been largely fought and won. However, five ships of the van of the Combined Fleet, which had been cut off by Nelson's attack, used boats to help them turn by towing them through what little wind there was and came back under the French Rear Admiral Dumanoir le Pelley to support the centre. This attack by fresh ships, when the *Victory* and the *Temeraire* were shattered hulks unable to manoeuvre, was thwarted by *Minotaur* and the next astern and the last ship in Nelson's windward column, *Spartiate*, which raked the bows of Dumanoir's ship, and fired broadsides into the three following French ships. However, the Spanish *Neptuno* (there were three ships named for the god of the sea at Trafalgar, one for each nation), which had been at the very head of the French and Spanish fleets, was now isolated at the tail of Dumanoir's squadron. The *Minotaur* fully engaged her and, after an hour's struggle, *Neptuno* surrendered. This is how the battle and its aftermath were recorded on board the *Minotaur*:

observed 4 French & one Spanish ship bearing down towards the *Victory* & two of the Enemy that had hauled our wind as did the Spanish. Commenced firing on the headmost ship, bearing a Flag at the Mizzen. Passed the four French ships within pistol shot keeping up a brisk Fire. Hove too abreast of Spanish ship being on different tacks shot at several ships to leeward commenced firing on her. At 4 wore ship & got along side of her again. *Spartiate* close to us firing at the same time, observed her mizzen mast go. At 5 her main top mast shot away. At 5.12 she struck her coulours to the *Minotaur*, sent an officer on board to take possession. She proved to be the *Neptuno* of 84 guns and 750 men.

Our damage sustained, 3 men killed 22 wounded the spare fore top sail Yard & fore top sail yard shot away, main top mast & head of the fore mast badly wounded 5 shot between wind & water sails & rigging much cut, & 2 of the wounded men since dead. At 5.15 the *Achilles* French ship blew up with a tremendous explosion wich closed the scene of action. Took the sprit sail yard for a fore top sail yard. Received 24 prisoners & 2 officers sent the second Lieut of Marines & 68 men on board the Prize. Made the signal for being in shoal water. Sounded in 13 fathoms answered signal to take possession of ships that had struck. Took the *Neptuno* in tow. Three of the Enemy ships in the N.E. Quarter totally dismasted but not secured . . .

Apart from the logs, which were of course, contemporary, most of the above accounts were written some weeks or even years after the battle, when its folklore had begun to settle around what happened. However, more immediate accounts of the battle do exist, for example in the following letter dated 1 November, which has recently been presented to the National Maritime Museum. It is notable for its quirky spelling and lack of punctuation, which probably took Ramsgate-born Henry Blackburne, a seaman in the 64-gun *Polyphemus* in the middle of the lee column, all of those eleven days to write. Blackburne gives yet one more version of Nelson's famous signal:

Honerable Mother

this Coms with my dutiful respects to you hoping you are in Good health as i am present thank God for it and for his Goodness to spair me to see the 21st of October over and to help us in fighting Against our Enimes that day when they were so superier in Number to us both in men and ships but we may well say the Lord was on Our side when men rose up against us to destroy use for if the Lord had not been on our side they would have swallowd us up the Combined fleet of france and Spain sail'd out of Cadis on the 20th of October and see them to Leward of us on the 21st at Break of day Consisting of 33 Sail of the line 5 frigats and 2 Brigs formed in a Line on the Starbord tack and at six bore up and mead all the sail we Could and saw the Enemies fleet in a Confused State on the Larboard tack the *Victory* Lord Nelson made the teligraph signal to prepare for Battle and Hope Every English Man would beheave with his Usual hersiom [sic] and exert every means to destroy the Enemies of there Country Lord Nelson wish was told our Ships Compy and returned by the *dreadnaught* then on our Larboard beam observd the *Royal Sovering* Break the Enemies Lines in the Center and Place him Self a Long side of a Spanish 3 Dacker receving at the same a havey fire from numbers of the Enemies Lines the *Victory tonant* and *Bellisle* also standing on to Break the Enemies Lines also we were a Bout the Eight Ship in action in the Same Line was a bout an houre after the *Royal Soverign* fired the first Shote the Ships was Engaged were the frinch *berwick* and Spanish *agumaut* and Le archille we bore up to tak off the firey Edge from the *Belisle* that was totally dismasted by the *archille* and others and would have Certainly gone Down had we not gone to hir assistance we lay along side of the *archille* untill we Dismasted hir and set hir on fire and about sun set Blew up with a great Explosion about 2 Hundred men saved Besids Giveing and Receiving Shote from many Others for they were all around us But Before Dark I had the Pleasure to see most of them Stricke and the Rest to run away but there arose such a trable storm that Night and we all Being in such a Crippld Condition we could daw nothing with them But Burn and Destroy them and the rest were Wrecked on shore if the weather had Been fine we would have taken and destroy'd the whole, Give my Love to My Brothers and Sisters and all Enquring friends so no more from your dutifull son Henry Blackburn . . .

Many diagrams of the Battle of Trafalgar show the ships of Nelson's two columns sailing down upon the Combined Fleet in neat lines, but from the two fleets sighting each other at dawn, it took more than six hours for Nelson's fleet to form up. At 6 a.m. Nelson gave the order to form in two columns in the published order of sailing: at 7.23 a.m. he ordered various ships to take station

without regard to the order of sailing and at 8 a.m. he reinforced
this with an order to take station 'as are most convenient': clearly
in the prevailing light airs there was difficulty in conforming to a
set battle plan and the rearmost ships had not all taken up their
stations when the leading ships broke through the crescent-shaped
formation of the Combined Fleet. Some ships sailed better than
others and in the lee column there was something of a race to come
into action, with Collingwood in the *Royal Sovereign* repeatedly
chivvying his ships to 'make more sail'. As Captain Robert Moorsom in the 74-gun *Revenge* described events: 'all our ships were
carrying studding sails and many bad sailers a long way astern, but
little or no stop was made for them. Admiral Collingwood dashed
directly down supported by such ships as could get up and went
directly through their line. Lord Nelson the same and the rest as
fast as they could'. To *Revenge*, who sailed well, Collingwood
signalled to 'keep a line of bearing from him, which made me one
of the leading ships through the Enemy Line . . .'

In the weather column, the ships astern of Nelson's *Victory*
bunched up as they pressed into action with all sail set. As for
Nelson's memorandum quoted above and the published order of
sailing, it seemed, at least to Moorsom in *Revenge*, and, according
to different accounts between sixth and tenth of the fifteen ships of
the lee column, that

> I have seen several plans of the action but none to answer my
> ideas of it – indeed scarce any plan can be given; it was irregular
> & the ships got down as fast as they could, & into any space
> where they found the Enemy without attending to their place
> in the Line – A regular plan was laid down by Lord Nelson
> some time before the Action, but not acted upon; his great
> anxiety seemed to be to get to leeward of them, lest they should
> make off for Cadiz before we could get near . . .

In another letter Moorsom wrote: 'I am not certain that our plan
of attack was the best, however it succeeded'.

The situation was evidently confused and each witness gave 'as
near as I can my idea of the attack, but it varied so much in
different parts of the line, that anyone person can scarce give an

account of it . . . but I fancy it will be found that the weight of the action fell on a few ships only'.

According to Moorsom 'in about three hours they gave way', but this would only have been about 4 p.m. Elsewhere, the battle still raged and at about a quarter to six in the evening it was punctuated by an explosion in the French *Achille*, which blew up with great loss of life. About 160 of her people were rescued from the water by the schooner *Pickle*, one of the smallest ships at the Battle of Trafalgar – though where the *Pickle* at 120 tons and 73 feet long put so many prisoners is source of amazement. One of them was a woman, perhaps the only substantiated case of a woman at the battle, though there were probably many more in the ships of all three nations. Robert Moorsom gives this account of the rescue of Jeannette, as she became known:

> I must tell you an anecdote of a French woman the *Pickle* Schooner sent to me about Fifty people saved from the *Achille* which was burned & blew up amongst them was a young French woman about five and twenty & the wife of one of the Main Topmen when the *Achille* was burning she got out of the gun room Port & sat on the Rudder chains, till some melted lead ran down upon her, and forced her to strip & leap off; she swam to a spar where several men were, but one of them bit & kicked her till she was obliged to quit & get to another, which supported her till she was taken up by the *Pickle* & sent on board the *Revenge* amongst the men she was lucky enough to find her Husband – We were not wanting in civility to the lady; I ordered her two Pussers shirts to make a Petticoat & most of the officers found something to clothe her; in a few hours Jeanette was perfectly happy & hard at work making her Petticoats – she was sent ashore at Gibraltar – The Spaniards were all released at Gibraltar, but the French we have brought home; in the squadron we had about Eight Hundred taken out of different ships . . .

Many accounts of the battle end with the death of Nelson, however Nelson's last order had been to prepare to anchor at the end of the day: it was a wise precaution, as he clearly recognized that a storm was brewing. On 23 October the remnants of the

Combined Fleet, led by the Breton Commodore Baron de Cosmao-Kerjulien, made a brief sortie, the main effect of which was to cause the British to cast off some of their prizes which were then wrecked on the Spanish coast. For many then the aftermath of battle was a struggle for survival which lasted several days.

The storm overwhelmed the damaged ships, British, French, and Spanish alike. For William Thorpe, one of the prize crew sent on board the Spanish *Neptuno*, the prospects were bad. In the next few days, the prisoners were enlisted to help pump ship, she was retaken by her crew, and both British and Spanish worked hard to save the ship from wreck, but she broke up on the Spanish coast. Thorpe helped in the rescue of some of the crew, was imprisoned, and was finally exchanged under cartel for other prisoners in British hands. As he recounts the triumph and misadventure:

Oct 21st The 2nd Lieut. Lieut of Marines & 48 men on board the *Neptuno* – at ½ past 5 p.m. took possession of the ship – sent the first Lieut of the *Neptuno* on board the *Minotaur* to deliver his Captain's sword who was killed in the action and the second badly wounded. Also sent 25 men on board who then seized the other prisoners fire arms and magazines – Afterward found she was very leaky, – having no shot plug on board, – sent on board the *Minotaur* for some, received six and proceeded to plug up the shot holes that appeared most dangerous, – Whe where obliged to make the Prisoners ply at the Pump as at this time she had 5½ feet water in her hold.

22nd At day light began to clear away the wreck, got the Mizen Mast Fore Yard and Main top Gallt Mast over board and cut away a number loass [loose?] spars and rigging – at half past three p.m. the *Minotaur* took us in tow the wind continued to increase to a hard gale, – soon after the Hawzer broke, whe where now left to the mercy of the waves the Gale continued to increase the ship a mere wreck on a lee shore possessed by the enemy, –

23rd At 12 Night the Main Mast whent by the board, stove in the Poop and Quarter Deck, – killed one of our seamen and the Spanish Capn of Marines who was lying asleep in his cot. – Whe then shoared up the Quarter Deck and the broken beams to prevent the Deck falling in upon us, – about three oclock

cleard away the best Bower Anka on account of seeing Cadiz
light show close under our lee, having only 18 Fathoms water,
at ½ past 3 oclock let go the anka and brought her up. Veered
the whole Cable service in the Hawze and remained in that
situation till Daylight. Whe then saw a squadron in shore
consisting of 5 sail of the line, 3 Frigates and a Brig which
proved to be the Enemy, – Thus situated whe expected assistance from our own fleet but looked in vain, – at 10 oclock,
rigged a spar to the stump of the main mast and an other to the
[mizen] set a top Gallant upon each and got an other the Fore
Mast, in lieu of a fore sail, – at 3 oclock cut our cable and stood
toward our own Fleet with all sail whe could set, – but the
enemy was gaining upon us fast from Cadiz, – whe cleared away
our sternchasers and the magazine, – The prisoners observing
this rose upon our people and retook the ship – in doing which
they met with little opposition – indeed it would a been
madness to resist, a slight resistance was made by some who
narrowly escaped with their lives, – They now wore ship &
stoad toward Cadiz at 4 p.m. *Le Hermione* French Frigate of 44
Guns took us in tow and towd us to the Harbour Mouth where
whe brought up amongst some of their disabled ships

24th ... and rode till 3 oclock following Day when whe
parted from our Ankors and not having an other Cable bent to
bring her up they let her drive ashore, near St Martins bay – at
this time the confusion on board is inexpressible it becoming
Dark, and ignorant what part of the coast whe where cast upon,
– expecting the Ship every moment to go to Pieces, the
Spaniards naturally dispirited now showed every simptom of
Dispair they run about in wild Disorder nor made the last effort
to extricate themselves from the Danger that threatened them at
Daylight our people conveyed three ropes on shore, one from
the Cat Head, one from the Bowspirit and another from the
Fore Mast head, – by the assistance of wich, a number of men
got safe on shore whilst others where imployd constructing a
raft for more expediously landing, as well as to convey such as
where unwilling to risk themselves by the ropes, when the raft
was completed 20 men ventured on board and arrived safe on
the shore, but the raft was Driven so far upon the rocks that it
was found impossible to get it of again, – those on board seeing

this sad Disaster, far from giving way to dispair immediately set about making an other, which certainly was our last resource, as whe had not any more spars fit for that purpose, when finished whe launched it over board and 20 men embarked on board it who arrived safe one Spaniard excepted who was washed off by the surf, – then made fast a rope to the raft on shore and there being one already fast from the ship, the People Dragged It of to the ship, when 28 men embarkd on board, all of whom arrived safe on shore, the raft was again Dragged on board and 28 men imbarkd 6 of whom was washd from the raft, (Spaniards) by the surf and perished, – The raft was much damaged upon the Rocks it was again dragged of to ship but Fate had decreed that all who remained on board should perish – the raft laden shoved off from the Ships side but ... every soul perished, – no further attempt could be made to save those unfortunate men who remained on board, all perished. Whe where marchd Prisoners to Port St Marys being about 4 miles from St Martins Port where whe where wreckd, whe where lodged in Prison and treated kindly by the Spaniards tho our lodging was on the ground, – whe remained here 3 days

On the 27th whe where marched 11 miles to a small town in the Isle of Loyans Passed a little town calld point Royal about nine miles from St Mary's whe where here lodged in Prison and served with a pint of wine and some bread The next day 28th, whe where marched to Cadiz distance about nine miles where whe where again lodged in Prison and received a Quarter Dollar per man to subsist us twenty four hours the following day 29th they marchd us to the Waterside and put us on board two Spanish gun boats, and by them carried on board the *Hermione* French Frigate, appointed to carry us to the Fleet, to be exchanged, remained on board two nights when our allowance was a Pint of Wine and Bread, the next day whe where put on board the *Sirius* Frigate, and again shifted to the *Swiftsure* 74 Guns – carryd to Gibraltar and Joined our own ship to the great joy of us all our loss amounted to four killed by the falling of the masts rigging and drowned, – Tho the suffering of our People where great, yet no instances of cruelty or even unkindness can be alleged to the Spaniards those who arrived safe on shore looked upon our men as their Deliverers and there where instances of Grattitude and Kindness – that would do Honor to Any Nation – It is with regret the Spaniard goes [to] war with the English who he wishes always to consider his Friends it is from the unfortunate situation of affairs on the continent he is compelled to act a part so foreign to his interest and contrary to the Publick wish. – Whoever therefore considers the destructive consequences of war if his heart is not callous to Humanity will feel for the sufferings of the Widows Orphans and Friends of the brave Fellows who fell on the 21st October 1805

The counter-attack from Cadiz on 23 October was repulsed by the British who, nevertheless, were forced to give up their prizes in order to defend themselves. However, in the final phase of the campaign of Trafalgar, on 4 November a British squadron led by Captain Richard Strachan, known as 'Mad Dick', captured the four ships of Dumanoir's squadron off Ferrol. Strachan's squadron was one of several which were looking for the French admiral Allemand, who had broken out of Rochefort with five ships in July. After capturing numerous prizes and two British warships in the Atlantic, Allemand sneaked back into Rochefort. Strachan, meanwhile, did not even know that Trafalgar had been fought and won, and this is how he reported this last battle, on board the *Caesar*:

West of Rochfort 264 miles, Nov 4 1805 . . . Being off Ferrol, working to the Westward, with the Wind Westerly, on the evening of the 2d, we observed a Frigate in the N.W. making Signals; made all Sail to join her before Night . . . we came up with her at Eleven at Night; and at the Moment she joined us, we saw Six large Ships near us. Captain Baker informed me he had been chaced by the Rochfort Squadron, then close to Leeward of us. We were delighted. . . . the Moon enabled us to see the Enemy bear away in a Line abreast, closely formed; but we lost Sight of them when it set . . . steering to the E.N.E. all night . . . at Nine we discovered the Enemy of Four Sail of the line in the N.E. under all Sail . . .

There followed several hours of complex manoeuvring, but

at half-past Three the Action ceased, the Enemy having fought to admiration, and not surrendered till their Ships were unmanageable . . . you may judge my surprise when I found the Ships we had taken were not the Rochfort Squadron, but from Cadiz . . .

Fittingly the names of the ships in Strachan's squadron and the accompanying frigates were a roll call of the nations, places, and ships whom the British had fought in recent years and the heroes they made of themselves – they could not even be bothered to hide a rebel name: *Caesar*, *Hero*, *Courageux*, *Namur*, *Bellona*, *Æolus*, *Santa Margarita*, *Phoenix*, and *Revolutionnaire*. The French 74-gun *Duguay Trouin* was taken into British service as the *Implacable* and survived until 1949 when she was sunk, with honour, in the English Channel, flying the ensigns of France and Britain. A section of her stern hangs in the Neptune Hall of the National Maritime Museum.

Meanwhile the news had to be taken to London. The ship chosen for this task was the schooner *Pickle*. *Pickle*'s crew presented in microcosm the cosmopolitan mix of the men who had fought for the Royal Navy at Trafalgar. Half of her thirty-odd crew were Englishmen, mostly from Devon and Cornwall; a quarter were from the rest of the British Isles, mostly from Ireland; and the rest were from a variety of nations, including two from America. The second in command, George Almy, hailed from Newport, Rhode Island. The ancestors of her captain, Lieutenant John Lapenotiere, had come to England with William of Orange. Racing home, Lapenotiere landed at Falmouth and rode the 256 miles to London in thirty-seven hours, arriving at the Admiralty at about 1 a.m. on 6 November.

The *Euryalus*, carrying copies of the despatches and a prisoner, Villeneuve, arrived off Falmouth three weeks later. On board was Second Surgeon Alexander Ross, who at the height of battle went on board the *Mars* to assist with the wounded there. Ross was under the influence of Blackwood, one of Nelson's particular friends, and his letter is the beginning of the myth that had already begun to fix on Nelson:

the loss sustained by our fleet is small compared with that of the enemy as we had only two ships dismasted during the whole action which was 4 hours and a half. The joy excited on account of this signal victory is however much diminished by the loss of Lord Nelson while this gallant hero with that presence of mind and resolution by which he was ever distinguished on such occasions was carrying destruction among the enemy he was unfortunately wounded in the Breast with a musquet ball. After he had lived long enough to receive the pleasing information of the enemy's defeat he expired in the arms of Victory he thus fell for his country no less regretted for his Public services, than for his private virtues; his heroic conduct in succeeding ages will be read with true pride in the glorious annals of Britain . . .

The brunt of the action had been borne by about half the British fleet, which had suffered less than five hundred dead, the largest number being in the *Victory*. In the French and Spanish fleets there were ten times that number, two and half thousand wounded, and several thousand prisoners. Ross had more detailed news of the butcher's bill, as it affected the Duff family from Scotland:

I am very sorry to inform you that Captain Duff of the *Mars* 74 had his head severely crushed by a shot in the heat of the action. I went onboard the *Mars* a little after he fell to assist the Surgeon, as there were above 100 killed and wounded two days after the action his body was committed to the deep. Mr Alexr Duff of Park was mortally wounded and died a little after the action. His leg had been amputated before I came on board and I only came [in] time enough to see him breath his last. I remained on board the *Mars* a week after the action during which time we lost our masts and rudder and marvellously escaped being driven on Shore on the enemy's coast I afterwards had the good fortune to join the *Euryalus* with Captain Duff's son [fourteen-year-old Norwich] and Mr. Thomas Duff of Park [Alexander's sixteen-year-old brother] who came with the *Euryalus* to England after the *Euryalus* had gone to Cadiz under a flag of truce to land some officers of distinction on Parole, she received dispatches for the Admiralty and we were disired to carry Admiral Villier [sic] now the enemy's commander in chief with his aide camp along with us to England. We arrived at Falmouth this morning and have safely delivered all the prisoners to be taken care of excepting Villiers [sic] whom we will deliver at Portsmouth . . .

The campaign was not quite over. Roused from his bed in the early hours of the morning, the octogenarian Barham spent the next few hours despatching reinforcements and supplies to Collingwood from other squadrons and from the homeports. Only at 9 a.m., after writing all these orders, did Barham write to the King, apologizing because he had been 'engaged in giving the requisite orders for dispatching reinforcements . . . not only to renew the blockade of Cadiz, but to complete the measures which his truly great and much lamented predecessor had in contemplation'.

There is a sad footnote to the campaign of Trafalgar. Nelson's close friend, Cuthbert Collingwood, was, as his name suggests, born in Northumberland. He had entered the Royal Navy in 1761 and as a midshipman fought at Bunker's Hill during the American War of Independence. He distinguished himself at the Glorious First of June, where Howe chose him to take home news of victory. Some ten years older than Nelson, he had served with him in the West Indies, where they became close friends, and Collingwood had several times succeeded his friend in appointments. Thereafter their careers remained closely entwined, Collingwood always knowing his friend's mind but perhaps never quite able to imitate Nelson's flashing genius. At the Battle of St Vincent, for example, it was Nelson who impetuously turned his ship downwind and ran alone upon the leading Spanish ships in order to stop them reuniting with their convoy, and it was Collingwood who followed his friend, but by the slower method of tacking through the wind. After Nelson's frantic chase to the West Indies, it was Collingwood who watched the Combined Fleet in Cadiz and then served as second in command at Trafalgar until Nelson's death, after which he took command of the damaged British fleet and its prizes. It was Collingwood too who in the midst of a storm wrote the Trafalgar despatches with their eloquent prose and ordered thanksgiving throughout the fleet: 'Almighty God, whose arm alone is strength, having of his great mercy been pleased to crown the exertion of His Majesty's Fleet with success, in giving them a complete Victory over their enemys . . . that all praise and thanksgiving may be offered up to the throne of Grace, for the great benefits to our Country and to mankind . . . his constant aid to us in the defence of our Country's liberties and laws'.

Collingwood had been one of the first to reimpose the blockade of Brest in 1803, and he never set foot in England again. In fact, he spent so much time at sea that though he took a ceaseless interest in the upbringing and education of his two daughters he rarely saw the girls. He was never allowed home after Trafalgar, and instead the Admiralty sent him into the Mediterranean to continue the blockade on the remains of the French fleet at Toulon. There his companion was Bounce, his dog, and there, worn out, he died in 1810. Only then was he allowed to join his friend in St Paul's.

*Chapter Eight*

# Britannia Rules

Decisive battle and command of the sea are rare events, compared to the jostling for strategic advantage, the squadron actions and the single-ship fights, and the navy's willingness to take battle ashore. So few sea fights can be ranked with Trafalgar for their decisiveness. Anyway, as Julian Corbett pointed out, by the day of Trafalgar Napoleon had already marched from Boulogne, and his battles at Austerlitz and Ulm established French hegemony in Europe for the next ten years. And even after Trafalgar, British supremacy at sea was not absolute, as can be seen from French naval activity in 1806.

## VICTORY NOT ABSOLUTE

Nelson's victory at the Battle of Trafalgar was crushing, but, notwithstanding the myth which has grown up, it was not annihilating and nor was it the final victory which popular historians and enthusiasts for the Nelson era would like to believe. France had plenty of ships available still and many more building.

In 1805 and 1806, in addition to Villeneuve's and Missiessy's breakouts into the Atlantic, at least seven other squadrons sailed from France. Even as the storm raged off Trafalgar, Linois was in the East Indies with a squadron and Allemand and his Rochefort squadron were in the Atlantic. Strachan thought he had found Allemand when he fought his action in November 1805 against the remnants of the van of the Combined Fleet. Instead Allemand's squadron of five line-of-battle ships and five frigates captured three British warships, the largest being the 54-gun former East Indiaman *Calcutta*, as well as forty-three merchant ships and over twelve hundred British prisoners. Allemand returned with his prizes and booty unmolested to Rochefort on 23 December 1805.

Meanwhile, only a few days after Trafalgar, ignorant that there had even been a battle, Commodore L'Hermite sailed with a squadron of four ships from Lorient. He took and destroyed several British slave-ships and merchant vessels off West Africa, and, on 6 January, captured the British sloop of war *Favourite*. L'Hermite was loose in the South Atlantic and marauding there and in the West Indies for most of 1806, and the *Favourite* was not recaptured until January 1807.

Then, on a winter's afternoon, Admiral Sir William Cornwallis' blockade was driven from the coast off Brest, and the French ships there, which had lain inactive for most of the momentous year of 1805, sailed on 14 December. Cornwallis, known in the fleet as 'Billy Blue', was a popular but unlucky officer, who despite active service since entering the navy in 1755 and having been an admiral since 1793, never commanded in a successful fleet action. The French fleet which now evaded him consisted of two squadrons, commanded by Admirals Leissègues and Willaumez. Leissègues had orders to take troops to San Domingo (now Haiti), where the slaves had revolted against their French masters: he was then to raid shipping in the North Atlantic before returning to Rochefort or Lorient. Willaumez was ordered to proceed to the South Atlantic and then to raid the West Indies. Both French admirals hoped to clear the coasts of Europe without being detected, but almost immediately the French plan began to unravel. On 15 December the squadrons were still in sight of each other, Leissègues steering west and Willaumez steering more southerly. Willaumez had seen a British convoy heading north from Gibraltar, escorted by the 64-gun *Polyphemus* and the frigate *Sirius*, which he chased, capturing a pair of transports from the convoy. In turn Leissègues was seen by Captain Charles Brisbane in the frigate *Arethusa*, escorting a convoy from Cork to the West Indies. Brisbane sent the main body of his convoy on its way, and despatched the sloop *Wasp* to raise the alarm with the British squadrons off Rochefort, Ferrol, Cadiz, and Gibraltar, and the frigate *Boadicea* to warn Admiral Cornwallis off Ushant. Brisbane himself feinted to the north and Leissègues followed him, chasing all day and the next. Leissègues's squadron may have been the cream of the French navy but they had not been to sea for months and *Arethusa*, making sail to the west, soon outsailed them.

Off Cadiz was Admiral Thomas Louis in the 80-gun *Canopus*, with his flag captain Francis Austen. Louis was one of Nelson's original band of brothers, who had commanded *Minotaur* between 1794 and 1799 and fought her at the Battle of the Nile in 1798. When he was promoted admiral he had briefly commanded the blockade off Boulogne, and then hoisted his flag in *Canopus*, under Nelson's command off Toulon. Later, off Cadiz, when Nelson was preparing for a long blockade by sending small squadrons away alternately, to replenish livestock and water, Louis had the misfortune to be sent to Gibraltar to water in mid-October, thus missing the Battle of Trafalgar. After the battle, however, his squadron was used to blockade the remnants of the Combined Fleet. (Francis Austen was not only brother to Jane Austen, but had another brother in the navy, Charles. Both Francis and Charles, who had successful naval careers, feature in Jane Austen's novels and their experiences influenced the great authoress's writings.)

Louis was superseded in command of the blockading squadron by Admiral Sir John Thomas Duckworth in the *Superb*. History knows Duckworth as Sir John, but his sailors called him 'Old Tommy'. As a junior officer he fought in the American War of Independence, and later commanded ships in the fleets of Howe and St Vincent, including *Orion* at the Battle of the Glorious First of June, 1794. As commander, captain, and admiral Duckworth served in the West Indies, and in 1803 he took the surrender of the French army in San Domingo: this experience may have influenced the outcome of events as they unfolded in 1806. Duckworth's flag captain was Richard Keats. He had been ignominiously put ashore by the mutineers of the *Galatea* in 1797, but he was a popular officer and had commanded *Superb* since 1801, first under Sir James Saumarez, then in the Mediterranean under Nelson, and he had taken part in the chase to the West Indies. *Superb* was one of several ships in the navy whose crews had been kept together for years under one captain, and they were evidently happy, united, and very effective. Keats was one of Nelson's favourite officers and it was to him that Nelson had first confided his battle plan, in the garden of his house at Merton, for when they met the French. However, *Superb* was still on her way from Portsmouth to Cadiz when she met *Pickle* flying north with her momentous news of the battle and the death of Nelson: for Keats it was a great shock to have missed the battle and to have lost his friend and commander-in-chief. As *Pickle* continued northward, Keats and every man in the *Superb* 'was conscious that he had missed a rendezvous with history and . . . suffered a personal loss'. So four men, Louis, Francis Austen, Duckworth, and Keats, had each something to prove.

When Duckworth heard of Allemand's squadron to the westward, he lifted his blockade of Cadiz, but searched in vain. As he was returning to Cadiz he met the *Arethusa*, who told him of another French squadron. Now Duckworth searched to the north, where he found Willaumez. In the chase both squadrons were drawn out over fifty miles, with *Superb* far ahead of other British ships and up with the rearmost French ones, when, unaccountably, Duckworth called off the pursuit. He then despatched *Amethyst* to England with intelligence of the strength of the French, and he sent *Powerful* to the East Indies to inform and reinforce the squadron there under Admiral Pellew. Whether he was so far to the west that it was the nearest port, or whether he remembered Nelson's actions in the previous year, Duckworth took the remainder of his squadron to the West Indies, arriving on 12 January 1806 at Barbados for water. Before he had finished refitting his ships for their homeward passage, on 1 February the sloop *Kingfisher* brought him news of French ships seen steering towards San Domingo. Immediately the British squadron made sail and for Duckworth, having missed bringing Allemand and Willaumez to action, it was third time lucky.

He arrived off San Domingo on the morning of 6 February 1806 and there, at last, he found an enemy: Leissègues with five line-of-battle ships, four frigates, and several merchantmen. Leissègues's ships had had a rough, slow crossing of the Atlantic and arrived only had a week before to land troops, and refit for the return crossing: the French admiral hurriedly rejoined his ship in a small boat. Slipping their cables, the French formed a line of battle led by the 130-gun *Impérial*, claimed to be the strongest and most beautiful ship ever built, and ran before the wind, according to both British and French reports, at about eight knots. This was a welcome sight to the approaching British, after so many months and years of blockade duty and frustration from never being able to bring the enemy to action, and Duckworth signalled, 'This is glorious'. The British hardly needed further orders as Duckworth shaped his course 'so as to make an action certain' and

> telegraphed the squadron, that the principal object of attack would be the Admiral and his seconds; and at three quarters past nine, for the ships to take stations for their mutual support, and engage the enemy as they got up; and a few minutes after, to engage as close as possible, when at a short period after ten the *Superb* closed upon the bow of the *Alexander*, the leading ship, and commenced the action ... [at] half past eleven ... the French Admiral, much shattered, and completely beat, hauled direct for the land, and ... ran on shore; his foremast only standing, which fell directly on her striking ... not long after the *Diomede*, of 84 guns, pushed on shore near his Admiral ... About fifty minutes after eleven, the firing ceased; and upon the smoke clearing away, I found *le Brave*, bearing a Commodores' pendant, the *Alexander* and *le Jupiter*, in our possession.

The running battle between seven British line-of-battle ships and five French had lasted two and half hours, during which three of the latter were captured and two driven aground. Only then did Duckworth return to his station several thousand miles away.

However, in Duckworth's absence, four frigates under the command of Captain La Marre La Meillerie, survivors of the Battle of Trafalgar, had escaped in an easterly storm on 26 February 1806. La Meillerie lost the 18-gun brig *Furet* to a watching British ship, but the *Furet*'s capture delayed his pursuers and enabled his squadron to disappear into the Atlantic. La Meillerie seems to have had a fruitless cruise from Senegal to Cayenne and Puerto Rico and was returning to Rochefort when, on 27 July, he met the line-of-battle ship *Mars*, belonging to Keats' squadron, which had returned to European waters from San Domingo. Had La Meillerie's been a British squadron of four frigates, no doubt they would have taken on a lone 74-gun ship, but instead they ran, all night and the following day. By evening the *Mars* had overhauled the *Rhin*, which surrendered to superior force, but La Meillerie, having sacrificed one of his ships, got safely into port.

Meanwhile, news of the escape from Brest of eleven sail-of-the-line and four frigates reached London on Christmas Eve. Immediately two British squadrons were ordered to put to sea, one of seven sail-of-the-line under Sir John Warren from Portsmouth and another of six ships under Sir Richard Strachan from Plymouth – though the departures were delayed by westerly gales in the Channel. Showing once more his brilliant grasp of strategy, the elderly Barham sent Warren to the West Indies and Strachan to St Helena and the Cape of Good Hope. Warren was too late to catch Willaumez, but instead, on 13 March, found Linois returning, well laden with booty, from his three years in the East Indies. Linois's cruise had not been wholly successful but now his luck ran out. He made the mistake of chasing Warren, believing his squadron to be a convoy of merchant ships, but when Warren turned on him, the 98-gun *London* and 80-gun *Foudroyant* made short work of the French *Marengo* and *Belle Poule*.

In March, Commodore Leduc sailed from Lorient: he had different orders, to attack the Arctic fisheries. Adopting a tactic similar to La Meillerie's, in order to escape observation, he sacrificed a small brig to a chasing British frigate and sailed north. However, these waters were even less hospitable than the usual cruising grounds of French squadrons, and though a score of whalers were taken and destroyed, on 18 July off the Faroes the 40-gun *Guerrière* made an easy capture for Captain Lavie in the slightly smaller British *Blanche*. This French raid caused consternation in the whaling ports, but little significant damage: however, the state of the French ships when they struggled back to Lorient on 22 September demonstrated the real differences between the French and British navies, for while the British could keep at sea for months at a time, the French, returning with scurvy and weather-damaged ships, could not.

Meanwhile Willaumez, having avoided both Duckworth and Warren, was thwarted when he found the British had recently captured the Cape, and after some weeks of futile cruising in the South Atlantic he took his squadron to Brazil to replenish. By June he was in the West Indies where, following a series of indecisive manoeuvres, he again escaped capture. Warren, who had returned briefly to Portsmouth in June, was now despatched to the West Indies to hunt him down, narrowly missing him off Barbados in July.

Strachan's squadron had also returned to England, but sailing again in May 1806 from Plymouth searched the Atlantic. By 18 August they were within sixty miles of Willaumez, but a great hurricane intervened. Strachan's squadron survived the storm, but Willaumez's ships were scattered in every direction, dismasted or badly damaged. Willaumez himself steered for Havana in the 80-gun *Foudroyant* under jury rig, which he reached on 15 September despite having his entry into port challenged by the 44-gun frigate *Anson*. *Impétueux* was chased into the Chesapeake and stranded, where she was burned by the 74-gun ships *Belleisle* and *Bellona* and the frigate *Melampus*, all ships of Strachan's squadron which had survived the hurricane. Of the other French, the 74-gun ships *Patriote* and *Eole* and the frigate *Valeureuse* also reached the Chesapeake, where they were blockaded by British ships from Halifax. This blockade eventually led to the notorious incident between the American frigate *Chesapeake* and the *Leopard*, described later in this chapter. Of the remaining French ships, the *Veteran*, commanded by Napoleon's younger brother Jerome, had deserted before the hurricane, and the *Cassard* and Willaumez in the *Foudroyant* eventually returned to France.

L'Hermite, after his operations on the African coast, refitted in Brazil and then cruised for prizes in the West Indies. However, on 20 August his squadron was overwhelmed by the hurricane which dispersed Willaumez's. The *Cybèle* took refuge in the United States, but the *Régulus* and *Présidente* steered separately for France; on 27 September 1806, Admiral Louis found and took the *Présidente* after a running battle. Only two ships of L'Hermite's squadron returned safely to France: the *Régulus*, in October 1806 and the *Cybèle* in 1807.

A fifth French squadron attempted to put to sea in 1806. On 24 September, Commodore Soleil sailed with five frigates from Rochefort, but they were seen by Commodore Samuel Hood in the early hours of the next day. Hood came from a family of successful sailors: he was one of Nelson's original band of brothers who had fought with him at Aboukir, commanding the *Zealous*, and it was he who had so annoyed Napoleon by erecting a 'symbol of insolence' when he manned and fortified HMS *Diamond Rock* off Port Royale. Soleil fought hard and suffered accordingly against

Hood's 74s, but four 40-gun frigates were taken and added to the Royal Navy. The battle is remarkable for Hood's sang-froid when he reported to the Admiralty: 'I received a severe wound in my right arm, (since amputated, and doing well I hope,) which obliged me to leave the deck . . .'

By the end of the year the French forays had been halted and the remaining ships blockaded in Cadiz, the Chesapeake, or the French Atlantic ports. Many brave actions had been fought, but the enemy had been defeated as much by superior seamanship as by gunnery. Duckworth's quicker passage of the Atlantic, his speedy refit of his ships and the better health of his crews compared to Leissègues's speaks volumes. So too does Strachan's survival of the great hurricane which shattered first Willaumez's ships, then L'Hermite's: Strachan's ships not only survived but were able to find their rendezvous off the Chesapeake and destroy or blockade the remnants of two French squadrons. Louis' 80-gun *Canopus* was a particularly well-run and seaworthy ship, which in the space of two years had taken a full part in the campaign of Trafalgar, including Nelson's chase to the West Indies, imposed a winter blockade on Cadiz, been on a second chase to the West Indies with Duckworth, fought at the Battle of San Domingo, and in 1807 was still seaworthy enough to be sent to the eastern Mediterranean.


## COCHRANE

Most of the British operations in 1806 were reactions to French manoeuvres, but there were plenty of opportunities for British offence too. One of the young officers who excelled in seamanship, aggression, and restless energy was Thomas Cochrane. In 1805–6 he commanded the new fir-built 32-gun frigate *Pallas*, and in March 1805, on his first cruise in her, he captured three valuable prizes, including the Spanish *Fortuna* carrying half a million dollars in gold and silver. It was typical of Cochrane that he should return to Plymouth with gold candlesticks five feet high fixed to each masthead, behaviour that at once taunted his superiors and excited their jealousy. To return with this booty Cochrane had had to outrun three of Missiessy's line-of-battle ships. They had threatened to overhaul him in a rising sea, and in these conditions they could carry more sail and would surely have run Cochrane down, but he suddenly clewed up his sails and clawed off to windward. The French ships shot past him and it was many miles before they could turn in pursuit, and in the following night Cochrane escaped. The *Pallas* became popularly known as the *Golden Pallas*.

Perhaps one of the finest examples of Cochrane's aggressive spirit and his seamanship occurred in the spring of 1806. Having, in his words, 'nothing better in view', he raided the French coast. In April he sent away most of his crew in boats to cut out a French corvette, but meanwhile was attacked by three other French warships: he had only enough men on board to operate the *Pallas*'s two bow guns, but he chased his opponents, ran them ashore, and captured a handsome new prize, the 14-gun *Tapageuse*. In May he destroyed several signal posts, and a battery of guns, in order to deny the enemy intelligence of his movements. Then he was ordered into the Aix Roads, where the remnants of Allemand's ships were sheltering. A lesser officer might have been content with a distant observation but Cochrane took the *Pallas* close inshore where Allemand could not ignore him, and sent a strong force (the same ships which were to be captured by Hood) to drive him off. In the two-hour fight which followed, tacking between the shoals and firing broadsides intermittently, it was the French *Minerve* which ran aground, in home waters. The force of the collision as the *Pallas* came alongside her drove the *Pallas*'s guns inboard and brought down much of her rigging. Nevertheless Cochrane was preparing to board the *Minerve* when two other, undamaged 40-gun frigates threatened to cut him off, and he was forced to retreat in his damaged ship. Throughout this and many other similar actions, in the historian James's words, Cochrane 'viewed his opponent through a diminishing medium: they were never, in appearance, too ample for his grasp, or too powerful to be subdued by his skill and intrepidity'.

## JOHNSON THE SMUGGLER

William Clarke was an officer in the Royal Marines who served from 1803 to 1816. He came into contact with many famous men of the period, and was eye-witness to many events which have now become history, including Hood's actions off Rochefort, the second Battle of Copenhagen (1807), the landings on Walcheren (1809), war in the Baltic, the Peninsular War, and one of the last sorties of a French fleet, in 1813. Somehow promotion evaded him, and he was invalided from the service after he lost a leg, though this and his lack of promotion does not seem to have embittered him. After a short period in the 110-gun *Ville de Paris*, under Admiral Cornwallis, Clarke was sent to command the marines in Samuel Hood's *Centaur*. Hood, we know, was commanding a squadron on blockade duty off Rochefort and the neighbouring coast, where towards the end of 1806, as has been already told, he captured an entire squadron. First, however, there was some boat work, one outstanding regular action, and another rather more irregular.

'Captain' Thomas Johnson (he was never in the Royal Navy) was – and still is – a shady figure of the Great War of 1793–1815. Johnson's main occupation seems to have been as a smuggler, in which he acted as procurer and spy, seemingly working principally for the British, often based in Holland. He served time in the prisons at the Fleet and at Flushing, from both of which he escaped, and apparently spent some time in America. What is sure is that for some time during the various attacks on the invasion fleet at Boulogne in 1804 he collaborated closely with Robert Fulton, who then went by the pseudonym of 'Mr Francis', and that for some time after Fulton had returned to America, they corresponded about their respective inventions. Fulton had devised a submarine, in which he tried to interest the French, as well as different types of floating mines, which, confusingly to the modern reader, were called submarine torpedoes, or plain 'infernal machines'. Johnson too was an inventor – or 'projector' in the language of the early nineteenth century – who had devised a submarine boat, though this may have been no more than a specially ballasted rowing boat, with a low freeboard and a waterproof covering. Intriguingly, Johnson may have first learned about submarines and mines while in prison in Holland.

A contemporary document records: 'For ten years the Navy was interested in Johnson's experiments, and as late as 1812 Melville, the First Lord of the Admiralty, considered a proposal by Johnson for a submarine boat which would be built of wrought iron, capable of containing three men with provisions for six days, and so strongly built and as to defy the effect of a twelve pounder at point blank range. Johnson wanted the Navy to buy his secret for £100,000, and even reached a draft agreement, which was very similar to an earlier secret agreement which Melville's father had struck with Fulton. However, when the war ended the Navy lost interest in Johnson's boats, and when Johnson reverted to his original profession of smuggling, he was chased down the Thames by customs officers and his boat was burned.'

Clarke was witness to another of Johnson's experiments in 1806, when the *Centaur* was off Rochefort. Hood, 'whose zeal, skill and enterprise were never surpassed even in the British Navy, could not remain long quietly looking at the Enemy, and both they and ourselves were soon in something like perpetual motion, and boats and small craft were in constant activity'. Clarke may not have known what he was witnessing, but his report seems to be fairly accurate, writing about

a most notorious smuggler of the name of Johnson, whose escape from either the Fleet Prison or Newgate by Escalade and some other most extraordinary feats of desperate enterprise (worthy the Buccaneers of former days) rendered him at the time a sort of 'public character'. This Man in command of a small cutter was sent out to Sir Samuel Hood to attempt the destruction of some of the Enemy's Ships in Basque Roads (Rochefort) [and] he was provided with Gigs or fast pulling Boats and Machines of particular construction, partly I believe of his own invention, one of which called a catamaran was filled with combustible materials and could be so far sunk in the water as to render the person conducting it scarcely visible above it, this Machine was to be attached to the cable of a ship whilst lying at anchor and allowed to drop under her Bows, where by the aid of Clockwork it was to explode after a given time and it was expected it would drive in her Bows and cause her immediate destruction: Well ! this fellow was with us I don't remember exactly how long, but some weeks, anchoring his vessel near the French Squadron most nights, and waiting for a favourable opportunity of carrying his scheme into execution,

but ! something or other according to his own account, always
presented some obstacle, either the Moon was too bright, and
would cause his premature discovery, or, it was too dark to
enable him to secure his 'infernal machine' in its proper
position; and at last Sir Samuel's patience began to tire indeed.
I have no doubt he considered him a Humbug from the first, as
he professed to row round the Enemy's Ships night after night
making the necessary observation to secure the success of his
plans . . . the Commodore resolved to send an Officer with him
who could form some judgement respecting what might be
expected from him: so Sibley our First Lieutenant accompanied
him one night and on that occasion *he did* row close to the
*Majesteuse*, the French Admiral's Flag Ship, if I remember right,
round her, yet however time passed on, and nothing more was
done and he and his vessel were ordered home, and the
Frenchman remained in whole Ships and whole Skins . . .

Just why Johnson's infernal machines did not work is not clear,
but given his persistence, over many years, his scheme seems to
have been more than just a scam, though this did not stop Clarke
reflecting what must have been the common view in the *Centaur*:
'The Cutter was I believe his own and the Government paid so
much per Month for her, *if so*, his dilatory proceedings are
sufficiently accounted for, delay not promptitude was his *interest*
the only object likely to be pursued by such a character . . .'

## SMALL BOAT ACTIONS

Meanwhile an opportunity arose for the proper business of naval
and marine officers on blockade duty, though Johnson was again
accused: 'During his stay he very nearly caused us a serious loss
by a false report, and his desertion of us at the time of Trial, he
reported to the Commodore that *a very large* French Man of War
Brig had anchored off Rochelle, that he had been sufficiently near
her to see the Men on her Deck, and could not be mistaken. Sibley
instantly requested and Sir Samuel granted permission to attempt
her capture with the Boats'.
Edward Sibley had been a midshipman under Alexander Hood

in the *Royal George* on the Glorious First of June in 1794, had spent eight years in the East Indies, and had served with Samuel Hood in the *Centaur* since 1804. The remainder of his career, bar a couple of years, was then spent in boat actions and in small ships, where he enjoyed steady success against privateers and in taking prizes. The action in the entrance of the Gironde is typical of his career and the scores of similar actions by other unsung heroes. Johnson was supposed to have guided him into the river, but had disappeared on a jolly of his own:

> it was arranged accordingly that [Johnson] was to anchor his Cutter between the French Squadron and our intended object of attack which being about one of his usual anchorages was not likely to create any suspicion of our intentions and when sufficiently dark, we were to quit the Squadron, and rendezvous alongside his Vessel, when he was to join and lead us to glory. Accordingly with eight Boats under the command of Sibley (with whom I was) we reached the Cutter about 10 o'clock when, to our utter dismay, the gallant Smuggler was gone, his Mate or first officer informed us that finding the night favourable for operations he was gone to see what could be done, he (the mate) said that there was a Brig, and that appeared to be all *he* knew, however we insisted on his accompanying us, and away we went, and pulled and pulled, without meeting anything until near day break, and were about to return when we saw a Brig sure enough and now we were inclined to forgive the Traitor, and away we dashed.

However Sibley and Clarke were to be disappointed, for when they boarded the brig they found that 'all was still as death; he was an American Merchantman, a Pistol went off by accident which awoke the Captain who poor fellow wondered what in the name of God all the row meant'. It was now daylight and the wind and the current favoured the French, who were alerted to this danger in their midst:

> now we had to pass at no great distance from the Enemy's Squadron some of which having espied us got under Sail to cut us off, and it became doubtful whether they would not do so before we could join our ships, which were nearly becalmed;

fortunately a breeze sprang up and brought them in so fast that the French Ships were obliged to allow us to pass, or risk an action with our Squadron which with their usual courtesy, they declined and we returned unharmed, but cursedly cross and venting invectives both loud and deep against Johnson who, doubtless would as soon have betrayed one party as the other, provided the balance of interest was in his own favour . . .

However, they had learned from the American that there was a convoy under the protection of two brigs in the roads where earlier in the year Cochrane had succeeded in cutting out the *Tapageuse*, and another boat action was planned. Clarke was very fond of Shakespeare, and quoted him when describing the boats

stealing along with muffled oars like poor old King Lear's Troop of Horse shod with felt we left the Frigates about 9 o'clock the boats in two lines . . . after pulling [rowing] some time we made sail, the wind blowing strong, and the boats keeping excellent order . . . it was now exceedingly dark, blowing strong with Thunder and Lightening . . . and began to fear we should miss our objects, if, we had not already passed them, when Sibley cautiously gave the order 'Oars' (that is cease rowing) . . .

Through the gloom they had made out the two warships stemming the tide in the swift river, and the two divisions of boats each pulled hard for their respective targets. The appalling weather favoured their approach until a vivid flash of lightning betrayed them. The Frenchman

opened her broadside upon us and followed it up by a rapid discharge of Musketry, and when we at length reached her side, and grappled the Boat to her, Muskets with bayonets fixed were darted into the Boat, and we found we had not yet cleared away the principle obstacle to our entrance.

The problem was that the Frenchman had

netting laced up to her mastheads and secured down to her hull, barring all entrance until Sibley, whilst clinging to the rigging, with a most fortunate stroke with his sword, severed the lacing line and down came the netting.

The boarders now rushed the ship and a desperate struggle ensued, though

> it was too terrible to last long, and the Frenchmen who were able ran below, and left us masters of the Deck! when we gave three hearty cheers, to give notice to the party which we hoped were in possession of the other Brig, but we heard no return to our cheering.

The prize proved to be

> *le Caesar* of 20 Guns commanded by Captain Hector Fourré, who poor fellow was bayoneted fighting in his shirt, and was found dead by the main mast. We missed Sibley, and suspecting where about he had fell, I went as soon as some kind of order was restored, in search of him, and found him fallen and insensible, under a heap of killed and wounded just where he had boarded, he had received seven pike and sabre wounds and had been trampled upon by those who so gallantly followed him.

In the darkness the other boats had been scattered, and a prisoner had cut the cable so that they were being carried on the tide higher up the river and another brig was firing on them, as were a number of batteries on shore. After a running battle in which the British in the *Caesar* were handicapped by not knowing the waters, a strong breeze blew up and the boarders in their prize, but without most of their boats, made for the open sea, where 'we joined the frigates at about nine o'clock in the morning [when] they manned their rigging and received us with three times three truly British cheers'. Sibley recovered, despite wounds to his head, face, and side, and was promoted to commander, but poor Clarke was not even named in the official despatches.

## THE DARDANELLES

Duckworth, it will be remembered, while fighting a battle off Haiti in the Caribbean, was supposed to be blockading Cadiz, several thousand miles away across the Atlantic. Collingwood, who had inherited Nelson's vast command, was not best pleased, because while Duckworth was absent, a French four-frigate squadron had escaped. A few months after he had returned to his proper station Duckworth was sent to the Dardanelles. Turkey had turned pro-French and expelled the Russian Ambassador (who was temporarily at least an ally), and the British business community had fled: Duckworth was ordered to demand the surrender of the Turkish fleet and, if the Turks would not give it up, to bombard the city, in the same fashion that the Danes had been dealt with. His mission clearly demonstrated the ubiquity and flexibility of sea power, but was also something of a mission impossible, and he was heavily criticized afterwards for failure.

The Dardanelles are formidable enough to ships under power, as the British and French were to find out a hundred years later, but Duckworth had the added difficulty of needing a settled southerly wind in order to stem the four-knot current and pass the several batteries en route, as well as orders from Collingwood which were equivocal. Further, his principal ally, Russia, was about to change sides. Duckworth was ordered to take diplomatic advice and not to provoke the Turks unnecessarily. So, at

> A quarter before nine o'clock AM Febry 19th [1807] the whole of the Squadron had passed the outer Castles, without having returned a shot to their fire, which occasioned but little injury. This forbearance was produced by the desire his Majesty's Minister expressed to preserve every appearance of amity, that he might negotiate with the strongest proof of the pacific disposition of our Sovereign toward the Porte: a second battery on the European side, fired also with as little effect.

A mile within the strait it narrows to about two miles wide and there

> At half past nine o'clock, the *Canopus* ... entered the narrow passage of the Sestos and Abidos, and sustained a very heavy carronade from both castles, within point blank shot of each ... As [our ships] continued to pass in succession ... I was happy in observing, that the very spirited return ... had so considerably diminished its force, that the effect on the stern-most ships could not have been so severe.

The next obstacle was a Turkish squadron:

> Immediately to the NE of the castles, and between them and Point Pesquies, in which a formidable battery had been newly erected, [was a] small squadron, of one 64 gun ship, and five frigates; all Turkish. The van division of our squadron gave them their broadsides as they passed, and Sir Sidney Smith with his division closed into the midst; the effect of the fire was such that in half an hour the Turks had all cut their cables to run onshore. The object of the Rear Admiral was then to destroy them, which was most rapidly effected; as in four hours the whole of them had exploded, except a small corvette, and a gun boat which it was thought proper to preserve.

Some of the Turkish cannon were of exceptionally large size, so that had their

> stone shot, some of which exceed eight hundred weight, made such a breach between wind and water, as they have done in our sides, the ship must have sunk; or had they struck a lower mast in the centre, it must evidently have been cut in two.

Despite this damage, the high level of seamanship in the British fleet soon had the ships ready for action again: 'no accident occurred that was not perfectly arranged in the course of the next day'.

Seamen and marines stormed the batteries, but they were not permanently occupied: 'the battery on the Point, of more than 30 guns, which had it been finished, was in a position to have annoyed the squadron most severely ... was taken possession of by the Royal Marines and boats crews of the rear-division ... and the guns were immediately spiked'. Under the circumstances it was a remarkable achievement for Duckworth to traverse the Dardanelles, and 'on the evening of the next day, the 20th came to anchor at ten o'clock ... about eight miles from the City of Constantinople ... had it been then in our power, we should have taken our station off the City immediately, but that could not be done from the rapidity of the current'. Once there, however, the Porte dealt with negotiations by simply ignoring Duckworth's demands or by flat refusal. Duckworth was perplexed by this diplomatic technique, and concerned for his return passage: he would have the current with him but now needed a northerly wind, and if his ships were damaged, he anticipated difficulty in passing the narrows again. After some days' fruitless inactivity, his fears were confirmed during his return to the Aegean, 'The fire of the two inner castles had, on our going up, been severe; but I am sorry to say, the effects they had on our ships, returning, has proved them to be doubly formidable; in short, had they been allowed another week to complete their defences throughout the channel, it would have been a very doubtful point, whether a return lay open to us at all'. Quite so: probably the best he could have done would have been to occupy Tenedos and Lemnos and blockade the straits, as the Russians did later in the year and other British commanders were to do during the next century.

One of the few officers to come out of this debacle with some honour was Sidney Smith. As a young officer Smith had served in North America and the West Indies, where in 1780 he was promoted to lieutenant. In the interwar years, after the American War of Independence, he served in the Swedish navy fighting against other British officers who had found service in the Russian navy. Smith's brother was a diplomat and Smith, using these connections, travelled in France and North Africa, working rather shadowily as a government agent. When the Revolutionary Wars broke out he was in Smyrna, whence he hurried to joined Hood at Toulon as a volunteer. He took part in the evacuation of Toulon and some, unfairly, blamed him for failing to burn the French fleet entirely. Smith seems to have been the archetypal 'James Bond' who combined a successful naval career and promotion to flag rank with life as a secret agent. In 1796, he was captured during a cutting-out expedition off le Havre, and for two years he was a prisoner in the notorious Temple, escaping in 1798 in an incident with closed carriages and hooded ladies which reads like an event in the life of the Scarlet Pimpernel. Next he was given command of the *Tigre* as senior officer in the Levant, a role he thought was independent of Nelson, who scorned him as 'the Swedish knight'. However, in his successful defence of Acre in 1799 he halted the advance of the French army, and became the first man to defeat Bonaparte in a land battle.

In 1805 Smith had commanded an inshore squadron which attempted to execute the plans of the inventors Fulton, Johnson, and

Congreve. Keith complained bitterly that Smith had appropriated all his small craft for these purposes 'which intended service seems to have no end ... the projectors of these projects ... will not abandon them; for the authors of them ... never will, so long as they are maintained in luxury at the expense of government'. Smith was given an advance of £30,000 from the secret fund for these operations – worth several millions in today's money – and, it seems, he was never able to properly account for it, so that when the Great War ended he was forced to exile himself in Paris, where in 1835 he was still campaigning for recognition and prize money for his people, and, perhaps, a little for himself: 'as the only surviving Flag Officer of the squadron detached by Lord Collingwood to force the passage of the Dardanelles' and for having been detached 'to destroy the Turkish fleet stationed at Point Pesquies above the Forts oppose our passage and which was necessary to secure our return'.

Smith died in Paris and his handsome tomb there is decorated with a magnificent relief carved by the great French sculptor David d'Angers.

## COPENHAGEN, 1807

While French squadrons were loose in the Atlantic, France was also busy building new ships and new alliances to challenge the British. The historian James calculated that France and Spain had something like forty-five line-of-battle ships in ports from Brest to Toulon, and could add perhaps as many again from the fleets of Austria, Portugal, Holland, Denmark, Sweden, and Russia. Even if none of these ships ever sailed they could occupy 'the attention of an equal number of British ships; and every division that escaped to sea would, in all probability, be pursued by at least two squadrons of equal force'. As news came of a treaty between the Russian and French emperors, and an alliance of the northern powers, the British government decided on desperate measures and asked the Danes to hand over their fleet, which, since the first Battle of Copenhagen in 1801, had been built up to over sixteen line-of-battle ships. The Danes naturally refused.

In mid-July, therefore, Admiral James Gambier sailed from

Yarmouth, his destination the Swedish island of Vingo, where the British fleet usually anchored for water and to buy provisions from Gothenburg. The fleet was received cordially enough and there was even time for a little sightseeing, according to William Clarke:

> we . . . passed Cronborg Castle and anchored in the Sound early in August, Our (the *Centaur's* Station) was near the Town of Elisnore [sic], where I went on shore several times, and visited amongst other places what is known as Hamlet's Gardens, and you, who know my veneration for our immortal Shakespeare, will believe with what sensations of enthusiasm and delight I viewed the spot rendered for ever classic ground by his unrivalled pen. We were received with every rite of friendship and hospitality, and were supplied with whatever refreshments we required and a pretty return we shortly made . . .

The army under Lord Cathcart sailed a little later, and when the expedition assembled it consisted of twenty-five sail-of-the-line and more than forty frigates, sloops, bomb-vessels, and gun brigs, nearly four hundred transports, and about twenty-seven thousand troops, more than half of them Germans in British pay.

Diplomatic negotiations made no progress. The British demand was for the Danes 'to deliver up to us (in trust) the Danish Navy, to prevent its falling into the hands of the French, guaranteeing of course, its return when such danger should cease to exist', which the Danes refused 'with a becoming spirit'. However, the British negotiator 'dealt only in words but a far more potent negotiator was at hand to back him, Lord Cathcart with seven or eight and twenty thousand men were desembarked within a few miles of Copenhagen on the sixteenth of August, and by the eighteenth the City was invested and preparations were commenced for Bombarding it both by Land and Sea'. The defences of Copenhagen were similar to those which had confronted Nelson six years before, including the powerful fortress of Trekronen, several blockships and floating batteries, and numerous gunboats, and, as before, the Danes fought bravely and put up a stout resistance. The navy took a full part in the siege: Danish

> Gun Boats were very active and found some warm employment for Boats and small craft, detachments of Seamen were landed

from the Ships to assist in transporting the heavy Guns, Mortars, Ammunition and stores from the landing places to the Batteries preparing for them, and all was activity and bustle, the Fleet was so distributed as to afford aid whenever and where ever it was in their power to give it, Commodore Sir Richard Keats and a Squadron occupied the great Belt on the opposite side of the Island of Zealand, Sir Samuel [Hood] with another Detachment moved in towards the further end of the Sound near the Town of Drago [Drager], on the Isle of Aurack [Amager]; so that if you glance your eye on the Map of Denmark, you will see that the Fleet as completely surrounded the Island as the Army did the City . . .

In Gambier's words,

The Mortar Batteries which had been erected by the Army in the several positions they had taken round Copenhagen, together with the Bomb Vessels which were placed in convenient situations, began the Bombardment on the morning of the second of September with such power and effect, that in a short time the Town was set on fire, and by the repeated discharges of our artillery, was kept in flames in different places, till the Evening of the fifth; when a considerable part of it being consumed, and the conflagration arrived at a great height, threatening the speedy destruction of the whole City . . .

Sir William Congreve's new-fangled rockets were amongst the weapons used.

Even when fire threatened the destruction of the whole city, a Danish request for an armistice was declined until the surrender of the Danish fleet was also promised. Eventually when

the Navy took possession of the Naval Arsenal, Officers, Seamen and Marines, were landed and immediately commenced fitting out the Danish Fleet. The *Norge* a fine seventy four fell to the *Centaur's* lot . . . the greatest activity prevailed in the Arsenal . . . we brought away early in October . . . Sixteen Ships of the Line, thirteen Frigates, and Six Brigs of War. The excellent arrangement in the Naval Arsenal gave great facility in expediting the equipment, and each Ship having a separate Store House assigned for her rigging stores etc all of which was

in the most complete and efficient order, the Ships themselves
lying alongside the various jetties ready to receive them, besides
those brought away we towed out of the Harbour an old Line
of Battle Ship and a Frigate and burnt them and destroyed
another Ship of the Line which was building and nearly
complete ...

Perhaps more valuable, the British seized masts, yards, timber, sails,
cordage, and other naval stores: the total booty was said to have
filled nearly a hundred transports.

Copenhagen 1807 was not, however, a noble passage of British
arms, and there were 'many, who could not be persuaded either of
the legality, or the expediency, of the attack upon Copenhagen ...
with respect to the merits of the expedition to Copenhagen, morally
and politically considered, the British public was for a long time
divided in opinion.' The loss to the British army and to the British
afloat was small compared to the thousands of men, women, and
children in the city injured or killed, and the destruction of
property. Clarke wrote:

Our attention was directed late one night to the Cathedral
Church the body of which appeared to be in flames, its beautiful
spire towering majestically above them: towards it we could
distinctly trace flying through the gloom of night the burning
fuzes of numerous shells, whilst the rockets rushed through the
air to the same destination with the roar of a distant hurricane!
From time to time, portions of ruins appeared to fall and dense
columns of smoke arose soon again to be succeeded by fresh
forecasts of increasing flames; at length between three and four
o'clock in the morning the body of the sacred Edifice being a
complete ruin, its magnificent spire which as yet, had appeared
erect and uninjured dropped perpendicularly to the ground.
Hundreds of Families which but a few days previous had been
living in peace and comfort, without the least anticipation of
approaching danger were thus ruined and rendered houseless
and hundreds of their numbers (including many females and
children) killed: or crippled and rendered a burden to themselves, their kindred and their Country for the remainder of
their existence. And this is Civilized and Christian Warfare ...

The Battle of Copenhagen had a dramatic impact on the balance of power in the Baltic, and when the Russian Emperor died the anti-British alliance collapsed. The battle also had more lasting effect: a century later everyone, especially the Germans, knew what Admiral Fisher meant when he threatened to 'Copenhagen' the German fleet in its harbours.

## THE PENINSULAR WAR

The Peninsular War showed a definitive example of the use of maritime force to complement land operations, revealing what has been called 'the beauty of naval operations'. The war commenced, following the withdrawal of Sir John Moore's army at Corunna in January 1809, with the re-insertion of an army under Wellington through the port of Lisbon in May the same year. Corunna was a forerunner of Dunkirk, when, against all odds, the navy carried off 28,000 men of the Allied armies. Sea power demonstrated one of its advantages: Soult, the French commander-in-chief, had difficulty in bringing his guns overland, while Moore's army was resupplied with arms and ammunition. Now the Peninsular War became a campaign sustained by sea power and one which used frequent and imaginative manoeuvre from the sea. Napoleon lost control of the peninsula when he could no longer guarantee sea-borne supplies for his army. Rapid manoeuvre by land, which was the hallmark of the Emperor's campaigns elsewhere, was not possible in the rugged, mountainous terrain of Spain, and once his soldiers spread out so that there was sufficient forage, they were vulnerable to attack by Spanish and Portuguese guerrillas. It was a French marshal who complained that the Anglo-Portuguese army was always concentrated and could always be moved because of the support it received from the Royal Navy, while he lived from day to day, foraging 'from the most wretched villages'. While Wellington veered and hauled across Spain, the navy's operations along the north coast of Spain actually preceded him, and by August 1812 the navy possessed Santander as an advanced base of operations.

Captain Home Popham's operations in the 74-gun line-of-battle ship *Venerable* typify the work of the navy during the Peninsular

War. In addition to two battalions of marines, he had a large quantity of small arms which he used to supply Spanish guerrillas. Popham infuriated the French with his raids, because no sooner had they marched in one direction than he would re-embark his seamen and marines and appear at another, his object 'to distract the enemy by rapid movements, followed by strong demonstrations ... the primary object of all our attentions is to assist Lord Wellington'. In response Napoleon ordered that all churches, convents, and strong houses situated near the mouths of creeks and rivers between Santander and San Sebastian should be fortified: it was a splendid compliment to the Royal Navy. One of Popham's officers, Robert Deans, describes one such distracting demonstration at Castro Urdiales starting on 6 July 1812:

> Anchored off Castro, sent two guns on shore and mounted them on a height at long range distance from the castle of Castro – landed the marines to protect them – about 10 they commenced firing from our guns – but found they did little mischief – the distance being too great. The castle did not even return the fire. About 200 guerrillas in possession of the hills above the Castro – About noon the enemy advanced with two field pieces, but halted ... and sent forward a party of cavalry – which were beat back by our marines – covered by an 18 pound carronade ... they attempted to cross the bridge over a small river ... but the fire from our gun was so directed that they were obliged to abandon their intentions, and retreat on their main body – we embarked our marines at night ...

The castle of Castro, according to Deans, was immensely strong, with walls nine feet thick, and the French had also strengthened a convent. From the sea Deans 'saw a deal of skirmishing between the guerrillas and the enemy, but little fighting on either side', then

> on the 7th we attacked the castle with the ships and obliged them to abandon their guns. They were still obstinate and would not strike their colours, notwithstanding we sent a flag of truce in the afternoon, to demand it – in order to prevent our injuring the town, which we were necessitated to fire upon – and by which ... innocent inhabitants alone were sufferers. On the night of the 7th we kept them awake by boats with guns

Nelson fought on land almost as much as at sea and his two best-known wounds, the loss of the sight in one eye and the loss of an arm, were inflicted in amphibious operations. In this melodramatic picture he is shot through the arm as he attempts to land at Tenerife in July 1797. [BHC0498]

Scots officers were comparatively rare in the Royal Navy but earned a large share of fame: Adam Duncan, victor of Camperdown, 1797. [PU 3079]

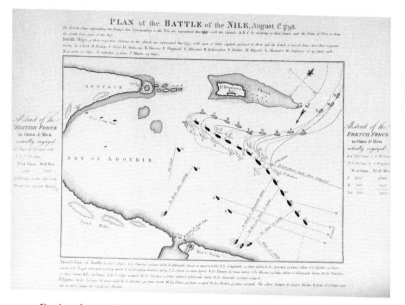

During the Battle of the Nile, the French were at anchor and thought themselves safe. One of Nelson's battleships went aground and acted as marker while his squadron doubled upon the French fleet and took or destroyed all but a handful. [PU 4026]

Lady Hamilton captured men's hearts through her 'Attitudes', flimsily dressed poses of classical heroines and goddesses. In this picture by Reynolds the artist seems to be aware of the rumour that she had given birth to twins and by etching in one more faintly than the other hints that the child died or was given away at birth. [PW 3633]

John Ross is best known as an explorer, but he was also a consummate seaman and a fighter. His clash in Cadiz Roads against a squadron of Spanish gunboats was so fierce and so successful that the Admiralty would not believe his report until a delegation of his men went to see the Port Admiral in Plymouth and tell the story themselves. In boarding one gunboat Ross was separated from his crew, but instead of surrendering he carried on and captured it single-handed, despite receiving many wounds. [PW5886]

One of the secrets of Nelson's success was taking his officers into his confidence and sharing with them his ideas. Before Trafalgar he called his captains on board *Victory* in two groups to explain his plan for dividing the enemy. Nelson never adopted the new-fashioned way of wearing the cocked hat fore and aft. [PU4500]

This plan of the Battle of Trafalgar was based on an original drawn up on board the frigate *Euryalus*, temporary flagship of Collingwood after the battle, and prison to the French Admiral Villeneuve. The straggling nature of the combined French and Spanish fleet helps explain the victory Nelson was able to obtain by concentrating his ships into two divisions. [PU 5715]

Daniel McLise, a popular Victorian painter, carefully researched all his pictures. Here for painterly effect he has transferred the death of Nelson to the upper deck but other details are historically correct and McLise has included two blacks and two women, who his research told him were part of the ship's company of HMS *Victory* at Trafalgar. [PAJ 3164]

The storm after the battle, by Clarkson Stanfield: after the battle the fleet was struck by a violent storm in which most of the prizes were lost and the damaged ships struggled to make Gibraltar. [D 2575]

The Battle of Trafalgar was not the end of war at sea: a few days afterwards
Sir Richard Strachan captured four escapers and brought them into Plymouth
Sound just a few hours after the despatches from Collingwood had arrived
announcing the victory itself, and the death of Nelson. [BHC0574]

Enemy codes or signal books were always great prizes. When the
USS *Chesapeake* was captured in 1813, the action was over so quickly
that the Americans had no time to sink this signal book, which had clearly
been prepared by stitching lead shot into its spine. In both the First and
Second World Wars the capture of German codebooks made a
decisive contribution to the tide of battle. [F3562]

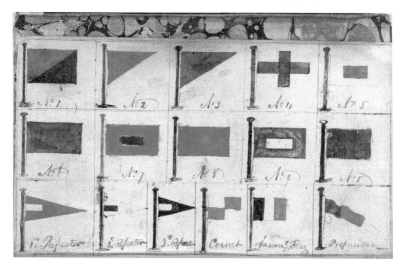

Contrary to popular belief, the Royal Navy highly prized steamships from their beginning. After George IV used the Post Office steamer *Lightning* on his state visit to Dublin, the navy soon took over all similar ships, initially using them as tugs for tactical manoeuvres and for carrying urgent despatches overseas. The *Lightning* survived, under various names, until 1888. [BHC0619]

Captain Frederick Marryat, better known as a novelist, was the first to use a steamship in action: the East India Company ship *Diana* in the Rangoon River in 1824. [B7870]

The nineteenth-century Arctic explorers were even hardier and more daring than their twentieth-century imitators like Scott and Shackleton. In the winters of 1829–1833 John Ross was shipwrecked in the Arctic, but by his force of personality and leadership he brought all his people back, bar one man who died of a pre-existing illness. After his ship *Victory* had been crushed in the ice he made an icehouse which he called 'Somerset House', then the home of the Navy Board in London. [PU6142]

Seamen and marines frequently fought ashore, and in the Russian War of 1854–56 they manned a considerable number of guns at the siege of Sebastopol: Diamond Battery was named by the men of HMS *Diamond* and commanded by Captain William Peel, who later won the Victoria Cross. [BHC0634]

and rockets and . . . planned an attack to begin in the morning following.

The plan was for the marines and seamen to carry the place by storm from the rear of the town, but

> whether they had dreaded this or no cannot be determined, but they surrendered the place that day – and we embarked 150 prisoners – all that remained in the fort . . . on the 10th we left Castro in charge of the spaniard and after embarking our marines, weighed and proceeded to Bilboa inlet, where we anchored off the village of Sanlucar.

There was another compliment for the navy, this time from Wellington, who wrote that 'Home Popham, with a few hundred marines and guerrillas of the north has succeeded in preventing [the French] from despatching anything to Marmont's assistance' and to Popham himself he wrote: 'congratulations upon the success of your operations . . . I trust you will not discontinue them'.

## BANDA NEIRA, 1810

In the years following Trafalgar, the British, through the agency of the Royal Navy, garnered colonies from France and from her allies. Cape Colony in South Africa and Curaçao in the West Indies were taken from the Dutch and Heligoland in the North Sea from the Danes, and Crete and the Ionian islands were annexed, as well as French possessions in the Indian Ocean, the West Indies, and North Atlantic. Frequently officers acted on their own initiative, though this was clearly exceeded when forces intended for India were diverted to capture Buenos Aires: euphoria in Britain at the news quickly turned sour when local forces rebelled and threw off both their former Spanish masters and the would-be British ones. On the other hand, Captain Cole's capture of Banda Neira, the last of the fabled Spice Islands, when he outwitted a far superior force, was very much approved of by the British government.

Captain Christopher Cole was an unusual officer, one of a handful of Welsh officers in the navy, and brother of a vice-chancellor of Oxford University. He was from a talented and numerous family: three older brothers were also in the navy, one joined the army and two entered the Church. Cole himself went to sea as a midshipman in 1780 and, aged twelve, soon saw action off Martinique and at the Battle of Chesapeake Bay. By 1810 he had many years of experience in the East Indies and commanded the 36-gun frigate *Caroline*. He sailed from Madras with a small squadron and a hundred or so European troops, and at Penang he was reinforced with twenty artillerymen and two field-pieces.

He had already formed his plan for taking Banda Neira, and commenced to train his people in using their hand weapons and scaling ladders. The voyage took two months, and his original plan of attack was to run in at daybreak for a frontal assault, but his ships, and boats, were spotted and fired on by a small battery on the evening of 8 August. His report belied his achievement: 'I have the honor and happiness of acquainting you with the capture of Banda Neira, the chief of the Spice Islands on the 9th Aug., by a portion of the force under my orders in consequence of a night attack, which completely surprised the enemy, although the approach of the ships had been avoidably discovered the day before'. Bad weather also disrupted his plans, and some of his marines and the larger part of the detachment of the regiment from Madras had been dispersed in the night, but this did not deter him: 'The attempt was now to be made with less than 200 men, consisting of the seamen and marines and about 40 of the Madras European regiment, or our labors in the boats through a dark and squally night, in the open sea, might have ended in the severest mortification . . .'

However, the weather now acted as excellent cover for his movements and 'the confidence I had in the handful of officers and men about me, left me no hesitation: and, with a degree [of] silence and firmness . . . the boats proceeded to the point of debarkation' where 'a dark cloud with rain covered our landing within a hundred yards of a battery of 10 guns; and . . . accompanied by thunder, lightning, and rain . . . the battery was taken in the rear'. With daylight, however, the alarm was raised and, heavily outnumbered, Cole's position became critical. He circled the town and raised his scaling ladders against Fort Belgica when his small party 'swept the ramparts like a whirlwind'. He now dominated the town and the sea batteries from the landward side and a well-placed shot into Fort Nassau, the last remaining fort, persuaded the Dutch governor to surrender. Meanwhile, the first lieutenant of the *Caroline* brought in the ships of the squadron, barely manned, drifting now on the morning breeze, and not knowing what to expect until he saw 'The day now beaming on the British flag' flying from Fort Belgica. Cole with less than two hundred men had taken a well-defended place mounting a hundred and twenty guns and defended by seven hundred regular, disciplined troops and over a thousand militia, several thousand miles from his base and many more again from Britain.

## CORFU, 1813

By the end of 1813 the Peninsular War was running in Britain's favour, the tide of the war in America was also in Britain's favour, and almost everywhere else British arms, or the arms of her allies, and, of course, the navy, were winning. In the Mediterranean there was unfinished work, in particular in the Adriatic. French or French-sponsored troops were active, the Greeks were in revolt against their Turkish rulers, and piracy was incipient. There Vice Admiral Sir Thomas Fremantle was sent to command a squadron of frigates. Fremantle was one more officer who had joined the navy at the outbreak of the American War of Independence. He had led the way into Toulon in 1793 and in the following year served under Nelson at the siege of Bastia. In 1797, while commanding the *Seahorse*, he took part in the attack on Santa Cruz, under Nelson, where he too was severely wounded. (The wounded Nelson refused to be taken on board the *Seahorse* lest he frighten Fremantle's wife by returning without news of her husband.) Later, Fremantle took part in the Battle of Copenhagen in 1801, commanding the *Ganges*, and was also at Trafalgar, in the *Neptune*. From 1810 onwards he served mostly in the Mediterranean, dying in Naples in 1819.

Captain Bridges Taylor of the 38-gun frigate *Apollo* was one of Fremantle's more active and successful officers on the station, and

even while away watering his ship, he left behind his boats, under
the command of Captain Garth of the *Cerberus*, to continue operations. Superlatives are normally absent from naval reports of the
period, but what happened next caused Taylor to write to Fremantle 'enclosing two letters from Captain Garth relating brilliant
exploits performed by two boats of the *Cerberus* under Lieut
William H Montague with the barge and first gig of the *Apollo*
under Lieut William H A Nares which I had left with him to assist
as the blockade during the absence of the *Apollo* to the Southward
watering'. The boats had already captured a ship which had run
herself aground beneath a Martello tower and for good measure
had captured the tower and removed its gun. Next they had no
hesitation in attacking a heavily defended convoy from Otranto to
Corfu. Midshipman Hutchinson, with just seven men in the gig,
captured a vessel mounting three guns and with a crew of forty
men, and Nares captured another gunboat and four merchant
ships.

Garth wrote glowingly of the bravery and good conduct of all
the men and officers, his only regrets being the loss of some men
and not capturing all the convoy:

> Notwithstanding this strong force aided by more Gun vessels
> from Faro, and the cliffs covered with French troops they were
> attacked in the most determined and gallant manner ... The
> gun vessels had each a twelve pounder in their boat and two
> four pounders ... with troops for Corfu, four of the convoy
> were also taken and had they been further from shore, I have
> no doubt but the greatest part of them would have been
> captured ...

It is a measure of how busy the navy was that although minor
operations of the Royal Navy 1803–1815 occupied half a volume,
250 pages, of Laird Clowes' seven-volume history of the navy, this
superlative boat action off Corfu was now commonplace and only
covered just half a page.

# THE ADRIATIC

Senior naval officers of the era frequently made both official and unofficial reports to their superiors. Official despatches were usually written by clerks and on receipt in London would be read to the assembled Board of Admiralty, when a secretary would write the reply, following the board's oral instructions. The private letters, often more revealing than the official ones, contained a wide range of general information, and the principals, in this case Fremantle and the First Lord of the Admiralty, might write their letters in their own hand. Fremantle remained in command of the Adriatic until 1814, and in a private letter to the First Lord of the Admiralty in parallel with his public despatch he wrote: 'I venture to trouble your Lordship with a letter to avoid the bulk of which a copy of my public dispatch to Sir Edw Pellew would occasion ... I anchored here (Fiume) with the *Milford Eagle* and *Havannah* on the 26 [August] at the same time [as] the Austrian troops marched into the town'. He had already taken this possibility into account: 'Your Lordship will have heard that I had, under the prospect of war being declared by Austria, taken all the places on their coast ... and destroyed all the cannon to open a communication on that coast ... [and am confident] ... of dispossessing the enemy of all the remaining ports in their country'. He also 'dispatched the *Eagle* to Zante and the *Havannah* to Sicily for troops and arms'.

Meanwhile the *Milford* was kept ready to re-embark General Nugent: should his 'posts be forced he may retreat upon Fiume under the protection of our guns, this enables him to employ the whole of his force, whilst a party of our marines do duty in the town ... The *Elizabeth* has a station off the Cabo d'Istria and I expect every day to hear of a communication being opened from there to ... one of the Austrian advanced posts'. General Nugent's force was quite small, less than two thousand men, but using Fremantle's ships he was able to outmanoeuvre the enemy: 'they have been successful in every attack that has been made upon them'. Just as in Spain, the regular troops were operating with guerrillas where 'All Istria has revolted and the peasants ... made prisoners [within] a few days the garrison of Pola amounting to

600'. And what was left of French ships were bottled up, without crews, and one ship on the stocks in the arsenal at Venice destined never to be finished.

Fremantle also negotiated on behalf of his government with the rebels, although his views of them and their shifting alliances were scathing.

> An envoy from the Bishop of Montenegro Came to me a few days ago, but very little dependence can be placed upon such a banditti as the Montenegrins, who begin with acquiring arms, money, provisions, and protection. I did not lend myself to the Bishops proposals on the plea of not being vested with sufficient powers, more especially as I was made acquainted that such a line of consideration would be most acceptable to the Austrian Government. Colonel Danese a native of Dalmatia has been furnished with letters from Gen[eral] Nugent and myself . . . to concert measures for raising that country against the common interest . . . Desertion from the enemy is very great, I calculate that 5000 Croats have joined the Austrians, some even in regiments with their officers, the number of prisoners amount to more than 1000 . . .

Fremantle had already served as a member of the Board of Admiralty as a captain, and was anxious to be in London again if there was to be a peace: 'I received three days ago their Lordships permission to return to England, and although I am very anxious to do so I shall consider it my duty to wait events, as my going away at present might have an influence while so good an understanding prevails'. Finally, having reread his letter and filled every margin, Fremantle found an unused area of paper and so wrote a postscript: 'I have sent to take possession of Pola, if it succeeds we shall have one of the finest posts in the Adriatic; it can be defended, will serve for an attack if found necessary, and will be the very best rendezvous for our ships during the Winter Months.'

Fremantle did go home, leaving Captain Charles Rowley in the 74-gun *Eagle* to command in the Adriatic. Rowley also wrote direct to Melville, the First Lord of the Admiralty, from an anchorage that was 'during the depth of winter, and what is reckoned the worst season of in the Adriatic [in] perfect safety'. There he was able to put into motion a plan of 'annihilating the maritime Trade of Venice, Trieste, and the Coast of Istria; as well as destroying the Italian Coasting Trade with the upper parts of the Adriatic'. He stationed men of war close inshore with flotillas of small boats able to cross the bars that lined the mouths of the rivers into the northern Adriatic and enter the canals which led to Venice, thus achieving 'the total impossibility of the Maritime Force of Venice becoming of any use whilst Ships are thus placed ... Men of War cannot come out of Venice but only Frigates may come out of the Port of Chiazza drawing fifteen feet'.

The campaign in the Adriatic was a minor one, and it was only possible because the navy was victorious elsewhere and ships and men could be spared, but the campaign also illustrated all the advantages and possibilities of sea power. Relatively junior officers acting under direct orders from London, but at the end of a long line of communication, used their initiative to prosecute the war according to the most general principles, making alliances and deploying resources as they thought best. The inherently flexible nature of sea power enabled a handful of ships and a few thousand men to hold down many more thousands of the enemy and to choose at will a point of attack where, temporarily, the enemy could be outnumbered and overwhelmed. Even when numerical superiority did not exist, the moral advantage the navy felt gave it the self-confidence to accept great odds – and to win.

## THE WAR OF 1812

One of the causes of renewed war with the United States of America was the impressment by the Royal Navy of seamen from American ships. What had started as a rebellion in the thirteen colonies in 1775 was by 1781 a general war involving Britain's traditional maritime enemies, the French, Spanish, and even the Dutch, and the inevitable consequence of this expansion was the need for a larger fleet and that meant more men. Keith, for example, while in command of the *Perseus* and in the Savannah River in May 1779, had authority to press seamen from merchant ships and indeed any others:

Whereas His Maj[esty's] Ships suffer at present for want of Seamen . . . which are absolutely necessary for the protection of the Inland Navigation as well as any efforts which may be required against the Rebels; You are to impress one man out Seven which may be found on board any vessel of Trade or privateer which may come into Port or be met with at Sea near her intended Port, taking care not to distress any Vessel so as to indanger the property of the King's subjects, neither are you to take any men out of transports, victuallers, or others employed in the Service . . . in port in these parts you are to apply to the Governor, or chief Civil Officer for permission and assistance, as also to the commander of the Troops, to take up and impress all idle Seamen . . . that maybe found Straggling ashore.

It was this kind of impressment which set the seed for later conflicts between Britain and the United States.

In the years after independence there was a large increase in American-flagged merchant ships, not least because as neutrals they could trade profitably where British and French ships could not. Estimates vary as to how many thousands of British seamen were drawn annually into the American merchant marine during the wars with France between 1793 and 1815, and likewise how many seamen, supposedly British, were impressed from American merchantmen by British warships. Identifying who was British and who was American was made more difficult by differing concepts of nationality. In American eyes, a man could become an American citizen by a simple act of declaring himself so, whereas under British law an individual always remained a subject of his King and could not forswear his nationality. The situation was open to abuse, and false certificates of identity as American citizens circulated widely; and in those days it was not easy to distinguish a man's nationality by his accent. Individual loyalties were not fixed and men swapped ships for better pay or prospects without regard to inconvenient flags, so desertion from British ships, whether by British seamen or wrongly impressed American seamen, was rife. Early in 1807, for example, while HMS *Chichester* was hove down at Gosport, Virginia, the desertion of five sailors and the recruitment of three Americans attracted little comment.

The desertion of five sailors, four British and one allegedly American, from the *Melampus*, however, had rather different consequences. She was part of a British squadron which was blockading the remains of a French squadron in Norfolk, Virginia, where they had been driven after a hurricane in the Atlantic. Norfolk was a neutral port which the British used as much as the French for water and provisions and recreation, and according to one story the men from the *Melampus*, who had now joined the USS *Chesapeake*, took advantage of their new status to insult drunkenly some British officers ashore, thus foolishly giving good intelligence of their whereabouts. Then, when the 50-gun *Leopard*, commanded by Captain Salusbury Humphreys, arrived from Halifax, Nova Scotia, with a list of deserters and orders from his commander-in-chief, Vice Admiral George Berkeley, to search for and recapture them, wherever they might be found, the *Chesapeake* was about to sail for the Barbary coast, passing through the British blockade.

The *Chesapeake* appears to have not been fully ready for sea, still less for action, and what happened next is told by James Atkins, Sergeant of Marines, one of the boarding party, in a letter to his uncle James Atkins, ironmonger at Windsor, dated 25 July 1807 from 'the far distant and much talked of shores of America':

As a rupture between England and America seems almost inevitable, and as I imagine that to you a knowledge of the first cause of such rupture might be not altogether unacceptable, I beg permission to state the following; being stationed off this coast, namely the entrance of Chesapeake River, blockading two French line of battle ships and one frigate belonging to that French Squadron of which we, under the command of Admiral Sir Richard Strachan, were so long in chase of when they, as well as ourselves, were separated in so dreadful a manner by that terrible hurricane on 19th August last, when we were not from them the distance of 10 leagues. Three of our ships, the *Bellicose* [*Belleisle*], *Bellona* and *Melampus*, made for this port, where they arrived in time to fall in with a part of the disabled enemy, one of whom, the *L'Impetueux*, they destroyed; the other two got safe into the place where they have ever since remained; we here patiently as possible wait for their coming out or a war with the Yankees when we will fetch them out . . .

It seems that Berkeley's orders to Humphreys were explicit:

In consequence of a positive information being given to Admiral Berkely [sic] at Halifax that the American frigate the *Chesapeake* had on board a number of English deserters in their service . . . H.M. Ship *Leopard* had orders, when the American sailed to overhaul her, to muster her ship's company and take the deserters, which order was fully executed by Captain Humphries on the 22nd . . .

The *Chesapeake* was simply not ready for action, and after several hails and some warning shots the *Leopard* fired three broadsides. After one shot to maintain her honour, the American surrendered. However, Humphries did not want a prize, only the men on his list 'according to the customs and usage of civilised nations on terms of peace and amity with each other'.

According to Barron he had no British deserters on board, but, Atkins wrote, 'We went on board, and the American officers presented their swords which, however, Britons refused to accept: we mustered the ship's company and found many English in their service but as our orders were only to secure the deserters, we in consequence secured only 4 belonging to the *Melampus*'. According to the historian James the men were one British deserter from the *Halifax* and three American-born deserters from the *Melampus*, including a black man. Twelve other British subjects were discovered in the *Chesapeake*'s crew, but they were not on Berkeley's list and therefore not taken.

Atkins was frank in his own views of the affair: 'we had the satisfaction of seeing the poor Yankee who the day before went past with flying standard as Commodore to Tripoli (up the straits) return past us again, skulking close into the shore like a dog with his tail burnt and with nothing appearing but his sides well hammered'. The immediate consequences were riots in Norfolk:

should a war between the two countries occur, is the first beginning of it to which I were an eye-witness; and if I do not survive to see the conclusion I have witnessed the beginning; and I think begin we shortly shall according to the Prato which Jefferson uses in his proclamations. We have been here the 9 months past and they have regularly supplied us with every necessary until this period and in consequence of the above mentioned affair, they have outlawed us and denied us everything. The Mobility on the shore of Norfolk have destroyed our water casks, plundered our merchant ships etc., all of which we bear with as much patience as Britons can do when such outrages are committed. I assure you we but very ill brook it; we only wait for an order when we will give Mr Yankee a receipt in full for their impudence and our casks destroyed. Our country expects our exertions to chastise such insults and she will have it. Such is the cowardice of them that they do not dare to come out; although they have two French 80 gun ships and 1 frigate of 44, 5 large American frigates and 11 gun-boats: our force is only 2 74's and 1 frigate . . . At the very moment I write this our tender has brought us news that our boat with two officers and three men has been seized and made prisoner by the American troops encamped here and that they have been sent to Norfolk . . .

Commodore Barron of the *Chesapeake* was tried by court martial and found guilty of not clearing for action, and suspended from duty for five years. Stephen Decatur accused him of cowardice, and when the two men met in a duel the American hero Decatur was killed. The meeting of the *Leopard* and *Chesapeake* was not, however, the cause of war. Rather, a weak American president, Jefferson, instituted what he called a commercial war, declaring an embargo preventing American goods from leaving American ports for the warring countries. The American squadron in the Mediterranean, which Barron was going to command, was recalled, and Jefferson adopted a policy of maintaining small craft only in American waters. The British government disavowed Berkeley's orders and recalled him, while insisting upon the right of impressment, and, noting that measures were being taken equally against Britain and France, lifted the naval blockade. However, the French grew increasingly antipathetic and seized American shipping in French ports, arguing that if they were Americans they should have been at home and so therefore they must be disguised British merchant ships. Then just as the Americans grew bellicose and the British, with victory at sea in the long war against France in sight, grew less ready to appeal to the sword, Commodore John Rodgers in the American frigate *President* attacked the British sloop *Little Belt*. The exasperated British government chose to regard this as tit for tat in the *Leopard* affair and took no action.

Before the Great War most trade had been in British ships, but during the war the American merchant fleet had multiplied as the Americans profited from their neutral status and traded with both sides. There was trade in seamen too, and both Britain and France accused the Americans of harbouring deserters. If anything, Napoleon's closure of Continental ports hurt the Americans rather more than British orders, but American politicians confused several issues. So, overcoming ties of kinship between the two English-speaking peoples, in June 1812 President Madison declared war on Britain.

For British officers there could be no doubt as to the final result, but there were some surprises in store, not least that the American frigates were better and more heavily armed than their British counterparts. There were some inconclusive chases and actions and then, in August 1812, the American Captain Isaac Hull in the 44-gun *Constitution* met the 38-gun *Guerriere*, Captain James Dacres. Even when she was captured in 1806, *Guerriere* was said to be in a deplorable state: certainly in 1812 her masts were rotten and she was undermanned. Dacres however had little choice but to give battle, and he was comprehensively outsailed and outgunned by Hull's *Constitution*. American joy at this victory and British shock were both exaggerated, but the shock was sufficient to cause the elderly former First Lord of the Admiralty, Lord Barham, to write to his friend's son and ultimately his successor in office, Robert Dundas, 2nd Viscount Melville, who replied:

We are indeed unaccustomed to discomfiture at sea, & I regret the late capture of the *Guerriere* much less on account of the mere loss of the ship, than from its shaking our confidence in the superiority of our largest Frigates over any other Frigates whatever, even the strong American vessels of that description. Sir John Warren [who had been sent to command a new combined North American station] has with him the *San Domingo* & *Poitiers* of 74 guns, the *Africa* of 64, and ten of our largest Frigates all on the Halifax station; he also carried out with him authority to take the *Dragon* of 74 from the Leeward

Islands, which we have replaced by a 50 gun ship. Sir John Duckworth has also his 50-gun ship & three of our largest class of Frigates at Newfoundland; so that the American Coast is not quite safe to American cruisers. We must keep them under, let our exertions be ever so great or inconvenient to us in other respects ... With such a force, which must be increased if necessary, our Frigates might certainly cruise in pairs ...

## THE USS *CHESAPEAKE* AND HMS *SHANNON*

After a series of defeats, British self-esteem was restored when Captain Philip Broke of the 38-gun *Shannon* met Captain James Lawrence of the similar sized USS *Chesapeake* in June 1813. Broke had been in command since 1806, with a crew he had kept together and trained in gunnery – and he had a passion for gunnery. The *Chesapeake* sailed from Boston flying a banner which read 'Free Trade and Sailors' Rights', but when she met the *Shannon* in the entrance, the fight was over in a few minutes. Such was the ferocity of the broadside and boarding, however, that *Chesapeake* suffered more casualties than *Victory* did at Trafalgar in several hours of fighting, and for the watchers on the shore, she disappeared from American possession in what seemed a single roll of thunder.

## HILLYAR'S ANXIOUS SEARCH

By 1813 the blockade of the Americans' coast was so tight that their frigates could rarely put to sea. An exception was Captain David Porter in the 32-gun *Essex*, who had escaped from the east coast in October 1812 and sailed to the Pacific, where he broke up the British whaling trade, capturing several hundred tons of shipping and scores of men. With the Spanish colonies officially neutral in the war between the USA and Britain, Porter was able to use Valparaiso as a base, but in February 1814 he was found by Captain James Hillyar in the 36-gun frigate *Phoebe*, with the 18-gun ship sloop *Cherub*. Hillyar had had secret orders to take members of the North-West Company to the Columbia River where he would meet a force of Canadians, and together they would wipe out any American settlements on the Pacific coast. The orders were typical of the period, giving wide powers of discretion to Hillyar and much latitude in interpreting what he had to do and how. Only after delivering the partners of the North-West Company safely to their destination would he be free to hunt for the *Essex*:

> ... take under your especial charge the ship *Isaac Todd*, and proceeding round Cape Horn make the best of your way to the River Columbia, on the North West Coast of America, where you may expect to meet a force dispatched from Canada across the Country of about 100 men of the North West Company who is instructed to be on that coast in May and remain there until the month of August.
>
> The principal object of the service on which you are employed is to protect and render whatever assistance is in your power to the British Traders from Canada and to destroy and if possible totally annihilate any settlements which the Americans may have formed either in the Columbia River or on the neighbouring coasts . . .
>
> After your arrival on the North West Coast, you are to continue for two months on this service; or for longer period if the state of your Provisions will allow, and the object of your mission shall seem to require your doing so, but when you leave the Coast you will take care to clear it if possible of all the Enemys force, and so place the British Settlements in the most respectable situation that your means will allow.
>
> On so distant and particular a service as this is likely to be, the strictest attention to the health, comfort and good . . . of your ships company will be in a peculiar degree necessary, and we rely [on] your zeal and prudence in using every occasion to promote these objects. We also most strictly enjoin you to take especial care in any intercourse which you may have with the native inhabitants . . .

Once he was free of his duties on the Columbia River, Hillyar started his search of the vast ocean, and 'after nearly five months' anxious search and six weeks' blockade', brought the *Essex* to action. Later Porter accused Hillyar of a breach of neutrality, though as one of the informants makes clear, Porter was not above breaching

Spanish neutrality by mounting an operation against Hillyar's ships. In fact both sides received assistance from the shore and both should have respected the neutrality of the place. On 15 March 1814, Andrew Blest, one of Hillyar's informants, wrote: 'We have been informed that the boats of the *Essex* to the number of ten full of men well armed proceeded out of Harbour on Saturday night. It is said that their intention was to board the *Cherub* at anchor. A canoe the owner of which is friendly to us passed thro them near the Playa anchorage ... The Governor expressed his surprise and indignation at hearing of it declaring that they should not pass the fort by night ...'

Meanwhile Porter's preparations for sea did not go unnoticed, and Hillyar was getting frequent reports: 'Last night the American Frigate made some movements which I think were to see if we made any signals ... I think it impossible for her to get off unseen. Capt Porter was on the hill yesterday and at the 4 Gun Battery continually. This morning he has also been looking out. From this anxiety and from what I can hear of his paying off all his accounts, I am inclined to think he certainly will attempt to put to Sea very shortly ... I will not fail to communicate to you everything that may occur. Be on your guard early in the Mornings ...'

Hillyar had with him the 18-gun *Cherub*, and Porter had a prize which he had commissioned as the *Essex Junior*. *Phoebe* was a crack ship whose company had been together with Hillyar some years, and though she sailed worse than the *Essex*, she was armed with long 18pdrs, which outranged the *Essex*'s 32pdr carronades. On 28 March *Essex* parted her cables in a southerly wind and making sail tried to pass to windward of *Phoebe* and weather the southern tip of the harbour, but as the wind freshened at the point, her main topmast broke. The *Essex* anchored close to a Chilean battery to make repairs while the *Phoebe* started a long-range bombardment. In two hours the *Essex* surrendered: she survived the voyage to England and was taken into the Royal Navy under the same name, though never fitted for sea.

The last American warship to be captured, appropriately since she had anticipated the war by attacking the *Little Belt*, was the *President* in January 1815, which ran into a squadron commanded by John Hayes, one of the best seamen in the navy. She was badly damaged first by stranding and then by gunfire after a day-long chase, but the Royal Navy so admired her that they took her apart and built a replica, and the name *President* survived in the Royal Navy until modern times. When tension between the two countries arose again in the 1830s, the British sent a clear message to the Americans by sending HMS *President* to North America wearing the flag of Admiral Sir George Cockburn, the man who had burned Washington.

The War of 1812 was a one-sided affair. The United States Navy had less than a dozen warships, of which the *President* was the largest and most beautiful, rated as a frigate but pierced for fifty-four broadside guns, while the Royal Navy had 600 warships and its officers and men were hardened and experienced by twenty years of nearly continuous warfare. On the balance sheet, the Americans took seventeen British warships (including two taken by privateers), while the British captured fifteen American warships and many more privateers, and by the war's end, the coasts of the Chesapeake and Delaware were blockaded by the Royal Navy and American trade had collapsed. The Royal Navy took 1,400 prizes, and British and Canadian privateers hundreds more, while American privateers took 1,350 British merchantmen and warships a further 240, but of these at least 750 were retaken and less than a third made it back to American ports. Only New York and New England were kept open – by the British – so that grain could be supplied to Wellington's armies in Europe. Those American ships which were not already at sea were bottled up in their ports, and a British admiral had led the forces which burned Washington, giving rise, after its hurried repainting, to the name White House. When the USA realized that Canada could not be captured 'just by marching', and a British counter-invasion across Lake Champlain was defeated, it was clear that this was a war which neither side could win.

## JOSIAH TATNALL

The wars between Britain and the United States between 1775 and 1815 and the tension between these two English-speaking countries did indeed have the character of a civil war, as can be illustrated through the life of Josiah Tatnall. Josiah was born in 1795 in Georgia, where the family had been settled since the seventeenth century. The Tatnall family was largely loyalist during the American revolution and kept up links with family in England. In the War of Independence, Josiah's grandfather, like some others, returned to England but refused to serve the British crown while there was a possibility that he might be asked to do so against his fellow North Americans. Josiah's father was a revolutionary who in 1801 was elected Governor of Georgia, and when he died Josiah was sent to his grandfather, and he was educated in England between 1805 and 1811. However, returning to America in a convoy under British protection in 1811 Josiah was appointed midshipman in the American navy and was sent to the USS *Constellation*.

As late as 1813, the ease with which Rear Admiral George Cockburn and a few hundred seamen and marines had gained control of Chesapeake Bay suggested that the opposition was not highly motivated: indeed, Cockburn reported that parts of the population were 'anxious to show assistance'. However when Vice Admiral Sir John Borlase Warren arrived with reinforcements and determined on taking Portsmouth Navy Yard, where the *Constellation* had been blockaded, this 'was not pushed home with the resolution ordinarily displayed by the British Navy'. *Constellation*'s seamen and marines were manning the batteries at Craney Island, and when the attacking British boats grounded in shallow water nearly a hundred British seamen and marines were killed, drowned, wounded, or imprisoned. The largest boat was known, from the number of her oars, as the *Centipede*, and it was Midshipman Tatnall who waded out with some of the crew of the *Constellation* to take prisoners and capture this prestigious prize.

Tatnall had a distinguished career in both the United States Navy and in the Confederate States Navy. In 1831 and again in 1832 he was congratulated by British merchants in the West Indies for services rendered to British shipping. During the Mexican War, in 1846, Tatnall in the USS *Spitfire* commanded the so-called mosquito fleet at the bombardment of Santa Cruz.

In 1857 he was flag-officer of the American East India Squadron and a frequent visitor to the new British colony of Hong Kong. On a diplomatic mission to Beijing in 1859 he chartered a British steamer, the *Toey-wan*, because his own ship the *Powhatan* drew too much water to allow him into the Pei Ho River. Subsequently the *Toey-wan* herself had to be towed off a sandbank, where the falling tide threatened to capsize her, by the British Rear Admiral James Hope. Hope was about to use more forceful means to pass the forts at the entrance to the Pei Ho. In the course of a confused and, for the British, disastrous battle in which they lost many men, Tatnall 'in view of the aid [which Hope] had tendered [him] the day before' used the *Toey-wan* to tow Hope's reserves into the fight. While doing so the Chinese sank Tatnall's barge, stranding the crew on board the British flagship, where they volunteered to serve the British guns. Tatnall had to remind his men that they were neutrals, but seeing what had happened he added that blood was thicker than water. His remark resonated, and *Blackwood's Magazine* reported that 'Gallant Americans! You and your Admiral did more that day to bind England and the United States together than all your lawyers and pettifogging politicians have ever done to part us . . .' The theme was taken up when British merchants at Honolulu wrote to Tatnall in 1860 that we were 'united in blood, civilisation and commerce'.

Tatnall is also known for his command of the CSS *Virginia*, after her fight with the USS *Monitor*. *Virginia* was reconstructed from the burnt-out hulk of the USS *Merrimac*, which the retreating federal forces had tried to destroy: the Confederates had turned her into a formidable armoured fighting ship but when the Union army began to advance again, Tatnall blew her up rather than let her fall into enemy hands.

After the American Civil War, Tatnall lived in exile in Nova Scotia between 1866 and 1870 before being partly rehabilitated and allowed to return to die in Savannah. So Tatnall's family had the distinction of having the same property confiscated and restored twice: by the British authorities in the American revolution for refusing to take arms in defence of the state of Georgia against the rebels, and in the American Civil War for refusing to take arms against the state of Georgia in support of the federal government. Tatnall lived his last years in some poverty, though when British officers learned this, they raised a subscription for him, remembering that blood is thicker than water. Out of this kind of episode grew a special relationship between the two navies.

## THE HUNT FOR NAPOLEON

The navy, which at its height during the Great War comprised more than 150,000 seamen and marines, was being rapidly paid off when Napoleon escaped in February 1815 from Elba and returned to France. In the rearmament which followed, many ships did not get to their distant stations before Napoleon had again been defeated, on 18 June 1815 at Waterloo by the British, Prussian, and allied armies. Napoleon fled Paris in July, apparently hoping to find a ship to take him to the United States, but he could not evade the British cruisers which so closely blockaded the ports of France. The ships on blockade duty off the French coast now began to hunt for Napoleon, and even in London Melville was well informed, for instance receiving a note via Jersey from an agent that 'Bonaparte will imbark on board one of the frigates at Brest . . . his effects have already passed [on the road] and that the Troops on the Coast are kept ready to protect him on his journey from the Royalists'.

In fact the royalists closed the road and Napoleon was forced to divert further south where, on 15 July, he surrendered to Captain Frederick Maitland of HMS *Bellerophon*. In 1814 he had refused to surrender to the British because 'their policy centres on the destruction of my fleet'. Now, appropriately, he surrendered in the Basque Roads, which the navy had spent so much effort and so many lives so assiduously blockading.

Napoleon was taken to Torbay and from there, on 8 August, Admiral Sir George Cockburn, in the *Northumberland*, took him to St Helena. The long war was almost over. Under the terms of the treaty many possessions were returned to France and the navy helped royalist Frenchmen to take back some colonies governed by republicans. One of these was Durand Linois, who as an admiral had been comprehensively bested by the navy on so many occasions; now as a count he was Governor of Guadaloupe, where, whatever his other qualities, he remained a staunch pro-Bonapartist. In the last operation of the hundreds which had been conducted over the previous quarter of a century of war on a global scale, the navy carried troops there and on 10 August 1815 the French surrendered.

## WAR'S END

The Treaty of Paris of 1815 was very favourable to France: generous politicians thought that a good settlement for royalist France was the price of a permanent peace after a quarter of a century of exhausting world war. France got back all her overseas possessions except Tobago, St Lucia, Mauritius, and the Seychelles. Britain's gain, however, was enormous. The French revolution and its excesses, and the fear of the spread of revolution, were largely over: France herself was exhausted and her traditional enmity of Britain was suspended, at least for the time being. So too was the danger of a single monarchy in Europe and there was no longer a risk that the rest of the world, even the United States, would become a breakfast for Bonaparte.

George Canning, the British Prime Minister, was content that the US President, Monroe, should steal his idea that the old imperial powers should be excluded from the New World. Indeed, it was the Royal Navy, not the US Navy, which policed the Monroe Doctrine in its early years, for Britain was undisputedly the one world power, and her navy was supreme. The actual forces deployed for much of the nineteenth century when Britannia ruled the waves were surprisingly small and inexpensive, though there was always a powerful reserve fleet at home which could occasionally be used to remind the world of what was possible for Britain and her allies, or impossible for her enemies.

Without the victory of sea power, little of this would have been possible.

# Chapter Nine

# The Long Peace

The period 1815 to 1914 is sometimes known as the long peace, though if this gives the impression that nothing happened, as far as the Royal Navy is concerned little could be further from the truth. Under the Pax Britannica, free trade between nations prospered; slavery and piracy were suppressed; the Monroe Doctrine which protected the Americas was pronounced in Washington but effectively policed by the Royal Navy; the new republics of South and Central America developed without the interference of European powers and independence from Spain was brought about by British naval officers, chief amongst them Thomas Cochrane; Greek independence from the Ottoman Empire was assured by Codrington's victory at Navarino; the Royal Navy helped to create modern Italy by securing Garibaldi's passage of the straits of Messina in 1860; and the coasts and seas of the world were charted and the knowledge gained freely shared with all. Meanwhile the British Empire grew to encompass one-fifth of the world. And while the long peace was punctuated by several small wars and two years of bloody war involving the great powers of Europe, there were revolutions in technology and in personnel affairs in the navy itself.

So the Royal Navy enjoyed a century of supremacy at sea which made Britain a world power, and for long periods the only world power – a position similar to that which the US Navy enjoys in the twenty-first century. There were brief challenges at sea from France, but few others until the emergence of the German navy. Britain was able to avoid involvement on the European continent yet act as a mediator in many crises, and, as overseas trade grew, an empire developed too. Yet despite becoming global trader, missionary and advocate of democracy, British use of sea power was largely altruistic.

## ALGIERS, 1816

However, there was unfinished business for the Royal Navy in North Africa. For centuries Barbary pirates based in Algiers, Tripoli, and Tunis had plagued European shipping in the Mediterranean and ranged as far north as Britain to capture slaves. The Barbary pirates had learned to avoid British ships, but they levied ransoms on other countries' flags, including merchant ships from the United States of America. In one disgraceful incident in 1800 the Dey of Algiers was able to insist not only on the payment of tribute but that William Bainbridge in the American frigate *George Washington* should wear the flag of Algiers to carry the Sultan's tribute across the Mediterranean to Constantinople. The inevitable consequence was a short series of American operations between 1801 and 1805, not wholly successful as far as American arms were concerned. Beginning as they did during the Peace of Amiens and a temporary rundown of the Royal Navy, the Americans were able to recruit a number of British seamen to help man their ships, through a Scottish agent in New York. Once in the Mediterranean they also needed to use British bases to replenish their ships, which lasted until Edward Preble was detected recruiting more British seamen and was forced to leave Gibraltar for a base at Syracuse. Eventually the USA won a treaty which did not require further annual instalments, but paid a ransom for the release of white American slaves.

When the wars in Europe resumed after the Peace of Amiens, so too did the depredations of the Barbary pirates. St Vincent and Nelson tried to check them and the Americans tried again in early 1816. With the war over, however, it was time to settle some scores, and an Anglo-Dutch fleet rendezvoused at Gibraltar in August 1816 under the command of Admiral Lord Exmouth, the former Edward Pellew. After his service as Commander-in-Chief, East Indies, he was promoted vice admiral and held the North Sea command from 1810 until 1811, and then was appointed to the Mediterranean with the *Caledonia* as his flagship. Returning to the Mediterranean, he was ordered to suppress the Moorish pirates and to enforce terms on the Dey of Algiers, who refused to comply.

Colour Sergeant Robert Griffin, who served in the Royal Marines from 1805 to 1828, and who had already witnessed the surrender of Bonaparte, was present at the bombardment of Algiers when Pellew decided to coerce the Dey into compliance. Griffin describes what happened:

> On the 27 of August we came to an Anchor off Algiers with the following ships under the Command of Lord Exmouth & Admiral Milne. The *Queen Charlotte* 110 Guns the *Impregnable* 90 *Minden Albion* & *Superb* 74 Guns each. The *Leander* 50 *Severn* 40 *Glasgow* 40 *Hebrus* 36 *Granicus* 36 & 6 Dutch Frigates The *Prometheus* 20 Bombs the *Infernal Fury Beelzebub* and *Hecla* – Brigs the *Britomart, Mutine, Cordelia, Heron, Jaspar* & *Express* 5 Gun Boats, 2 Cutters, 1 Schooner, 3 Transports. We sent in a Flag of Truce which the Enemy refused & at ½ past 2 they fired one gun at the *Superb* which was instantly returned by the *Queen Charlotte's* Broadside when a most Tremendous Fire commenced on both sides which lasted ten hours without ceasing a moment.
>
> We destroyed most of their Batteries and did Great Damage to the Town. Burnt 9 Frigates & Corvettes & 35 smaller vessels with great quantities of Stores of all descriptions. We then warped out of the reach of their guns to repair our damages & prepare to attack them again the next day – but they sent a Flag of Truce & made peace on our own Terms – They are never more to make Slaves of the Christians of any Nation & to give up all the Slaves in the Country and to give us all the Money they have received for Slaves during the present year and to make good to the Consul the losses he sustained by Imprisonment . . . and the Dey has asked his pardon before our Officers & his own Ministers. They had about 10000 Men Killed & Wounded. We had about 800. They had 3 times the Number of Guns we had . . .

Over a thousand Christian prisoners were freed, an indemnity of half a million dollars was paid, and the Dey finally agreed to end slave-taking. It was not quite the end, for two Tunisian pirates captured a German ship in the North Sea in 1817, but it was the beginning of the end. Many thought that Algiers should be annexed, but this was left to the French to accomplish two decades later. For his achievement at Algiers Pellew was elevated to a viscount: in the late twentieth century the Royal Navy named two ships of the same class after him, the Type 14 frigates *Pellew* and *Exmouth*.


## THE NAVY IN THE MEDITERRANEAN

British policy in the Mediterranean in the nineteenth century was governed by the slow collapse of the Ottoman Empire, which stretched from the Danube, southwards over the Balkans and Greece to Asia Minor, Egypt, and westwards along the coast of North Africa to the Atlantic. Britain's position in the so-called 'Eastern Question' was complex, acknowledging the virtual independence of some parts of the Ottoman Empire, while supporting Turkey against Russian advances and in her control of the Dardanelles, thus preventing the Russian Black Sea Fleet from entering the Mediterranean. The dichotomy in this policy changed only with the opening of the Suez Canal (1876) and the occupation of Cyprus (1878) and Egypt (1882).


### NAVARINO, 1827

By the 1820s the independence of the Greeks, who had revolted against the Turks, was a liberal cause in Europe. The poet Byron (grandson of 'Foul Weather Jack') and Thomas Cochrane (again!) were freelances in an insurrection which the Turks tried to put down bloodily. In 1827 Britain, France, and Russia attempted to impose a truce on both parties. Despite an armistice the Turks, under an Egyptian general and advised by French officers, sailed to burn villages in southern Greece and to attack a Greek force led by Cochrane. The Turkish fleet was anchored in a strong defensive arc when an allied fleet under Admiral Sir Edward Codrington sailed into the Bay of Navarino. Codrington's orders from his government were unclear, but he was prepared to use force to impose an armistice, and warned the Turks that if fired on he would reply.

Codrington stood in the long line of succession of naval officers:

he had entered the navy in 1783 and was Admiral Howe's flag lieutenant in the *Queen Charlotte* at the Glorious First of June in 1794. Strangely he was unemployed from 1797 until 1805, but he was brought back in time to command the *Orion* at Trafalgar and from 1808 onwards he commanded the *Blake* for six years, in the Mediterranean, during the unsuccessful Walcheren expedition of 1809, and off the coast of Spain during the Peninsular War. Next he commanded *Forth* and *Havannah* during the War of 1812, supplying the marines and the army when they captured and burned Washington. In 1826 he hoisted his flag in *Asia* as Commander-in-Chief, Mediterranean Fleet. At first his fleet was employed in the suppression of piracy in the Levant, but then he was expected to take a leading part in the interpretation of allied policy in the Greek war of independence, culminating in the Battle of Navarino in 1827.

Navarino was last fleet action fought only under sail. Codrington's fleet sailed into the landlocked bay and anchored in silence, Codrington opposite the Turkish flagship, a French squadron ahead and a Russian astern. Then when a boat from the frigate *Dartmouth* went to order some Turkish fireships to move away it was greeted by musketry and soon fire became general. The Turks did not understand the concept of force majeure, and, whereas a fight between European ships might have ended in honourable defeat, the Turks fought until the bitter end: whereas at Trafalgar Codrington's *Orion* had suffered 1 killed and 23 wounded, at Navarino *Asia* suffered 172 killed and 481 wounded. Codrington, however, emerged victorious and was showered with honours and gifts from England, France, Russia and Greece, whose struggle for independence was the main beneficiary of the battle. The battle also secured Codrington's fame, but politicians at home were pusillanimous and he was temporarily disgraced.

A letter from Lieutenant Alexander Anderson of the Royal Marines, in *Albion*, describes the battle:

[I am] alive and in perfect health. On Saturday 20th (the morning before the Anniversary of Trafalgar) about ½ past two o'clock we entered Navarin ... for the purpose of desiring the Egyptians to return home and in case they refused to do so we

intended using more forcible means than words but before we
could make our errand known to Ibraham Pasha ... [there]
commenced a general action which lasted till 6 o'clock. The
*Albion* was very dangerously but at the same time very nobly
situated being open to the fire of two lines of Battle Ships and
two Frigates neither of which were out of Musket shot one of
the Frigates had her jib-boom over our quarter but she did not
remain there long before we boarded and carried her she caught
fire alongside and we had some difficulty in cutting her adrift
before she blew up as it was two or three of our men were
blown up in her, after this we very soon silenced one of the line
of Battle Ships the other line of Battle Ships and the Frigate
kept up a fire till the last though they were so cut to pieces that
they could only fire now and then. We lost our Capt. of
Marines in the beginning of the Action. We have 10 Killed and
51 wounded. In the English Squadron there are 3 Capt. of
Marines and one Lt. Killed a number of Midshipmen one Lieut.
of the Navy and one Captain the number of men I do not
know but I believe the other line of battle ships have suffered as
great loss as ourselves ...

It was a hard-won victory, as Anderson tells us:

On Saturday night we all remained at our quarters ready to
renew the fight at daybreak, but as soon as day appeared we
found the line of battle ships had hoisted the English Colours
and the frigate had blown up. Vessels were blowing up all night
and all the next day, about 10 o'clock Captain Campbell ...
Lt. Botter [Boteler], Lt. Hurdle and myself with a few Marines
boarded the line of battle ship and took the swords of the two
principal Officers and made prisoners of them and the remainder of the officers this ship was in a horrible state, she had
hardly one nail above another. We cut her adrift and allowed
her to drive on shore – about 2 o'clock I went away in one of
the boats Commanded by a Lieut. for the purpose of cutting
adrift some fire vessels ...

Anderson nevertheless was ready for more action:

the boats assembled round the Flag ship and waited above an
hour for orders when to our no small annoyance the Admiral

came to the gangway and said we were to return to our ships and wait till night. When he burnt a blue light we were to assemble round his ship again, but as he did not burn one we did not go. However I do not think that it is all over yet for I dare say the batteries will have a slap at us as we go out . . .

The allies exchanged compliments:

Our Admiral sent a letter of thanks to the Russian and French Admirals, directly the Russian Admiral received it he read it and then said whatever honours he might receive hereafter from his Sovereign he would give this letter the preference. After the Action the French Admiral asked . . . who commanded this ship, The 'Albion', [and] when he was told, he said she fought as if she were manned by Devils . . .

The direct results of the battle were the independence of Greece in 1829, the invasion of Algeria by the French in 1830, and the declaration of independence by Egypt in 1841, which events led to the next phase of war in the Mediterranean.

## THE BOMBARDMENT OF ACRE, 1840

When Egypt revolted against Turkey and invaded Syria, Turkey turned in despair to Russia for help to suppress the rebellion. Britain and France did not like this extension of Russian influence, so the kaleidoscope of alliances changed a third time and Britain led a coalition consisting of Austria and a reluctant France in support of Turkey. A strong British fleet was sent under the command of Admiral Sir Robert Stopford to the eastern Mediterranean. Stopford was something of a politician who served sixty years in the navy but somehow missed most of the major engagements of the Great War, and who, when he was appointed Commander-in-Chief, Mediterranean Fleet, had spent the previous seven years ashore on half-pay. His deputy was Sir Charles Napier, or 'Black Charlie'. Napier had had a rather different war: he had been at the taking of *Marengo* and *Belle Poule*, and the burning of Washington. He used the peace to take service in the Portuguese navy but having overlooked the formality of asking permission to enter a foreign navy was struck from the Navy List. He was restored in time to be given command of *Powerful* and appointed second-in-command of the Mediterranean Fleet. Napier was a strong advocate of steam, and perhaps it was no coincidence that when the fleet was sent on the Syrian campaign it was assisted by steam-driven paddle ships.

The campaign turned upon the siege of Acre, a fortress which when manned by Sidney Smith had defied even Bonaparte. Stopford worked his ships inside the shoals of the harbour and under the guns of the fortress, and after three hours' bombardment the magazine blew up with a dreadful roar.

To Lieutenant Frederick Kerr, writing to his brother Lord Henry Kerr in October 1840 on board the paddle ship *Gorgon*, 'The place seems very strong, with about eighty guns to seaward'. *Gorgon* was a major development in the design and construction of steam warships. She was built with teak frames imported from India, she had the most powerful engines yet fitted in a warship, with additional bunkers for coal which for the first time were outboard of the engines thus giving more protection, she was bark-rigged and a good sailer, and could carry 1,600 troops as well as a heavy, mixed armament. For a brief spell, until a sister ship *Cyclops* was built, *Gorgon* was next in size only to Brunel's *Great Western*. Many designs were based on the *Gorgon*, and she was not broken up until 1864.

Notwithstanding the strength of Acre,

On the 31st. we were sent with three more steamers to Acre, taking about 1,000 Turkish troops. We arrived off that place the same night, and the following morning stood in-shore and fired our 10-inch guns with shell into the town, keeping at a considerable distance for fear of getting a shot in our machinery or boilers. However, the fire was returned, and their first shell burst just beyond us ... We fired away for about three hours, and then paddled out. In the afternoon we returned and not knowing our distance exactly, got well within range of their guns, which was against our orders, which were to keep out of range. This time their fire was more extensive, and the shot whistled about us in style, some passing close over the paddle-

box, others between the funnel and mainmast, but as luck
would have it, none touched. I felt myself give an involuntary
bob when the sound of the shot came very close . . . This
evening the fleet hove in sight, and anchored about sunset under
Mount Carmel. There were seven English line-of-battleships,
with Sir Robert Stopford's flag and Commodore Napier's broad
pendant flying on board the *Princess Charlotte* and *Powerful*,
and five frigates and sloops. The Austrian squadron consisted of
two frigates and a corvette, and the Turkish of one line-of-
battleship, with the flag of Admiral Walker, who is a Captain in
our service, and a very fine fellow indeed.

The steamers could be used as gunboats or tugs:

The plan of attack was all arranged, and the steamers were to
tow the ships in if there was no wind. However, there was a
little on the 3rd and the ships weighed about 9 o'clock, the
steamers throwing shell into the town, as usual. The Admiral
went on board his son's steamer, the *Phoenix*, to be able to see
and direct manoeuvres better. They did not return the steamers'
fire. The ships bore down about 1 o'clock and firing commenced about half-past two from the forts and ships with great
vigour, about three all the ships were engaged and keeping up a
tremendous fire, steamers firing between the ships just within
range. This continued till about four, when a most tremendous
explosion took place in the town, evidently caused by one of
our shells going into a magazine. It was the most awfully grand
sight I ever saw, equal for the time, I should say, to any eruption
of Vesuvius. Immense stones came tumbling down upward of a
minute after it occurred, and an immense cloud of earth and
dust, about four or five hundred feet high, moved slowly with
the breeze, completely hiding the ships as it passed them . . .
The wall looked like a large bit of plum pudding with the plums
picked out . . . There were a great many Frenchmen in the case,
they say, encouraging the garrison to hold out to the last, but
nothing could withstand the fire of the British ships.

The French had not been wholehearted allies and, Kerr wrote,
'will be very much annoyed at our success, as letters have been

found in the Citadel dated 27th September, urging them to hold out, and not to think so much of English prowess.'

Another witness to the bombardment of Acre was John Blackmore, whose uncle, Captain Wilmot of the *Alliance*, had been killed while mounting a gun in a breach at the previous siege in 1799. In the Great War the Royal Navy's gunners had specialized in short-range bombardment and great rate of fire, and Blackmore's diary shows that nothing of that skill had been lost, testifying that that the British could fire a broadside of three rounds in fifty seconds. According to Blackmore, when the magazine blew up 'The noise was like thunder [and] our ship felt as if there had been an earthquake'.

The earthquake was felt worldwide, for as the Prime Minster, Palmerston, remarked, the bombardment of Acre was

> an event of immense political importance as regards the interests of England not only in connection with the Turkish Question, but in relation to every other question which we may have to discuss with other powers. Every country that has towns within cannon shot of deep water will remember the operations of the British Fleet on the Coast of Syria in . . . 1840, whenever such country has any differences with us . . .

## FIRST FOR STEAM

Captain Frederick Marryat's claim to fame is as an author who wrote sea stories and historical novels for children in the first half of the nineteenth century. However, he entered the navy in 1806 and served under the fabulous Lord Cochrane, and, as a midshipman in *Impérieuse*, took part in Cochrane's attack in the Basque Roads in 1809. So when in his sea stories he took Cochrane for his model, he was able to draw on his own, intimate knowledge of the navy and his personal observations of the great hero, anticipating C. S. Forester and Patrick O'Brian by more than a century. When he was elected a fellow of the Royal Society in 1819 for his work on improving Sir Home Popham's system of signalling, his service also included time in *Centaur* under Sir Samuel Hood. Later he was commander of *Beaver*, guard ship at St Helena, and when he was sent to the East Indies in 1823 in the *Larne* he played a distinguished part in the First Burmese War.

Marryat's claim to fame as a naval officer is that he was the first to use steam at sea for the purposes of war. By the 1820s there were many examples of the successful application of steam in paddle ships, for example the ferry service from Portsmouth to Ryde and on short voyages to Ireland and to the Continent. The First Lord of the Admiralty, Lord Melville, and his Controller of the Navy, Sir Thomas Byam Martin, were well aware of the advantages which steam would bring in the English Channel to help prevent any French invasion, in the packet service to help make the mails more regular and reliable, in the battle fleet to manoeuvre battleships into line, and in the exploration of the great rivers of the world.

Expeditions in steam-driven paddle ships were sent to the River Congo in 1817 and the Arctic in 1819. Melville and Byam Martin planned in secrecy to buy steam engines, to modify ships to take the engines and, essential before developing a steam navy, to stockpile coal at depots around the world. Melville had strong commercial and family interests in India, and he secretly agreed to sell two of the navy's steam engines, which were to be replaced with two more modern engines as the technology rapidly improved, to the East India Company. Consequently the paddle ship *Diana* was fitted out in India for operations on the Irrawaddy River in Burma. At first *Diana* was viewed as an auxiliary to tow ships, but, as her usefulness became apparent, Marryat mounted guns on her and transferred his operations to her. In his diary for 1824 he wrote:

> April 13 Came down [Hooghly to Calcutta] in *Diana* Steam Vessel . . . April 15 Weighed and made sail . . . *Diana* Steam Vessel in company . . . April 23 Taken in tow by Steam Vessel – Engineer fell under traversing beam of the Engine and severely wounded. Took him onboard amputated his leg . . . 29 May On Service in Steam Boat . . . 31 May Towing the *Liffey* down the River . . .

Progress in steam propulsion was rapid, and it was soon recognized that steamships were an essential and integral part of the fleet. Ambitious officers like Kerr, who eventually became a full admiral, actively sought appointments to steamships, recognizing that 'it is a very desirable object in these days of steam to know something about it'.

Another early example of the use of steam came in 1834 when the paddle steamer *Rhadamanthus* became the first British steamship to cross the Atlantic. Until *Rhadamanthus* went to the West Indies, operations had been governed by the prevailing winds. The Admiralty issued some very specific instructions and when they heard that a senior officer 'had ordered the *Rhadamanthus* to tow the *Blanche* to Morant Point Jamaica' they were quick to remind him that she was to be used to give an operational advantage in the face of contrary winds and not to overcome the ordinary problems of seamanship: 'it is their intention to keep the *Rhadamanthus* as far as possible for carrying Troops in times of difficulty, and for other cases of emergency, and that you are therefore to give directions to prevent her being used as a Steam Vessel for ordinary purposes . . . and as far as may be to avoid using her Steam power, when she can use her sails'. The problem was technical and logistical rather than any aversion to use of steam, and the order was given 'both with a view to saving the consumption of Coals and the wear and tear of the Engine and Boilers'.

One of the difficulties of extending Melville's steam plan was the provision of adequate stocks of coal. Another arose through the professional pride of the engineers who, apparently, did not wish to share their knowledge with either the officers on deck or the mere shovellers of coal. This problem was largely overcome when it was decided that 'that the Engineers should be directed to instruct the Stokers to enable them to work the Engines . . . the Engineers of the *Columbia* [are] to instruct the Stokers to enable them to work the Engines; and [I] shall send for the first Engineers of all the Steam Vessels, and recommend its general adoption'.

The Navy's first wooden-hulled steam vessels were well designed and robust. *Driver*, for example, laid down in June 1840 and launched on Christmas Eve as the first of a class of eight ships was, at 203 feet long, the largest paddle sloop built by the navy until after the Russian War. She had a beam of 45 feet, intended to accommodate larger bunkers and to provide a more stable platform, and she was armed with one 110pdr and two 10in swivel-mounted guns as well as four 32pdrs. Many early steamers were long lived, and though the *Driver* was wrecked after only twenty years' service, in 1861, other ships of her type, occasionally rearmed and re-engined, were so well built that they lasted up to thirty and forty years.

*Driver* is significant in the history of steam and of the navy. After being commissioned in 1841 she was employed on the East Indies and China stations, until ordered to New Zealand for the wars there. When she returned to Portsmouth on 14 May 1846, her five-year commission was one of the longest since the Great War. Out of a ship's company of 145 the *Driver* had lost 32 men by death and 47 by invaliding, and the only officers who left England in *Driver* and returned in her were the first lieutenant, master, surgeon, and purser. She had sailed and steamed 75,696 miles, and, by returning home across the Pacific Ocean, she became the first steam circumnavigator.

## JOHN FRANKLIN

As a boy in *Polyphemus* John Franklin fought at the Battle of Copenhagen, 1801. He became a surveyor under Matthew Flinders in *Investigator* and when she was wrecked he took passage in the East Indiaman *Earl Camden*, where he served as Nathaniel Dance's signal officer when Linois was repulsed. He reached England in time to join the *Bellerophon* and fight at Trafalgar, again as signal officer. He concluded his war as busily as he had started it, at the Battle of New Orleans, in a bloody boat action, helping to cut a canal across the neck of land between the Bayou Catalan and the Mississippi, and commanding a naval party at the brilliant defeat of a body of Americans strongly entrenched on the right bank of the river.

Franklin was one of about one in twenty officers who were fortunate to find employment after the war, and in 1818 he commanded the hired brig *Trent* on an expedition to the north. In 1819, when William Parry was exploring Lancaster Sound, Franklin went overland from the shores of Hudson's Bay to the Coppermine River, reaching Point Turnagain in 1821 and a new furthest west, on the coast, of 109° 25′ W, in an overland journey of 5,550 miles. In 1825–27 he undertook a second expedition to the north, along the Mackenzie River, still seeking the elusive North-West Passage. From 1830–33 he commanded the *Rainbow* on the Mediterranean station and then became Governor of Van Diemen's Land. However, in 1845 he volunteered to return to exploration and at the age of sixty set off for a third expedition to the north. He was never heard from again.

Franklin had sailed on his second Arctic expedition as his wife lay dying, and he had married Jane Griffin soon afterwards, in 1828. Jane seems to have been a particularly determined lady, and it was her letter writing, lobbying, and appeal to Victorian society at large which inspired some twenty expeditions to search for her missing husband. Jane never gave up hope of finding her John.

## THE RUSSIAN WAR, 1854–56

The outcome of the Syrian campaign and the bombardment of Acre had been a temporary halt to Russian expansion, but the Eastern question was not resolved. So, when Russia invaded the Danube provinces and destroyed the Turkish fleet in the Black Sea, Britain and France declared war. The events which followed are frequently referred to as the Crimean War, though since it was a global war fought on four fronts it should be known by its contemporary name, the Russian War.

The British and French arrived in the Crimea in 1854, and when they landed acted timorously: the privations of the army before and during the subsequent sieges of Sevastopol and Florence Nightingale's single-minded efforts to relieve them are well known. The British admiral had been opposed to a landing on an exposed coast, and Balaklava was taken as base, though the harbour was not large enough to save the fleet from the winter gales. However, a naval brigade was landed and took part in much of the fighting. In the first landings, nearly half the artillery, 74 guns of five types and 680 rockets were manned by the navy, and the seamen were busy for six days landing the guns with sheers and dragging them up the heights, allegedly with a fiddler on the gun. At the Siege of Sevastopol, 47 of 123 guns were the navy's. Elsewhere sailors helped to build a railway, and at the town of Eupatoria the initial garrison was made up entirely of sailors and marines, supported by naval guns and rockets. There, in October 1854, an impromptu patrol of thirty mounted Royal Marines charged and defeated a force of Cossacks.

Elsewhere, the sailors enjoyed their usual reputation for working with steadfast cheerfulness and untiring courage, and two of their officers, Captain William Peel and Midshipman Edward St John Daniel, were awarded the Victoria Cross. Summing up their service, Lord Raglan wrote, a little ungenerously perhaps, 'I attach the greatest value to the services of the seamen and marines, and am fully sensible of the advantage the army has derived from their effective co-operation'.

In the Pacific the war was fought on an oceanic scale. The British admiral received news of the war while he was in Callao, Chile, and sailing north-west via Hawaii he slowly gathered forces, both British and French, and followed two Russian warships to Petropavlovsk on the Kamchatka peninsula. There, however, in perhaps the only incident of its kind in the history of the navy, Price, the British admiral, shot himself. Later entrenched Russians repulsed the allied assault on Petropavlosk, subsequent manoeuvrings were inconclusive, and the British and French failed to bring any Russian ships to battle. However, the Admiralty reinforced the Pacific squadron, and, wary of an alliance between America and Russia, created a base at Esquimault while the Russians, fearful of a repeat attack, evacuated Petropavlosk. The Americans responded by strengthening San Francisco, where massive, multi-tiered forts and fortified islands stand today as a silent tribute to the Royal Navy's long reach.

In the White Sea, operating without allies and without support from the army, the navy was successful. There, Captain Edmund Lyons, son of the Admiral Sir Edward Lyons commanding in the Black Sea, reported from *Miranda* to the senior officer of the White Sea Squadron an attack on Kola in August 1854. The operation was a classic of its type. Sending boats before him to sound the channel, it was 'necessary to pass many points well adapted for defence, and one in particular, where, from the narrowness of the Channel, a Ship has to pass at 50 yards distance from precipitous, and, in parts, overhanging cliffs, whence serious loss might be inflicted without any risk to the Enemy, in consequence of its being impossible to elevate the Guns sufficiently'. Lyons saw how easily these positions could hazard his return downriver and since an attack by boats was impracticable, decided that it was 'advisable to make every effort to get the Ship up to the Town . . . This was only accomplished by great exertions on the part of the Officers and Ship's Company and with considerable difficulty owing to the narrowness and intricacy of the Channel, and the violence of the spring tides, which combined caused the Ship to ground frequently. At 6.30 P.M. however on the evening of the 22nd, we got into position within 500 yards of the Battery and the nearest part of the Town . . .'

Once off the town, Lyons attempted to negotiate, waiting

till daylight the following morning when, no answer having been sent and observing that the Battery and the other defences were manned, and everything prepared for action on shore, I hauled down the Flag of Truce, and opened Fire on the Battery stockade, and loopholed houses, which was instantly returned by Guns and Musketry. The Guns were shortly dismounted and the Battery reduced to ruins, but, although our shells burst well in the loopholed houses and stockade, an obstinate fire of Musketry was kept up from various parts of the Town; this allowed me no alternative and I was therefore obliged to destroy it; it was soon in flames from our Shell and red hot shot, and burned furiously, being fanned by a Fresh Breeze. The Ship at this time became critically situated, the violence of the Tide causing her to drag the Bower and Stream Anchors and the two kedges laid out to spring her broadside, and the passage being too narrow for her to swing, she grounded at less than 300 yards of the burning Town, fragments from which were blown on board; however, by keeping the sails, rigging, and Decks well wetted until the Ship was hove off, no bad consequences ensued . . .

An action at close quarters was inevitable and Lyons

sent the Boats and Marines . . . to drive out the enemy who had returned to the Battery and were keeping up a fire of Musketry from its ruins, and to bring off the Guns ... The Battery was found to be a heap of ruins, with one gun buried under them and the other broken by Shot. On the return of the Boats, I sent Lieut. Mackenzie, with the same party, to destroy some Government Buildings and Storehouses, which being separated from the Town would not otherwise have been burnt.

In the twentieth century the Royal Navy was to return to the White Sea and the Kola peninsula under very different circumstances.

Though studies of the Russian War have concentrated on the war in the Crimea, and the army's administrative problems there, by far the most decisive of the different campaigns was in the Baltic. After the Great War, Russia had dominated the area, occupying Finland and Poland, influencing Denmark, allying herself with Prussia, and threatening Britain's traditional ally, Sweden. The Russian navy when it was mobilized each summer often outnumbered the peacetime Royal Navy. Elsewhere, of course, Russia challenged British influence in Persia and India. So the navy's immediate aim in 1855 was to destroy the Russian squadron lying at its outpost of Reval and then as the ice melted move towards Kronstadt. When the popular but by now elderly and irascible 'Black Charlie', Vice Admiral Sir Charles Napier, arrived in the Baltic with French allies, however, he found that the Reval squadron had been withdrawn to join the main Russian fleet.

Napier established a blockade which crippled the Russian economy and then he inspected the two large Russian fortresses, Kronstadt and Sweaborg, which protected St Petersburg and Helsinki respectively, but he thought they were too strong to attack without gunboats and mortar vessels. Smaller forts were taken from or evacuated by the Russians, leaving as the only worthwhile object of a campaign Bomarsund, in the archipelago between Finland and Sweden. The Grand Duchy of Finland had only been wrested from the Swedes in 1809 and its capture might be the price of Sweden joining the war. Many raids on the Finnish coast took place and in August Bomarsund fell: Napier, however, was sacked.

In 1855 Rear Admiral Sir Richard Dundas commanded the fleet on its return to the Baltic: whereas Napier had suffered a want of seamen and had been advised to recruit Norwegians and Swedes, but not to let them serve together, Dundas now commanded the first all-steam fleet. Napier's hydrographer, Captain Bartholomew Sulivan, who had also acted as his chief intelligence officer and planner, also returned, and he persuaded Dundas that an attack on Sweaborg was, after all, possible.

To understand Sulivan's role it is necessary to examine his background: his father had fought with distinction in the Great War, and ashore in the War of 1812, where he had commanded a division of seamen at the Battle of Bladensburg in 1814 and again at the Battle of New Orleans. Young Sulivan had his first experience of survey work in the *Beagle* in 1828–29 and 1831–36 off the coast of South America, and was on another survey, in command of *Philomel*, 1842–46, when in 1845 he took a major part in an unusual naval operation, the Battle of Obligado, fought eight hundred miles from the sea. General Rosas, who previously had helped Darwin and the officers of the *Beagle*, had established himself in the Argentine, and helped by an Irishman, Admiral Brown, had attacked Uruguay and Paraguay. Britain and France were allies, assisted by Guiseppe Garibaldi, then a freedom fighter for the Uruguayans, who commanded a motley flotilla. Rosas' forces were concentrated at Obligado, strongly defended by batteries and blockships, where the River Parana was a mile wide but only seventeen feet deep. Sulivan not only surveyed the river under the noses of Rosas' gaucho troops, but displayed conspicuous personal bravery in entering one of the first forts and spiking its guns. Then in 1847–48 he organized the dockyard militia in Portsmouth.

In 1854, Francis Beaufort, Hydrographer of the Navy, had written to him about his 'purpose of assisting with the important operations of the Baltic fleet, by making such skilful and rapid reconnaissances, as well as occasional hydrographic surveys, wherever it may be considered necessary' and exhorted him to

> keep all our surveying rules and habits always in your mind, so as to render everything you do more or less subservient to the great object of improving our charts; never to defer to the following day writing the remarks and observations that you may have collected, as they may be of lasting value long after the campaign in which you are engaged has passed away; to give

descriptions of the characteristic features of the land, or of the leading peculiarities of the different districts of the Baltic navigation . . . and to take great care to establish the connection of some one permanent and conspicuous object with your triangulation or bearings by which you may subsequently adjust any new work, or by which any new labourers may bring every fragment of fresh information into harmonious agreement with former acquisitions. Considering you as one of the Admiral's eyes, and knowing that through it he will see everything that he ought to see, I feel sure that at the end of the campaign he will exclaim, as Sir William Parker did in the China Sea, 'Without those admirable surveyors I should have done nothing' . . .

The ship Sulivan was given to command was the *Lightning*, built in 1823 and one of the very first steam-driven paddle ships: he was assisted by Commander Arthur Cochrane in the *Driver*. The paddle ships operating at the edge of the retreating ice surveyed the Baltic as far as Kronstadt and then turned to a more detailed survey of Bomarsund and the Gulf of Bothnia.

In 1855, as soon as the ice cleared, Sulivan, now in the newer and more powerful paddle ship *Merlin*, surveyed Kronstadt and Sweaborg again, quickly determining that Sweaborg was vulnerable to the allies with their gunboats and rockets. Despite difficulties with the specially converted barges which were used as mortar vessels and the embarrassment of going aground with his commander-in-chief embarked, Sulivan's plan was completely successful and the fortress and arsenal complex ruined without the loss of a single allied life.

The plan for 1856 was to threaten St Petersburg, the capital of Russia, by steaming directly to an assault on Kronstadt using nine armoured floating batteries, two hundred and fifty gunboats, and a hundred mortar craft. The bloody siege and capture of a remote city, Sevastopol, on the edges of his empire in September 1855 had had little effect on the decision by the Tsar to accept the allied terms in early 1856. What concentrated minds in St Petersburg was the threat that the Royal Navy, which had fired Copenhagen in 1807, burned Washington in 1814, bombarded Algiers in 1816, destroyed Acre in 1840, taken Bomarsund in 1854, and ruined

Sweaborg in 1855, was now preparing to attack the capital. The Tsar sued for peace.

Under the peace treaty agreed in Paris in March 1856, the allies withdrew from the Black Sea, which was partly neutralized, the Danube was declared an open waterway, Turkey kept its provinces in Europe, and the Åland Islands were declared neutral. Meanwhile the British government decided to complete the naval building programme, with accompanying publicity, and assembled a Royal fleet review at Spithead on St George's Day 1856. The build-up was intended to influence the peace process and to remind the world, again, of Palmerston's words after Acre, that 'every country that has towns within cannon shot of deep water will remember the operations of the British Fleet . . . whenever such country has any differences with us'. It was effective: Britain fought many more small wars in the second half of the nineteenth century, in China, New Zealand, Japan, and Africa, but there was no major war for another sixty years.

## THE SLAVE TRADE

Amongst the growing number of advocates of the abolition of the slave trade in the early nineteenth century was no less than Charles Middleton, otherwise known as Lord Barham, the First Lord of the Admiralty, who had masterminded the campaign of Trafalgar. Barham had become an abolitionist either from a conversion experience when commanding *Arundel* in the West Indies, 1759–60, or from the influence of his wife, Margaret Gambier, and her friend Elizabeth Bouverie, both evangelical Christians of Huguenot descent, and he had made his home at Teston in Kent, as Hannah More put it, 'the Runnymede of the Negroes'. There Barham's secretary, a former surgeon's mate in *Arundel*, wrote anti-slavery pamphlets and William Wilberforce found a home from home. Wilberforce was a close friend of Pitt the Younger, and it was Pitt who as Prime Minister who had elevated Middleton to the peerage and his last great office.

There must have been some satisfaction at Teston when in 1807 Britain abolished the slave trade in British vessels. Then, in the

Treaty of Ghent in 1815 which ended the war between Britain and the United States of America, the countries promised each other mutual support in the abolition of the trade. The tenth and last article of the treaty read, 'Whereas the Traffic in Slaves is irreconcilable with the principles of humanity and Justice, and whereas both His Majesty and the United States are desirous of continuing their efforts to promote its entire abolition, it is hereby agreed that both the contracting parties shall use their best endeavours to accomplish so desirable an object'. Meanwhile, in Paris in 1815 Britain pressed the other great powers, Austria, France, Prussia, and Russia, for a universal ban on slavery itself. The British even proposed an armed and international police on the coast of Africa, but this idea was far in advance of its time. True, Sweden had banned the slave trade in her ships in 1813, and the Netherlands in 1818 (following the joint operation with Britain at Algiers in 1816 to end the trade in Christian slaves). True also, France passed domestic laws in 1816, the USA in 1820, Spain in 1823, and Brazil 1830, but these nations only paid lip service to the idea. The United States was less than half-hearted in the application of the relevant law, and the first slave trader was not punished by death, as the law provided, until the Civil War.

Slavery itself was abolished in British colonies in 1833, and meanwhile Britain reached a number of unilateral agreements, in some cases paying handsome compensation, but issues regarding rights of search, the use of flags of convenience, and false papers hindered the imposition of laws. These agreements included mutual rights of search, but it was clear that the Royal Navy was going to do most of the searching. Also, in 1824, Britain declared slave-trading to be piracy, alleging that there was 'an intimate connexion between slave-trading and all the atrocities of a piratical life': this implied a right to stop and visit any ship flying whatever flag to ascertain that it was bona fide. Other nations feared the powers this gave the Royal Navy, wondering whether the principles of belligerent rights, contraband of war, and blockade would be extended in peace.

However, senior naval officers such as Cockburn and Napier welcomed the experience which the war on slavery gave young commanders, and advocated the imposition of a close blockade on the slave ports. Subsequently boats with landing parties were often sent inshore to destroy slave depots (known as barracoons), slave-raiders were chased up rivers, and chiefs who traded in their people were placed under ever closer supervision. Several British colonies in Africa grew out of this activity. Distant blockade was not forgotten and ships were also stationed in Brazilian and Cuban waters to catch slavers as they arrived from Africa with their terrible cargo.

It was exhausting and disease-ridden work, mostly undertaken by junior officers in small vessels, and the islands of St Helena and Ascension, both well offshore, proved invaluable resorts for crews to recuperate. Ascension, which had been garrisoned by the Royal Marines to prevent the French mounting any attempt to rescue the exiled Napoleon, was commissioned as HMS *Ascension*, where ships could fish and harvest turtles, and a farm was established to grow anti-scorbutic food. A seventeenth-century rhyme ran: 'Beware and take care of the Bight of Benin, There's one comes out for forty goes in'. By the nineteenth century the casualty rate was less, but the graves of Comfortless Cove on Ascension bear testimony to the men who died in the cause of anti-slavery.

The Royal Navy's war on slavery was global, one of the longest and more successful in its history; as Lecky wrote, an 'unweary, unostentatious, and inglorious crusade of England against slavery may probably be regarded as among the three or four perfectly virtuous pages comprised in the history of nations'. Of course the war could only be won when the causes of slavery were addressed, but by the 1860s the dreadful cross-Atlantic trade was more or less suppressed. The Royal Navy then turned its attention to slaving on the East Africa coast and 'blackbirding' in the Pacific.


## THE CAREER OF ALBERT MARKHAM

Albert Hastings Markham may well stand as a cipher for the Royal Navy in the later part of the nineteenth century. Unquestionably, Markham had huge physical and moral courage, but he was not a noted thinker. He was, however, a member of a number of inner circles, including royalty and freemasonry, and seems to have led a charmed life which protected and promoted him until he reached his natural level of incompetence. This protection has extended into history and assessments of his career have tended to forgive Markham even for having rammed and sunk his commander-in-chief's flagship and drowning one of the few reforming admirals of his age.

As a midshipman on the East African coast Markham attacked Arab slavers from an open boat. He repeated the action when an acting lieutenant in 1862, again under sail and oar, but this time off the coast of China: his actions were indistinguishable from countless similar deeds during the previous several hundred years. Markham reported:

> In obedience to your orders to search for pirates, I dropped down the River from Ningpo ... in the Lorcha *Vivid* ... at noon the next day ... two lorchas were seen alongside each other. I immediately ordered the men (20 in no.) under cover and stood towards them – one of them on our approach shoved off to meet us, at the same time hoisting the Pirate Flag (red triangle with black border). When about 400 yards off she opened fire upon us ... I ordered the men up and returned the fire with the 12-pdr howitzer and small arms, the Pirate was evidently surprised and made off for the Main Land distant about 4 miles, keeping up a fire upon us from her large guns, gingalls and muskets. The other lorcha now hoisted American Colours and a house flag and stood towards, keeping however out of danger ...

A notable feature of this action was that Markham had a Chinese crew to manage his lorcha, and, like galley slaves of another age of warfare, they needed encouragement. When the wind dropped he took to a small boat and continued the chase until, forty yards from his enemy, his one-man crew

> refused to scull the sampan any further, and I was compelled to return to the lorcha. I then opened fire upon her with case and carried away her large scull, and reduced her to a sinking state, she was also on fire abaft, but still kept up a heavy fire on us her men being all under cover. By force I compelled the Chinese Crew to work, and when close to the pirate threw stink pots and bags of powder on our deck. I was in the act of boarding when they blew themselves up. Afterwards recovered 12 men

from her. The action lasted from noon till 3p.m. After seeing
the pirate junk sink I proceeded to the other lorcha, and she
proved to be the *Spic* seized that forenoon. Her master and one
European passenger were murdered before I arrived. I placed a
crew on board and in company proceeded to this place, where I
arrived on the morning of 4th inst. We had 5 men wounded.
The pirate probably lost 25 men.

Only the handwriting and the style of English had deteriorated
since earlier encounters in the century. For this episode, Markham
was promoted to full lieutenant, though a wise and cautious
Admiralty added the condition that he must first pass his professional examinations.


## THE SOUTH PACIFIC

Nine years later Markham was an acting commander when he was
tasked with a cruise among the South Seas islands where the natives
were proving restless. Commodore Stirling was senior officer of
ships and vessels on the Australian station, a vast area covering three
oceans and a score of archipelagos, thinly patrolled from a base in
Sydney. Standing orders seemed reasonable enough: commanding
officers were

to afford the Consuls all the assistance and support which they
can properly give, taking care to act in accordance with law.
They are also to afford protection to the free intercourse and
commerce of British subjects trading in those islands. Captains
and all officers of ships visiting the South Pacific Islands are to
see that the spirit of the regulations contained in Admiralty
Instructions is fully carried out. Allowance should always be
made for the uncivilized state of the islanders, and every care
taken to prevent jealousy or ill-feeling, the greater number of
the murders and outrages committed by them being the result
of intemperate conduct on the part of white people on previous
occasions. As a rule the display of arms should be avoided where
the natives are known to be friendly, and where their suspicion
would be aroused by such display; but commanding officers

must be guided by their judgment on this point; and at places where the habitants are of an unfriendly or doubtful character, sufficient force should always be at hand to prevent any hostile attempt on the part of the natives . . .

In October 1871, Markham was despatched in the 3-gun screwship *Rosario* on an imperial policing mission, with unlimited powers and indeterminate length: he was told to return to Sydney before his provisions ran out. He was instructed to 'visit each island of the New Hebrides and Santa Cruz groups, and communicate with every missionary, planter, or other person from whom reliable information can be obtained relative to the murders of British subjects which have recently taken place there, and to the alleged kidnapping of natives which is supposed to have led to these acts. You are to report fully all the information you can gather'. On Norfolk Island Markham was given special instructions to communicate with Bishop Patterson, but by the time he had arrived the bishop had already been murdered, although, possibly as a sign of his clerical rank, not eaten. Markham's investigation found that 'that the bishop landed in a canoe, and almost immediately after stepping on shore, was clubbed to death . . . the attack on the bishop and party was made entirely in retaliation of wrongs and murders suffered by them at the bands of white people, whom I imagine to be those concerned in the nefarious practice of kidnapping natives for labour. The body of Bishop Patteson was afterwards brought alongside the schooner, though denuded of everything but the boots . . .'

It was ever the lot of lonely, often junior officers to interpret their orders, but these events seem to have temporarily disturbed Markham. On one island he fired at random amongst the natives he saw on the beach, set fire to their village, and destroyed their canoes. Though he later claimed that he had fired 'over' rather than 'amongst' the natives, even his apologists admit that he killed some twenty-five people. On another island, while investigating the murder of a crew from an English ketch, Markham

went on shore . . . into the native village, about a quarter of a mile from the beach, where after some little difficulty, . . . I succeeded in obtaining an interview with the chief of Vasalai, who came out from the bush accompanied by several of his men. On being questioned, he did not deny having murdered two white men and three black, belonging to the *Wild Duck*, but he said it was done on account of their attempting to carry off one of his tribe, though when I asked him to point out their graves, as he told me their bodies had afterwards been buried, he seemed almost paralysed with fear and incapable of answering; and I have no doubt they were all eaten, which I have subsequently discovered to be the case.

Markham

tried to point out his crime, and attempted to show him what his conduct should be on future occasions, and having admitted that he had done wrong in murdering these men, and taking into consideration the provocation that they had received, and the lapse of time since the murders had been committed, I thought the best punishment I could inflict upon them would be by levying a fine on the whole village of 25 pigs, threatening to land my men and destroy the village if the fine was not forthcoming in a very short time. He seemed much pleased at my leniency, and promised compliance. Having waited an hour, during which time only four pigs had been brought in . . . the chief and all his men had ran away and concealed themselves in the bush, being afraid that I would take their lives. I sent out several times to try and reassure them, which proving unsuccessful I had no alternative but to land our men and destroy the village and several canoes, which was speedily effected . . . [I have] no doubt that the punishment inflicted on the inhabitants of Vasalai will have a very good effect upon the whole of the natives of this island, and will, I trust, in some way put a stop to the kidnapping of natives by white men, as I have told several of the chiefs that were brought before me by Mr. Goodwell, that in future they are to make prisoners any white men that should attempt to carry their people off by forcible means, at the same time acquainting the missionary or the first ship that may arrive of the fact . . .

Markham's proceedings in the *Rosario* gave great offence to philanthropists in Britain, and questions were put in the House of

Commons. However the First Lord of the Admiralty, Mr Goschen, held that by allowing the offending natives to compound by the payment of a few pigs for the murders which they admitted having committed, Markham had behaved leniently. On the other hand, the Pacific islanders do seem to have had some justification for behaving 'frightfully' towards those who were kidnapping them for slave labour to dig guano.

## ARCTIC EXPLORING

The search for Franklin had helped open up northern Canada, but after Franklin's death and the failure of various exploration parties to discover any new sources of wealth, still less a practicable North-West Passage, the appetite for exploration was temporarily sated. However, by 1875 Markham's cousin, Clements, was secretary of the Royal Geographical Society: he was an armchair admiral who had largely taken over the role John Barrow had played in the first half of the nineteenth century. The Prime Minister himself, Disraeli, announced that the purpose of a new expedition would be 'to encourage that spirit of enterprise which had ever distinguished the English people', while the Royal Geographical Society wanted exploration of the polar region for scientific purposes, 'not a foolish rush to the pole', and devised some bizarre experiments. Disregarding both sentiments, the instructions drawn by the Admiralty contained the fatal order to go as far north as possible.

An old sloop, *Alert*, was selected, and a whaler, purchased for the service and strengthened for ice navigation, was renamed *Discovery*. The command was entrusted to Captain George Nares, who had distinguished himself as captain of the *Challenger*; and Albert Markham was selected as second-in-command. The expedition set off for Smith's Sound at the far northern end of Baffin's Bay. The *Discovery* was left to winter in Lady Franklin Bay, but Nares pressed on in *Alert* until he encountered impenetrable pack ice and was forced to camp on an open coast, the most northern winter quarters yet formed. There his officers issued orders to each other's sledges, as though they were Nelson's frigate captains, and competed to fly the most heraldic sledge pennants. Apart from these touches, however, they had not improved on technique since John Ross and his contemporaries fifty years before.

The dogs which were to have pulled the sledges escaped or died, and substituting brawn for brain, Markham took a party northward on foot. Sickness had already broken out during the winter, and on his two-and-a-half-month journey, dragging heavy loads, Markham narrowly escaped death by the oldest of sailors' enemies: scurvy. Instead, he reached a new furthest north, and was promoted to captain for this achievement.

Thirty years later Nares wrote to Robert Scott, passing on the succession which had begun two centuries before: 'My dear Captain Scott, I am commissioned by the Members of the Arctic Expedition of 1875–76 to request you will accept from them, for use during your Antarctic cruise in the *Discovery*, the accompanying Union Jack, with their hearty wishes for a successful voyage and a safe return Home', and Scott replied: 'I only hope that we may do something to keep up the English reputation in Polar adventure which was so gloriously upheld by you all thirty [sic] years ago'.

Meanwhile, fate played once more with Markham. As captain of the navy's experimental school, he could have stayed at his desk in Portsmouth, but in July 1885 he took the school's torpedo tender, *Hecla*, to sea for trials. Off Land's End he was involved in a collision with a passenger steamer, drowning a dozen civilians, but was acquitted at a court martial of any blame. In reality, fate was only saving 'Old Marco' for another roll of the dice.


## GEORGE TRYON AND STEAM TACTICS

Now a rear admiral, Markham was appointed second-in-command of the Mediterranean Fleet, working for the fierce and innovative Sir George Tryon. It was an appointment due more to Markham's rank in freemasonry than to any empathy between these two officers; they did not make a good partnership and Tryon sent Markham off on a series of independent cruises. Occasionally a ship would be detached from Markham's squadron, as when *Inflexible* was sent to investigate an earthquake on Samothrace in February 1893, the effects of which were found to be 'much exaggerated', but Markham's main preoccupation, as revealed in his log of the new-fangled telegram, was in finding where his mails were and in establishing where the next coals were – his squadron needed 2,000–2,500 tons every three to four weeks. Only occasionally the telegram log shows concern for the movements of the rival fleet of the French.

Admiral Sir George Tryon was physically a giant of man; by many accounts he was brusque and bullying, though much of his abruptness with his officers could be put down to his intellectual impatience. There was no formal school for the study of tactics and strategy and the Royal Navy relied on its reputation for success. Such campaigns as the navy had been involved in, had, with the exception of the Russian War (1854–56), been small-scale affairs. Seamanship, the art and science of manoeuvring ships under steam or sail, remained of a high order, and no one could fault the navy's courage, individually or corporately. Ships still moved primarily under sail, especially on long voyages. Steam was increasingly used in confined waters and when ships were in company, however, and the navy was developing one of its periodic schisms.

On one side were officers such as Admiral Philip Colomb. Like many of his contemporaries, he had had few opportunities to distinguish himself and he was made a 'yellow admiral' in 1886, in other words promoted into retirement. He was, however, an innovator, who, for example, introduced the use of flashing lights and the Morse code at sea. The advantages of steam when applied to manoeuvres and operations under sail had been noted as long ago as the 1820s, when Captain John Ross had written the first treatise on steam navigation and rules of the road in order to avoid collisions at sea. The problem was this: when changes in formation had been ordered under sail, ships were expected to take up their new stations as best they could, but speeds were slow, the number of options – shortening or increasing sail, tacking or wearing – was limited, and ships were of a more or less uniform type, so (allowing for the vagaries of wind and water) movements were predictable: but when similar orders were given to fleets of ships powered by steam the results were less predictable. It was rare in the navy of the late nineteenth century, which was undergoing great technological change, to find large classes of ships or the same classes of ships being built from year to year, and as a result squadrons and fleets were composed of ships with widely differing characteristics of speed, acceleration, and turning. One nineteenth-century navigation notebook gave details of a score of ships each with different characteristics, propeller revolutions for given speeds, maximum degrees of helm, and turning circles which varied by several hundred yards. (The turning circle was seaman's shorthand for the lateral distance which a ship would move when reversing course.) Colomb's answer to this chaos was what became known as 'equal speed manoeuvres': if the speed were fixed by the flagship, then using helm alone ships' movements, especially in close quarters, would be more predictable. Colomb's *Manual of Fleet Evolutions*, published in 1874, enabled a series of complex, spectacular balletic movements for which British fleets became famous. No one apparently gave much gave a thought to what would happen if the choreographer was lost, if flag signals or signal halyards were shot away or signalmen killed in action, never mind where, in mastless steam ships, all the flags were to be hung. In effect the navy had produced the means of introducing the perfect line of battle, but it was known to its detractors as the goose-step.

Tryon opposed the goose-step and wished to instil in his captains a greater self-reliance. Using a little-known flag signal, TA, Tryon wanted his officers to follow him into battle without further orders. The spirit which Tryon wished to instil in his fleet was recognizably that which had persisted throughout an earlier age, and to some extent still exists in the modern Royal Navy:

1. While an order should be implicitly obeyed, still circumstances may change and conditions may widely vary from those known, or even from those that presented themselves at the time orders were issued. In such cases the Officer receiving orders, guided by the object that he knows this Chief has in view, must act on his own responsibility.

2. (a) Orders directing the movement of Ships either collectively or singly are invariably accompanied, as a matter of course with the paramount understood condition: 'With due regard to the safety of HM Ships'. (b) When the literal obedience to any order, however given, would entail a collision with a friend, or

endanger a Ship by running on shore or in any other way, paramount orders direct that the danger is to be avoided, while the object of the order should be attained if possible.

3. An Admiral leading a Fleet relies with confidence that, while the 'Order' of the Fleet is maintained, each Ship will be handled and piloted with all the care and attention that is exercised in the guidance of the leading Ship. He relies that this will be the case more especially when the Fleet is approaching land or a harbour . . .

4. Ships following a Leader in a Column should in manoeuvring avoid turning on a greater arc than that of the Leader; if there is any error or difference it should be due to turning on a smaller arc.

5. When in line ahead any error from the exact station of a Ship should be rather in the direction of being ahead of station, but when in line abreast any error should be in the direction of being astern of station rather than ahead of it.

6. The neighbourly duties of Ships in a Fleet to each other are duties which must be kept constantly in mind.

7. Risks that are not only justifiable, but which ought to be incurred, during War are not justifiable during Peace.

## THE SINKING OF THE *VICTORIA*

On 22 June 1893, while bringing the fleet to an anchorage off Tripoli, Tryon seems to have made an error of judgement. Two columns of ships were steaming in parallel, the starboard column led by Tryon in the *Victoria* and the port column by Markham in the *Camperdown*. Tryon ordered the leading ships to reverse course (by sixteen points, or 180°) by turning inwards and the rest of the columns to follow their leaders in succession. This would have been a safe if spectacular manoeuvre if the columns had been sufficiently far apart, reckoned to be ten cables (2,000 yards). In fact the columns were six cables (1,200 yards) apart. Whatever manoeuvre Tryon had in mind, the leading ships turned towards each other and inside each other's turning circle. Markham had hesitated in obeying the order so that *Camperdown* turned slightly later than *Victoria* with the result that he rammed his commander-in-chief on the starboard bow, and she capsized, drowning 358 officers and men including Tryon. Markham's telegram to the Admiralty contained more than a little degree of pathos:

> ... Rear Admiral Tripoli to Admiralty Regret to report that while manoeuvring this afternoon off Tripoli Victoria and Camperdown collided. Victoria sank 15 minutes afterwards in 80 fathoms bottom uppermost. Camperdown's ram struck Victoria before the turret starboard bow. Following officers drowned Commander in Chief ... 255 men saved [later changed to 261] ... Awaiting instructions Markham ...

The court martial of the surviving officers found 'with the deepest sorrow and regret that ... this collision was due to an order given by the then Commander-in-Chief, the late Vice Admiral Sir George Tryon, to the two divisions in which the fleet was made to turn sixteen points inwards, leaders first, the others in succession, the columns at that time being only six cables apart'. However, the court also felt 'strongly that although it is much to be regretted that Rear Admiral Albert Hastings Markham did not carry out his first intention of semaphoring to the Commander-in-Chief his doubt as to the signal, it would be fatal to the best interests of the service to say he was to blame for carrying out the directions of his Commander-in-Chief present in person'. The new-fangled telegraph enabled the collision and the court martial to become the scandal of the season in London, and as the facts emerged, the mood changed, even against Markham who had so far lived a charmed life. In October that year when the Admiralty reviewed the proceedings they minuted

> their Lordships concur in the feeling expressed by the Court that it is much to be regretted that Rear Admiral A. H. Markham did not carry out his first intention of semaphoring to the Commander-in-Chief his doubts as to the signal; but they deem it necessary to point out that the Rear Admiral's belief that the Commander-in-Chief would circle round him was not justified by the proper interpretation of the signal. The evidence shows that it was owing to this misconception that the

precautions, which mistrust of the order given by the Commander-in-Chief should have prompted, were not at once taken by the Rear Admiral, and that he did not order Captain Johnstone to reverse the starboard screw, and to close the watertight doors, until after the ships had turned eight points inwards and were end on . . .

There were ironies as well as controversy surrounding the collision. First, Tryon, who wanted to instil a spirit of independence in his subordinates, had so cowed Markham, and others, that they did not dare to question his orders and they had relied too much on their commander-in-chief to pull a rabbit out of a bag. Another was that Tyron was not using TA when he ordered the manoeuvre, though the collision brought to an end any further experimentation along these lines: thereafter, the goose-step became the order of the day. A third was that one of the survivors of the collision was Commander John Jellicoe, who had been lying sick in his cabin, thus avoiding any association by omission or commission with what had happened: twenty years later Jellicoe's excessive reliance on flag signalling would be criticized by some for failing to deliver a great tactical victory Nelson-style.

However, Markham's naval career was finally over.

## WALTER COWAN

Meanwhile a new school of naval officers was developing, brought up not on the highly skilled but mindless steam tactics, but in small wars ashore, in India, Egypt, Africa, and China. Among these was Admiral Sir Walter Cowan, whose words and deeds will feature often in the remainder of this book. Amongst other achievements Cowan was awarded the Distinguished Service Cross twice in his remarkable career, at an interval of forty-six years, a record unlikely ever to be beaten.

Cowan entered *Britannia* as a naval cadet in 1884, and served in the Mediterranean, the Atlantic and Indian Oceans, and the Red Sea, until in 1895 he volunteered for *Barrosa* on the Cape station, where he saw active service during the Brass River and Benin expeditions. In 1898 he commanded the gunboat flotilla on the Nile during the operations in the Sudan. He commanded *Princess Royal* at the Battle of Jutland and then was appointed commodore of the First Light Cruiser Squadron. He continued to command the squadron and the naval force in the Baltic during the anti-Bolshevik operations in 1920–21. He retired as a full admiral in 1931 after a series of senior interwar appointments, including Commander-in-Chief, North America and West Indies (1926–28). However, at the age of sixty-eight, when the Second World War broke out, he persuaded his friends, mostly his former subordinates, in the Admiralty to employ him for the duration of the war in the rank of commander. He served as liaison officer with a commando brigade in the eastern Mediterranean during 1941 and was then attached to an Indian regiment in the Western Desert. He was captured at Bir Hakeim in 1942 and repatriated the following year, when he promptly rejoined the commandos. Cowan loved what he called 'turbulence' and liked to collect other people's flags. By the end of his long and eventful career he had collected quite a few.

## AFRICA

Cowan thirsted for action and in 1894, while a lieutenant, volunteered for the third-class cruiser *Barrosa*, on the Cape station, which included East and West Africa. He took part in a number of minor operations against lawless tribes on the west coast, including the Brass River expedition, one of the last punishment expeditions before full colonial rule was established. Then the *Barrosa* was sent to the opposite coast of Africa.

Arriving in Zanzibar, Cowan wrote:

we found a most pleasing atmosphere of turbulence up and down that coast and went on to Mombasa and found that *St. George* and *Phoebe* had landed their men and were marching for [a town called] Gaze so we followed with all speed, but the rebels bolted without fighting, so the Admiral [Rawson] and all the expedition climbed into us and we took them to Mombasa, picked up 70 Porters there and took them to Malindi and Kilifi for *Swallow* and *Racoon's* provisioning and back to Mombasa, rather on the qui vive and the next night about 1 a.m. we were pitched on shore in a hurry on the news that the place was being attacked, but that didn't come off and we returned on board dripping with sweat . . .

The next day Cowan and his captain trekked to a mission station to find that all was quiet, only to hear, next day, that it had been looted and burned. The admiral then decided to root out the trouble at source: 'we went for Mwele the stronghold of [a native leader called] Mbaruk the root of all this unrest'. The force consisted of

390 Bluejackets and Marines, 60 Soudanese, 50 Zanzibar Askaris, of very moderate fighting value, and 700 Porters, all under the command of Rear Admiral Harry Rawson . . . With him came General Matthews the C in C of the Sultan of Zanzibar's Army, to which he had been promoted from Lieutenant R.N. some years before, and Arthur Hardinge the Consul General of British East Africa who delighted in coming on our small wars.

They landed at Gaze and it took them five days to march to Mwele, 'a goodish way inland through good open country . . . so different to the Niger'. There followed one of the comic incidents in war:

General Matthews was shot through the shoulder, and the orderly through the head. Picking up the pieces when it was over a wounded prisoner said that they had orders to shoot the two fattest men amongst the English and there was no question that . . . General Matthews answered that description, in fact I should say General Matthews was probably the fattest white man in British East Africa.

The action was sharp and short.

Next day we got to the Mwele stockade up a wooded hill and so sited that getting right round it with the force we had was almost out of the question, to cut off their retreat unless they meant fighting it out; one way and another there were over 40 of these stockades or Bomas besides the main one, stout logs of timber about 7 feet high and though we trundled up our 7 pr. the only piece of Artillery we had, to within 80 yards, its shots didn't often penetrate. Our attack was from three sides, the enemy never let drive until we were within 50 yards of his loop-holes and then quite a storm of it, but bad shooting, the whole thing took two hours and then we were in. Mbaruk bolted early and his son Nasran hung on in command and was shot at 10 yards range as we stormed in. Above the main stockade flew a red and white swallow tailed banner which I greatly longed for . . .

Cowan got both the banner and an antelope horn, and it was the end of the war in East Africa.


## THE FASHODA CRISIS, 1898

General Gordon, 'Chinese Gordon', was 'the finest specimen of the heroic Victorian type, a Bible-taught Evangelical, fearless, tireless, incorruptible': he fought in the Crimea and at the capture of Peking in 1860, and served in the Chinese army. Later he devoted his military career to the suppression of slavery and the establishment of order over vast tracts of the hinterland of Africa: he was murdered in 1885 during the Mahdist revolt in the Sudan. By the summer of 1898 he had been avenged and the reconquest of the Sudan, by an Anglo-Egyptian force led by their British Sirdar, Kitchener, was almost complete, when an incident occurred which almost brought Britain and France to the brink of war. Kitchener, advancing southwards through the Sudan, fighting most of the way, met a French patrol consisting of a handful of officers and some hundred Senegalese infantry who had marched eastwards across Africa, laying claim to a huge swath of the continent. In part Kitchener's advance had been made possible by laying a railway along which he brought up forage and supplies for his men and animals, but he was strongly supported on the Nile by gunboats, which were used as ferries, troop barges, mobile gun batteries, headquarters and hospital ships, and generally to surprise, overawe, and outflank the enemy. They were shallow craft with high superstructures, protected by light armour and loopholed for rifles and Maxims, and their main armament consisted of 12pdr or 6pdr guns. Some of them had been brought out from England in sections, carried on the railway over the desert, rebuilt on the banks of the Nile, and hauled over the Nile cataracts: one of these historic craft, the *Melik*, is still there. Their complements consisted of one or two Royal Navy officers and a couple of Royal Marines, with local crews. So, at Fashoda, where Kitchener met the French, over fifteen hundred miles from the sea, there also flew the White Ensign.

The Fashoda Crisis is now a footnote in the history books, but at the time war between Britain and France seemed very likely. Walter Cowan's is one of the best descriptions of the Battle of Omdurman, and he was at Fashoda:

about Six days after the Omdurman battle down the River appeared the old paddle steamer *Tewfikish* formerly one of Gordon's Flotilla but since the fall of Khartoum in the Dervish service. Seeing Turkish flags everywhere and coming unawares all in amongst our Gunboats she hurriedly surrendered and was then asked her business. She was bespattered and riddled with bullets and said that some Turks were at Fashoda and had killed and wounded some forty of her crew. All they could say about the flag flying at Fashoda was that it had three colours . . .

Kitchener quickly assembled an expedition of five steamers including Cowan's *Sultan*, but Fashoda was a further four hundred miles up the White Nile and it took nine days to get there against the current: the steamers were designed to use coal and nearly half the journey was taken up in cutting wood.

Not all resistance was at an end:

one morning before breakfast coming round a corner of the river the *Sultan* leading and I in my bath on the sun deck, there was a bang and a shrapnel shell burst just over our funnel and there about 300 yards off was a steamer lying on the bank with a force of about 500 Dervishes camped round her and two Flags planted in the middle. I abandoned my bath and in Pyjama trousers, Khaki tunic, helmet, pistol and a pair of slippers my mother had worked me we ran in at them with all guns going, shoved *Sultan's* nose well up on the mud and leapt for the shore while one of the others landed half a Sudanese Battalion just above. I greatly wanted the two Flags so had aimed to put her nose in opposite where they flew and managed to get them. The Steamer was the old *Safia* of Gordon's day . . .

This action took about twenty minutes and in an hour Cowan had resumed his breakfast and the journey south up the river. Five days later a new enemy appeared.

on nearing Fashoda a steel rowing boat flying a gigantic French Flag appeared coming down towards us, in it a Senegalese Sergeant and two men in bright red jerseys and bringing a letter from Major Marchand the leader of the expedition announcing his formal occupation of the Sudan in the name of France and welcoming us to Fashoda . . . we made fast to the bank near by to Gordon's old fort where was flying the French Flag.

Kitchener protested at the French incursion, pointed out to the French officer in command that the Anglo-Egyptian force outnumbered his by about one to ten, hoisted the British and Egyptian flags, entertained the local ruler (some of whose people were in the British ranks), and gave a demonstration of firepower from his machine guns and cannon. As if this was not enough, the Cameron Highlanders who were with him were allowed to play the bagpipes.

The *Sultan's* contribution, wrote Cowan, 'was the firing of a war rocket and that I think was the King's biggest thrill . . . This ceremony over and our rights asserted and as an act of grace the French [were] allowed to keep their Flag flying over Gordon's old Fort'. Sixty miles higher up the Nile, Kitchener placed an outpost at the junction of the Sobat River, flowing out of Abyssinia, and returned downriver with Major Marchand en route to Cairo, leaving Cowan in command of that part of the Nile.

Cowan patrolled the river to cut off French communications and prevent reinforcements, and on his first patrol was rewarded with another flag:

we sighted a native walking up the bank . . . carrying a spear with the French Flag – we caught him and asked him for his letter – guessing of course that he had one – which he then produced and another French Flag as well – Marchand had told him that no one would dare touch him if he showed it. The letter was from Marchand to the Abyssinian General giving all details of our Force and proposing another plan for a joint attack on us . . .

Soon the remaining French at Fashoda became difficult. They developed a

truculent attitude and started raiding the villages and defying all the orders the Sirdar had laid down for so long as they remained in our territory. We remonstrated several times . . . to little avail so at last gave him an ultimatum, as he had begun throwing up earth works in our direction as well as disregarding our orders about interfering with the natives. He replied to the effect that we were treating him as an enemy before the outbreak of war and there was a great demonstration of fist shaking and clambering about on the ramparts . . .

Once the earthworks were nearly complete Cowan merely cast off, dropped down the river to outflank the French and threatened them from a new angle and at a range of less than 100 yards. He was ready to 'let drive but at that moment there was smoke down the river to the North, we hadn't heard anything from the outside world for some weeks – and it proved to be a steamer with Marchand on board returning with orders to evacuate his Force by way of Abyssinia'. Cowan was 'relieved and glad – there could have been no glory in annihilating seven gallant French Officers and a hundred-and-twenty very brave Senegalese troops', though his main regret was that if there were to be war with France he personally 'stuck as we were in the middle of Africa . . . might have been badly left out of [it]'.

When he wrote his autobiography Cowan had one of the French flags, still on its spear, but after the Second World War he presented it at a ceremony in Paris, as an act of reconciliation.

## STRATEGIC THOUGHT

By the end of the nineteenth century the Royal Navy had had hundreds of years of fighting experience and had developed its habit of success, its officers and men were superb seamen and explorers, and there had been no rival at sea since 1815. Politicians and the public understood how to wage naval war: build a fleet at least twice as big as any rival (the power standards), prevent the junction of enemy fleets (at Cadiz and Gibraltar), blockade the enemy in his ports (usually Toulon and Brest), and sweep up his shipping and his colonies. Actual experience of major war since 1856 whether at the operational or strategic level was, however, absent. At the tactical level a fighting admiral like Walter Cowan gained valuable experience of command in the riverine war in Sudan and during the Fashoda Crisis. Other officers like Jackie Fisher, Charles Beresford, Percy Scott, John Jellicoe, and David Beatty, all of whom would lead the navy in the new century, were blooded and gained essential experience of command at a young age in fighting ashore in Africa and in China. Andrew Cunningham, who was one of the greatest fighting admirals of the Second World War, enjoyed similar experience as a midshipman with the naval brigades during the Boer War.

However, in 1889, Sir George Goschen, First Lord of the Admiralty, told Parliament, 'there is not now, nor has there ever been, an established school for the study of [naval] strategy'. One year later, in 1890, *The Times*, in reviewing a new book, declared magisterially that it was 'almost a pioneer in its class, for, strange to say, the literature of the greatest Naval Power in history has no authoritative treatise on the principles of Naval Warfare'. The book was *The Influence of Sea Power upon History, 1660 to 1793* by a then obscure American, Captain A. T. Mahan. Mahan had fought on the Union side in the American Civil War, had plenty of sea service, spoke French, and had travelled widely outside the USA, but by the age of fifty his career was undistinguished. However, it was as a writer and lecturer at the newly founded US Navy War College that he found his metier, and there he began to influence American views on the need to build up the United States Navy. His *Influence of Sea Power* is his best-known work, but he wrote several other books on similar themes, and together they had a profound effect upon navies, politicians, and public in the USA, Britain, Germany, and Japan. In short, Mahan helped to relaunch the US Navy, which in the 1890s was rather in the doldrums, and subsequently, in his words, 'the American Republic broke free from her old moorings and sailed out to be a world power'. Then, for more than century, Mahan's theories, especially about big fleet actions, influenced the heart of American decision-making from Theodore Roosevelt down to the US Navy's maritime strategy during the Cold War. The Americans came to accept Mahan's theories unquestioningly and in 1948 the American politician Henry Stimson wrote that the US Navy 'had a particular psychology, which frequently seems to retire from the realm of logic into a dim religious world in which Neptune is god, Mahan the prophet and the United States Navy the only true church'. Mahan's work also stimulated the growth of the German navy; the Kaiser enthused about *The Influence of Sea Power* and placed a translation in every warship, ordering his officers to read it. It may be too much to blame Mahan for being one of the causes of the First World War, but it was a widely held British view, repeated as late as 1940, that he had played a part in bringing Germany and Britain into war with each other. However, he was perhaps the first to systematically examine the history of Europe and America with reference to the part that sea power had played, and he attempted to show how historians had overlooked the all-pervasive effect of sea power: his writings were more significant for their general stimulus to thinking about navies and sea power than for their particular conclusions. Unfortunately his ideas were also corrupted into a single theory about decisive battle at sea, which the Germans came to think of as *der Tag*.

*The Times'* judgement about there being no native British treatise about naval warfare was a little harsh, given the generations of knowledge which had been handed down within the Royal Navy, and the work of contemporary writers who had filled *The Times'* own pages. Not least among these correspondents were the Colomb brothers, especially Philip Colomb, a writer so prolific that Fisher called him 'column and half'. When Mahan published *Influence of Sea Power*, Philip Colomb was finishing a book of his own on the same subject, but he generously wrote to Mahan, 'I think all our naval men regard it as the naval book of the age, and it has had a great effect in getting people to understand what they never understood before . . . my book comes a long way behind yours in literary worth, for we have all been struck by the beauty of your style as much as by the force of your arguments'. A generation later and more objectively Julian Corbett confided that he thought that Mahan had raped history to support his case that the United States needed a navy.

Corbett's own book, modestly entitled *Some Principles of Maritime Strategy*, is the most important book for navies today. Julian Corbett's writings were lucid and original, informed both by his careful research and by his excellent prose style, in contrast to Mahan, whose prose is rather turgid. Corbett derived his principles from his study of the maritime and amphibious campaigns of the Elizabethans, and many of these are set out in his foreword to *The Successors of Drake*, in which he wrote:

> The real importance of maritime power is its influence on military operations . . . The great lesson that the period teaches is the limitation of maritime power. The power had been gained and appreciated, but to everyone's surprise it did not produce the expected results, and neither the Queen nor her Government could understand the reason . . . the real object of Essex and the military reformers was to form a corps ready trained and organised for service beyond the seas – a force that could reap where the fleet had sown . . . they viewed the fleet, not as a separate entity, but as an integral part of one great force.

With the names changed and the language updated these words could be a description of the modern concept of amphibious or littoral warfare.

Corbett came from a moderately wealthy background, qualified as a lawyer but did not practise, travelled widely in the 1880s and 1890s, and began his literary career by writing *Boy's Own* stories about Drake and Monck. From there he was quickly drawn into more serious writing and began his career as naval writer, strategist, and lecturer at the naval war college at Greenwich. Unlike Mahan, whose biography of Nelson emerged from his historical and theoretical writing, Corbett's early writings were works of fiction and biography, and only later did he turn to history and theory. He was a civilian, which gave him a certain independence of the factions which divided the British navy of his era, especially those for and against Fisher. However, his lectures at Greenwich were sometimes rubbished by naval officers who thought he needed to have served at sea in order to sea to speak, especially when he advocated that battles, or seeking battles, did not necessarily make good history or good strategy. The senior officers who were his pupils were surprised and did not wish to hear him say that 'without a supporting army, imaginatively led, the navy is not a decisive weapon'.

Corbett thought that Mahan and others were unduly influenced by battle: further his private summary of Mahan was 'shallow and wholly unhistorical'. In modern strategic parlance, Corbett's theories were manoeuvrist and Mahan's attritional. In the twentieth century the world would see that battles of attrition led nowhere except to the stalemate and the horrors of the trenches of the First World War. Corbett was much more subtle and original, for example, arguing against the theory of the decisive battle and that, 'the great dramatic moments of naval history have to be worked for and the first preoccupation of the fleet will almost always be to bring them about by interference with the enemy's military and diplomatic arrangements'.

Above all, Corbett understood that a navy was not a separate entity which could act independently, but that 'men live upon the land and not upon the sea, that great issues between nations at war have always been decided – except in the rarest of cases – either by what your army can do against your enemy's territory and national life, or else by the fear of what the fleet makes it possible for your army to do'.

Corbett's reputation after his death in 1922 was clouded by contemporary controversies, by a misunderstanding of his views about the relationship between navies and armies, and by the fact that some of his views were downright unpalatable for naval officers. He died before completing the *Official History of Naval Operations 1914–18*, and to their eternal shame the Admiralty, influenced by Beatty, introduced a note in the dead man's last volume that the principles advocated in the book were in conflict with theirs in 'tending to minimise the importance of seeking battle and forcing it to a conclusion'.

The First World War would be an opportunity for the two theories, of Mahan and Corbett, complementary and conflicting as they were, to be tested.

# Chapter Ten

# The First World War

The Royal Navy was at the height of its power at the beginning of the twentieth century. The French navy had not been a threat for years, the Russian navy suffered a crushing defeat by the Japanese at Tsushima in 1905, and the US Navy was not significant. However, the Kaiser and his naval chief, von Tirpitz, wanted a navy to help secure an overseas empire, and they wanted it even if it meant challenging the Royal Navy. German shipbuilding plans were indeed taken as a challenge to British naval supremacy and resulted in a naval arms race. The construction, launch, and successful sea trial in twelve months (October 1905 to October 1906) of a revolutionary battleship, the all-big-gun *Dreadnought*, soon led to Britain building two keels to every new German in an effort to use superior industrial resources to out-build the German navy – anticipating the Reagan–Thatcher policy by which the Cold War was finally won.

While relations with Germany deteriorated, those with France improved. Admiral Sir 'Jackie' Fisher brought the fleet home from its worldwide deployments, paying off older manpower-intensive warships. Britain joined in the Entente Cordiale with her long-time enemy, France, and an Anglo-Japanese Treaty allowed the Royal Navy to maintain only token forces in the east. Urgent steps were taken to create an empire navy by establishing navies in the former colonies, such as the Royal Australian Navy. The French navy was persuaded to concentrate its forces in the Mediterranean, while the Royal Navy took responsibility for the defence of the North Sea, and so northern France.

Meanwhile 'Jackie' Fisher was thrusting the Royal Navy into the new century with a breathtaking range of reforms: submarines, steam-driven turbines, oil power instead of coal, better torpedoes, and education. The only serious oversight was his failure to create a

naval staff, which he thought, perhaps subconsciously, would
restrict his genius: not everyone shared his greatness, and there were
many weaknesses in the hierarchy of the navy.

Then in 1914 the First Lord of the Admiralty, the young
Winston Churchill, suggested, as an economy measure, that the
usual summer exercise be cancelled and instead a mobilization of
the reserve or Third Fleet be practised. Mobilization was followed
by a fleet review at Spithead, of some four hundred ships, which
were supposed to disperse. However, the First Sea Lord, Prince
Louis of Battenberg, cancelled the order, so that when war was
declared all was ready at sea: 'Great Britain was as ready as ever to
play the old game, and had set the board with all the old skill'.


## THE ROYAL NAVAL AIR SERVICE

The Royal Navy, the world's leading sea power, also led the world
in the development of air power, using heavier than air machines
(unlike the Germans, who excelled in lighter than air vessels). The
navy had warmly embraced the concept of naval aviation, sending
the first pilots for training in 1910, and developments in naval air
were surprisingly quick: the first flight, by Lieutenant Charles
Samson from the forecastle of the stationary HMS *Africa*, was in
December 1911. Samson, in a Short biplane, used 100ft of specially
constructed decking: within a year runs of only 25ft were needed if
the ship, *London*, was underway. The first dedicated aircraft carrier,
the appropriately named *Hermes*, was converted to carry seaplanes
in the same year. By January 1914, when the Naval Wing of the
Royal Flying Corps had 135 aircraft of more than a score of types,
it was decided 'that the time had come when it must pass from the
experimental stage to take a definitive place in the Naval Organisation', even though 'the general opinion is that present experience
had been too brief'. In 1914, Lieutenant Longmore, RN (later Air
Chief Marshal Sir Arthur Longmore, RAF) was already testing anti-
submarine tactics, and the Naval Wing was rechristened the Royal
Naval Air Service. The RNAS officers were recruited from the navy,
used naval-style ranks (flight-lieutenant, and flight-, squadron-, and
wing-commander), and wore naval uniform but with bastardized

naval cap badges on which eagles replaced anchors. The RNAS had several roles: air defence (and an admiral, Sir Percy Scott, was put in charge of the anti-aircraft gunnery to defend London), photo-reconnaissance, gunnery spotting, anti-submarine warfare, and attacking airship and aeroplane bases. Several squadrons were deployed to the Western Front, where they distinguished themselves. The first strategic bombing was by a single naval aircraft, on airship sheds at Düsseldorf in October 1914, the pilot, Flight Lieutenant Marix, RN returning to his base by borrowed bike and hired car. By 1916 an independent bombing wing of the RNAS was stationed in France to conduct strategic bombing deep into Germany against targets such as steel and chemical works, munitions factories, and, of course, Zeppelin bases.

By 1914 Samson, who had already pioneered deck take-off, night flying, and airborne radio, was commanding No. 3 or Eastchurch Squadron RNAS. In August his squadron was sent to Belgium to support the Royal Naval Division, which attempted to seize Antwerp before the Germans. Samson promptly improvised two armoured cars to reconnoitre the advancing enemy, one of them a Rolls-Royce belonging to his brother, and they added a Maxim gun and side-armour made of boiler plate. In fact, because No. 3 Squadron's mixed bag of aircraft was unserviceable, most of their fighting was done in these cars.

## THE FIRST TANKS

Success, it is said, has many fathers, and the tank was no exception, but it is clear that the idea originated in the navy and that the First Lord, Winston Churchill, with his fertile mind and restless seeking for the offensive, was the midwife. The idea for the first tank seems to have been born when naval 12pdr guns were fitted to armoured cars. According to Eustace d'Eyncourt, the Director of Naval Construction,

> I first received instructions from Mr Churchill, in February 1915, who sent me notes ... of a proposal which he had discussed with Major Hetherington [variously described as 18th

Hussars, RNAS, and later Machine Gun Corps, and also referred to by his naval rank of flight commander] of the Naval Air Service. I looked into these proposals, which were for a very heavy machine which would have weighed more than 1,000 tons [sic], with wheels 40 feet in diameter, and it soon became apparent that this was not a practical proposition ... [I] suggested that we should try a smaller alternative arrangement which would not be quite so ambitious ...

After examining various designs, in March 1915 an order for twelve caterpillar-tracked vehicles was placed, while design work continued which quickly produced tanks 'generally on the lines of the present tanks now in use [he was writing post-war]'.

Churchill wanted these 'very large ships . . . to carry to the attack a large body of men say 100 each, safely across trenches and barbed wire entanglements'. He appointed d'Eyncourt, a naval architect, to the chairmanship of the Admiralty Landships Committee, and clearly intended that the RNAS should man them and carry the Royal Naval Division into action. Even after it was decided that 'the army and not the navy would have to fight these ships', naval officers continued to dominate the group that worked out the design and technical details. However, when Churchill left the Admiralty, his successor, Balfour, refused to take responsibility for 'any special liens of the late 1st Lord'.

Though it soon became the army which 'should decide the purpose for which these ships would be used and the armament required', this did not stop officers of the navy from recommending that large numbers should be produced and used in shock tactics. However, the first tanks were committed piecemeal to the battle and 'from the moment the Germans saw them they started making tanks probably more powerful and, if possible, in greater numbers than, than our own'.

## TYRWHITT AND KEYES

The spirit of the navy has remained constant from generation to generation, and this spirit had not atrophied in nearly a century without general war as the careers of two other famous fighting admirals of the First World War demonstrate.

Reginald Tyrwhitt was one of the war's outstanding admirals: his cruisers and destroyers, the Harwich Force, relentlessly patrolled the North Sea. His force sank a German minelayer on 5 August 1914 in the first naval action in the North Sea, regularly raided the enemy coast, and was the harbinger of operations by the Battle Cruiser Force and the Grand Fleet, including Heligoland Bight later in August 1914 and Dogger Bank in January 1915. By the end of the war, he and his ships had earned the reputation of having spent more time at sea and engaging in more actions than any others.

Only slightly younger than Tyrwhitt, Roger Keyes, coming like many officers from Anglo-Irish stock, was a child of imperial Britain, born in India, where his father was general commanding the Punjab Frontier Force. Keyes was motivated to join the navy by his reading of James' *Naval History of Great Britain*, whose six volumes certainly belong to the inspirational school of history writing. After two years in the training ship HMS *Britannia* moored in the Dart, Keyes was sent to sea aged fourteen, about the same age as the captain's servants and volunteers of a hundred years and more before, and for the next decade or so the conditions under which he served, almost all under sail, were not much different from theirs. In his action-packed life, his first command, aged seventeen, was of eight men in a cutter off the island of Pemba, East Africa, armed with cutlasses and pistols. Keyes' first modern ship was the destroyer *Opossum* in 1898, when these small, fast ships were the very latest thing in naval development and the place for a man with a love of action. Sent to command the thirty-knot destroyer *Fame* based in Hong Kong, then the scene of great turmoil, Keyes showed the ability to get himself into thick of whatever action there was. During the Boxer Rebellion, he boarded and captured other destroyers in the old-fashioned style with handgun and cutlass, captured and blew up forts, and, with his White Ensign, was the first man of the relieving allied troops to enter the besieged legation quarter in Beijing. Aged twenty-eight he was promoted to commander for his services. Although never an intellectual, he spent time in the Naval Intelligence Division, was

sent to Rome as Naval Attaché Southern Europe, and after commanding a cruiser in the Atlantic Fleet, was, to everyone's surprise,
appointed Inspecting Captain of Submarines in 1910. His benefac-
tor was Arthur Knyvet Wilson, who, as Controller of the Navy, had
ordered the first submarines: Wilson wanted a charismatic officer
who would integrate the submariners more with the fleet. Later in
the war Keyes helped organize operations in the Dardanelles and
raids on the canal at Zeebrugge and Ostend, and in the Second
World War he was placed in charge of Combined Operations, out
of which grew the organization and force for Operation Neptune,
the invasion of Normandy. Keyes, clearly, had inherited the stop-
at-nothing courage, initiative, and aggression of his predecessors.

Tyrwhitt and Keyes, commanding his submarines from a
destroyer, took part in the Cuxhaven Raid on Christmas Day 1914,
which stands out as a seminal event in naval warfare: with aircraft,
surface ships, and submarines operating in concert, it was the first
carrier battle group. The technology was brand new: the aircraft
were two years old, the submarines ten, and the destroyers scarcely
twenty. The objective was first the sheds and then ships in the
Schillig Roads. Seven aircraft started, but as they crossed the coast
they encountered dense fog which made location near impossible:
but in the Schillig Roads were seven German battleships and three
battlecruisers, and more cruisers and destroyers, which took alarm
and weighed so hurriedly that the battlecruiser *Von der Tann* fouled
another cruiser and both were severely damaged.

No German ships came out, but Zeppelins and seaplanes
attacked the supporting force, without success. The results were
meagre, but in the words of the official history 'the experience was
as valuable as it was encouraging'. The fact that British forces had
been able to operate with impunity so close to the German coast
was a victory for British morale, and the raid was a precedent for
the battles that were to come, Taranto and Pearl Harbor, in a
subsequent world war.

However, the aircraft fared rather badly on their return, suffering
as they often did at this stage of their development as fighting
machines from fuel shortages and oil leaks, and only two returned
to their parent ships. The others dropped short into the sea. One
crew was rescued by Commodore Keyes in the *Lurcher* and three

others by Lieutenant Commander Nasmith, commanding HM Submarine *E11*. Nasmith had just taken one aircraft in tow when two more alighted beside him, and a Zeppelin attacked with bombs. Displaying the coolness and bravery for which he was to become famous the next year in the Dardanelles, he rescued the aircrew and dived. The remaining seaplane crew was briefly interned in Holland.

Later raids were no less inventive. This is how Walter Cowan describes subsequent operations in the North Sea:

After 2 years and 5 months in *Princess Royal*, I was made Commodore and given command of the 1st Light Cruiser Squadron still in the Battle Cruiser Force, with *Caledon* as my Flagship; the other ships were *Royalist*, *Galatea*, *Inconstant*, and *Phaeton* . . . There were 2 Squadrons of us with the B.C.F., the other the 6th L.C.S. [Light Cruiser Squadron] commanded by Jack Alexander Sinclair in *Cardiff*, and whenever the B.C.F. put to sea we two were the first out and last in and as a rule scouting 10 miles ahead of them, ears pricked and hearts full of hope.

Other times, one or other of our 2 Squadrons would go out and over to the German coast to trail our coats up and down the line of their minefields . . . Each of my ships had an aeroplane sitting on a platform above the forecastle: we would go over and fly them off to bomb the Zeppelin sheds at Tondern and had one or two successes that way. The pity of it was that they could never fly on again, we used to send them off as near to the target as we could and than thrash and zig-zag about at full speed until they re-appeared with our Destroyer escort; when they did, each aircraft would make for a Destroyer and plunge down into the sea hoping for the best and the Destroyer would run up alongside and drag the Pilot in-board, and then save as much of the wrecked plane as could be managed in a few minutes. It used to be a nerve straining tough finish for the Pilot at the end of a raid like that.

Flying them off was always an anxiety, all the run they could get was perhaps 20 feet of the platform they perched on. The way we did it was to set them all warming their engines up and then when each had signalled he was ready, all ships would turn into the wind together at full speed and up they would go, but always there was rather an alarming droop as they became airborne and cleared the forecastle head . . .

The aircraft used in these operations were Sopwith 1½ Strutters, which had the distinct disadvantage that they could not climb fast enough to catch any watching Zeppelin. Soon, however, a new, faster aircraft was taken to sea, the Sopwith Pup, its markings painted grey to delay detection, intended to climb behind the Zeppelin and fire on it from above and behind. The pilot still had to ditch in the sea, hoping a destroyer would pick him up. This is how Cowan, with suitable hunting analogies, describes the tactic which seems to have surprised the Zeppelin L23 on 21 August 1917:

There was generally a Zeppelin watching and reporting our movements from a safe distance and in those days we had no A.A. guns, so it was a continual fret not being able to cope with them. Time after time I was over there and shadowed by one of them, with sometimes an escorting aeroplane, but at last the Admiralty prepared the Cruiser *Yarmouth* to carry a suitable aeroplane which could fly off and climb quick, and attached her to my Squadron to see what we could do.

We went over in baddish weather and with this aeroplane covered up so that it could not be seen from the air. The usual Zeppelin came out with an escorting plane and we manoeuvred about keeping *Yarmouth* in formation until at last the enemy plane ran out of fuel and had to go home, then we uncovered ours, turned into the wind and up it went, but rather erratically as the controls were all salted up and rusty from the journey over. Anyhow he soon gained height and the Zeppelin, like a heron with a hawk after him, made for home and began to clatter with its wireless. Our plane dived to perhaps 200 yards and missed, then up he swung again, and this time came down and let drive with his incendiary bullets at 25 yards and wasn't far from following them into the Zeppelin's fabric himself; then there was a streak of fox coloured smoke and in no time nothing was left of her, one man dropped out and fell into the minefield and our plane hurtled down alongside a Destroyer and the Pilot was dragged on board all well, but he had had the greatest difficulty with his rusted up controls. I asked for the V.C. for him, as it was the first time we had dealt with a Zeppelin in that way, and it was gallantly done: he got great cheering from us all. Flight Sub-lieutenant Bernard A. Smart was his name, and he was awarded a D.S.O., not, as I hoped the V.C. . . .

Smart seems to have led a charmed life and was still attempting self-drowning several months later when the Royal Navy, having started the war with a primitive carrier battle group attack, mounted what one historian has called 'the first carrier strike . . . the first and faltering exhibition of a weapon which . . . was to play a major role in annihilating the maritime power of Japan'. Aircraft development was very rapid at this time, and yet another new mark of aircraft, the Sopwith Camel, was available and embarked in the aircraft carrier *Furious*. After several attempts were thwarted by bad weather, on 19 July 1918 the German airship base at Tondern was once again subject to low-level bombing, with the destruction of two airships, a large captive balloon, and some ground facilities. Thereafter the Germans retreated to Ahlhorn, far from the sea. However, bad weather and turbulence across *Furious*'s deck prevented the returning aircraft from landing on. Four aircraft flew on to Denmark and were interned, and three ditched in the sea, but only two pilots were picked from the water, one of whom was, of course, Smart.

About this time occurred the first and one of the few recorded incidents of a submarine shooting down an aircraft, as Cowan related:

Zeppelins came to their ends in different ways, one of our bombing raids on Tondern accounted for 3 of them, and we lost 3 planes with their pilots, but they survived. Another became disabled near to one of our patrolling submarines and flying very low was finished off by her and the survivors absorbed down the conning tower . . .

On 1 April 1918, the RNAS, which had performed so gallantly and devised many innovative operations during the war, was amalgamated once more with the Royal Flying Corps to become the Royal Air Force. A single air force had been advocated, for different reasons, by such eminent and influential figures as

Churchill, Beatty, and Smuts, though probably none of them anticipated what the effect would be on the navy. The most deleterious was the loss of nearly every experienced aviator to the RAF, which seriously impinged on the navy's readiness for the next war. The RAF units serving with the fleet were given the ungainly titles of Air Force Contingents, which in 1924 the navy rechristened the Fleet Air Arm. The navy was not to regain full control of its own air force until 1937, but that story is to be told later.

## BATTLE OF THE FALKLANDS, 1914

On the outbreak of the war, the German Pacific Squadron was cut off from the fatherland. Leaving China and crossing the empty Pacific, the squadron under Admiral von Spee raided harbours for coal and threatened British shipping off South America. The British Admiralty had divided its forces, exposing Admiral Cradock and the South American Squadron, giving him conflicting orders and a mixed squadron of elderly ships. Off the Chilean port of Coronel on 1 November 1914 these ill-matched squadrons clashed. Von Spee, whose two largest ships, *Scharnhorst* and *Gneisenau*, were crack gunnery ships, was inshore of Cradock and had the advantage of calmer water, the outlines of his ships being obscured against the coast, and the smoke from his guns, drifting towards the British, making spotting the fall of shot difficult for Cradock's ships. Held at long range, the silhouettes of the British ships were sharply defined against the setting sun. In growing darkness the Germans were almost invisible to the British, even when the heavy seas and spray did not wash their sights, and the cruisers *Good Hope* and *Monmouth* were sunk at about 7.30 p.m. with few survivors. This is how Lieutenant Frederick Giffard, writing to his mother, described the battle, using information which he gleaned from German sources:

> The Germans heard that the [cruiser] *Glasgow* was there and went to look, never hoping to catch four [of] our ships together. The fight ... was very one sided, and after about ½ hour the *Good Hope* was burning fiercely, with showers of different

coloured flames due to wood I suppose. They left her and went for the other ships . . . it was nearly dark . . . and never saw her again and reported her ashore. They did not know till some days later that she was sunk. The *Monmouth* was badly knocked about and the [cruiser] *Nurnberg* was sent to torpedo her. The *Nurnberg* – it was so dark – at first thought she was German, but when the *Monmouth* fired at her knew better and fired some 50 rounds at her and I think a torpedo. The *Monmouth* sank, and though the Germans tried they could see no one in the water, and it was far too rough to launch a boat . . .

This was a blow to British prestige, which, in the words of Julian Corbett, 'let loose all the latent energy and resource of the oldest and most powerful of the navies'. All available cruisers were ordered to concentrate in the River Plate, and from Britain, two of the latest and fastest battlecruisers, *Inflexible* and *Invincible*, were detached from the Grand Fleet and hurried south under the command of Admiral Sir Frederick Sturdee: both battlecruisers still had some dockyard mateys working on board. Sturdee had remarkable orders: an almost free hand, and, as Commander-in-Chief South Atlantic and Pacific, the largest geographical command ever entrusted to a single admiral. The British force concentrated at the Abrolhos Islands, nominally Brazilian but freely used by the Royal Navy as an anchorage and place of rendezvous, and then on 28 November steamed on southwards, with the ships formed in a scouting line at twelve-mile intervals. Reaching the Falkland Islands on 7 December, they began at once to coal. In parts of his letter Giffard's sentiments are surprisingly pro-German, but here is how he described the first Battle of the Falklands, starting on the morning of 8 December 1914:

We were coaling in preparation to seeking them. A difficult job where such enormous areas of water are concerned. And they were just going along after rounding Cape Harbour, so as to prize the Falklands and they walked right into it, as soon as they saw our tripods and our sisters they could hardly believe it, and then they had to and turned away South at full speed . . . as soon as they saw us they knew that their number was up . . . All our ships were getting up steam as fast as possible, and one the *Cornwall* was soon ready and went out to keep an eye on them. We got under way at 10, which was jolly good, the stokers worked like good'uns, and you may be sure that any success we have in this war will be due very largely to our engineer staff. When we got clear we saw the enemy hull down on the Southern horizon, belching thick black smoke ... We tooled along at 20 knots keeping them slightly on our Starboard Bow. Soon however, they divided up, the German admiral ordering his light ships to make for South American ports whilst the *Scharnhorst* and *Gneisenau* did their best against us big ships. They were both smart ships, and the latter had held the Kaisers prize for battle practice for two years running ... We went to action stations at 12.34 and within a couple of minutes all was ready, people at their stations, hoses running over the decks and 3 ensigns flying from our masts. My station was in the after Conning Tower just above the mainmast, in connection with the after Torpedo Quarters. At 1 pm we opened fire from our fore turret at the *Leipzig* and fired several shots after her as did the *Invincible* at one other ship. They were in line abreast steaming away, and we two in quarter line. No hits were I think got at this period, but they went jolly close to them. Our shell [in the First World War shell, not shells, was the adopted plural] threw up huge mountains of water the peaks rising to over 300 feet above the water. They were magnificent to watch. About this time their small cruisers separated and our little fellows went after them and bagged two after a stubborn fight. Our fellows were all admiration for their fighting, and said amongst other things that the *Nurnberg*, after she had finished her ammunition and was sinking, her crew collected on the upper deck and sang patriotic songs.

The *Scharnhorst* and *Gneisenau* turned up to port and we followed ... Their firing was beautiful to watch – perfect ripple salvos all along their sides. A brown coloured puff with a centre of flames masking each gun as it fired. Of course we were playing at long bowls, it was to our advantage. But ... They straddled us time after time. One could hear the shell coming with a curious shrill whine which gradually got deeper and then pop, pop as they burst in the water. As the range was so long we heard this shell before they got to us, as the velocity had fallen to below 1100 feet per second (the velocity of sound) . . . We were all blazing away now, and our guns shook us up considerably . . . About 2 they drew out of range due to a sudden alteration of course which we did not notice at once. So we had to start all over again and chase them. We had a spell to, and the upper deck was covered with men hunting for splinters as mementoes. There were several splinters of shell from short shots bursting.

By this time we had one hit on the fore turret, which burst without doing any damage, though some small splinters got into the conning tower, and one gave the navigator a small scratch on the right eyebrow. He had a fine black eye afterwards. My cabin was in an awful state. Everything upset in the middle, due to the blast of our own guns. The Wardroom was also wrecked in a similar manner, and there was a lot of wine spilt all over the deck. We got into range again about 3, and they opened fire first, but we got going this time properly. They were on our starboard beam to the Southward. At 3.40 they turned 16 points to starboard, and we turned together to port. At 4.20 the *Scharnhorst* who had dropped out of the line at 4.10 turned over and sank with appalling suddenness. She had been getting a list for some time we could not stop and save any as the *Gneisenau* was still going strong. There cannot have been many left in her as she turned over so suddenly. There was nothing to be seen in the water with glasses but she was 3 to 4 miles away. The *Gneisenau* was getting into trouble about now, her foremost funnel being all any how, and at about 5.30 she stopped firing, we closed, she opened again, so did we. Then she stopped, we closed again and then she fired one gun – her last round. We put some more into her and then she stopped. We closed and she gradually turned over and at 6pm sank . . . The water was fearfully cold and many of them must have drowned from sheer cold . . . Most of them could not sleep that first night – the scenes on their ship were so terrible. To see ones best friend suddenly torn to bits, or rush on deck one huge wound covered with blood and just have time to send his love home is terrible. Although there was practically no damage to be seen it was impossible for them to get from one end of the ship to the other, there was no upper or main deck left at all, and the lower

(armoured) deck was full of holes and very hot. That is the
result of long range plunging fire ... Over 2000 of them must
have been killed or drowned with all their cherished possessions,
and their good ships ... They said our 12" shell made their
whole ship shake and they could feel the decks rippling like a
caterpillar ... We had one man killed and two wounded from
a splinter from the main derrick which was shot away at about
3.30pm But we only had two hits on our ship, possibly due to
our good and rapid shooting. The *Invincible* got many more
hits. But it was all luck, as they were pitching in the waters all
round us most of the time, some within 10 yards. So we were
very lucky ...

Although the German cruiser *Dresden* escaped from the Battle of
the Falklands, only to be hunted down later, and the *Königsberg* hid
ignobly in the Rufiji delta in East Africa for several more months,
temporarily tying up more British forces, the German navy's
attempts at commerce-raiding using surface ships was brought
swiftly to an end. In the words of the official historian, 'the wonder
is they did not cause more mischief than they did ... the impotence
of the Germans while their chance lasted is remarkable'.

## THE ROYAL NAVAL DIVISION

While Jellicoe and the Grand Fleet were preparing for a new
Trafalgar against the Germans in the North Sea, the navy maintained the same aggressive spirit which had characterized its operations in the Great War of 1793–1815, forming from surplus
recruits and Royal Marines the Royal Naval Division, which fought
first at Antwerp, then in the Dardanelles, and later on the Western
Front, where it became one of the crack formations of the British
army. The title of naval brigade was often applied to a force much
smaller than the army would have graced with the title of brigade:
in the navy it could be any size of force, and Beatty claimed to have
commanded a brigade of just two men. However, in the First
World War, there were so many men employed in brigades that
they formed an entire division, and the division's battalions were

given the names of famous admirals. The RND was something of an elite, attracting a distinguished officer corps which included the poet Rupert Brooke, Arthur Asquith, the Prime Minister's son, and Bernard Freyberg, who won the Victoria Cross. Forty per cent of the Royal Navy's casualties in the First World War occurred not at sea but ashore in the Royal Naval Division.

Operations began on 25 August 1914 when the Royal Marines temporarily occupied Ostend. Meanwhile, the Admiralty found maybe for the first time in its history that it had more men than it needed, so in mid-September several hundred reservists began training for operations ashore. By the end of September the Royal Marines were redeployed to Dunkirk, with Commander Samson's aeroplanes, and a number of armoured cars, initially to guard the port. Soon they were moved again, this time to defend Antwerp, where they were joined in early October by two of the newly trained naval brigades: they were in action for just two days before being ordered to withdraw, and in the confusion some men crossed the frontier into neutral Holland and were interned.

By the end of February 1915 the Royal Naval Division had re-formed and retrained and was sent to the eastern Mediterranean, reaching Lemnos, a familiar anchorage in British naval history, on 11 March 1915. They took part in diversionary operations to draw the attention of the Turks away from an unsuccessful attempt by British and French ships to force the Dardanelles. The plan according to the admiral commanding the Eastern Mediterranean Squadron given on board the battleship *Queen Elizabeth* on 15 March was similar to the one Duckworth had used a century before: 'to silence the defences of the Narrows and of the minefield simultaneously, so as to enable sweepers to clear a passage through the Kephaz mine field; if this is successful the attack to be at once continued on the remaining defences until the fleet has passed through the Dardanelles'. However, the forts at the entrance gave unexpected resistance, there were British losses, and the Turks, thoroughly alerted to Allied intentions, had time to reinforce the Dardanelles.

After a short spell in Egypt, the Royal Naval Division returned to the Gulf of Saros to take part in the main landings at Gallipoli, and the seamen and marines of the division suffered heavy losses alongside the Australians and New Zealanders. Ships also suffered, as described by a signalman, Jordan, in the *Inflexible* in a letter home to his sister, Daisy, written on signal forms and dated 12 September 1915:

> we was struck by several large shell from the Forts . . . [and] . . . set on fire, which after a struggle was put out and we kept hard at it, setting fire to the Forts a treat. It made one feel a bit sick when the French ship *Bouvet* went (two explosions and no ship left, in a matter of seconds) quite early in the day. Just as we were getting the better of the Forts towards the evening and the firing was slacking a bit (all day the shells were coming down like hailstones from Forts and Land Batteries on both sides) we had the bad luck to strike a mine, which lifted us and dropped us and left us in rather a bad condition about ten miles inside the Dardanelles . . . on our way out we passed the *Ocean* and *Irresistible* in difficulties, the *Ocean* sank but the *Irresistible* was wrecked . . .

The attack on the Dardanelles was a failure and in the evacuation in January 1916 the Royal Naval Division was amongst the last to leave. After operations in Salonika and in the Aegean islands, the division left for France in May 1916, landing at Marseilles. By July 1916, the RND was under the control of the army, who rather unimaginatively rechristened it the 63rd (R.N.) Division, but throughout the First World War the division was paid for by the navy, and the battalions retained the names of famous fighting admirals. As in the RNAS, the RND kept its naval ranks, and it also retained its customs, keeping time by a ship's bell, and using naval speech, including 'going ashore' and cooking in a 'galley'. This greatly annoyed some senior army officers, one of whom at least seems to have adopted a murderous attitude to the men under his own command. In truth, one of the elements in maintaining the elite nature of the RND was its piratical attitude to war in the trenches, and the RND was often compared favourably to the crack Commonwealth divisions.

The RND had arrived in France in time to take part in the last battle of the Somme campaign, capturing Beaucourt and hundreds of prisoners. Later it chased the German army back to its Hindenburg Line, and fought in the mud of the Passchendaele offensive. During the last great German counter-offensive, in the spring of 1918, the RND fell back almost as far as its starting position in 1916, but recovered to take a full part in the last victorious advance: it was still fighting, near Mons, when the Armistice was declared.

On 6 June 1919 the Royal Naval Division attended its final parade on Horse Guards Parade, where it was addressed by the Prince of Wales, and where a handsome monument by Lutyens was raised to its memory.

## LIFE IN THE BATTLE CRUISER FORCE

For most of the First World War the main body of the British Grand Fleet lay at Scapa Flow in the Orkneys under Sir John Jellicoe, while the Battle Cruiser Force was based further south, at Rosyth in Scotland, under the command of Sir David Beatty. Beatty was another of the charismatic, daring, and assertive officers of his age. He had served with distinction in the Sudan from 1896 to 1898, where he first met Churchill, and in China during the Boxer Rising of 1900. At the age of thirty-eight he was the youngest officer for more than a century to achieve flag rank.

The Battle Cruiser Force consisted of fast ships, intended to help locate the enemy fleet and decoy them onto the main body of the Grand Fleet. Some of their speed had been achieved by sacrificing armour, and in Beatty's attack on the German High Seas Fleet at Jutland his ships suffered major losses. Both sides claimed victory: in practice the Battle of Jutland was a German tactical victory, but a strategic victory for the British that discouraged German offensive fleet action for the rest of the war. However, Jellicoe was blamed for the lack of a clear British success, the dashing Beatty was his natural successor, and he was appointed Commander-in-Chief of the Grand Fleet in November 1916 when Jellicoe went to be First Sea Lord. Subsequently Beatty too became First Sea Lord, from 1919 to 1927.

Meanwhile at Rosyth the Battle Cruiser Force held itself in readiness: 'leave for the men was very restricted as we lay there at 4 hours notice only, and, very often less and there is no doubt the

monotony of it all told on them. Periodic visits over to France were
arranged for parties of about 40 with 2 or 3 officers and every now
and then they dropped in for quite a battle and generally acquitted
themselves well'. This is how one such visit was described by an
engine-room rating who visited the trenches: 'The dugout was a
sandbag affair about 8 ft long 6 ft wide and 4 ft 6 in high. The
machine gun and rifle fire and an occasional art[iller]y bang made
such a row that sleep, to me at least, was impossible. The Canadians
on our immediate left kept up a lively machine gun fire all night'.
The visit included some action:

> At 4.30 AM a sentry put his head in with the news that the
> wind had veered round to NE direct from the German lines
> and that there were signs of a Gas Attack [but] The wind
> suddenly veered round again so nothing came of it. At 5 AM
> word was passed to 'Stand To' and immediately everybody
> manned the parapet in readiness for an attack from the German
> lines, it being found Fritz's favourite time for attack . . . During
> this time a continuous rain of rifle and machine gun fire had
> been falling. I fired another 47 rounds from a Lewis Rifle and
> about 20 rounds from a rifle; nothing serious occurred until
> 6.15 AM when 9 men were killed by a large whiz bang [high-
> velocity shell] and 4 by rifle fire, and several wounded. It being
> still dark they were at once sent down to the B.H.Q. the dead
> for burial, and the wounded dressed and sent on the base.
> About 6.45, one of the Sub Lieuts gave me a snipers spring rifle
> and a periscope, though which I could see three men working
> on the German parapet. I fired two rounds and two of them
> apparently fell and the other disappeared but whether they were
> injured or not it was impossible to say . . .

Meanwhile in the Battle Cruiser Force itself:

> We used also to have Boxing tournaments every few months
> and very good ones. David Beatty greatly encouraged it and
> every one of our ships had good entries and quite often would
> be found well known high class professional boxers from the
> outside world, disguised generally as stokers. In my *Princess
> Royal* for instance was Jimmy Wilde. At the end of each
> tournament after the prize giving, D.B. would always address

them about Battle Cruiser happenings and give them a review of the war and perhaps his forecast of the future, the burning question always was when will they come out. They did come out now and then, but generally not far enough to be compelled to fight, there were many disappointments like that, but at last one lovely evening at the end of May came the signal for 1 hour's notice. I had been playing tennis at the Hood's all the afternoon ...

In two years of war the Battles of Heligoland Bight, the Falklands, and Dogger Bank were the only major engagements between the British and the German fleets. However, British and German tactics were complementary. The Germans hoped that by raids on the English coast they would draw the British battlecruisers to sea where they would then be led on to the German High Seas Fleet, and if the Grand Fleet sailed it would be ambushed by German U-boats. The British hoped that Beatty's battlecruisers would draw the High Seas Fleet onto the well-disciplined Grand Fleet, and this is pretty well what happened at the end of May 1916.

## THE BATTLE OF JUTLAND

The Commander-in-Chief of the Grand Fleet at the Battle of Jutland was, of course, Admiral Sir John Jellicoe. Jellicoe's career had been busy and eventful, and he shared with contemporaries the experiences of campaigning ashore. He fought in the Egyptian War of 1882, and while commanding an expedition during the Boxer Rebellion in China of 1900 he had escaped death though severely wounded. Jellicoe was also one of the survivors of the collision of the *Victoria* and *Camperdown* in 1893: this was actually a multiple escape, because, by being sick in his cabin on board the flagship, he was not called upon to contradict the fearsome George Tryon, his Commander-in-Chief, and thus no blame could be apportioned to him at the court martial. Subsequently he became something of a protégé of Jackie Fisher and, as Controller of the Navy, helped Fisher in his modernization of the fleet, including the building of

*Dreadnought.* At the outbreak of war in 1914 Jellicoe was sent north to take over command of the Grand Fleet from Admiral Callaghan, though even as he waited on the jetty to be ferried to the flagship, he was telegramming the Admiralty asking that this cup should be taken from him.

After finishing his tennis, Cowan describes the how the fleet deployed and the battle developed:

> At nightfall, we slid quietly under the Forth Bridge and made for a rendezvous signalled by the Admiralty over towards the Jutland Coast with the 5th Battle Squadron attached, all new modern warships, the fastest we had *Barham*, *Valiant*, *Malaya*, *Warspite*, and *Queen Elizabeth* . . . That next afternoon we were . . . steaming along with Jack A-Sinclair's Light Cruisers far out on the Starboard bow and the 5th B.S. Hugh Evan-Thomas about a mile also on our Starboard bow. There was smoke in sight away to starboard and a merchant ship being signalled by *Cardiff* A-S's Flagship, and almost immediately from him came the signal 'Enemy in sight' and their Battle Cruisers hove up. My first ejaculation was 'That d-----d 5th B.S. is going to take the bread out of our mouths', they were the nearest and seemed to have the inside turn had they at once gone the shortest way at them to close the range, but I believe their Admiral expected a signal from D.B. and there was just that pause, and then the way they led round put them rather a long way astern of us with the result that instead of being able to join us in battering away at their Battle Cruisers at the head of their Battle line they got rather heavily hammered by the German Battleships, but all these events have been so profusely written about by people far wiser and better qualified to judge than I am that I think I will not further enlarge upon it. What I have written here is just my own observation of what I saw, and felt and with no thought of criticism . . .

Cowan's modest observations were fairly accurate, and this by a man who

> When that war began I copied out and kept on my person or under my pillow and for many years after it was all over, Nelson's directive about those sort of doubtful moments. 'Some-

thing must be left to chance, nothing is sure in a Sea fight beyond all others but in case signals can neither be seen or perfectly understood, no Captain can do very wrong if he places his ship alongside that of an Enemy.'

Beatty had evidently read the same text:

D.B. of course led us over to get at them and the Battle began. To begin with the Germans shot very well indeed, but directly we began hitting them it soon deteriorated though in the first 40 minutes we lost 3 out of our 9 Battle Cruisers with all hands, through plunging fire going through their decks and exploding the magazines. *Queen Mary* next astern of us went first, our Signal Boatswain snapped out to me 'Something has happened to *Queen Mary*, sir', I looked round and saw a billow of soft white smoke and her stern sliding beneath the water, and a Destroyer dashing in to the pool of oil to try and pick up some of them.

All this time we were driving Northwards and watching for the Grand Fleet speeding South to meet us, but next came Hood with his 3 Battle Cruisers from Scapa and he swung them most beautifully round to station them ahead of *Lion* with all 3 of them blazing away at the Enemy, and then a salvo hit *Invincible* and blew her in half; it was shallow water there and as we roared close past her the two ragged ends of her rested on the bottom and her two sharp ends were leaning together like the beginning of a card house and one man climbing out of the wreckage of the control top.

*Lion*, *Princess Royal* and *Tiger*, were all getting a fair good knocking about. *Lion* in particular, and on fire in one or two places; I suggested to O. de B. Brock that we should offer to change places with her for a bit to take some of the weight of the battering off her, but it was not agreed to. *Indefatigable*, also blew up just before *Invincible*.

Then the advanced screen of the Grand Fleet hove in sight and out in front of all of them raging along with all guns firing that would bear, heading straight for the German Battleline was one Armoured Cruiser. I said to O. de B. 'I will bet anything that is Robert Arbuthnot,' and so it was, in *Defence*, there were 4 of that class, but in the smoke and clatter, it was hard to tell which was which, but it was just what one reckoned his form, to fly straight at their throats, regardless of any odds. 3 quick salvoes struck her one after another and down she went, you could not imagine any quicker more spectacular example of successful gunnery.

With the Fleet now in sight and within striking distance, we felt like throwing our caps in the air, it looked a certainty we had them. The Germans a half beaten, wholly rattled Fleet with most of their torpedoes fired and a good deal of their ammunition, confronted by our splendid, fresh, and preponderant Battle Fleet all wild for blood after nearly two years of monotonous waiting. The Germans had planned to trap D.B's Force and here they were trapped themselves, and their spear head of Battle Cruisers well nigh fought to a standstill . . .

The Grand Fleet was a highly regimented force. Whereas Beatty had fought his part of the battle with too few orders and thus the battlecruisers and the fast battleships had failed to support each other, the Grand Fleet could not be fought without voluminous instructions and orders. In both cases the orders were passed by signal flag, a technology which was scarcely reliable when ships fought under sail and short ranges, and certainly unsuitable to the high-speed, long-range fighting of the First World War. Cowan was rightly critical of Grand Fleet Battle Orders:

Just about then, we were swinging round to Starboard battering the head of their line to the Eastward and that desperation [sic] pompous business of the Battle fleet deployment had begun, it was ever rather beyond my intellect to grasp the value of it, there were sheets of directions and diagrams to govern and explain it and the whole business took 40 minutes to complete. What we were longing for was for one of their Divisions of 8 to tail in astern of us, to just give a bit more weight of gunfire to crumple up the head of their line . . .

Then:

As we were swinging round there was rather a bunching up mostly of Destroyers and Grand Fleet light craft and in the middle of it all on our starboard hand appeared the German light Cruiser *Wiesbaden*, half disabled and smoke and steam gushing out everywhere. She was too far gone to be a worthy target for a Battle Cruiser I thought, and so told my ship to leave her alone and at that instant out shot one of our screening Destroyers *Onslow*, going straight at her and torpedoed her at close range. I asked the name of her Captain and it was John Tovey . . .

Jack Tovey was to serve with distinction in the next world war, 'showing the same unvarying form all the way'.

The battle itself was indecisive.

Night fell and we had not pulled it off, but there was still hope for the morning which would be, as D.B. signalled to us, the anniversary of Lord Howe's Glorious 1st of June. The present Lord Howe was then with him in *Lion* . . . All through the night there was confused fighting and torpedo attacks and by the trend of it it seemed they were working round the stern of our line to make for Hiorn's Reef and I believe the Admiralty wireless during the night expressed that opinion . . . Next morning we were somewhere about the middle of the North Sea and nothing in sight except a certain amount of wreckage and floating bodies from yesterday's fight, and so the hope of an annihilating victory died . . .

'It was', Cowan wrote, 'a bitter disappointment for us in the Battle Cruisers. We had found the enemy, fought them, and led them up into the jaws of our main Fleet and had lost 3 out of our 9 Battle Cruisers with near to 4,000 men in doing so . . .'

In Cowan's battlecruiser, *Princess Royal*, the damage was extensive:

our damages when the signal 'Return to Base' was made one turret was punched through the armour of the redoubt and out of action. 2 out of the 3 struts of the tripod mast carrying the control top, etc. were shot through by a heavy shell and so rather hanging by a thread and an anxiety in case a sea got up. 25% of the auxiliary armament out of action as well as of the main. Several heavy shell bursts inside and below – one in the middle of the canteen store. *Princess Royal's* consumption of eggs used to be 5,000 a day, we had, I think, 2 days supply on going to sea and these, were with the bodies of the two canteen

servers in the middle of it all blown to pieces. Fore and aft the
upper deck, casings and funnels riddled with shell splinters.
Engines and boilers as good as new, a big shell through the
Admiral's cabin and pantry, that is about all I can remember.
Casualties just over 100 . . .

In the *Lion* there were many more casualties:

as she lost the whole of the Marine Turret's crew through a
charge igniting in the gun house and, but for gallant prompt
action by the mortally wounded Marine Major Harvey, the
magazine must have blown up as well. She had 75 dead; I
remember so well as we steamed along astern of her watching
the bodies being brought up and laid out on deck, it seemed a
very long row, before the last was up . . .

Beatty's judgement of the battle was that 'we have been deprived
of striking one Great Blow for the Freedom of the World for which
we have waited so long. But the Prestige of the Grand Fleet was
too much for them and our Glory lies in that. The disappointment
is great but that is a small thing compared with the Result'. Many
had thought that Jellicoe would be the new Nelson, and certainly
the British public had expected a Trafalgar when the Grand Fleet
met the German High Seas Fleet. Controversy still reigns as to the
result of the Battle of Jutland. It is, however, too much to claim
that Jellicoe had displayed anything approaching naval genius.
Perhaps Fisher's comment when he heard the news of the Battle of
Jutland sums up the battle: 'They've failed me, they've failed me! I
have spent thirty years of my life preparing for this day and they've
failed me!'


## A-HUNTING WE WILL GO

Jutland had a cathartic effect on the Royal Navy, and a reaction to
regimented battle lines soon set in. For example, Cowan moved to
command a cruiser based at Harwich from where he conducted
aggressive patrols: 'We were not often idle in those days and my
first year in that Squadron *Caledon* averaged 100 miles a day'. Then
in November 1917,

'HMS *Victoria* sinking by the bows after ramming *Camperdown*'.
George Tryon tried to break out of the straitjacket of 'steam tactics' and
experimented with tactical manoeuvres by using as few signals as possible,
but when his subordinates did not understand or did not question evident
mistakes the result was disastrous and set back tactical development in
the Royal Navy by many years. [PU 6306]

HM submarines in Portsmouth harbour: the Royal Navy waited until the
technology was mature and then built, in some secrecy, the largest submarine
fleet in the world, which was ready by the start of the First World War. [N 3311]

The forecastle of the battlecruiser *Lion*, showing Admiral Sir David Beatty and his officers in some characterful poses, including Beatty with his rakish hat and non-regulation six-buttoned reefer jacket – which no one dared mimic. [P39959]

HM destroyers *Attack* and *Hydra*, taken from HMS *Inflexible*: the Battle of Jutland was not just a contest between dreadnoughts, and many flotillas of destroyers on both sides took part. This photograph gives some idea of the hazy weather and poor visibility in which the battle was fought. [P39965]

The Royal Navy was at battle stations when HMS *Cardiff* led the surrendered German High Seas Fleet into internment on Thursday 21 November 1918: Admiral Beatty told the ship's company of his flagship, 'they are out, and they are now in.' [BHC0670]

During the Norwegian Campaign and at Dunkirk in 1940 and again at Crete in 1941 the Royal Navy established that it would not abandon the army: at Dunkirk over 330,000 British and Allied troops were rescued from the beaches. [BHC0672]

*Above.* Using Gibraltar as its base, the Royal Navy formed 'Force H', which could swing into battle either in the Western Mediterranean or in the North Atlantic, and with this strategic advantage battleships and carriers took part in the relief of Malta and the hunt for the *Bismarck*. [BHC1582]

*Left.* Britain's greatest fighting admiral since Nelson, Admiral Andrew Brown Cunningham, fought the last battleship campaign in the Mediterranean, and revolutionized war at sea by integrating carriers into the battlefleet and ordering the Fleet Air Arm's attack on Taranto. [BHC2641]

The five-day fight of Operation Pedestal, to convoy ships and aircraft to Malta, was the culmination of one of the greatest convoy battles ever, and a turning point in the Second World War. [BHC1575]

Despite rough weather, freezing temperatures and the midnight sun which favoured the attack of German U-boats and aircraft operating from nearby bases in northern Norway, 811 merchant ships were escorted through the Barents Sea to aid the Soviet war effort: 53 were lost to enemy action and the weather. [BHC1576]

The oil tanker *Ohio*, taken over from the American Eagle Oil and Shipping Company, which made several successful voyages to the besieged island of Malta, seen here under tow into Grand Harbour with heavy damage received during Operation Pedestal. [P39677]

Convoy HXM 290, seen looking aft from the starboard bridge wing of HMCS *St Catharine*: the Royal Canadian Navy rapidly expanded into being the fourth-largest navy in the world and took over much of the North Atlantic convoy-protection duties. [N38538]

The great invasion convoy to North Africa, which assembled in the Atlantic from the USA and Britain, was possible because the Royal Navy and its allies had gained command of the seas. [BHC1565]

In April 1944 two fleet carriers, *Victorious* and *Furious*, and four escort carriers, *Emperor*, *Fencer*, *Pursuer* and *Searcher*, with a strong force of bombers and fighters, carried out a highly successful attack on the heavily defended German battleship *Tirpitz*. [BHC0687]

*Above.* Operation Neptune was the naval part of Operation Overlord, commonly called D-Day, the largest amphibious operation ever undertaken. It was under the command of Admiral Ramsay, who four years before been responsible for the miracle of Dunkirk.
[BHC1554]

*Left.* The succession passes: a continuous line of seamen have passed their knowledge and traditions down the ages and inspired each new generation.
[BHC1811]

the whole Battle Cruiser Force moved out and made for the Heligoland Bight, to the edge of the minefields. Reinforcements since our Jutland losses were *Repulse*, Battle Cruiser with Dick Phillimore, *Courageous*, and *Glorious*, new and very fast, heavily armed Light Cruisers carrying 15-inch guns very lightly built and I think about 18,000 tons and 90,000 Horse Power. The Vice Admiral Light Cruiser, Trevelyan Napier, flew his Flag in *Courageous*. At about 7 a.m. on the 17th, with the Battle Cruisers and William Pakenham in support of us, a whole lot of German craft hove in sight. They were Mine Sweepers, Destroyers and a Squadron of Light Cruisers. It rather seemed at first as if neither quite expected to meet the other just then, and we knew little about the minefields except that we were right on the edge of them, and it was never intended to risk the big ships amongst them . . .

This time there were no voluminous Grand Fleet Battle Orders to follow and what happened next was no goose-step:

Not knowing what we should meet in the way of enemy, there were no detailed orders as to who should go for what. The Destroyers, of course, dived in amongst the small craft and took their toll, and Jack Sinclair and I with our Squadrons settled down to hunt their Light Cruisers, looking to them to guide us through the minefields with *Repulse* and Dick Phillimore foaming along not far behind.

The Germans made great play with smoke screens and tried again and again with torpedoes. Their rear ship was well on fire and rather dropping back, but we just had not the speed to range up and get our A Arcs bearing. I think for 6 hours my telegraphs were at Full Speed, one ached to get nearer and finish them off before they could reach the shelter of Heligoland, but it was the old story of not being able to win without the horse and at last Heligoland hove up, with also a German Battle Squadron advancing 'fremissant au bouche' and splashing us about rather, so it was about time to turn for home. As we swung round, *Caledon* got such a punch in the ribs that I thought she was going to drop in half, but barring a biggish hole, she remained intact and then we all began to pick our way back through what we could figure out was the track through

the minefields, with gallant and faithful *Repulse* still in atten-
dance. I signalled to Dick Phillimore to say how well I knew
that wherever we got to he would be there too ... We got back
clear of the mines after dark, rather a relief as a shell had gone
through our chart house and defaced the chart, hitting my
Captain, Stewart Harrison-Wallace, on the foot and cutting a
signalman in half.

Once in clear waters and darkness we stopped and buried
the dead, with the Destroyers steaming round us to keep any
submarines down. There were very few casualties, except in the
two leading Flag ships, Jack Alexander Sinclair's and mine,
though one other Cruiser had a shell on her bridge which killed
the Captain and knocked the deck steering position about. We
saw her all of a sudden swerve right out of the line and
wondered why.

They gave a posthumous V.C. to one of my men, a shell
burst amongst the crew of our foremost 6-inch gun leaving only
2 standing up to keep the gun in action, one with most of his
stomach laid bare, he was a loading number and went on with
it, and rallied another man or two to keep up the fire, but very
soon collapsed and died. His name was J.H.Carless and he
belonged to Walsall in Staffordshire, where afterwards I went to
unveil a memorial bust of him ... at dawn next morning we
got amongst the Grand Fleet which had come down in hopes
that the German Battle Squadron would persevere in their
pursuit of us, but they did not ...

In fact Jutland had been the one and only chance of a decisive
fleet action, and last time which two surface fleets would meet on
such a scale. The era of the battleship was fast drawing to a close.

## SUBMARINES

For submarines, the Royal Navy in the nineteenth century had had
a policy of wait and see. This was an active not a passive policy,
and Commander (later Admiral Sir) Arthur Knyvet Wilson, known
as Old 'Ard 'Art, had recognized the submarine for its potential
during the American Civil War. However, once the submarine had

been proved in France and in the United States, the Royal Navy could no longer delay the introduction of the technology. Wilson, and others, urged the building of a British prototype or the purchase of a foreign design: despite growing entente, the Royal Navy could hardly turn to France, and, in any case, the best designs were in America. Consequently, negotiations with the Electric Boat Company resulted in the launch in 1901 of Holland Boat, HM Submarine *No 1*. It is Wilson, of course, who is often accused of having said something like submarines were underhand and damned un-English and recommending the hanging of their crews as pirates, but there is no evidence for this and an examination of the record, and more importantly his actions, shows quite the opposite intention.

Ostensibly the first submarines were intended to devise anti-submarine tactics, but in secret the navy was building an offensive submarine fleet, and by the start of the First World War it had the largest and most modern fleet of submarines in the world. Both Fisher and Churchill backed the new submarines: the new submariners formed an elite force, which attracted many young officers with the prospect of early command (for example, the first commanding officer of the first submarine was Lieutenant F. D. Arnold Forster, the son of a member of the Board of Admiralty), and in the First World War some of the Royal Navy's most aggressive officers were submariners.

The first warship sunk on the open sea was the light cruiser *Pathfinder*, by the German U-boat *U21*. This did little to affect British sweeps across the North Sea, but when Lieutenant Max Horton in the British submarine *E9* sank the German cruiser *Hela* the Germans withdrew into the Baltic. Then *U9* sank three elderly British cruisers off the Hook of Holland, and the Royal Navy lost three times as many men (1,459, most of them recently called-up reservists) as at the Battle of Trafalgar (449 killed). The incident also temporarily drove the Grand Fleet of Battle out of Scapa Flow and to the west coast of Scotland at Lough Swilly.

British submarine operations into the Baltic suffered from lack of communications with the Russians. There was more success when submarines were sent to reinforce the faltering Allied attack on the Dardanelles. Lieutenant N. D. Holbrook in the relatively primitive *B11* scored a first when he sank the old Turkish battleship *Messudieh* off Constantinople in December 1914 and so won the first Victoria Cross in submarine service. Then in April, May, and June 1915 Lieutenant Commanders E. C. Boyle in *E14* and M. E. Nasmith in *E11* won Victoria Crosses for their efforts. The Germans, however, retaliated by sending the *U21* from the North Sea into the Mediterranean, where she sank two old British battleships, *Triumph* and *Majestic*.

After many months of stalemate, which saw the Germans increasingly sinking merchant ships without warning in defiance of the rules of war, unrestricted U-boat warfare broke out in February 1917. In that month German U-boats sank 105 ships, over 300,000 tons, with the loss of several hundred merchant seamen. The Germans had found a weapon with which they thought they could impose a blockade on the British Isles, and they came perilously close to success, but by the end of the war over 200 German submarines had been sunk. Losses continued at a horrendous rate for the rest of the war and only declined as the British reverted to the convoy system which they had used so successfully in previous major wars.

The Royal Navy, which had started the war with seventy-six submarines, lost fifty-four from all causes, but new construction enabled it to finish the war with a hundred and thirty-seven. It had also gained a new tradition: when Horton returned to Harwich from his successful patrol in 1914 he flew a skull and crossbones flag to indicate that he had sunk an enemy warship. The tradition was still strong in 1982 when Commander Chris Wreford-Brown in the nuclear submarine *Conqueror* sank the Argentine cruiser *Belgrano* south of the Falklands and returned to base in Scotland flying (after much internal debate in the Ministry of Defence about its political correctness) the skull and crossbones. But between Horton's and Wreford-Brown's exploits there was to be a lot of sea time and excitement which would justify flying the pirate flag.

## THE BATTLE OF MAY ISLAND

The First World War had quickly proved the potential of the submarine as a weapon of war, even though early submarines were slow compared to surface warships. Admirals were keen to explore the potential of the new weapon, and it seemed logical to have submarines accompany the fleet on the surface, diving to attack the enemy fleet when it was spotted. Diesel engines of the period simply could not provide enough speed for a submarine on the surface to keep up with battleships, so the K-class was the Royal Navy's answer: steam-driven submarines, using turbines when surfaced and electric motors whilst submerged. Built with great haste during wartime, the K-boats pushed submarine technology to the limits. They were fast (twenty-four knots), long thin boats, but with their hinged funnels, they took a long time to prepare for a dive, and they had a poor reputation for mechanical reliability. *K13* fulfilled the worst fears of the superstitious by sinking on her maiden dive, but she was salvaged and renamed *K22*. She then joined the 13th submarine flotilla.

The ironically named Battle of May Island centred on a tragic series of accidents, costing the lives of over 100 submariners and involving the K-class of submarines, during a night exercise. On 31 January 1918, Admiral Beatty took the Grand Fleet to sea for exercises and nine K-boats sailed from Rosyth, along with the battlecruiser squadron. Manoeuvring off May Island in the dark, the rudder of *K14* jammed and she turned broadside on to *K22* (ex-*K13*), who rammed her and was in turn rammed by the battle-cruiser *Inflexible*. The remaining ships of the 13th flotilla turned back to help and were promptly run down by the 12th submarine flotilla. An accompanying light cruiser sank *K17*, and *K4*, who was rammed by both *K6* and *K7*, also sank.

This tragic accident has left us a harrowing first-hand account. Signalman George Kimbell was ill with a stomach bug on board *K17* when disaster struck. He had been warned that there was about to be an alteration of course and was paying a last visit to the heads before settling down for the night when

> there was an almighty crash either in the midship torpedo room
> or the control room. The lights went out and the order close all

watertight doors. Now I was trapped in the passage [between the control room and the engine room] like a rat in a trap I could hear water rushing in somewhere forar'd. I knew it was no use going on so I returned to the after watertight door and knowing there was a big spanner on the bulkhead by the door. Getting this down after a struggle I knocked on the door [and] heard someone say who's there and I said it's Kimbell I'm trapped let me out. They soon done that and shut and clipped the door again ... The Engineer had a quick calculation ... [and] this is what he decided: release all the air when I give the signal and that will be when there is a good pressure, then knock off the clips and the pressure should force the hatch open and hold back the water if we are under [water] ... we got on the steel ladder and hung till your head is clear of the steel hatch then let go I was the third one to follow and all I remember was I was shot out like a rocket ... I think all those in the engine room managed to get out but only five of them that were rescued ...

Kimbell's ordeal was hardly over when he bobbed to the surface of the Firth of Forth on a January night. Fortunately, and unlike many sailors, he was a strong swimmer:

It was a night I'll never forget I was the last to get picked up and I really do think it was by the hand of God ... when the stern half sank there was a lot of us together and it was awful to hear the cries for help ... Now comes the most awful experience, I don't want another like it. The cries had disappeared in silence and thinking what's going to happen now I was alone in those dark waters ... I disposed of my vests and pants, being wool they were dragging on me these were all the clothes I had on when we were first in the water ... Suddenly I faintly saw some big bow waves approaching me from the left. These I thought must be the big ships so I turned and went back to where the boat sank. I have no idea how long I was in that area but it was now that my troubles began, and I was getting so weak that I had to float on my back to get a sort of rest and it [was] then that I saw a white light but had no idea how far it was away ... Setting out once more for the light it was now that I began to loose all hope of being saved and I must have been almost at death's door as all my past life came before my eyes from a little baby to that very moment. I remember being on my back and the light I had been trying to reach shone in my eyes and I heard a voice say 'Eh, here's another one' when a rope fell close to me. I grabbed it and was nearly within reach of rescue when I fell back into the water. Coming up again another rope was thrown to me and this time it fell across my chest . . . that was all I knew until I came round and found myself on submarine *K-7* . . .

The night had been very dark and the submarines had been run over by the fleet as it speeded up to pass May Island and to avoid a reported German U-boat. Kimbell had survived being trapped, run down, and drowned, and probably only a covering of oil prevented him from dying of hypothermia, but he had also swallowed plenty of the oil:

how on earth had I escaped the whole force of the big ships, destroyers and light cruisers . . . some how I twisted the rope round the standing part . . . in fact they thought I was dead as they had a job to get [me] free of the rope. It was two hours before I actually revived enough to mutter one or two words . . . when the doctor had succeeded with the oil fuel I was wrapped in a blanket with two others and given very small sips of rum to get the circulation moving and then put near the hot boiler plates . . .

The concept of submarines as fleet escorts was a sound idea, but it was beyond the technology of the early twentieth century.


## Q-SHIPS

Q-ships were one of the desperate measures attempted against U-boats. The idea was simple: each Q-ship was disguised to resemble a merchantman, and when a U-boat, whose normal method of sinking was by gunfire from on the surface, came within range, false deck fittings would suddenly reveal guns, which would rake the unwary submarine. A number of U-boats fell into such traps, but the enemy soon became wiser, and the countermeasure was to sink without warning. The first Q-ship was ordered by – who else? – Winston Churchill in November 1914, and eventually 180 Q-ships were fitted out between 1914 and 1918. They were credited with helping to destroy eleven U-Boats, and one of the most successful Q-ship captains was Gordon Campbell, a colourful individual and self-publicist who was highly decorated for his services. After the war he enjoyed popularity as an author, journalist, and broadcaster, and one his books, *Mystery Ships*, which was about the Q-ships, was published in 1928. *Mystery Ships* was translated into several languages and presumably read by his former opponents, the Germans. Campbell's autobiography, *Number Thirteen*, was published in 1932.

The Royal Navy also operated decoy ships in the Second World War, when they were known as special-service freighters. Many doubted the wisdom of repeating in a new war a particular tactic about which the enemy was fully informed. However, eight freighters were fitted out, allegedly on Churchill's orders, and Campbell was brought back from retirement. The first special-service freighter sailed in December 1939 and the remainder in early in 1940. None of them ever sighted a U-boat or accomplished any useful purpose at all, and two of them, *Williamette Valley* and *Cape Howe*, were torpedoed and sunk, with great loss of life, in the Western Approaches in June 1940. The Germans were far too wary to be caught by a ruse which had been so well advertised between the wars. Indeed, Dönitz, a U-boat commander in the First World War and commander-in-chief of Hitler's U-boat fleet in the Second, issued standing orders that U-boats were always to make their attacks in diving trim and to be specially beware of lone ships which straggled a convoy. Even by the end of the First World War the use of Q-ships was as a tactic worn threadbare.

Indubitably the officers and men of Q-ships required great personal bravery, but their contribution towards defeating the U-boat menace was small. Q-ship tactics might have deterred some U-boats from attacking lone merchant ships, but on the other hand they were one more inducement to the Germans to begin unrestricted warfare, a policy which might have starved Britain.

## THE INTRODUCTION OF CONVOY

Early in the First World War the British established an effective
distant blockade of German ports, while the Germans conducted
their U-boat war more or less according to the rules of war. The
threat or fear of submarines in the North Sea had already affected
tactics on both sides, restricting the fleets to defensive postures
and making the area south of Dogger Bank impassable for the
Grand Fleet. By the end of 1916 German U-boats had sunk only
twenty-four warships, but over two million tons of British merchant shipping. Huge numbers of light craft had been deployed
on patrol duties, and a considerable portion of the RNAS was
used on anti-submarine patrols. Jellicoe, however, would not,
either as Commander-in-Chief of the Grand Fleet or as First Sea
Lord (from December 1916), spare destroyers from the Grand
Fleet for convoy duties. Then at the start of 1917 the Germans
declared that their trade war would be unrestricted, and in one
month, April 1917, nearly a million tons of shipping was lost
worldwide.

The countermeasure, convoy, was well known and had been
used successfully for centuries. However, Duff, Jellicoe's head of
anti-submarine warfare, 'shared Admiral Jellicoe's views, for he
believed that unless the escorting ships bore a very large proportion
to the number of ships in each convoy, the system would be an
additional danger rather than a protection' and he had had printed
a memorandum which said that

> whenever possible, vessels should sail singly, escorted as con-
> sidered necessary. The system of several ships, sailing in com-
> pany, as a convoy, is not recommended in any area where
> submarine attack is a possibility. It is evident that the larger the
> number of ships forming the convoy, the greater is the chance
> of a submarine being enabled to attack successfully, the greater
> the difficulty of the escort in preventing such an attack. In the
> case of defensively armed merchant vessels, it is preferable that
> they should sail singly rather than in a convoy with several other
> vessels. A submarine could remain at a distance and fire her

torpedo into the middle of a convoy with every chance of
success. A defensively armed merchant vessel of good speed
should rarely, if ever, be captured. If the submarine comes to
the surface to overtake and attack with her gun, the merchant
vessel's gun will nearly always make the submarine dive, in
which case the preponderance of speed will allow of the merchant ship escaping.

It would take thirty years more, another world war, and a Nobel-
prize winner, to prove him wrong – albeit with simple arithmetic –
but Duff, and Jellicoe, could hardly have been further from the
truth. Historians do not agree how convoys came to be instituted
in the First World War, but by April 1917 one out of four
merchant ships leaving Britain was being sunk and it was estimated
that if losses continued at this rate, the war would be lost by
November.

However, when in April the USA declared war on Germany,
partly because British naval intelligence had intercepted and leaked
the Zimmermann telegram in which Germany urged Mexico to
declare war on the USA, the most important effect was the promise
of extra destroyers for escort duties. The Royal Navy did have over
four hundred such ships, but Jellicoe continued to argue that none
could be spared, while Lloyd George, the Prime Minister, urged
that the destroyers should be released from the Grand Fleet and
used for convoy. The logical inconsistency between requiring the
destroyers to escort major warships but not to escort merchant
ships, and the simple fact that military transports were usually
escorted seem to have been missed. An exasperated Lloyd George
went personally to the Admiralty on 30 January, but Jellicoe had
already agreed (on the 27th) to introduce convoys on an experimental basis and on short sea routes, across the Channel, to Scandinavia,
and then to and from Gibraltar.

By the end of the summer of 1917 a convoy organization was in
place and in the six months from April to October only ten ships
out of 1,500 in convoy had been sunk. The facts spoke for
themselves.

After the war Jellicoe appears to have attempted to rewrite
history, telling Duff that

I had an interview with Newbolt [author of the official history of the war at sea] last week over a revised chapter on the Convoy System, and I discovered what is really in his mind on the subject. He told me quite frankly that in his view, it was the expressed intention of the Prime Minister to visit the Admiralty (about April 25th, 1917 [after a meeting of the War Cabinet on the 23rd in which he had advocated convoys]) that caused you to recommend the trial of the Convoy in your Minute ... In fact, it was due to Ll.G. that we started it. I told him that so far as my opinion was concerned, I felt certain that it was the heavy daily losses at that time that led to the change, and that I recollected your coming to me in evening of one of those days and saying that the losses were so heavy that you considered we should try Convoy – as even a big disaster to a trial convoy would not be worse than the losses we were suffering. Will you let me know what your recollection of this matter is? Newbolt says, that when Ll.G.'s Memoirs are published, we shall find that he will claim to have brought in the Convoy System. I replied that he also claimed with equal untruth, to have solved the munitions question ...

Not even the loyal Duff could agree entirely with his former boss:

The first suggestion I heard that LlGeorge's visit to the Admlty was primarily in connection with the Convoy Organisation, was when the chapter on Convoy came under discussion. My impression was that he came to look into Admlty Organisation generally; in fact, I recollect you telling me that I must be ready to answer, and I understood the outcome of his visit to be that Oliver and I became members of the Board. There is no foundation for the belief that his visit was in any way the cause of my suggestion that the time had arrived for starting Convoy. It must be obvious that if Ll.G. came with the intention of forcing Convoy on an unwilling Admlty, he would have dealt with you and not with the Director of a Division of the War Staff, who – as I remember telling him – had no executive authority. My minute of April 30th had no connection whatever with Ll.G's visit. It was the direct result of (1) The serious and progressive loss of ships weekly (2) The assured prospect of additional naval forces becoming available as the organisation developed. These two factors changed the situation and warranted the introduction of convoy without delay. Had the losses remained stationary, the risk would not in my opinion have been justified until the measures in course of development had been brought into use. I have no doubt there are many Downing Street candidates for the credit of Mercantile Convoy – Ll.George, Hankey, Clement Jones, etc, etc. But it is very easy to be wise after the event and one hears no mention of Downing Street follies, such as Sea-lions on which we were forced to waste time and energy . . .

## SEALIONS AS SUBMARINE HUNTERS

It is not clear what all 'the measures in course of development' were, but one of them certainly involved sealions as submarine hunters, as this letter from Jellicoe's Admiralty in May 1917 shows:

Sir,

I am commanded by My Lords Commissioners of the Admiralty to acquaint you that they have approved of a series of trials being carried out in the Solent in regard to the capabilities of Sealions in tracking Submarines.

2. Rear Admiral R.A. Allenby (Retired) is in charge of these trials, and Their Lordships desire that you will place a Submarine at his disposal for the trials and furnish him with all necessary facilities for this purpose.

3. Rear Admiral Allenby's requirements for the trials are as follows:

A stable or shed with water laid on, salt for choice,

A *suitable* launch with small boat in tow, which launch should carry a cage with two animals. The launch should be as noiseless as possible. A suitable cage would require to be built, also a sloping gangway to be fitted for the animals to climb on board, unless the launch had a low gunwale (3 feet).

A Submarine of any class would suffice to train the animals. Preliminary trials at anchor on the surface, later submerged. There are no data to enable a definite opinion to be expressed as to how long the training with submarines would continue, but a decision might be arrived at, one way or another, in about a fortnight provided weather conditions were favourable.

4. You are requested to report to the Admiralty by telegraph when the trial will be ready to commence, observing that the sealions will not be ready before the 25th instant.

Whatever Duff meant to imply in his reply to Jellicoe, it is evident that the Admiralty did take the sealion experiment seriously and a Commander Crowther was ordered to 'to take charge of these trials and make all arrangements and everything is to be based at Blockhouse. He is to give me a date as soon as possible to comply with paragraph 4 of Admiralty Letter'.

Convoy, however, was the proper answer to the U-boat menace.

## ZEEBRUGGE

Since Jutland the Grand Fleet had waited two years at Scapa Flow for the German High Seas Fleet to venture out again. Life for the sailors of the Grand Fleet had become routine and boring, and there was even some criticism of the navy for apparently sitting at anchor doing nothing whilst the army did the fighting. Meanwhile, Zeebrugge, a forward operating base for German U-boats, caught the attention of Roger Keyes, Vice Admiral Dover Patrol, whose qualities as a fighter have already been touched upon, and he proposed to block the exits to the Bruges canal there and at Ostend.

His plan was for a diversionary attack to draw the enemy fire while three hulks, *Thetis*, *Intrepid*, and *Iphigenia*, were to be scuttled at Zeebrugge. Under cover of darkness, behind an immense smoke screen generated by Wing Commander Brock RNAS, who had called in his family's expertise as manufacturers of fireworks, a large raiding party from the old cruiser *Vindictive* would be landed on the mole to destroy the heavy guns which covered the harbour and to prevent German reinforcements, and two redundant submarines filled with explosives were to be blown up under the viaduct connecting the mole to the shore.

The attacks took place on the night of 22/23 April, and when the news was released, British newspapers of the day were euphoric. While the Germans claimed to have defeated the raiders (the raid on Ostend failed because a moved buoy misled the blockships) and that they could still use the canal at Zeebrugge, aerial photographs showed two of the blockships in position across its mouth. More importantly the raid seemed to be a decisive blow against the U-boats which had been trying to starve Britain out of the war. On a wave of public emotion Keyes became a national hero.

Fisher, who as First Sea Lord had forced through the modernization of the Royal Navy before the First World War, and had been so bitterly disappointed in the way in which Jellicoe had repaid his faith in him, wrote to Keyes: 'you have earned the gratitude of the whole Navy. We feel vindicated. We can put our heads up again'. Churchill, a friend and admirer of Keyes, found one of his great phrases to describe the episode: 'The raid on Zeebrugge may well rank as the finest feat of arms in the Great War, and certainly as an episode unsurpassed in the history of the Royal Navy'. Even Lloyd George thought that it was 'the one Naval exploit of the war that moved and still moves the imagination of the Nation'.

Keyes was established as a world expert on such operations and during the Second World War both Churchill and the United States Navy called upon his experience.

## ARMISTICE, 1918

Defeated at sea and on land, the Germans sued for peace, and on 11 November 1918 their plenipotentiaries signed an Armistice in preparation for the eventual peace treaty. Under the agreement, they would hand over their fleet to the Royal Navy, their High Seas Fleet to be surrendered in Scotland and their submarines at Harwich. The fleet was duly met at sea and escorted into the Firth of Forth. In *Queen Elizabeth* gunnery orders for Thursday 21 November 1918 read: 'Before meeting German Fleet, Ship's Companies will be at [battle] stations. Turrets and Guns are to be kept in the securing positions, but free. Guns are to be empty with cages up and loaded with Shellite ready for ramming home. Directors and

Armoured Tower will be trained on. Range and Deflection will be kept set continuously'. According to another source, the whole of the Grand Fleet was at action stations 'in case of any funny nonsense', and when they anchored off Rosyth, 'Our Commander in Chief then made the following signal to them: "THE GERMAN FLAG WILL BE HAULED DOWN AT SUNSET TODAY AND NOT HOISTED AGAIN WITHOUT PERMISSION"'.

This scene was repeated at Harwich:

> At Harwich, we sailed on four successive mornings to receive the surrender of the submarines. It was an amazing, thrilling and never to be forgotten sight to see as dawn broke, the horizon dotted with little black objects, which as we approached with ships at action stations, developed into the enemy U-boats that we had been fighting to destroy for four gruesome years, and that had caused the death of so many of our gallant merchant seamen. We escorted them into harbour without trouble, although I believe that one or two had sunk themselves deliberately on the way across. They secured to buoys and the crews transferred to their accompanying Depot Ship for return to the Fatherland. In charge of the transfer was a Lieutenant, a pretty tough character; he armed himself with a poker and any German who displayed surliness or was slow in obeying orders, quickly felt the error of his ways . . .

Thus ended the German Kaiser's boast of being 'emperor of the Atlantic' and one more challenge to the Royal Navy.

## Chapter Eleven

# The Interwar Years

## THE BALTIC

In 1918, just as after the previous Great War in 1815, there was unfinished business for the Royal Navy and there were active and bloody operations for the fleet. Russia had collapsed into anarchy, the Tsar and his family had been killed, and Russia's vassals struggled for their independence, while revolution threatened to envelop Finland, and German armies were still in the field in the Baltic states.

While the Treaty of Versailles was being negotiated by the great powers, Walter Cowan was sent to the Baltic, and, in the face of many difficulties, was responsible for enforcing the terms of the Armistice and for restoring order there, which meant challenging the remnants of the Russian fleet. In the course of these operations Lieutenant Augustus Agar won the Victoria Cross for his attack on the Russian cruiser *Oleg*, and there was a night raid by British coastal motorboats on the island fortress of Kronstadt, which had in previous wars defied the Royal Navy's best – or worst – intentions. Cowan decided upon an attack upon Kronstadt using a flotilla of coastal motorboats or CMBs, 'their length 40 feet, armament, 2 torpedoes, crew 2 Officers and 3 men, speed 35 knots, and draught about 12 inches, very noisy when going all out'. He kept these boats as secret as possible and set about planning to strike at Kronstadt and the Russian ships there, choosing 18 August for his attack, the official last day of summer, a festival day when, he hoped, a certain proportion of the garrison would be drunk.

It was a well-coordinated sea and air attack:

The plan was . . . for the aeroplanes arriving over the harbour 2 minutes before the attack on the ships and dry dock by the

C.M.B's so that the noise of the aeroplanes would drown that of the C.M.B's and also distract the enemy's attention . . . I had all my Force out along the edge of the minefields in support and for the C.M.B's to fall back on, and to the minute the attack went in, and then came the watching and waiting to see what came back.

The attack was pressed home:

8 C.M.B's went in led by Commander Dobson, a veteran C.M.B. Officer, the others were Lieutenant Bremner, Brade R.N.R. Dayrell-Reid, McBean, Howard, Napier and Agar. The targets were the submarine depot ship *Pamiet Azov*, she was sunk. The Battleships *Andrei Pervossani* and *Petropavlosk*. Both these ships were torpedoed, but as they had less than 2 feet under their bottoms where they lay, they could not sink. To blow in the caisson of the big dry dock. The boat detailed for this was so shot about that her torpedo could not be fired. One boat to guard against any interference by Destroyers from the Eastern harbour and one to attack the Destroyer guardship at the entrance but this torpedo passed under her bottom. 2 boats were detailed for each battleship.

As Dayrell-Reid's boat was swinging round to go for the *Petropavlosk* he was shot through the head and fell over the wheel and controls, he was over 6 feet high and Steele his 2nd in command was small and lightly built, they were then well within 100 yards and swinging round. By a tremendous effort he swayed Dayrell-Reid clear, seized the wheel, steadied her up and fired his torpedo so close into the ship that part of the explosive blew back on to the Forecastle of the C.M.B. where it was when just afterwards she came alongside my *Delhi*. He just had room to wrench her round before ramming *Petropavlosk* and gained the open sea.

The failure to blow in the dry dock caisson was a disappointment, but my main object to disable the 2 battleships was accomplished and with the *Oleg* already sunk, only *Rurik* was left of the larger active ships.

The boat told off to deal with her broke down at the entrance and had to be towed out of action. All boats had a waiting rendezvous to return to after delivering their attack.

3 boats were sunk or blown up, 2 Captains killed, Lieutenant Brade R.N.R. and Lieutenant Dayrell-Reid, Lieutenant Bremner whose boat was sunk was pulled out of the water by another already badly damaged, and with Captain and Sub-lieutenant killed; he himself was wounded 11 times and again sunk and in the end pulled out and taken prisoner by a Russian Destroyer, as also was Lieutenant Napier, Captain of the other boat sunk and a kinsman of old Admiral Napier who strove to reduce Kronstadt at the time of the Crimean War.

Dawn was breaking as they withdrew and how anxiously we watched to see how many would come back over the minefields. The first one to show up was 88 and she came alongside *Delhi* with Dayrell-Reid still alive with 2 bullet holes through his forehead. The Surgeon Commander went to him at once and we got him inboard, he lived for 2 hours and when he died we put him on the quarter deck covered by my silk Rear Admiral's Flag which my faithful gallant Captains of the 1st Light Cruiser Squadron had given me, and which I had last flown when bringing the German Fleet in to surrender. He was a man without fear or any thought of it in his composition, every now and then you find such a quality and when I gave them all their objectives I felt that he had only to live to achieve the utmost I hoped of him. He had served under Roger Keyes in the Dover Patrol, and when next I saw him, I found that was the way he summed him up.

5 out of the 8 boats came back and the personnel casualties out of the 8 were 50%, and His Majesty granted the V.C. to their Leader, Commander C.C.Dobson as well as to Sub-Lieutenant Gordon Steele, Dayrell-Reid's 2nd in command. I had big brass replicas of the V.C. made and nailed on to the boats that had won them. I believe one of those boats is now in some Service Museum in England. [The Imperial War Museum at Duxford.] I give the substance of my remarks to the C.M.B. and Aircraft personnel the day after return from the Raid

Cowan's speech stands as an example of the words which many a commanding officer must have given to his people on the eve of battles, or, as in this case, its aftermath:

This action was a very complete example of gallant unselfish and perfectly disciplined co-operation between Sea and Air. To begin with though the enterprise might have been attempted 'Blind' i.e. without aerial reconnaissance and photographing, and going by hearsay and local charts, I should have hesitated to order it and unquestionably the losses would have been heavier and the results probably far less, but by reason of the very perfect photographs taken and enlarged by Lieutenant Whippey R.A.F. and the constant patient and resolute reconnoitring carried out under fire, and the correct and intelligent reports resulting, made what the outside world would have called a forlorn hope into a legitimate and practicable operation which has met with far greater success than I ever hoped. And this success is the result of cool matter of fact and businesslike direction, preparation and organisation by the two Leaders, Commander C.C.Dobson, R.N. and Major D.G.Donald, R.A.F. followed by gallant confident leading and backed as I well knew it would be, by cool disciplined dare-devil gallantry from every one of you.

The result I feel will be assessed by those best qualified to judge to be as brilliant and completely successful a combined enterprise by Sea and Air Forces as the last 5 years of war can show. And what has brought these results, is unselfishness, strict attention to every detail of equipment, of drill and of discipline, and the determination of all to 'Play for the Side'.

The losses are heavy, but there is not one single incident to regret or that could have been avoided. The 3 boats that were Lost, went most gloriously, the open sea gained and fighting most indomitably to the finish. I venture to think the end of those 3 boats will have as great an effect in keeping the remainder of the Bolshevic Navy quiet as will the devastation you have wrought in their harbour, the strongest Naval Fortress in the World ravished and blasted by under 50 splendidly disciplined dauntless Britons. Those who are dead, we can only envy. The sorrow is for those who loved and belonged to them.

Between you, you have written another very brilliant chapter in our Navy's History, and its faultless execution is due to your splendid discipline, and also to what is our Service's strongest and fairest characteristic, namely the sympathy, trust and understanding between all Ranks.

Cowan's speech on that shortening August day to his ship's company is one of the best to have survived in the archives of the National Maritime Museum. On receiving the report of this operation the Commander-in-Chief of the Grand Fleet, now Sir Charles Madden, commented: 'This successful enterprise will rank among the most daring and skilfully executed of the Naval Operations of this War. On no other occasions during hostilities has so small a force inflicted so much damage on the enemy. Rear Admiral Sir Walter Henry Cowan deserves generous recognition for the able foresight, planning and preparation which led to this great Naval success.'

Summing up the effect of Cowan's operations in the Baltic, Field Marshal Mannerheim, who used the opportunity to rescue his country from the jaws of socialist revolution and the clutches of the Soviet Union, wrote:

> My dear Sir Walter, Thanking you my dear Admiral for your kind letter, I cannot refrain from writing once more to you to express my deep admiration for the splendid way in which small crafts from the Naval Forces under your command entering the harbour of Kronstadt delivered the Baltic from some of the most dangerous units of Bolshevik sea power.
>
> Deeds of that kind have in times past built up the fame of the English Navy and this feat has once more shown to the world that when England strikes it strikes hard.
>
> I know that my feelings of admiration and respect for the men participating in the plucky raid are shared by every true soldier in this country, and that we all deplore the loss of some of the gallant officers and men who had their share in this splendid achievement.
>
> I am believe me my dear Sir Walter
> Sincerely yours,
> G. MANNERHEIM.

Little more can be added to these encomiums about a glorious passage of arms which so typified everything that the Royal Navy could and did do.

## SECRETS TO AMERICA

Eustace Tennyson d'Eyncourt was probably the leading naval architect of his age. Trained at Armstrong's yard at Elswick and at the Royal Naval College, Greenwich, d'Eyncourt worked in civilian yards where he made his reputation both for his technical competence and for his skill in securing foreign orders. In 1912 he was appointed the Admiralty's Director of Naval Construction and became responsible for the British wartime shipbuilding programme, including the later, larger, and more successful submarine designs and the first aircraft carriers, as well as for the development of tanks and airships, for monitors, and for the two unique so-called light cruisers which mounted four 15in guns. These cruisers, *Courageous* and *Glorious*, were thought up and modelled over Christmas 1914 and, like the *Dreadnought* before them, built in record time. D'Eyncourt was, of course, a confidant of both Fisher and Churchill, but he was not a member of the venerable Royal Corps of Naval Constructors. He seems, however, to have been better than most outsiders at integrating himself, though he regarded himself as the creature of the First Sea Lord rather than of his direct employer, the Controller of the Navy. When he retired in 1924 he rejoined Armstrong's until they amalgamated with Vickers in 1927, and then for twenty years acted as a consulting naval architect and played a leading role in numerous institutions such as the National Physical Laboratory, the Worshipful Company of Shipwrights, and the Royal Institution of Naval Architects.

The Royal Navy had pioneered naval aviation in the First World War, both tactically and technically, and in 1918 was the only navy with operational aircraft carriers: d'Eyncourt and his fellow constructors had played a major part in getting aircraft to sea. As for the carriers themselves, 'secret patents exist . . . in connection with certain contrivances in aircraft carriers. As this is so, I think the position is clear; no other portions of aircraft carriers are considered secret, but foreigners are not permitted on board A.C.C.s nor civilians except by special permission'. The Royal Navy was, however, prepared to sell its secrets to its new ally, the United States Navy, or to swap them for related information. The Secretary of the Admiralty wrote to the American naval attaché in London:

> I am sorry to have been so long in replying to Commander Morris' letter of the 31st March [1922] in which you asked that the United States Navy might purchase the rights for the latest landing devices and arresting gears used on British Airplane carriers. The subject has required consideration in conjunction with the Air Ministry.
>
> I now write to say that although the proposal is one which goes beyond the ordinary exchange of information of Naval interest with friendly Nations, the Admiralty are willing, in the case of the United States of America to agree to this proposal . . .
>
> The Admiralty desire to make it clear that this agreement covers all details of the landing devices and arresting gear employed, but not the disclosure of any other details of Aircraft Carriers nor any details of aircraft employed for deck-landing purposes. This applies to the design of aircraft attachment in connection with the arresting gear which are actually employed in British Aircraft. Those attachments are particular to the aircraft in question, and there will be no difficulty in designing attachments suitable for U.S. machines.
>
> The Admiralty would be glad if all possible steps could be taken to keep secret the fact that these rights have been acquired from Great Britain and they will expect that the United States Navy Department will consider favourably any request that the Admiralty may make in the future for details of any important invention which the United States may make in connection with Naval Aviation . . .

The naval attaché replied that in 'the question of reciprocal information to be given . . . in return for information regarding the arresting gear' he wanted confirmation 'in writing that only information of corresponding value and within a limited period would be asked for'. In addition, and in keeping with his former achievements in foreign sales, d'Eyncourt had acquired a commercial interest in various secret patents and on 5 January 1923 Captain Hussey USN wrote to d'Eyncourt:

Dear Sir Eustace, The arrangements for the purchase of the Arresting Gear Patent are now complete. It covers the payment of a sum of money to you and Messrs. Narbeth & Hopkins for the use by the U.S. Navy of your Patent (British Secret Patent No. 10,000/21) and for the preparation and supply at your own expense of drawings, specifications and instructions, showing how to adapt the Patent to fit up a typical vessel selected by the U.S. Authorities. No drawings of any British Aircraft carriers are required. This payment is to be regarded as purely personal to yourselves . . .

It is a curious comment on British ingenuity that while many advances in aircraft carrier design were British, it was the Americans who exploited these advances: they included the tail hook and arrester wire, the steam catapult, the mirror deck-landing sight, the angled flight deck, and the ski-jump.

## POWER STANDARDS

The surrender of the German fleet in 1918 and its scuttling in 1919 left Britain again with an overwhelming superiority at sea, although there was a significant difference from 1815. In 1815 Britain had also been industrially and financially supreme. In 1918 she was exhausted financially and, in sharp contrast to a hundred years before, the growing industrial and financial strength of the United States of America was obvious. There was an increasing realization that planning against the USA, in either military or industrial terms, was a luxury which Britain simply could not afford. Simultaneously there was some resentment at the wealth and power of the United States of America and suspicion of her motives: why should an essentially continental power require any navy at all?

For more than a century and a half British naval policy had been measured by standards of power. One of the first public statements of these standards was in 1770 when the Earl of Chatham, in a debate in the House of Lords on the Spanish seizure of the Falkland Islands, declared that 'the first great and acknowledged object of national defence in this country is to maintain such a superior naval force at home that even the united fleets of France and Spain may never be masters of the Channel', and there were many more statements over the next two centuries about what the standard should be. For example, the second Lord Melville observed in 1813 that, 'in 1796 [against] the united forces of France, Spain and Holland . . . we still preserved a superior and conquering navy', i.e. a three-power standard. When Melville wrote this he was contemplating a French enemy in possession of the ports of Holland and Italy as well as of France and able to build, by his reckoning, a force of 106 ships-of-the-line by 1816, 'an equal naval force [to ours], at least as to the number and magnitude of ships'.

However, after the defeat of France, Sir George Cockburn was able to assure the Duke of Wellington in 1828 that the British navy had a superiority of not less than two to one over the French, measured in all classes of warships. In 1841 the First Lord minuted that a three-power standard of continuing superiority, against France, Russia and the United States of America, was essential. In the mid-1800s, however, the USA turned inward upon itself, ceasing temporarily to be a naval power. In 1868 Admiral Sir Alexander Milne wrote that 'before the introduction of armour-clads, it was an accepted rule that we required, and we actually maintained, a navy not far short of double that of France'. However, during most of the nineteenth century the standards were internal to the British Admiralty and government of the day and, if recognized, were not widely or overtly acknowledged.

Power standards were never fixed or absolute numerical standards, but could be applied quantitatively, qualitatively, or geographically, thus misleading a Select Committee on the Naval Estimates in 1888 to state that 'no complete scheme had ever been laid before the admiralty, showing apart from the financial limits laid down by the Cabinet, what, in the opinion of naval experts, the strength of the fleet should be'. One of the few public announcements was on 7 March 1889, during the debate in the House of Lords over the Naval Defence Bill, when the First Lord of the Admiralty, Lord Hamilton, announced that the fleet must be 'at least equal to the naval strength of any two other countries'. Even this statement needed interpretation but it was sixteen years before another First Lord, Lord Selborne, did so: 'the two-power

standard only applies to battleships. It has never applied to cruisers
... and has never applied to any two particular nations, but always
to the two strongest naval Powers. The two strongest Powers of
Lord George Hamilton's Board in 1889 were France and Italy'.

After the Battle of Tsushima between the Russian and Japanese
navies in 1905, a three-power standard became possible again,
but by 1908 the standard was set against the next two navies,
France and the USA, plus 10 ten per cent. With war looming,
the standard could be freely reinterpreted: thus it could become the
German navy plus 60 per cent. In terms of number and quality
of modern warships, this was one of the highest standards against
which Britain tried to build, leading to an attempt in 1909–10
and again in 1913–14 to reach thirty modern super-dreadnoughts
by building six per year, the maximum capacity of British warship-
building yards.

In geographical terms, the setting of power standards increasingly
reflected a sense of realism in British naval policy that large naval
powers like Japan or United States of America could not be
challenged close to their home bases: thoughts 'of opposing the
navy of the US in the Caribbean and the North Atlantic close to
its bases must be abandoned ... [and] in years not far distant we
shall be quite unable to oppose the navy of Japan in its own waters.
It is best to recognise facts but not always to proclaim them from
the house-top'.

But with war against Germany increasingly likely, Britain needed
allies at sea as well as on land. Britain's diplomatic measures were
quickly taken: the Hay–Pauncefoote agreement with the United
States in 1901, the Anglo-Japanese treaties of 1902, 1905 and 1911
(the early treaties were intended to form an alliance against a
perceived threat from a Franco-German alliance), the Entente
Cordiale with France in 1904 and a treaty with Russia in 1907
were all recognitions that the Royal Navy alone could not assure
British security.

In 1919 Jellicoe was sent on an Imperial Mission intended in
part to drum up support for an idea which had been mooted before
the First World War: an Empire Navy. He reckoned that post-war
British naval requirements were for a navy built to a standard of
100 per cent of either France or Germany, in order 'to be certain

of being able at any "average moment" to meet them with decisively superior forces at their "selected moment" . . .' The navy would also need a force of battleships to counter the USA, but in view of the 'great distance which separates us from the United States' the need was for only 'a fleet of capital ships of a strength of 70 per cent of that of the United States'. Soon his ideas would be tested in an international forum, but first his successors in London had to answer a yet more fundamental question.

## BATTLESHIP VERSUS SUBMARINE

In London there was a public argument raging about the very future of battleships. Admiral Percy Scott, hero of the Boer War, who had taught the navy how to shoot and taken charge of the air defences of London during the 1914–18 war, had decided the day of the battleship was over. Furthermore, he campaigned loudly that no more money should be spent on such behemoths, and that submarines and aircraft should be built instead. The Admiralty responded that these were only complementary to surface ships, and that 'possessing only submarines the British Empire would be unable to [prevent] . . . war on commerce' since 'submarines are not the most effective vessels for attacking other submarines'. The Admiralty used similar arguments regarding aircraft. In practice, the Admiralty relied too much on the counter-measures which it thought would be effective, and Scott's ideas were several generations ahead of his time and the available technology. Nevertheless he managed to thoroughly rile the sea lords, Beatty became personally involved and asked Chatfield to draft papers of rebuttal, and an inquiry was set up to investigate the navy's construction policy. The inquiry was a subcommittee of the Committee of Imperial Defence, and Scott was called as one of the witnesses, but refused to attend such an obviously biased inquiry and instead wrote to the newspapers.

What happened next had the air of a comic opera about it. Beatty asked the secretary of the Admiralty Board, Oswyn Murray, about 'the power of the Admiralty to take notice of Admiral Sir Percy Scott's letter to "The Times" revealing the contents of a secret and confidential letter sent to him from the Committee of Imperial Defence and referring in disrespectful terms to it'. Murray told Beatty, 'I think that the only step open to the Admiralty would be (1) to write a letter conveying censure to Admiral Sir Percy which would probably provoke a rude reply (2) to treat his behaviour as conduct justifying forfeiture or suspension of his retired pay . . . (3) to treat his action as behaviour justifying his removal from the Retired List . . . [but] I know of no precedent for taking such a strong step . . . for what may be regarded as, at the most, contumacious behaviour'. Murray pointed out that a retired officer had been censured before the war for writing a letter to a newspaper, 'and in reply he informed the Board that he was no longer serving under their command and that he entirely declined to accept their censure'. For good measure he added that Admiralty did not even have the power to compel him to give evidence to the subcommittee on Imperial Defence, as it was not a Royal Commission nor a committee of the Houses of Parliament. 'Nor', Murray added, did the Admiralty have 'any power, except in the case of war or emergency, to call him up and thus render him amenable to the directions of the Board'.

Beatty clearly thought that a new precedent should be established. For him it was not just a question of ill-informed retired officers speaking out of turn, but a key issue of what the navy was for, what it had achieved, and what it needed for survival. He saw that 'both Canada and Australia are sensitive to the possibility of aggression by Japan . . . and that if the Japanese were to become the predominant naval power in the Pacific both countries would seek a close union with the USA'. This, thought Beatty, would mean 'nothing more or less than the dismemberment of the Empire. The Empire therefore depends on the maintenance of an efficient and sufficient Navy . . . Are the steps necessary to achieve this contained in the paper on Naval Policy and Construction dated 22nd November and the other papers sent to the Cabinet during the last 17 months? Are not these the considered opinions of the Board of Admiralty based on the lessons of the War?'

This spat was a personal matter between Beatty and Scott, and one of the latest manifestations of the schisms which had periodically rent the navy. In pre-war days this latest schism had been between the modernizers and the traditionalists. Scott belonged to the 'Fishpond', that circle of modernizers, also known as the materialists, who were led by Fisher and supported his reforms of the navy: the modernizers also placed their faith, often blindly, in the ability of technology to overcome all odds. The traditionalists, led by the permanently irate Admiral Charles Beresford, who was also a personal rival of Fisher, thought that some mysterious spirit of the seamen and their officers, embellished with a degree of Teutonic-style staff training, would be a battle-winning factor, and they chose to disparage those who put their faith in material. Scott had consistently supported Jellicoe, another swimmer in the 'Fishpond', even while Beatty was rewriting the history of Jutland to cast himself in a better light.

## HERBERT RICHMOND

Further insight into the schisms is contained in a private letter from Captain Roger Bellairs to Admiral Herbert Richmond in December 1920. At the time of writing Bellairs was naval assistant to Beatty, the First Sea Lord, and Richmond was at the Royal Naval College, Greenwich attempting to revive naval thinking by re-establishing the War College. Bellairs had served Jellicoe on his staff in the battleship *Iron Duke* at the Battle of Jutland. Later he joined Richmond in the East Indies, where his career began to run out of steam and he ended, as a rear admiral on the retired list, for many years writing staff histories in the naval historical branch.

Richmond was one of the navy's rare intellectual firebrands. He joined the Royal Navy as a cadet in 1885, saw service in Australia, and tried life as a hydrographer before specializing in the torpedo branch, at that time the technical and experimental branch of the Royal Navy. He was fascinated by all that was new and leading edge, and volunteered in 1901 for service in the new-fangled submarine, but was refused. He also missed the formative experiences of serving ashore in Africa or China which helped to shape the destinies of many of his contemporaries. Precociously bright, from a family of artists, his curiosity was spurred by a family friendship with Julian Corbett, and he started writing naval history at an early age, though it took him fifteen years of loving labour to produce his first book, the three-volume *The Navy in the War of 1739 to 1748*. His career followed a roller-coaster pattern: after each plum appointment his outspokenness caused him to be relegated to some backwater – for instance he commanded the revolutionary new battleship *Dreadnought* but from her he was sent to command a small squadron of second-class cruisers. Nevertheless, he exerted great influence throughout the navy. His acerbic letters on the cadet training system, of which he had, of course, personal and recent knowledge, helped Corbett to write prominent articles critical of training and education of the fleet, and these helped to bring about one of Admiral 'Jackie' Fisher's revolutions, the so-called Selborne Scheme for manning the Royal Navy with well-trained technically minded young officers.

Richmond himself had met Fisher in the 1890s, and had originally been in the Fishpond, but in advocating the creation of a more effective naval staff, he offended the egocentric Fisher and indeed other senior officers when he called the navy's organization for war as 'beneath contempt'. It was a sign of his increasing unemployability that on the eve of Jutland he was sent to Italy as a liaison officer, and, on his return, to command the old, slow, and very dispensable battleship *Commonwealth*, defending the Thames against a German raid, while every other ambitious captain commanded a unit of the Grand Fleet.

Richmond's criticism of Jellicoe's tactics at Jutland may have temporarily rescued his career, though the honeymoon with Beatty was soon over when it became clear that Richmond held other, renegade ideas about the size of battleships. Richmond's appointments continued to send him further and further away from London and the Admiralty. He was effectively banished to be Commander-in-Chief in the East Indies 1923–25, where Bellairs joined him, and then became the first commandant of the new Imperial Defence College, 1926–28. This latter appointment actually suited him well, as he was a strong advocate of joint warfare and of inter-service and intra-Empire cooperation. However, he opposed the independence of the air force, arguing that aviation should be integral to land and sea power. Like others of his generation he was offended by the concept of mass bombing, and argued for a limitation on the size of warships and for the defence of trade routes. He retired from the navy in 1931 and took the Vere Harmsworth Chair of Imperial and Naval History at Cambridge, the only naval officer and indeed the only naval historian (rather than imperial historian) to have ever done so; more remarkably, in 1936 he became Master of Downing College.

Beatty may not have been best pleased to know that his naval assistant and one of his admirals were in private correspondence. Of the first meeting of the Subcommittee on Imperial Defence about battleships, Bellairs wrote to Richmond: 'The greater proportion of the meeting was taken up by the Prime Minister . . . pointing out the extreme gravity of the position, political and financial . . . If we were to enter into a race with America, and if it was held that the outcome of the race depended on the building of units each costing £9,000,000 besides the tremendous other additions to expenditure in the way of Docks and attendant craft, it was difficult to say what would be the outcome'.

Beatty, the First Sea Lord, had replied to the Prime Minister that the programme of warship building 'had only been put forward as the considered Admiralty opinion of the measures necessary if we were to carry out the Government policy and maintain a "One-Power Standard" . . .' Winston Churchill, who might have been expected to be the navy's ally, was as Chancellor of the Exchequer in the early interwar years strongly opposed to defence expenditure and apparently agreed: 'whilst emphasising that it would be a deplorable thing for us to give up our sea supremacy, stated that he could not off-hand ascribe to the view that our sea supremacy depended now on a building programme of battleships, and that all the so-called Pre-Jutland types were obsolete'.

Bellairs continued his letter: 'The outcome of the meeting was that it was decided to make an eleventh hour appeal to America to ascertain if some agreement on building programmes could not be reached . . . it is extremely improbable that such an agreement can be arrived at, and under these circumstances the Committee of Imperial Defence will meet again on Monday next and sit practically continuously with the object of thrashing out the whole matter'.

Bellairs added his own thought:

The more I look into this question the more desirable it seems to me that we should pause and think. The net result of a battle-ship building programme will be that services in every other direction will be starved. Sir Percy Scott's question – 'what is the use of the present type of battleship?' – has not, so far as I am aware, been answered even in official papers by the Naval Staff. It is not correct reasoning to say that under Atlantic or Pacific strategy the battleship must be maintained as being the most powerful unit afloat and which all other units are finally supported by. This is to look at the question entirely from the gunnery point of view. The battleship may carry the heaviest gun, but, as you have pointed out, this does not make it a strong unit. Its sea-keeping qualities under present conditions, and in the face of the submarine menace actually make it a weak unit. There would appear to be a certain amount of confusion of thought when you hear the question asked whether or not the Capital Ship is obsolete. So far as one can see at present there must be a capital ship of a type with high offensive powers and which include high sea-keeping power. The real question is is the so-called Post-Jutland type capable of carrying out the requirements of the Capital Ship? It would seem that the answer is emphatically no, and that we had better save our money, rely at the moment on our present fleet, and meanwhile devote ourselves for at least a year to study and scientific research, with the object of overcoming the submarine and obtaining the capital ship necessary for the new strategic situation.

He added in manuscript to his typed letter 'also thereby "dishing" the American and Japanese programmes'.

Against this background, Beatty may have been quite relieved that the first of a series of conferences to consider the limitation of naval arms was called in Washington.

## NAVAL ARMS TREATIES

The inevitability of accepting parity with America formally entered British naval thinking as the Admiralty prepared for the Washington

Naval Conference of 1921–22, and from the negotiations in Washington yet one more definition of the power standard emerged: 'The naval policy of the government as approved by parliament and implemented at Washington', said the First Lord in his statement accompanying the 1922 naval estimates, 'is to maintain a one-power standard, i.e. our navy should not be inferior in strength to that of any other power.'

The USA had ended the war with a building programme that would provide the US Navy with twenty-five capital ships less than ten years old by 1925. In order to match this, Britain would have to replace her older fleet by laying down seven ships as the war ended and by continuing to build and launch at the rate of four per year, an intensity of construction which exceeded her building capacity at the height of the pre-war arms race and, of course, would coincide with post-war calls for economy. However, British government policy also contained a ten-year rule which presumed that Britain would not be engaged in any great war during the next ten years, and that no expeditionary force would be required for this period. In these circumstances the naval staff thought it was impossible 'in the present unsettled state of international affairs to arrive at any final conclusion as to the naval strength which will be required in the future'. Gradually the naval staff came round to the idea of accepting a power standard expressed in terms of parity with the US Navy.

There were four naval arms conferences between the wars, Washington in 1921–22, Geneva in 1927, and London in 1930–31 and 1935–36, and they dominated British naval planning and policy. It was hoped that a successful arms-control agreement would save money, maintain the effectiveness of the British fleet, and control future shipbuilding by other nations. Most importantly it would 'stop the clock' with the British navy supreme. 'The main object of the conversation' which the navy hoped to achieve 'would be to induce the USA to make a concession and to abandon her intention to build a great navy.'

Specifically the British delegation hoped to obtain a power standard of 3:3:2 compared to the US Navy and the Japanese navy. However, when at the start of conference the Americans unexpectedly offered a slightly higher ratio, 5:5:3, and also to cut back its so-called 1916 programme, the British immediately accepted. Beatty, the First Sea Lord, was well content with this windfall and returned to England, leaving his deputies, Chatfield and Domvile, to work out the details.

Near contemporaries, these two were contrasting characters. Barry Edward Domvile entered the navy in 1892, became a gunnery specialist and served in the Harwich Force and in staff appointments as Assistant Secretary to the Committee on Imperial Defence, Director of Plans Division, Director of Naval Intelligence, and President of the Royal Naval College. Besides keeping a scurrilous diary, he held right-wing, even pro-Nazi views and in June 1940 he was detained under the Defence Regulations. He was released from Brixton Prison in 1943, an unusual place for British admirals to spend their wars.

Alfred Ernle Montacute Chatfield entered the navy in 1886. His career was largely at sea; he specialized in gunnery, and his first major appointment was as captain of the battlecruiser *Lion* and flag captain to Admiral Beatty at the Battle of Jutland. When first *Indefatigable* and then *Queen Mary* blew up, it was to Chatfield that Beatty turned and said, 'There seems to be something wrong with our bloody ships today.' After the war he served briefly as Fourth Sea Lord and then as Assistant Chief of Naval Staff and accompanied Beatty to Washington for the first naval conference. He was Commander-in-Chief of the Atlantic Fleet 1929–30 and of the Mediterranean Fleet 1930–32, and First Sea Lord 1933–38, when his principal achievement was to help prepare the fleet for the coming war. For the first few months of the Second World War he was Minister for Co-ordination of Defence, with a seat in the War Cabinet.

Included in the American proposals was the idea of a ten-year holiday on the building of capital ships, which caused concern in the British delegation about how the shipbuilding industry would survive such a moratorium. Eventually the five-power naval treaty signed on 6 February 1922 listed the ships to be scrapped by the British Empire, France, Italy, Japan, and the USA. It provided a ten-year holiday on construction of new capital ships, except as replacements for those twenty years old. It established ratios for the British, American, Japanese, French, and Italian navies, of 5:5:3:1.67:1.67. No replacement vessel was to exceed 35,000 tons or carry guns larger than 16in. Aircraft carrier tonnage was also limited, and no carrier was to be bigger than 27,000 tons. No lesser naval ships, except transports, should exceed 10,000 tons and merchant ships should not be prepared for arming (one of Scott's ideas had been for dual-role ships which would carry passengers in peacetime and be converted to aircraft carriers in war). The Pacific powers, Britain, Japan, and the USA, also agreed to maintain the status quo on fortifications and naval bases in the Pacific, drawing the area to exclude Singapore. Finally the treaty was to operate until 1936, unless a member gave a two-year notice of intention to terminate it.

The other naval disarmament conferences made less progress, and, of course, there was cheating. When, for example, an Italian cruiser was accidentally damaged by an explosion and underwent emergency docking in Gibraltar, Royal Navy constructors measured her and found she exceeded the Washington treaty limits. The navy kept this information to itself, hoping to use it as a lever to persuade the Italians in other matters, but it did not matter: the period 1930–39 was one of growing rearmament.

## THE INVERGORDON MUTINY

In the recurrent economic crises of the 1920s and 1930s, the government decided to cut the pay of the armed services. On 11 September 1931 the Atlantic Fleet arrived at Invergordon, where it received newspapers announcing the government's decision: in the case of officers the nature of the reductions appeared in detail, but with regard to the men it was stated only that whereas hitherto men who had joined before 1925 were on a higher rate of pay than those who joined in or after 1925, now the 1925 rates would apply to all. An across-the-board cut of one shilling a day meant about 10 per cent for the officers, but 25 per cent for their men. The consequences were ill considered.

On Sunday evening, 13 September, the officer of the patrol ashore at Invergordon signalled 'Trouble in the Canteen; request larger patrol': in the canteen a few men were making speeches about their reduction in pay. Order was restored, the canteen closed, and the men left in an orderly manner, although further speeches were made when the men arrived at the pier. When he heard about this, Rear Admiral Wilfred Tomkinson, who was in temporary command of the fleet, decided that 'no importance need be attached to the incident from a general disciplinary point of view'. Then, when he opened a letter from the Admiralty addressed to all flag and commanding officers, stating the principles on which the reduction in pay had been based and explaining the views of the Admiralty, he assumed that it had been received by all ships and made a signal on the Monday morning directing that it be explained by commanding officers to their ships' companies without delay. However, the letter had been received by only a few ships and it was not until late Monday or early Tuesday that its contents could be explained to all. The admiral's dinner was disturbed by news that fresh disturbances had broken out in the canteen, and though the men returned from their leave, they did so in a very disorderly and noisy manner, and once on board there was speech-making, cheering and singing until late.

At this stage, no one thought that these events amounted to mutiny. The officer of the patrol on Monday evening was Robert Elkins, who eventually became a vice admiral. Recalling the events forty-five years later he wrote: 'Nobody as far as I know mentioned the word "mutiny" at any time before it took place . . . the worst that I expected was a bust up in the canteen . . . it was not until I saw the temper of the men that I realised that something more serious was afoot'. After witnessing events on the second night of disturbances, he reported directly to Tomkinson, noting that, 'from what I saw of [the admiral] and his staff that Monday night, frankly I do not think they thought there would be a mutiny'. Ominously however, and again reflective of 1797, the captain of the fleet was heard to remark that he thought one of the speakers in the canteen was 'another nosey Parker' – Parker being the name of one of the ringleaders of the earlier mutiny.

When, on Tuesday morning, the mutiny did break out, according to Tomkinson, 'There was no feeling of any sort against the officers'; trouble was confined to the ratings below leading rate, the men were carrying out their ordinary harbour routine, but it was clear to Tomkinson that there was a considerable number of men in the capital ships *Rodney*, *Hood*, *Valiant*, and *Nelson* and in other ships who intended to prevent their ships sailing the next morning in accordance with the practice programme. In *Rodney* the men had taken a piano onto the roof of a gun turret to show that they were not working.

In words reminiscent of 1797, Tomkinson informed the fleet, this time by signal, that he 'was aware that cases of hardship would result in consequence of the new rates of pay, and [he] directed Commanding officers to investigate and report typical cases to [him] so that [he] could represent the matter at once to the Admiralty. [He] also informed the Admiralty by telegram that [he] thought that it would be difficult to get ships to sea next morning'. The Admiralty did still not understand the seriousness of the situation and loftily signalled that they 'confidently expected that the men would uphold the traditions of the Service by loyally carrying out their duties', telling Tomkinson that the fleet's practice programme should be resumed as soon as his investigations had been completed. 'These telegrams', said Tomkinson in his official report, 'caused me some concern, as they appeared to indicate that my previous telegrams had failed to convey to Their Lordships a true picture of the situation . . .'

By Wednesday the mutiny had affected more men and ships. Tomkinson recommended that a representative of the Board should come to see matters for himself, and made specific recommendations about how to alleviate the valid grievances of his people. The Admiralty replied that the Cabinet was now considering the matter, and when the ships were ordered to return to their home ports the mutiny collapsed as easily as it had begun.

'With regard to the causes of the outbreak,' reported Tomkinson, 'there is no doubt that first and foremost was the disproportionate [effect upon] the lower ratings who entered before 1925. Contributory factors were the unexpectedness of such a reduction . . . the suddenness with which it was announced . . . the short interval before it [took] effect, and the belief held by a large number that the reductions were contrary to previous affirmations by the Government that ratings on the pre-1925 scale would continue to receive it during the whole period of their continuous service. There was no other grievance.' For good measure, Tomkinson added, 'In my opinion the cause of complaint was well founded; the reductions do undoubtedly affect most severely the younger and lower paid ratings, and are disproportionate'.

It had been a polite mutiny, and if it was fanned by left-wing agitators, its outbreak was spontaneous, and its cause exactly as described by Tomkinson. After investigation, some men were punished and others discharged from the service, and Tomkinson was made the scapegoat. He probably did fail to take firm action when the incident first occurred on the Sunday evening, but then he had been kept in the dark by the Admiralty, and it is difficult to see how else he could have acted.

Chatfield was Commander-in-Chief of the Mediterranean Fleet when the mutiny broke out at Invergordon. News of the mutiny had spread rapidly to the Mediterranean, but thanks to improved communications news of its remedy followed quickly, and so Chatfield was able to suppress any signs of indiscipline. His signal to his fleet was similar to the message which St Vincent had sent to the Mediterranean Fleet all those years before at the time of the previous great mutiny at home:

> On meeting the Fleet for the first time after the very serious occurrences in certain ships at Invergordon . . . I wish to express to you all my high appreciation of your conduct at a time of severe trial . . . that the Mediterranean fleet would preserve under every circumstance, however difficult, its traditional reputation for loyalty and discipline was what I expected, but what I wish to pay tribute to is the immense service to the Navy and the Nation that resulted from the facts that the heavy sacrifices, demanded in the first instance, were received by you in a spirit of absolute loyalty, and that your representations were put forward in a manner which was no less compelling because they were properly made through your own officers . . .

Chatfield's chief of staff wrote to him with 'a small suggestion that may appear trifling with in comparison with other issues . . . but great with the men. I suggest that *all* naval officers serving at the Admiralty wear uniform when visiting ships . . . thereby informing the lower deck that there is a naval element at the Admiralty'.

His chief of staff recalled that during one visit by the board of Admiralty to Plymouth, when some petty officers had asked him why the board were all civilians and he explained that in the Admiralty everyone wore plain clothes, another petty officer had replied, 'Yes, but they are retired officers as they wear top hats.' Tomkinson had already implied that the admirals and their staffs in London were out of touch with reality; many other officers in their reminiscences had shown that they thought so too, as did Chatfield. So when Chatfield became First Sea Lord, as an outward and visible sign of change, he ordered the board, for the first time in decades, to put on their uniforms.

Chatfield's time at the Admiralty was spent preparing the navy for war and little more was heard of unrest in the fleet.

## THE BRITISH NAVY

A frequently asked question is: when did the navy become the Royal Navy? In early times the English navy was a personal possession of the monarch, as when Queen Elizabeth I wrote that she was resolved to have her 'owne Navie of Shippes and vesselles imployed on the Seas'. However, unlike the Royal Marines who are an integral part of the navy and whose title was formally granted to them, the title of Royal Navy has never been formally conferred. On his restoration in 1660 Charles II made a point of renaming *Speaker* and *Naseby*, which became *Mary* and *Royal James*, and one writer, Michael Lewis, claims that the King also conferred the title of Royal Navy on the fleet which he inherited from the Commonwealth.

Only after the Glorious Revolution does the name seem to slip into general use, about 1690, and in the archives of the National Maritime Museum a document of William III's time lists in 1695 the ships of 'his Majesties Royall Navy with their Dimensions etc'. One of the next early uses is in an engraving of van der Gucht entitled *His MAJESTY's Royal Navy* with a portrait of George I surrounded by the fleet from first rates down to pleasure and advice boats, and dated 1714.

The concept of a Royal Navy as the navy of Britain emerged

slowly, and it was only when Britain grew into an empire that the government in London began to try to persuade the colonies to pay for their own defence, and out of this desire grew the concept of the Royal Navy as the navy of the British Empire. It was an idea fraught with difficulties, about the size and proportion of any monetary contribution, the types of ships which would best contribute to the defence of the British Empire, and even the legality of colonial ships. In some minds the Royal Navy was a concept above governments, and Domvile, for example, even suggested in the interwar years that defence of the empire would be best assured by moving the office of the Admiralty from London to Singapore, where presumably it would grow some independent, supranational identity, rather like the modern NATO.

Even as late as the twentieth century the name was not fixed. Naval officers from about the late 1700s onwards might use 'RN' as post-nominal letters to distinguish themselves from others, but writers and senior officers in the twentieth century still referred to the British navy rather than the Royal Navy.

King George VI used both titles when, in 1936, on his accession to the throne he sent a message to the fleet, saying

> I recall with pride that as my dear father did before me I received my early training in the Royal Navy. It has been my privilege to serve as a Naval Officer both in peace and war. At Jutland, the greatest sea battle of modern times, I saw for myself in action the maintenance of those great traditions which are the inheritance of British Seamen. It is my intention always to keep the closest touch with all ranks and ratings of the Naval forces throughout the Empire and with all matters affecting them. I shall do so in the sure knowledge that they will be worthy of the implicit trust placed in them by their fellow countrymen and that in their hands the honour of the British Navies will be upheld.

The next few years would test that trust.

# Chapter Twelve

# The Second World War

At the start of the Second World War the Royal Navy was the strongest it had been for two hundred years: in commission and building, there were twenty battleships and battlecruisers, twelve aircraft carriers, over ninety cruisers of all types including Commonwealth ships, and twenty classes of destroyers, as well as seventy submarines and numerous escort and patrol vessels, minelayers, minesweepers, and netlayers. France was now an ally and her large modern fleet was based in the Mediterranean to counter another powerful fleet, the Italian. The German navy was a shadow of its former self, but included a number of pocket battleships intended for commerce raiding, and a huge U-boat building programme was underway. In the Far East, however, the Japanese were no longer allied by treaty and were fighting wars of colonization which threatened British outposts and influence. By the end of the war threats from all of these navies had been crushed. Instead the Royal Navy's nemesis came from the United States, which, stimulated by Japanese aggression in 1942, stretched out her industrial might and built an ocean-going navy which has ruled the waves ever since.

The war opened with the Royal Navy engaged in familiar operations, transporting troops to the Continent, enforcing a blockade against Germany, hunting surface and submarine raiders, and protecting shipping in convoys.

In Germany the leaders of its navy, Grand Admirals Erich Raeder until January 1943 and Karl Dönitz thereafter, were pessimistic about the outcome of the war. Noting that the Kriegsmarine was hopelessly outnumbered and unprepared for the war, Raeder had said that the navy could 'do no more than show that they know how die gallantly', and Dönitz was scarcely less morbid: 'we can be satisfied if we manage to end the war with a draw'.

The London Treaty of 1935 allowed Germany a navy 35 per

cent of the size of the British surface fleet and the same number of submarines as the British, but given Hitler's allocation of resources they would take ten years to build. Hitler did hasten some U-boat construction in the late 1930s, but he was convinced that war with Britain would not begin until the mid-1940s. Raeder, who had been appointed Commander-in-Chief in 1928, wanted a balanced fleet for war on Britain's sea communications, and the fleet he planned would have included 13 battleships or heavy cruisers, 33 light cruisers, 4 aircraft carriers and 267 U-boats, which, taking a realistic view of shipyard capacity, would not be ready until 1948.

As Poland was invaded, Raeder sent two battleships with their supply ships and twenty-one U-boats to their war stations. His strategy was to blockade Poland and mine the approaches to the Baltic, to attack merchant shipping, and to mine British ports. The war began with mixed fortunes for the German navy: despite an apparently sincere intent to adhere to international law, the passenger ship *Athenia* was sunk by *U-30*. More heroically, *U-47* sank the battleship *Royal Oak* in Scapa Flow, and the aircraft carrier *Courageous* was sunk by torpedoes in the south-west approaches. But by the end of the year the pocket battleship *Graf Spee* had been forced to an ignominious end by three British cruisers.

## THE BATTLE OF THE RIVER PLATE

As in the First World War, one of the first surface-ship engagements took place in the South Atlantic. The raider *Admiral Graf Spee* had sunk nine ships, over 50,000 tons, in the Indian Ocean before she was brought to account. Several groups of British and French warships were employed in hunting her down until, on the morning of 13 December 1939, three cruisers, Force G under Commodore Henry Harwood, found her off the River Plate. The ensuing battle showed that the Royal Navy had learned a great deal since Jutland. After meeting his captains Nelson-style on board his flagship, Harwood gave his orders in three crisp sentences: 'My policy with three cruisers in company versus one pocket battleship. Attack at once by day or night. By day act in two divisions . . . by night ships will normally remain in company in open order.' The three cruisers, the British *Exeter* and *Ajax* and the New Zealand *Achilles*, had not operated before, yet the following morning, no further tactical orders were necessary as the ships separated into their two divisions to divide the fire of their superior enemy. Second, though the *Exeter* in particular took terrible punishment from *Graf Spee*'s six 11in guns, she did not, as some of the battlecruisers at Jutland did, blow up: the navy had relearned some lessons about damage control and ammunition handling. The cruisers drove their foe into the neutral harbour of Montevideo and there, after several days of intrigue and bluff, the *Graf Spee* was scuttled by her captain.

Vice Admiral Kenneth Dewar's views of the Battle of the River Plate are revealing. Dewar had entered the navy in 1893 and specialized in gunnery: despite this he was also something of an academic and, between commands at sea, he had won the Royal United Service Institution's gold medal with an essay on the influence of overseas commerce on the operations of war, and he had served in the Plans and Naval Intelligence divisions of the Admiralty. He was also one of the founders of the *Naval Review*, a journal which still circulates privately among Royal Navy officers, and was also a strong advocate of naval reform and of improved staff training. He retired after an infamous incident in *Royal Oak* in 1928 when his senior officer swore at the Royal Marines bandmaster, but in the Second World War returned to the Admiralty as a historian. This is what he wrote:

> At the Battle of the River Plate, three British cruisers, two mounting 6-inch, and one 8-inch guns, defeated the armoured pocket battleship *Graf Spee* (11 and 5.9 inch guns) . . . In the River Plate action, wide scope was given to individual ships. The dash and flexibility of their tactics can, at least in part, be attributed to their Captains knowing what to do and being allowed to do it. Proof of this may be found in the fact that not a single course, speed or manoeuvring signal was made throughout the action. The *Exeter* attacked independently whilst *Achilles* had to conform to the Commodore's movements in the *Ajax* without the necessity of keeping station. Her Captain states that his main objects were to keep A arcs [the bearing on which her guns could fire] open, develop maximum fire, and avoid punishment by frequent alterations of course. Our ships might have

been wiped out one by one by the enemy's superior armament if they had not manoeuvred independently to dodge the *Graf Spee*'s salvos ... The division of the British squadron into two widely separated groups was a noteworthy departure from the orthodox battle line. Amongst other advantages, it forced the *Graf Spee* to divide her armament, thus decreasing her chances of hitting or of quickly shifting from one target to the other ... The River Plate was the first British action since the great victories of the Nile and Trafalgar in which initiative has not been cramped by signals or stereotyped fighting instructions ...

Quite apart from the doctrinal improvements which Dewar perceived, it was a much-needed boost to morale, and a victory in the spirit and style of Nelson.

## NORWAY, 1940

The Battle of the River Plate had another consequence. The *Altmark* was one of the *Graf Spee*'s supply ships and she was en route to Germany with British prisoners of war from the merchant ships which *Graf Spee* had sunk. Hunted by the Royal Navy, *Altmark* took refuge in the Inner Leads of the Norwegian coast, where Captain Philip Vian, in the destroyer *Cossack*, found her and boarded her in breach of Norwegian neutrality. The event is noteworthy for another act of delegation, the signal from the Commander-in-Chief simply saying, 'Altmark your objective. Act accordingly.' Famously, the boarding officer made himself known to the prisoners with the cry, 'The navy's here!'

The German war economy needed the iron ore which Sweden was exporting by rail to Narvik and thence by ships through the Inner Leads and almost entirely in Norwegian territorial waters. So the Admiralty prepared plans to mine these waters and to force the iron-ore carriers out into the open sea where they could be stopped. A strong German reaction was expected, and the British prepared to make pre-emptive landings at Scavenger, Bergen, Trondheim and Narvik. Then on 8 April 1940 British destroyers laid three fields of dummy mines, while a covering force led by the battle-cruiser *Renown* stood off in the Norwegian Sea.

The British plans for occupying Norway had their origins in Jackie Fisher's First World War plans to 'Copenhagen' the German fleet in its Baltic harbours when Winston Churchill was First Lord of the Admiralty. In 1939 Winston returned to office as First Lord and 'on the fourth day after I reached the Admiralty I asked that a plan for forcing a passage into the Baltic should be prepared by the Naval Staff': this plan was known as Operation Catherine. However, when Russia invaded Finland, a new plan known as R4 called for a British and French army of nearly 100,000 men to land at Narvik and to pass along the railway (there was no road) through northern Sweden and so to help the Finns.

Ironically, long-prepared German plans for the occupation of both Denmark and Norway were already underway, in part pre-cipitated by Vian's actions. By 6 April there were strong indica-tions of enemy activity in the Baltic ports, and on 7 April the Admiralty was able to send to the Commander-in-Chief of the Home Fleet an accurate account of German movements, though these were interpreted as preparations for a breakout by the German fleet into the North Atlantic. When actual sighting reports of the enemy's northward movements were received, and the main forces of the Home Fleet sailed on 7 April, it was already too late: the German operations achieved complete tactical and operational surprise.

In poor weather the British search for the German navy brought only fleeting and accidental contacts. Late on 8 April, the destroyer *Glowworm*, which had become detached from the fleet while searching for a man overboard, sent a sighting report on the heavy cruiser *Hipper* before heroically closing to attack and damage her. On 9 April, *Renown*, searching for *Hipper*, found the battleships *Scharnhorst* and *Gneisenau*, but lost the Germans in a snowstorm. The Luftwaffe attacked the Home Fleet, without sinking any ships, while the British submarine *Truant* torpedoed and sank the cruiser *Karlsruhe*. Next day, Fleet Air Arm Skuas, flying to their extreme range from the Orkneys, sank the *Königsberg* in Bergen, and the pocket battleship *Lützow* was torpedoed by the submarine *Spearfish* and put out of action.

Notable actions followed, particularly between the destroyers at the First and Second Battles of Narvik. The troops, who had been embarked in cruisers ready for unopposed landings in Norwegian ports, had been put ashore in Scotland when the cruisers were diverted to the mistaken mission of preventing a German breakout. So it was that armed seamen and Royal Marines from warships, following a centuries-old tradition, were landed first, in an attempt to counter the German invasion.

There were two naval battles at Narvik, and the destroyer *Havock* took a full part in all these operations. In the confused and changing situation the Second Destroyer Flotilla, consisting of *Hardy*, *Hostile*, *Hotspur*, *Havock*, and *Hunter*, had left Scapa Flow late on 2 April to take part in laying minefields off the Norwegian coast. In the Norwegian Sea the ships rendezvoused with the battlecruiser *Renown*, under the command of Vice Admiral W. J. 'Jock' Whitworth, and the 20th Destroyer Flotilla. *Havock*, commanded by the appropriately named Lieutenant Commander R. E. Courage, was then in the thick of the action:

The northern minefield was laid about 80 miles from Narvic [sic] early on Monday, 8th of April, by 20th D.F. screened by ships of 2nd D.F. According to instructions we were to patrol this minefield for 48 hours, but were recalled to join *Renown* later in the day. After joining up we acted in the capacity of a screen against Submarine attack but owing to bad weather we had to form single line ahead (*Renown*, 2nd D.F. and 20th D.F.). During the night the *Havock* was unfortunate when her starboard engine refused to function for a short time. This left us in considerable difficulty in heavy seas. Defects were made good and we resumed our normal position in the line at 0350.

Tuesday morning at 0430 Action Stations were sounded. The *Renown* had sighted two unknown ships on the horizon and was engaging them. The 2nd D.F. concentrated for a few salvoes; further fire from Destroyers was futile as the range was far too great. The fact that we did fire probably had some effect on the enemy . . .

The effect was the very early imposition of a moral ascendancy of the Royal Navy over the German navy: two modern battlecruisers, the *Scharnhorst* and *Gneisenau*, had run away from an elderly First World War battleship. However:

Owing to the heavy seas the Destroyers were unable to keep up with the *Renown*, who chased the enemy. The Admiral, seeing that we were out of it, ordered us to proceed northwards and patrol to prevent the enemy from reaching the Narvic area . . .

*Havock* was soon involved in other operations:

Captain D.2. received orders from Admiralty to proceed to Narvic and take the town. Admiralty indicated that a small force of Germans were there, one ship, with possibly a Destroyer. Acting on these instructions, Captain D.2. Issued orders to Captains of ships re Landing parties . . . and we proceeded up the Fjord; stopping off Trannoy Point (Pilot Station). Enquiries were made here by an Officer of the *Hardy* and it was found that there were at least 6 Destroyers and 1 Submarine in Narvic. The attack was postponed and Admiralty informed of the size of the force which could have been anything up to 3,000 men as well as Naval units. Whilst waiting for Admiralty's reply, Captain D.2. decided to attack at 0330, 10th April, and the necessary orders were given. Until midnight, patrol was established across the mouth of the Fjord. At 0030, all ships went to action stations and proceeded up the Fjord in a blinding snowstorm in single line ahead in sequence of *Hardy*, *Hunter*, *Hotspur*, *Havock* and *Hostile*, visibility being from a few yards to 1,000 at the most. Great credit is due to Captain D. on such a feat of navigation. Here the Asdic sets played a great part in keeping us in touch with each other as we found our way up. At about 0220 *Hotspur* and *Havock* nearly ran ashore, but sheared off in time . . . At 0242 Captain D.2. made by W/T [wireless telegraphy, or radio] 'Good luck, let them have it' . . .

Owing to bad visibility we could not find the harbour . . . then visibility improved, clearing away to Northward and the harbour was seen ahead. This we headed for. The *Hardy* entered first and at first could see only Merchant ships. Then at 0426 alarm bearing 010 was made by *Hardy*. *Hardy* attacked. *Hostile* and *Hotspur* went to Northwards . . . *Hunter* followed in after *Hardy* was clear. The *Havock* went in after some delay due to the slowness of *Hunter* . . . The first Merchant ship was assumed by Captain D. to be British. Havock passed round this ship in her attack and a revolver was fired at *Havock's* bridge by a man on the foc'sle – he was settled by one of our Lewis guns. During these attacks all ships fired torpedoes. *Havock* hit one Destroyer amidships also some Merchantmen. *Hardy* sank one Destroyer and Merchantman. This left two Destroyers in the harbour who were hit by our shell fire. *Hunter's* results were unobtainable.

Captain D. now ordered *Hostile* and *Hotspur* to fire their torpedoes into the harbour as opportunity arose. *Hotspur* fired all eight direct into the harbour. Fire from the enemy was now becoming intense (including floating onions and tracer bullets). Torpedoes now came from the harbour and *Havock* was extremely lucky as one passed right underneath but had the wrong setting. Full ahead and astern were employed to dodge others (43 knots being obtained). All ships survived first attack . . .

At 0530, the second attack was made. Before getting right into the harbour, three enemy Destroyers were sighted at 0557 coming out of Herjangs Fjord and were engaged by all ships. At first these appeared to be 1 Cruiser and 2 Destroyers, but were established as large and new Destroyers of the *Lerbechte Mass* class. The enemy being superior, we retired to Westward to engage them. One was hit badly, as she was only firing ragged salvoes from one gun. At 0603, two more Destroyers of the same class were sighted ahead of us. We were trapped between two forces. The fresh force was engaged and were observed to fire torpedoes up our line.

At 0605 *Hardy* was hit and flames were seen belching from her after boiler room. *Hardy* was run aground . . . smoke screens were being made by floats and funnels. In this confusion, *Hotspur* hit *Hunter's* stern and only *Hostile* was observed by *Havock* to come out. The next seen of *Hunter* was that she was hit by shell fire and slowly sinking. *Hotspur* was also hit and signalled that she might require assistance. The two enemy Destroyers parted and *Havock* took the foremost one and hit her after magazine with a 4.7[in] salvo. She was beached . . . and afterwards towed off by Germans and sunk in the second attack.

*Havock* and *Hostile* now returned to assist their sister Chatham ship. With the *Hardy* aground and still firing her guns, the remains of the 'Fighting Second' returned unharrassed by the enemy who had had enough. Whilst returning, the German Ammunition ship *Rauenfels* was met. *Hostile* put a shot under her bridge and *Havock* one in the bows. The crew abandoned their ship and *Havock* remained behind to board. As the ship was blazing, the party returned and *Havock* having been informed by the German Captain that his ship was empty, layed off about 500 yards and let go H.E. The result was an immense explosion which lifted *Havock* in the water. Much damage was sustained from flying metal and pieces of mines, torpedoes and shells were picked up on the deck. *Havock* now continued down to join the other two Destroyers . . . So ended the first Battle of Narvic . . .

Two destroyers had been sunk on each side but five more German destroyers had been damaged and several German-controlled merchant ships also destroyed, and for his achievement against a superior force Captain B. A. W. Warburton-Lee, who had been killed on the bridge of the *Hardy*, was awarded the Victoria Cross – the first of any service to be gazetted in the war. Perhaps the most serious loss to the German army ashore was the ammunition ship *Rauenfels*, which was carrying all their ammunition reserve, and the loss of another ship on the following day, *Alster*, which had aboard their motor transport. Effectively the Germans were stranded, though a second Battle of Narvik was necessary to finish off the German destroyers. For this the Commander-in-Chief decided to send overwhelming force in the shape of the battleship *Warspite*, nine destroyers and supporting attack by aircraft from the carrier *Glorious*. The effects of *Warspite*'s 15in guns and the relentless pursuit by her escorts of the enemy to the furthest ends of the fjord saw the destruction of nine destroyers and a U-boat, thus giving a second opportunity to occupy the vital port and railhead from the Swedish iron mines. An opportunity which was passed up: this was the opinion of one then junior officer, Mike Gretton:

Victor Crutchley was Captain of the *Warspite* [in] the Second Battle of Narvik. In the afternoon, a Norwegian skied down to the ship . . . and told us that the Germans had fled Narvik town. I persuaded with out any difficulty Rupert Sherbrooke to

make a signal to Jock Whitworth [the admiral in command]
asking permission to land and take the town. Victor fell in his
Marines on the QD [quarterdeck] and was aching to get going
but Jock said no. The whole campaign would have been altered
if we had landed and I am sure that we [could] have held on
until the Army arrived. They were at Harstadt, not far away.
The decision was typical of our flag officer at the start of the
war!

Also, next day, we went alongside *Warspite* to transfer
wounded. Not a word from Whitworth or his staff, but Victor
left the ship to the Navigator and came down to the QD and
gossiped with Rupert while we were alongside. We loved him
for that . . .

## THE FLEET AIR ARM IS BLOODIED

The navy had lost control of its air arm when the Royal Naval Air
Service was amalgamated into the Royal Air Force on April Fool's
Day, 1918. Many thousands of air-minded officers, all the official
records, and the responsibility for writing the official history, and
learning the lessons of the air war in the First World War, were
also lost to the navy. Bitter arguments about control of the Fleet
Air Arm were only resolved when Admiral Sir Ernle Chatfield
became First Sea Lord, determined to regain control over the Fleet
Air Arm. It was as illogical, he argued, to have the Royal Air Force
control the Royal Navy's aircraft as it would be for the army to
control the navy's guns, and he threatened to resign. He won his
argument in 1937, though this left barely enough time to prepare
the navy and its Fleet Air Arm for war.

In consequence the Fleet Air Arm was not as well trained or
equipped as it should have been. Nevertheless the pilots flew and
fought bravely, and Fleet Air Arm Skua dive-bombers were the first
aircraft ever to sink an enemy warship. At the Second Battle of
Narvik, one of *Warspite*'s seaplanes, a Swordfish, had attacked and
sunk the *U-64*. Then:

by the plan of attack, aircraft from the *Furious* [Captain T. H.
Troubridge] should have joined the battle at this stage . . . her

machines had come punctually over Baroy Island [at the entrance to the fifty-mile-long fjord]; but . . . the weather being very thick when . . . The striking force [arrived] over Narvik, ten machines under Captain Burch R.M., fought their way through the narrows into Ofot Fjord with a ceiling of 500 feet and snow squalls that occasionally reduced visibility to a few yards.

As they came to the open fiord, the weather improved; and they arrived at exactly the proper moment. They dived from 2,000 feet to drop their bombs at 900 feet – about a hundred bombs, of which one in three were 250-pounders and the rest 20-pounders. They claimed two hits with the larger bombs on German destroyers outside Narvik at the cost of two aircraft . . .

The next day, as Dewar wrote, 'as arranged between Sir Charles Forbes [Commander-in-Chief, Home Fleet] and the Admiralty, aircraft from the *Furious* attacked German shipping near Trondheim . . . Eighteen machines armed with torpedoes left the carrier . . . some ninety miles from the town . . .' Unluckily the German cruisers had gone. The *Furious*'s airmen found only a couple of destroyers and a submarine besides merchantmen. They attacked both destroyers, and believed they hit one; but several torpedoes grounded in shallow water and exploded before they reached their targets. The disappointing result caused Forbes to order a proper reconnaissance of Trondheim to attack the warships when they had reported what they found in the fjords. In the words of the official historian:

The result was disappointing indeed; yet it was not the airmen's fault, as Captain Troubridge of the *Furious* pointed out in his letter of proceedings. At the end of the month, when the *Furious* went home, he wrote of these young officers and men, 'All were firing their first shot, whether torpedo, bomb, or machine gun, in action; many made their first night landing on 11th April . . . and undeterred by the loss of several of their shipmates their honour and courage remained throughout as dazzling as the snow-covered mountains over which they so triumphantly flew' – a tribute that reminds us of Lord St Vincent's saying of an earlier Thomas Troubridge that 'his honour was bright as his sword' . . .

Subsequent attempts to recapture any part of the Norwegian coast were a failure, though Narvik was occupied by the Allies for a short while, but in May, when a general evacuation was ordered, the principle was established, which the world would see again at Dunkirk and at Crete, that the Royal Navy would never abandon the army. On this occasion the only casualties to the army while at sea in the care of the navy were to the rearguard from Namsos, whose ship was sunk. As Major General Carton de Wiart later reported, 'in the course of that last, endless day I got a message from the navy to say that they would evacuate the whole of my force that night. I thought this was impossible, but learned a few hours later that the Navy does not know the word . . .'

The navy's performance in the Norway campaign was marred by the loss of the carrier *Glorious* and her destroyer escorts, *Acasta* and *Ardent*, who were overwhelmed by the German battlecruisers *Gneisenau* and *Scharnhorst* on 8 June. There were only a handful of survivors out of over 1,500 men: quite why *Glorious* was not flying air reconnaissance that afternoon is a circumstance which has excited controversy ever since.

## DUNKIRK

The campaign in Norway was brought to a halt by the German decision to attack westwards through the Low Countries and France. In five days the Dutch army was forced to surrender, part of the French army collapsed, and the British Expeditionary Force and some Allied troops were outflanked by rapidly advancing armoured and motorized Germans. In what was almost a repetition of the Royal Naval Division's landing at Antwerp in the First World War, cruisers and destroyers took naval landing parties and Royal Marines to the ports of Holland and Belgium, with orders for the ports and installations to be destroyed. The Dutch royal family and gold reserves were evacuated, but for some time the authorities resisted Royal Navy efforts to fire the oil stocks. Nevertheless, some Allied warships and a large number of merchant ships escaped to England.

Meanwhile, most of the army was cut off on a small section of the Belgian and French coast, and on 19 May Vice Admiral Ramsay, Flag Officer Dover, was told to prepare for evacuation. Boulogne, further westward, had to be evacuated first, and there two battalions of Guards marched on board the navy's destroyers, while Royal Marines acted as their rearguard and ships' guns, firing over open sights, kept German tanks at bay. On 20 May nearly 30,000 non-essential troops were sent home and starting on 25/26 May a makeshift flotilla of small craft, many of them civilian, carried the wounded out of Calais, the last party leaving in the early hours of 27 May when the rest of the town was already in enemy hands.

Meanwhile Operation Dynamo, more simply known as Dunkirk, had been ordered. Initially it was thought that only a few thousand men could be rescued in the forty-eight hours which were available before the Germans sprang their trap. Thus the stage was set for what the official historian called

> an operation which has no parallel in the history of warfare; one of incalculable difficulty and hazard with the scales of success greatly weighted in the enemy's favour ... Yet its success far exceeded the hopes of even the most sanguine. The Germans had ... accomplished the rapid surrender of many armies and nations ... all had been laid prostrate under the swastika ... [and] it was not unreasonable for them to expect a similar surrender of the British and French armies encircled at Dunkirk ...

Over the next nine days a flotilla of nearly a thousand ships, including fifty Dutch barges which had been saved only a week before, some two hundred private motor boats, and nineteen RNLI lifeboats, rescued 338,226 British and Allied troops. Nine destroyers were lost and nineteen damaged, there were countless acts of great individual bravery most of which were never recorded, and the contribution of the little ships ensured that the spirit of Dunkirk entered the language and the national psyche of the British. Much of the success of Operation Dynamo was due to the bravery and skill of the men in the ships, the discipline and patience of the army, and the inspired leadership of Admiral Ramsay. Almost the only factor working in the British favour was the weather, and the navy's control of the Narrow Seas, where it was fighting in waters familiar to it since the sixteenth century.

One of the heroes ashore was Captain (later Admiral Sir) William Tennant, Senior Naval Officer, Dunkirk. Tennant had joined the navy at the brand-new college on the Dart in 1905 and, like generations of his predecessors, at the young age of fifteen. His service record reads like that of many officers in the preceding four centuries: the North Sea, the Mediterranean, the Levant, the Indian Ocean, and North America. Even the names of his ships would have been familiar to his antecedents: *Venerable*, *Implacable*, *Renown*, *Repulse*, and *Arethusa*. He had served most of the First World War in the Harwich Force and so was personally familiar with the waters through which he helped organize the evacuation of Dunkirk. Later in the Second World War he commanded the *Repulse* and survived her sinking by air attack at the end of 1941, was promoted to rear admiral, and commanded a cruiser squadron of the Eastern Fleet. He helped plan Operation Overlord in 1943 and in 1945 was Flag Officer, Levant and Eastern Mediterranean, ending his career as Commander-in-Chief, America and West Indies, 1946–49.

Keeping with tradition, Tennant's signal as he stepped aboard the last ship was suitably laconic, after three weeks' heroic effort: 'B.E.F. evacuated returning now. 2330'. Tennant, and the nation, were filled with a sense of deliverance, as he recorded later:

> that terrible twenty-three days for the B.E.F. of rearguard action, retreat and sleepless nights, ended on the beaches between Dunkirk and La Panne. When I arrived with my party of twelve officers and one hundred and fifty men, to be greeted by a good bombing, I asked the Generals I encountered how long we should expect to have for the evacuation before the enemy broke through and they replied: 'Twenty four hours, perhaps thirty-six!'
>
> So, fully expecting to be 'put in the bag', we plugged away at the evacuation and by the end of the week 330,000 men had been evacuated. This was perhaps the greatest deliverance the country has ever had, for nearly all her army were got back again. It was no victory. It was no miracle worked by the Navy and the hundreds of other craft. They did a good job. But it was all brought about by the mercy of God and the stupidity of the enemy . . .

A further 200,000 British, French, Polish, Czech, and Belgian troops were evacuated from St-Malo, Cherbourg, and the Biscay ports up to the end of June. While much equipment was lost, half a million trained men were brought back for the defence of Britain against a German invasion and to prepare for the landings in Normandy four years later.

There were two tragic footnotes to the evacuation from France. On 17 June 1940 the liner *Lancastria*, loaded with troops, was sunk in the Loire with the loss of about 3,000 lives, the single largest loss suffered during this period: for reasons of morale the news was kept secret. The other tragedy was to have strategic consequences: one of the aims of the evacuation had been to get the French fleet away and out of the Germans' hands. Many ships joined the Free French in Britain, but others sailed for French ports in North Africa. Fearful that they would eventually be handed over to the Germans, French ships in British ports were seized and in Alexandria Admiral Cunningham persuaded the French Admiral Godfroy to immobilize his ships. Cunningham and his captains achieved this through personal meetings which took place over several days. At Oran it was another matter: there was a lack of personal contact, and after agonizing, day-long negotiations, Admiral Somerville, commanding the newly formed Force H, opened fire on his erstwhile allies. The consequent loss of life embittered relations between the two navies, as well as within the French navy, for many years. However, the episode also convinced neutral nations of Britain's determination to fight on against the Nazi tyranny.


## SEALION

The German capture of Norway in May 1940 assured supplies of Swedish iron ore, but it also gave Hitler an obsession with defending Norway which handicapped the German navy. The Kriegsmarine's losses had been heavy: five cruisers and ten destroyers sunk or severely damaged. These losses told Raeder what to expect if the Germans tried to invade England.

However, the invasion seemed imminent. The Dutch and Belgian ports, which for so long it had been British policy to keep out of the hands of any enemy, and the coast of France from Calais to the Pyrenees, were now in the hands of a single and implacable foe. The German name for their invasion plan was Sealion, though there seems to have been little conviction to it. The army wanted to land on a broad front from Ramsgate to Lyme Bay; the Kriegsmarine reckoned it could only guarantee a safe crossing if the invasion was on a narrow front, but hoped that the air war would force the British to negotiate. The Kriegsmarine also reckoned that it would need one million tons of shipping, which, astonishingly, was ready by the middle of September 1940. However, the preliminary order for Sealion, which had been under consideration since May, was repeatedly postponed throughout September 1940, and in October it was decided to keep the plans 'purely as a means of political and military pressure on the English' and in January 1941 it was discontinued. The cause was not just the German air force's failure to achieve air supremacy, but at no time had the Germans achieved that essential precondition to an invasion: command of the sea.


## TARANTO

Command of the sea was more directly contested in the Mediterranean. Malta, a British base for over a century, was considered indefensible against Italian air power, and was abandoned for Alexandria, which, however, lacked the facilities of a modern fleet base. The Italian fleet from its central position was, on paper, stronger than any fleet which the Royal Navy could muster there, and before long would be augmented by German U-boats and the German air force too. All these advantages were set aside by a man who has been described as the greatest admiral since Nelson. Admiral of the Fleet Viscount Cunningham of Hyndhope, as he became, had served ashore as a midshipman in the Boer War, and during the First World War commanded with distinction the destroyer *Scorpion* in the North Sea and post-war in the Baltic, earning the DSO and two bars. A child of the British Empire, Cunningham was born in Dublin but of a Scots family, and he entered the Royal Navy in 1897. In his later years Cunningham preferred the nickname of 'ABC' (his initials) but earlier in his career he was always known as 'Cuts', a reference to his short temper and generally frugal nature. The start of the Second World War found 'ABC' as Commander-in-Chief, Mediterranean Fleet and after his victory off Cape Matapan, the Italian fleet never recovered.

Cunningham used his relentless aggression to establish an unbeatable moral ascendancy over his enemies. On land the war was going rather badly and Cunningham evacuated troops from Greece to Crete, where he sent Royal Marines reinforcements and defeated an attempt at a sea-borne invasion, but German paratroopers gained a foothold and eventually forced a further evacuation. During these operations the navy suffered heavily from enemy air attacks, but the navy would never abandon the army, and Cunningham told the generals: 'It takes three years to build a ship. It would take three hundred years to build a tradition.' He went on to a series of victories over the Italian fleet, to fight convoys through to Malta and Tobruk, to command the Allied landings in North Africa and Sicily, and to become First Sea Lord in 1943.

In the First World War the Royal Navy had several times attacked the enemy in his harbours using aircraft, though given the small payload which the planes could carry, these attacks amounted to not much more than experiments and inflicted little damage. Now that the Fleet Air Arm had been restored to the Admiralty's control, the world would see what aircraft carriers and naval aircraft could do. Cunningham had a long cherished plan to use his 'Stringbags', as his Swordfish torpedo-bombers were known, to hit the Italian fleet in its harbours. The attack was originally intended for Trafalgar Day 1940, but a fire on board the carrier *Illustrious* caused postponement until the night of 11/12 November.

By moonlight twenty-one Swordfish from Nos 813, 815, 819, and 824 squadrons flew off in two waves from Rear Admiral Lyster's flagship, achieving complete surprise and causing more damage to the enemy fleet than Jellicoe had achieved in his day-long battle at Jutland: three battleships were sunk at their moorings as well as damage and fires caused to other ships and installations. Meanwhile cruisers had entered the Straits of Otranto and destroyed a convoy. Cunningham reported: '*Illustrious* aircraft carried out most successful attack on Taranto. Estimated that one *Littorio* and two *Cavours* torpedoed and many fires started by bombs. Italian SOS's were intercepted from Straits of Otranto which indicates that the VA was not idle'. Cunningham's signal '*Illustrious* manoeuvre well executed' was, even by his own fierce standards, an understatement.

The news reached home when, to use St Vincent's words about his battle on 14 February 1797, 'A victory is very essential to England at this moment'. Or as the First Sea Lord, Admiral of the Fleet Sir Dudley Pound, wrote to Cunningham, 'Just before the news of Taranto the Cabinet were rather down in the dumps; but Taranto has had a most amazing effect upon them.'

## MATAPAN

The next major encounter was the Battle of Matapan in March 1941. An Italian battleship, several cruisers and destroyers had sailed to intercept troop convoys between Alexandria and Piraeus. Cunningham, warned by signals intelligence and anxious to bring about an engagement, arranged an elaborate deception. Taking care to clear his convoys off the sea, he set a trap south of Crete. An anonymous officer in *Havock*, whose last major action was off Norway, takes up the story:

At 1530 27th March we sailed from Alexandria ... with the Aircraft Carrier *Formidable* ... [and] *Nubian, Mohawk* and *Hotspur*. While at sea messages were intercepted that units of the Italian Fleet were at sea, these consisted of 4 cruisers escorted by one destroyer in a position 84 miles from Cape Passero steering 120 degrees at 15 knots. Cruisers were subsequently identified as probable 2 of the *Zara* class and one *Colleoni* class and when last reported at 1900 when visibility was bad were still steering 120 degrees. On completion of flying operations we were returning to Alexandria when we met the battlefleet leaving harbour. We were ordered to join the screen taking up position on the starboard wing steering 300 degrees at 20 knots to intercept the enemy if possible.

Our Light Forces consisting of the 3rd and 7th Cruiser Squadrons who had been operating in the Aegean proceeded through Antikithera Channel on the night 27/28th March in an endeavour to intercept the enemy. At 0802 *Orion* sighted 3 unknown ships 18 miles away, these were closed and 10 minutes later were identified as 3 enemy cruisers and 3 destroyers, 2 cruisers being of the *Zara* class and one 6-inch cruiser. At 0830 the Battlefleet were ordered to raise steam for full speed with all despatch and *Havock* ordered to form part of the 10th Destroyer Flotilla under the Command of Captain Waller in *Stuart* R.A.N. At 0900 enemy were reported to have altered course to port and steering a course North West, *Orion* was at this period trying to draw the enemy towards our Battlefleet. *Formidable* was now ordered to fly off Torpedo striking force this being an attempt to reduce the speed of the enemy ships and enable our Battlefleet to make contact. At 0930 a report was also received that 4 more enemy cruisers and 6 destroyers were also at sea to the southward of the enemy previously reported. The destroyers *Juno*, *Jaguar* and *Defender* were now detached from the Aegean to cover Kithera Channel.

At 1000 the Battlefleet were still steering 300 degrees at 22 knots and an hour later *Orion* sighted 2 enemy battleships of the *Cavour* class steering 160 degrees who opened fire on her and ships in company which included Captain 'D' 2nd Destroyer Flotilla in H.M.S. *Ilex*. It now appears that the enemy cruisers had retired on their heavy ships drawing our cruisers under their fire. At this point *Orion* and ships in company retired towards our Battlefleet with the Italian warships in pursuit and reports were now received of another Italian Battleship of the *Littorio* class in company with cruisers and destroyers.

At 1150 the course of our Battlefleet was altered to 280 degrees and at 1226 destroyers consisting of the 2nd, 10th and 14th Destroyer Flotillas were stationed ahead of the Battlefleet, speed 29 knots. Battle Ensigns were flown and we flew the Battle Ensign used in the first Battle of Narvik and all ships were ready for action ... The main enemy forces were now known to consist of the following: The Northerly group 2 *Cavour* class battleships, 2 *Zara* and 1 *Pola* class cruisers and 5 destroyers. The other group consisted of one *Littorio* class battleship, six cruisers and destroyers. This force was 60 miles to the westward of our forces at 1130 and the former 35 miles west of Gavdo Island.

The chase now continued throughout the afternoon and first dog [watch]. At 1823 the Commander in Chief reported that one damaged *Littorio* class battleship was bearing 292 degrees 50 miles from our Battlefleet steering 300 degrees at 12 knots. The *Littorio* was damaged by first Torpedo striking Force.

At 1830 second Torpedo Striking Force was flown off from *Formidable* and simultaneously a report was received that some of the enemy forces had concentrated around the damaged battleship. This force was in 5 columns reading from left to right were 3 *Navigatori*, 3 six[-inch] Cruisers, 1 *Littorio*, 2 *Nembo*, 3 eight-inch Cruisers and 2 six-inch cruisers screened by destroyers. During this dusk attack several hits were scored by torpedoes from the Torpedo Striking Force which greatly reduced the speed of the *Littorio*, the 8-inch cruiser *Pola* together with a destroyer was also damaged.

At 1900 destroyers were formed up by flotillas, the flotillas reading from left to right were 2nd, 10th and 14th.

At 2037 the 2nd and 14th Destroyer Flotillas were ordered to attack enemy battlefleet with torpedoes. The 10th Flotilla were ordered to form screening diagram number 17 on the battlefleet, we were in a position one mile on the starboard beam of the *Warspite*. The enemy battlefleet were now reported to be in a position bearing 286 degrees 33 miles steering 295 at 13 knots from the *Warspite*.

At 2205 *Valiant* reported surface craft bearing 244 degrees 8 miles which was on the port bow of the battlefleet. At 2220 our destroyers *Greyhound* and *Griffin* on the port side of the screen were told to take station on the starboard side of the fleet. At 2226 *Valiant* now reported surface craft bearing 178 degrees 4 miles distance and a minute later *Stuart* gave a night alarm bearing 250 degrees, and now a red Very's light was fired to port of our fleet, this probably being the Italian recognition signal for the night. At approximately 2228 *Valiant* and *Warspite* opened fire on enemy vessels simultaneously scoring a direct hit on the 8 inch cruiser *Fiume* leaving her burning fiercely and the *Warspite* hit what appeared to be a destroyer of the *Vincenzo Gioberti* class, firing was now observed to the westward of us on the horizon for a very short period, this from after reports appears to have been the remainder of the Italian fleet fighting amongst themselves. The *Stuart* was then engaging various targets but no hits were observed. The 8-inch Cruiser was now damaged by our Capital ships and destroyers were then ordered to finish off burning cruiser to the south east of the battlefleet, the battlefleet now turned to the Northwards to avoid possible torpedo attack from enemy destroyers . . .

Cunningham was frustrated: his flagship had run aground leaving Alexandria and her sea-water filters had been clogged, restricting her speed, and while the wind was from the east he had to keep slowing even further while *Formidable* turned into wind to fly off her aircraft. The enemy, though wounded, was getting away from him and so, though various reports had told him that there were up to three Italian battleships and many more cruisers at sea, he pressed on into the night, deciding to chance a night action against a theoretically superior force. Then, about 10 p.m., a radar contact was made ahead. Manoeuvring his battleships, *Warspite*, *Barham*, and *Valiant*, like destroyers, first into quarter line and back into line ahead, Cunningham rapidly closed the range on the radar targets to discover they were the 8in cruisers *Zara* and *Fiume*: opening fire at less than two miles, the effect of his battleships' 15in guns was devastating. Meanwhile *Havock* had her own share of glory. The battle had stretched out over 150 miles of the Mediterranean, with few orders given and most units acting on their own initiative:

At about 2310 we sighted an enemy destroyer right ahead turned to fire torpedoes but were unable to in so short a time, we closed her and gave her all we had and in addition fired one torpedo which hit her amidships. This destroyer turned out to [be] the *Alfieri* of 1750 tons, 400 tons heavier than us, we circled her firing another 3 torpedoes without results but our gunfire and the result of the first torpedo had set her on fire from end to end and shortly afterwards she blew up and turned turtle. We now proceeded to finish off [the] burning cruiser as previously ordered, turned to fire torpedoes and at the same time sighted the Italian cruiser *Zara* damaged but still underway, torpedoes were then fired at the *Zara*. At this moment we were illuminated by starshell from our own capital ships and came under the fire from their 6-inch guns but the salvoes fell well astern, we then retired under cover of a smoke screen. This mistake was due to our not burning fighting lights as a means of recognition and was unavoidable in the darkness and the swiftly changing situation. Fire was ceased almost immediately when the Capital ships recognized us in the light of the starshell and we returned to the scene of the action.

Shortly afterwards an explosion occurred on the *Zara* which may have been caused by one of our torpedoes striking home and otherwise an internal explosion. We now fired starshell to illuminate the *Zara* but starshell fell right illuminating what appeared at the time to be a *Littorio* class battleship but was later identified as the Italian 10,000 ton cruiser *Pola* apparently stopped and undamaged, fire was opened at a range of 6,000 yards and several hits were observed on the superstructure, we turned away making smoke and were greatly surprised that our fire had not been returned. We now retired at high speed to the north-eastwards at 0045, reporting the position of the *Pola*.

At approximately 0130 *Greyhound* reported that she had closed the cruiser *Pola* and had *Griffin* in company with her, we now returned to the scene of the action to reinforce *Greyhound* and on arrival at about 0230 found her and *Griffin* lying off the *Pola* who had her guns trained fore and aft and appeared undamaged except for a fire burning internally and superficial damage to the superstructure. Italian seamen were yelling for help on board and swimming in the water. Owing to our having no torpedoes remaining we were unable to add her to our nights bag and at 0330 we were joined by the 2nd and 14th Destroyers Flotillas who had sighted nothing all night. The destroyer *Jervis* went alongside the *Pola* and took off wounded . . .

In fact the *Pola* had been hit in the engine room with a torpedo during one of the Swordfish attacks earlier in the day: she had lost power but was otherwise undamaged. Captain Philip Mack, Captain of the 14th Destroyer Flotilla, took his ship *Jervis* alongside and boarded the *Pola* in fashion reminiscent of bygone days – armed with cutlasses, probably the last occasion on which this

venerable weapon was ever used in anger. Mack contemplated
towing the *Pola* to Alexandria but decided against it as the
approaching morning would find him still within range of enemy
land-based aircraft. They liberated some trophies, like much-needed
20mm Breda machine guns, and took over 250 prisoners of war,
the other survivors having already abandoned ship. While this was
going on:

> a large explosion occurred to the eastwards this in all probability
> being the *Zara* blowing up for the last time. *Jervis* now fired a
> torpedo at the *Pola* and she eventually blew up and turned
> turtle slowly to port and sank. Destroyers then commenced to
> pick up survivors and at 0445 after we had picked up 35 from
> the *Pola* all ships had to leave the scene of the action to
> rendezvous with the Battlefleet at 0700. The position of the
> remaining survivors was later signalled to the Italian High
> Command suggesting a Hospital ship be sent.
>
> We rendezvoused with the fleet at 0700 March 29th and
> formed an anti-submarine screen steering southwest, course was
> altered later to the eastwards and the fleet started on its return
> to its base . . . The Fleet arrived at its base at Alexandria on the
> evening of the 30th and we started another of our very brief
> spells in harbour . . .

Although the battleship *Vittorio Veneto* had escaped, Cunningham's fleet had sunk three heavy cruisers and two destroyers for the
loss of one aircraft and its crew. Cunningham was regarded by
some as being rather niggardly in his praise, but this was not one of
those occasions, as he signalled to the fleet:

> The skilful handling of our cruisers and the untiring efforts of
> the F.A.A. kept me well informed of the enemy movements,
> and the well pressed home attacks of the T/B aircraft on the
> *Littorio* [-class battleship *Vittorio Veneto*] so reduced the speed
> of the enemy fleet that we were able to gain contact during the
> night and inflict heavy damage. The devastating results of the
> battleships gunfire are an ample reward for the months of
> patient training. This work was completed by the destroyers in
> the admirable way we have come to expect from them. The
> contribution of the engine room departments to this success

cannot be over emphasised. Their work not only keeping their ships steaming at high speed for long periods but in the work of maintenance under most difficult conditions has been most praiseworthy. I am very grateful to all in the Fleet for their support on this and on all other occasions.

## MALTA CONVOY

For generations senior naval officers have often conducted their affairs between themselves and with, and sometimes about, their political masters at two levels, an official one, copies of which are often found in the public archives, and a private one, of which there are sometimes only chance survivals. The following letter written in January 1941 from Andrew to Jack is an example of the latter:

> Your passages with W[inston] C[hurchill] made me laugh some. I was quite sure you'd have a scrap with him. He's a great leader of the nation but I wish he'd leave naval policy in the proper hands. I have had a lot of trouble with him lately over his idea of sending Roger Keyes out here to command a party of cutthroats as an independent command. I eventually succeeded in getting R.K. disrated to commodore & I now hope he wont arrive ... I fear D[udley] P[ound] is having a lot of trouble with W.C. He doesn't stand up to him enough ...

Andrew was Admiral Sir Andrew Cunningham, Commander-in-Chief Mediterranean and Jack was Admiral Sir John Tovey, Commander-in-Chief Home Fleet. While Tovey was searching for German raiders in the Atlantic, whether pocket battleships or disguised merchant ships, Cunningham was arranging his forces in the Mediterranean. He ordered Operation Excess, which aimed to pass a military convoy to Piraeus with supplies for the Greek army, convoys from Gibraltar and Alexandria to Malta, troops in cruisers to reinforce the garrison of Malta, and an attempt to extricate eight empty ships from that brave but beleaguered island. The complex operation, which required meticulous planning, resulted in the first encounter with the German air force, and on 10 January heavy air attacks using torpedoes, high-level bombing, and dive-bombing developed. The experience convinced Cunningham that his essential purpose had become the war against the German air force and he urgently requested more fighter aircraft, anti-aircraft guns, and radar-fitted ships. The Germans responded with a concentrated attack on the aircraft carrier *Illustrious*, which was saved only by her armoured flight deck. This is how, in the same letter to Tovey, Cunningham described the German attack on her:

> We had a bit of a setback between Malta and Pantallaria. I never did like that locality and stiff with German dive-bombers it became a bit impossible. We had two lively periods of about ten minutes each. *Illustrious* bore the brunt of the first attack and they hit her 4 times with bombs that looked like flying elephants ... *Illustrious* had three fires going and her steering gear bust but made off for Malta at 26 knots. Then she started turning circles but got going again after an hour or so. We were attacked again at 1630 & *Illustrious* was a fine sight every gun going all out ... the *Fulmers* [Fulmars: *Illustrious*' fighter aircraft] came along and took a good toll. They have been trying to get *Illustrious* in Malta ever since and have inflicted additional damage. Malta has however shown its teeth, there are nearly 100 guns there now, & has I hope shaken them badly. Anyhow *Illustrious* sailed overnight & I am like a cat on hot bricks ...

*Illustrious* did get back to Alexandria and then went to the USA for repairs before joining the Far East Fleet.

## THE CAPTURE OF A FLEET

The tide of war began to turn in late 1942. The British Empire was, above all, an empire based upon sea power, and even if the Mediterranean was closed, the army in Egypt could be resupplied by convoys of troops and supplies from across the Indian Ocean and around the Cape, and from all parts of the empire, including Britain, Australia, India, and New Zealand. As a consequence of the influence of sea power German and Italian forces were duly

defeated at the Battle of El Alamein by British Empire forces
supported on their seaward flank by ships of the Empire's navy.

A vast armada sailing from Britain and the United States landed
an Allied army in French North Africa, Operation Torch, and
pushed eastwards. Cunningham's ships cut off further retreat or
escape and the Germans were forced to surrender: Cunningham
issued the order to 'sink, burn and destroy', words which, of course,
echoed both the orders which Anson had been given two hundred
years before and those which St Vincent had given to Nelson when
he was in the Mediterranean.

In July 1943 the Allies invaded southern Europe. The invasion
of Sicily, Operation Husky, involved nearly 3,000 ships of all kinds,
again commanded by Admiral Cunningham. In September the
Italian mainland was invaded at Salerno, leading to the overthrow
of the Italian dictator Mussolini, and an armistice with Italy. By
September Cunningham was feeling unusually lyrical, recording in
his memoirs that the sight of his old flagship, the battleship
*Warspite*, leading the surrendered Italians into captivity, was his
'wildest hopes of years back brought to fruition', filling him 'with
the deepest emotion [which] I can never forget'. His signal to
the Admiralty, however, was in the tradition of generations of his
ilk suitably laconic: 'Be pleased to inform their Lordships that
the Italian battle fleet now lies at anchor beneath the guns of the
fortress of Malta'.


## SPIRIT OF THE NAVY


Admiral Sir Walter Cowan, who entered these pages several chapters
ago, was sixty-eight years old when the Second World War broke
out, though mere age did not dull his determination to fight. First,
he volunteered to serve as an acting commander to his younger
brother, but when he heard that Roger Keyes was working up some
commandos for special operations he got himself transferred. Soon
he found himself in Alexandria, where he met Cunningham, who
as a young midshipman had been serving with the navy's 12pdrs in
the Boer War when Cowan was aide de camp to Lord Kitchener.
Later Cunningham had commanded the destroyer *Seafire* in

Cowan's Baltic squadron in 1920, where they had had a minor clash because Cowan would not accept that fog should delay destroyers, and then Cunningham had been Cowan's flag captain on the America and West Indies Station. Now Cunningham welcomed Cowan on board the *Warspite* with all the dignity due to an old chief, and took him to sea where he witnessed the Battle of Matapan.

Next Cowan took part in a commando raid at Bardia, and when part of his commando was sent to reinforce Tobruk, the admiral joined the 18th King Edward VIIth's Own Cavalry, an Indian regiment. Later, when an Italian armoured division overran this regiment Cowan was captured, but only after firing off all his ammunition, and even then he refused to put his hands up. Cowan had time to scribble a note that the honour of the regiment was intact, and, later, confided that 'If only I'd had a companion and some more ammunition I'd have captured that Italian armoured car'. Cowan spent some time in Italy as a prisoner of war, but under ancient rules of war he was exchanged for an Italian general and took passage home in a cruiser. He was soon out again with the commandos.

The islands of the Adriatic and the Aegean were the scenes of bloody guerrilla warfare. Following the Italian armistice in 1943, the German high command recommended the evacuation of the islands, but Hitler refused to 'on account of the political repercussions which would follow'. Churchill had similar ideas and wanted to occupy the islands and so he signalled the Commander-in-Chief: 'This is the time to play high. Improvise and dare.' Thus it became German policy ruthlessly to suppress risings by the Italian forces on islands like Cephalonia, while the Allied policy was to occupy key islands with the scant forces which were left over from more major operations.

Soon Cowan was involved in a form of littoral warfare which Drake, Nelson, and countless officers and men of the Royal Navy down the centuries would have recognized. After visiting the Italian front, Cowan 'with Tom Churchill . . . got into an M.G.B. [motor gun boat] . . . [and went] over to the island of Viz some time after dark, alongside the harbour jetty of Camiza, and there were welcomed by Jack Churchill, Tom's brother and Colonel of 2

[Army] Commando . . . The life there was one of frequent bombing by the Germans. It was the only island not in their possession, and we made it a very constant thorn in their flesh'. This was the same coast where Captain William Hoste had landed parties of seamen from his ships and frequently hauled guns to the top of precipitous hills, a thorn in the flesh of the French and their allies a hundred and thirty years before.

Similarly Cowan conducted raids working with

just the one Commando and some hundreds of Yugo-Slav partisans, with no great quantity of equipment or ammunition. At night all the troops and inhabitants went into dug-outs and places in the mountains, and our force of light craft lying alongside dispersed to anchorages under the land outside; Camiza was an awkward place to bomb, high land all round . . . we lived on the water front with Navy House next door, but had a Battle H. Q. a few mile a away in the mountains . . . Sometimes besides bombs they [the Germans] dropped incendiaries. One morning very early before dawn we were ringed with fire, and the Germans put out on the wireless that they had burnt the whole town and sunk every craft in the harbour, but this was by no means the case. They did however blast every window and door . . .

This is how Cowan describes the buildup to what was almost his last action:

With Tom Churchill's arrival began a steady stream of reinforcements and munitions, and day by day we became a bit harder a nut for the Germans to crack . . . They planned one invasion scheme after another, but just could not pull it off, and the two Churchills, masters of war, set and kept going what has ever been the most effective mode of defence, i.e. offence. Raids of all sizes by land and sea, and the Commandos delighted in it all. There would go out after nightfall perhaps in a schooner or an M.G.B. a small party, with one officer and be landed on a German held island, where friendly partisans would see to them and guide them to the group of Germans they were after, and, perhaps, they would hide up for a bit and get to know their habits before striking, and over and over again they would pull it off . . . and bring back prisoners. Sometimes the Partisans alone and sometimes our Commando men . . . Then whenever all things were favourable, or there were signs of German action against us . . . a major raid would be set going . . . Our first was against the island of Sholto, about 10 miles away. We got into the L.C.I's [Landing Craft Infantry] at night-fall and steamed for 5 hours, the navigating of the expedition conducted by 'Spider' Webb, Lieut. R.N.R., and most faultlessly he did it, being guided finally to the beaches by a single torch flashed by Captain MacMiniman of 2 Commando, who had been in hiding over there three days cheek by jowl with the German garrison, but very carefully guided and looked after by Partisans . . . These raids in one respect were mostly the same – very small landlocked beaches and then straight up the mountain side, sometimes a track, but as often, not.

This particular night we marched five hours at the rate of about 1000 yards an hour, and by dawn all detachments were where they were told to be, including a party of American Rangers, the counterpart of our Commandos, and a splendid war wise lot . . . Just at dawn they [the Germans] let drive at us, and we were all round their position in a village crowning a hill and crammed in on them to ensure them not breaking out again. Then 'according to plan' came the 'Spits', four lots of three, diving down with all guns going, and dropping their bombs exactly right and swooping away again, rather beautifully done, and the whole village smoke and dust and flying stones; quite a lot on us too, as we were in a very tight ring round them. Then a sort of Heath Robinson touch of modern warfare. We had a loud speaker outfit, and a most gallant Commando man – a German Jew – to operate it, and he addressed the Germans to the effect that if they did not at once surrender, the Spits would return and give them a second dose. After a minute or two a few of them showed up and began to trickle in, but not as quickly as we considered they should, so we whistled up the 'Spits' again, and at it they went with great good will and accuracy. Another word or two from the loud-speaker and they ceased fire, our men drove forward with the bayonet and that finished the business, we liquidated the entire force to a man.

In a small way, I reckon it was as perfect an example of a

Commando raid as there has been in this war. My first had been at Bardia two years before. Then, after a period for light refreshments, picking up the pieces and burying the dead, and having a look at the effect of our guns and bombs and doing a little utilitarian looting in the way of equipment and some food, the force formed up and Jack Churchill our leader got out his bagpipes, which on every raid and with a Highland claymore as well he carried into battle with him, and at the head of them all played us down to the beach and off we went back to Viz . . .

Cowan was awarded the DSO for his 'gallantry, determination, and undaunted devotion to duty as Liaison Officer with Commandos in the attack and capture of Mount Ornito, Italy and during attacks on the islands of Solta, Mljet and Brac in the Adriatic, all of which operations were carried out under very heavy fire from the enemy . . .'

## THE BATTLE OF THE ATLANTIC

In May 1941 the German battleship *Bismarck* sank the battlecruiser *Hood*, pride of the Royal Navy, but when she in turn was hunted down her sinking largely brought to an end German cruiser warfare in the Atlantic. Hitler's concern for a British invasion of Norway caused him to insist on the squadron at Brest being brought back to defend Norway. So in February the *Scharnhorst* and *Gneisenau*, which had had been tying down a portion of the British fleet, and acting as 'flypaper', that is distracting bombing raids from Germany to France, made a successful dash up the English Channel. Interestingly, Raeder had argued against this on the grounds that the crews were inexperienced and should not be exposed: another parallel with the French blockaded in their ports a hundred and fifty years before. Manpower shortages were hurting the Kriegsmarine: the navy had only 15,000 officers for a navy which had rapidly expanded to 500,000 men, and Dönitz, who commanded the U-boats, was running out of experienced crews. Naval manpower was being dissipated in garrison duties and in riverine and coastal operations in the Mediterranean and in Russia.

Then in late 1942, at last, a German naval squadron was able to bring a weaker British squadron to action on advantageous terms, but the cruisers *Hipper* and *Lützow* and their destroyer escort were driven from their quarry, an Arctic convoy, by a squadron led by the destroyer *Onslow*. Hitler raged. He raged for an hour and half on the theme that capital ships were a waste of men and material, and while he raged Grand Admiral Raeder could not get a word in edgeways. The subsequent order to draw up plans for decommissioning the German big ships was a turning point in the war and Raeder resigned after fourteen years in office.

The new German naval commander-in-chief, Dönitz, had shown what trade war and wolf-pack tactics could achieve, even if the main type of U-boat, the VIIC, was little different from the boats with which Germany had finished the First World War. Now he was able to give priority to the U-boat war, and to determine what U-boat types should be built and what strategy used. Overall, however, the U-boat campaign was defective. For example, Dönitz never developed any appreciable capability for operational research, which would have indicated the best use of the U-boats. He was unable to decide whether *Tonnagekrieg* (sinking ships wherever they were found) or *Zufuhrkrieg* (sinking laden ships as they approached Britain) was the better strategy. Nor did he appreciate that his coded signal traffic was seriously compromised, declaring instead that treachery was to blame for so many convoys being routed out of the way of his waiting U-boat packs. Lack of trained manpower was a serious problem too: by 1942 the original corps of 3,000 U-boat volunteers were dead, captured, worn out, or thinly dispersed throughout the fleet.

The U-boat war was fought in five phases. In the first, to August 1940, 215 merchant ships were sunk for the loss of 29 U-boats and 1,200 experienced submariners. The exchange rate might have been better but the detonator pistols of German torpedoes were defective, and many U-boats had been diverted to the Norwegian campaign. The second phase, which lasted about two years, was much more successful. These were the happy times for U-boats, operating from French Atlantic ports, whose achievements peaked, however, in October 1940: later this phase included several months' *Tonnagekrieg* against poorly organized shipping on the American east coast.

Meanwhile Dönitz himself was fighting two wars: an external war against the Allies and a domestic struggle for resources. As late as 1942 he was still dogged by torpedo failures: according to German estimates it took 806 torpedoes to sink 404 Allied ships. Ominously he began to lose his best U-boat captains, or 'aces', and once America had entered the war he could win neither *Tonnagekrieg* nor *Zufuhrkrieg*.

Between November 1942 and March 1943, in the third phase of the U-boat war, the U-boats sank 100 merchant ships, more than half a million tons: it was the nearest they came to cutting Britain's sea communications. But by May 1943, with the cumulative effect of extended air cover, radar in Allied escorts, repeated cryptographic insight into German plans, and more experienced escort commanders, German fortunes were reversed. Thirty-one U-boats were lost in three weeks: more than in all of 1941. According to a contemporary analysis, given 'the crippling losses of U-boats trying to attack convoys, Dönitz withdrew his boats from the North Atlantic . . . and sent several groups to the Central Atlantic to attack the stream of convoys working between United States and the Mediterranean . . . [but] this coincided with the entry into force of the U.S.N. Hunter-Killer groups'. The hunter-killer groups consisted of an escort carrier and several anti-submarine destroyers, which 'were employed, first in close support of convoys in threatened areas and later on in distant support operations. The results were brilliant and very few ships were sunk, while the enemy losses were disastrous'. The groups were, however, well cued by Ultra intelligence. The final phase of the U-boat war, beginning in November 1943, was, despite new equipment and new types of U-boats, a period of collapse and defeat. U-boat construction peaked and then fell precipitously: losses at sea exceeded 50 per cent of Dönitz's precious crews and over 400 boats.

The U-boat war did cause huge resources to be diverted to the Battle of the Atlantic, but the reality is somewhat different to the popular images. According to British and German statistics, only 131 of all commissioned U-boats successfully attacked six or more Allied ships. While a handful of aces sank nearly 800 ships, or about a third of Allied losses, less than 30 per cent of all U-boat patrols resulted in contact with an Allied convoy, and even at the peak of German success in 1942 only thirty out of 3,281 convoyed ships were sunk. 550 front-line U-boats saw nothing during their short careers: overall they were powerless to stop Allied landings in North Africa, the reinforcement of Britain, and Operation Neptune.

The war at sea had become, in Winston Churchill's words, a matter of 'seamanship and science', in which a leading scientist, who had been a sailor, took a prominent part. Patrick Blackett, who was descended from a long line of naval officers, had entered the navy as a youngster and served, in the First World War, at the Battle of the Falklands in 1914, at Jutland, and on some arduous patrols in the North Sea and English Channel. After that war the navy sent its young officers to Cambridge to be civilized and there Blackett, who had always had a mechanical bent, discovered he wanted to be an experimental engineer: later he would win the Nobel Prize for Physics, the only British officer ever to win such a prize.

In the Second World War Blackett had taken the lead in founding the science of operational research. He

> produced some interesting statistics about North Atlantic Ocean convoys based on the results of 1941–42, which was the period when the enemy was still well 'on top'. He analysed five factors which have an important bearing on the success or failure of the defence of the convoy under attack by U boats and upon the defeat of the U boat fleet ... (i) The number of surface escorts per convoy (ii) The size of the convoy (iii) The speed of the convoy (iv) The amount of air cover per convoy (v) The efficiency of the surface escorts ...
>
> First, it was found that an increase from six to nine in the number of ships in the close escort would lead to a reduction of losses of ships of about 25%. The need for a strong escort had been accepted earlier but the excuse had always been given that the additional ships were not available. This may have been true numerically but by a simple adjustment of duties whereby the size of the close escort in U-boat infested waters was increased, and in comparatively safe areas was decreased, the size of the escorts when and where numbers mattered critically could be substantially raised.
>
> This was only achieved after the North African landings had

finished at the beginning of 1943, when support groups which could reinforce the escort of threatened convoys were first formed from the existing escort forces. Support groups had indeed been conceived some time earlier but consisted of very short legged destroyers which, because convoys at that time could not refuel at sea, were useless for their purpose.

Secondly, it was found that an increase in the average size of convoys from 32 to 54 ships was associated with a reduction in losses of no less than 56%. This surprising conclusion was disputed hotly for some months.

But it is true and it brings an additional operational advantage in that with larger convoys, fewer convoys need be sailed, the number of escort groups can be reduced but the number of ships in the escort groups can be correspondingly increased. However, the view had always been held that the larger the convoy the more vulnerable to attack the ships in it were and in November 1940, a ruling was made that no convoy over 40 ships was to be sailed. So, as ships' sailings could not be delayed and as additional convoys could not be run for lack of escorts the ships necessarily excluded were sailed independently. These left overs were taken from the fastest and the slowest ships eligible for convoy. The results were disastrous, the loss rate of the slow ships sailing independently was 25%. In other words, each ship lasted four voyages. Even for the fastest ships, except for the high speed 'monsters', the loss rate was several times higher than ships in convoy. This order was not rescinded until June 1941.

Thirdly it was found that an increase in speed from 7 to 9 knots was associated with a reduction in loss of 43%. This conclusion was also closely associated with the presence of air cover, when speed became even more important because U-boats under air cover had to remain submerged. The conclusion did not come as a surprise but the extent of the decrease was greater than expected although there were ample statistics available of the no less startling effect of Air escort during the first World War.

Fourthly, Air cover for eight hours per day brought in the later stages of 1942, which is the only period for which statistics are adequate, a decrease in losses of 64%. In fact, less than a dozen ships were sunk in daylight in convoys with Air and Surface escort during the whole war, while in 1917 and 18 only five ships were sunk in convoys escorted by Aircraft, Airships and Kite balloons as well as by surface craft.

Fifthly, the results achieved by individual escort groups were analysed over a long period. Based on a comparison of the number of ships lost in convoy guarded by each group for the total number of days in which U boats were in contact with the convoy, it was possible to place escort groups into two classes. The figures show that during a comparable period the second class lost three times the number of 'ships per U boat' day than did the first. Thus, if all groups had reached the average standard of efficiency of the first class groups, a reduction of losses of no less than 61% should have been achieved.

The maths were Blackett's and they were new, but in the debate over large convoys versus small ones his arguments were decisive. However, many old lessons were also contained within his findings:

It is a melancholy reflection that it was not until 1943 that such facts were put across to higher authority by the efforts of the scientists in the operational research sections. And a closer look at the picture will show it even blacker, for the majority of these five factors had been proved time and time again in 1917 and 1918. The vital contribution of air escorts and supports to convoys was well recognised in 1917 and 1918, yet when World War II started, the first priority of the shore based maritime Aircraft was stated to be reconnaissance of Enemy Surface ships and Raiders. The value of speed was equally ignored by the government and the shipping companies. And finally, both escort groups and support groups had been a regular feature of convoy defence both in home waters and in the Mediterranean in World War I and reports made in 1918 emphasised time and again the need for group training both together and in conjunction with an escorting Aircraft . . .

These findings and similar work led one expert to credit Blackett with doing more than any other one man to win the Battle of the Atlantic. There were, of course, many heroes who went to sea in merchant ships and in warships and fought bravely against the U-boats and the weather, and many books about the Second World War have told their story, and the tales of survivors, but much of the convoy work was dull routine and the unsung heroes were the convoy commanders.

## CONVOY COMMANDER

Commodore Walter Boucher was typical of his generation. He had entered the navy as a cadet in 1904 and served during the First World War in the North Sea, the eastern Mediterranean, and the North Atlantic, winning the DSO and being mentioned in despatches in 1919 for his work in minesweeping. He qualified as an air pilot in 1925, was in charge of the flying training of the Fleet Air Arm and the training of naval observers in the Directorate of Training of the Air Ministry from 1929 to 1931, and served with the Naval Air Division at the Admiralty in 1933–34, commanding the aircraft carrier *Courageous* from 1935 to 1937. He was Director of Air Material at the Admiralty in 1938, and was then second naval member of the Australian Naval Board until 1940. Upon retirement he joined the Air Transport Auxiliary as a ferry pilot, but was persuaded that while he could ferry one aircraft at a time as a pilot, as a convoy commodore he could carry several dozens at once. As a commodore in the Royal Naval Reserve he commanded Atlantic and Arctic convoys, and his autobiographical memoir well describes the role of the convoy commodore and manoeuvring a convoy by night when under attack. At his first convoy conference he made a

little speech to the assembled ship's captains about such things as; leaders keeping touch in fog; use of navigation lights in fog by day or night; emergency turns by the convoy; &c., &c., ending up with a request to be informed at any time of anything about which I ought to know and which I obviously could not see, and finally our thanks to the control staff and all concerned. I was to sail as Commodore in the Norwegian motor vessel 'Abraham Lincoln', which was commanded by Captain Holmsen ... That ship, under that Captain, had been crossing and recrossing the Atlantic, in convoy, all the war, usually with a Commodore on board ... The convoy soon settled down into nice, steady, station. Our ocean escort joined us, and the Senior Officer steamed close alongside us and had a talk with me on the loud hailer. Then, we ran through a patch of fog, but, to our relief, it didn't last long. We soon had a following wind as we steamed through the deep blue, clear waters of the Gulf Stream with an occasional little patch of golden yellow gulf weed floating on the surface. After the small U.S. Navy airship had ceased patrolling round the convoy, U.S. Navy Catalina flying boats took over as air escort. At the first convenient opportunity, I exercised the convoy in making emergency turns, both by day and night, and about four nights later I was glad I had.

I was asleep ... when the whistle of the voice pipe shrilled in my ear ... 'Escort got something ahead!' called the officer of the watch ... cursing myself for ever having undressed at all; grabbing trowsers, sweater, coat, and pulling on a pair of sea boots as I made for the bridge snatching up my Convoy Form and binoculars on the way. The ship's alarm gong was sounding for action stations. One of our escorts was showing coloured lights. 'Crrump! Crrump! Crrump!' came from the distance ... A tiny light blinked out of the darkness ahead. 'Answer the escort!' I called, and the signalman on watch got busy with his shaded lamp. 'From escort,' he reported, 'forty five to port, please.' 'Reds and greens for forty five to port!' I shouted. 'Switch on!' 'Aye, aye, sir!' cried my yeoman, half way up the ladder to the bridge, and a moment later we were lit with a string of red and green lights up to the masthead signalling 'Turn together forty five degrees to port.'

I looked back among the convoy on each side waiting for the signal repeating ships in the convoy to switch on the same lights. One after another they did so, 'Do you think all ships in the convoy have got the signal by now?' I asked Yeoman Caterall. 'Oh yes, sir, I expect so – with the noise of the depth charges too.' 'Crrump! Crrump! Crrump! Crrump!' they went again. 'Switch off!' I ordered.

... there was always an element of risk at this point of an emergency turn. The turn had been sprung suddenly on to a large number of ships by coded light signals in the middle of the night. Not many seconds were allowed them to make up their minds about it, because, if long delayed, the whole object of the manoeuvre which was to avoid attack would be defeated. Again, if even one ship turned the wrong way, there would almost certainly be, not one, but several collisions resulting in ships damaged or sinking, dropping astern of the convoy to be sunk by the very 'U' boats they had tried to avoid.

To my great relief, the convoy swung round 'like one man', so to speak, each sounding two blasts as she put her wheel over. 'That's another escort joined in!' pointed the yeoman suddenly grabbing a signal lamp to answer Senior Officer of Escort. 'Another forty five to port, please,' came through. More coloured lights, more blasts on the whistle, and the convoy, darkened and invisible, turned their second forty five degrees to port like soldiers on parade . . . Flashes of guns split the darkness off our starboard quarter . . . Then, a searchlight pointed a thin finger of light ending in some dark object which had reared itself just above the surface of the sea. 'Got one, sir!' . . .

Such episodes became commonplace during the Battle of the Atlantic.

## ARCTIC CONVOY

Just as the demands of escort work in the Atlantic piled up, a new task in worse weather and with the enemy closer at hand was required of the Royal Navy: Arctic convoy. The German invasion of the Soviet Union made an ally of Stalin, who demanded supplies of war material to be delivered to Russia's Arctic ports, yet with the German air force in northern Norway, as well as submarines and surface ships, the convoys met furious and sustained opposition. The weather was a major factor: the icy storms of winter and dark nights meant attack from German surface ships but were preferable to the midnight sun of summer when they could expect day-long attacks by submarines and aircraft when retreat to the edge of the icepack gave insufficient sea room to manoeuvre. Yet the convoys were fought through, and only one was ordered to scatter, with the consequent slaughter.

Boucher was involved as commodore of a convoy which was attacked by the *Scharnhorst*:

By Christmas day it was darker at noon than it had been at midnight. The sky was overcast. There was a freezing south easterly gale which cut right through one and a very high sea. To touch bare metal meant leaving one's skin behind on it. The men at the guns and at other exposed positions were suffering torments. The galley however was doing well, they were hard at it with carols. In the saloon, the steward had written a reminder across the mirror in soap, 'A HAPPY CHRISTMAS' and we sat down there to enjoy an excellent joint of roast pork and a few jokes together, quite unconscious that the battle cruiser *Scharnhorst*, with a screen of five destroyers searching ahead of her were steaming at high speed towards us. They had left Altenfjord at 7 p.m. for a quick dash out, an easy kill, and a safe return at speed in the Arctic darkness.

So far, we had not been able to get any wireless news from home or elsewhere and then, by chance, someone switched on the Pacific service of the B.B.C., and we heard, by sheer luck, Christmas carols, beautifully sung by children of Dr. Barnardo's homes. They were helping us on our way, although they didn't know it. The wireless beam we heard passed near the Pole then round the world to the Pacific. Not only had we no wireless news, we had no knowledge of any supporting British forces. How it would have cheered us to know that Vice Admiral Sir Robert Burnett with his cruiser Squadron, had already left Kola Inlet where Murmansk is situated and was hastening to our aid. Besides that, the Commander in Chief Home Fleet, himself, Admiral Sir Bruce Fraser (made Lord Fraser of North Cape after that battle), was also speeding along from the south westward, where he had a following wind, to intercept and destroy the enemy. He was flying his flag in the Battleship *Duke of York* and was accompanied by the Cruiser *Jamaica* and had an anti-submarine screen of four Destroyers, *Savage*, *Scorpion*, *Saumarez*, and the Norwegian *Stord*.

They were a long way from us and as they subsequently reported a south westerly gale, while ours was south south easterly, they must have been the other side of the centre of what to us 'tramp steamers' was the storm . . . according to my orders, I should have to make a bold alteration of course to the eastward, i.e. towards the wind. It was blowing harder now, and the frequent snow showers blotted out most of the Convoy most of the time. There was a big sea and the ships were making very heavy weather of it. The *Fort Kullyspell's* starboard lifeboat had been smashed by the sea and a *Sherman* tank had started to move about her after deck . . . The Master of the *Fort Kullyspell* wanted me to heave to, but I told him that the tank could go over the side if necessary. The important thing was to get the convoy through, and I intended to do it if I could. Was I not given the princely sum of 5 shillings a day for commanding it! Such remuneration entails responsibilities!

To alter course more into the teeth of the gale would have done greater damage still to the ships with their deck cargoes, so we stood on as we were going. What we did not realize, until later, was that the course to the eastward would have taken us towards the advancing *Scharnhorst*. The gale was, therefore, an intervention of Providence . . . Sometime later – it was Boxing Day by now – I got an order from the C. in C. . . . to steer north . . . This left little doubt that the *Scharnhorst* was out and we were being sent up to the North Pole to hide. It suited us well, however, for the convoy rode easier farther off the wind and risk of severe damage was reduced, though the ships were rolling heavily.

That alteration of course took us 40 minutes to make . . . The only feasible way of doing this without throwing the convoy into confusion, or running a great risk of ships becoming detached and unprotected, was by a series of wheeling turns. These were made by coloured light signals. An apparently endless series of very heavy snow showers kept driving down making it impossible to ensure that all ships had ever seen a particular signal either switched on, or switched off which told them the moment they should turn . . . The convoy plunged and rolled along through the freezing darkness with all its guns manned. There was nothing to be seen. Nothing to be heard except the scream of the wind and the thunder of the waves against the hulls of the ships . . . when things began to happen quite suddenly.

Away in the darkness to starboard a huge orb of flame slowly grew – hung – then faded away. Nothing could be heard above the existing din. Captain D.17, signalled: 'Cruisers engaging enemy to S. Eastward.' As he was making it he streaked off with his flotilla in sheets of foam to join the fun, leaving the convoy to its own devices. More great orbs of flame appeared from the distant darkness to starboard as the guns of Admiral Burnett's cruisers exchanged salvo after salvo with their much more powerful enemy in an attempt to draw her away from the convoy regardless of the punishment they were taking.

We, in the convoy, could not tell how the battle was going, nor how many enemy ships were present. All we did know was that up to date we had not been attacked. In time, the gun fire ceased, and later still our destroyer escort returned to us and signalled the welcome news 'Scharnhorst retiring to S.E.ard.'

In fact the four destroyers who had formed an antisubmarine screen around the Duke of York had made a torpedo attack which slowed the Scharnhorst and enabled the Commander-in-Chief to sink her. But Boucher's convoy was not out of trouble yet. He received a signal: 'To Commodore of convoy from C. in C. Resume your course', but a new entertainment was only just round the corner, for he soon received another signal: 'We are surrounded by "U" boats. Attack is certain.' So far, the convoy had been saved by the miracle of the gale, which prevented it altering course into the arms of the Scharnhorst, but now, conditions for attack by U-boat were excellent:

There was a cutting, freezing wind, against which it was physical pain to look out. Blinding snow storms, and a very steep sea against which the convoy was making but little progress. We certainly did seem to be out of the frying pan into the fire. Or perhaps it was out of the 'fridge into the deep freeze.

All of a sudden, to our utter amazement, our second miracle flashed upon us. Without warning, the wind dropped. Then almost immediately, great white ribbons of light appeared in the sky. Three of them together. They were like immense paper decorations, starting near one horizon, going right over our heads, and finishing near the opposite horizon. They were of great beauty, never still, always twisting, untwisting and twisting up again. We were floodlit. It was light as day. Ships saw again each other for the first time. Everything was altered now. The former favourable conditions for submarine attack were reversed. Things were now distinctly bad for them.

There was far too much light for attack on the surface. On the other hand, although the wind had dropped, the high seas remained. Not only would the huge wave crests obscure the target when viewed through a periscope, but the submarine herself would break surface in the troughs of the waves . . .

Turning southwards, the convoy reached Murmansk, where Boucher rewarded the merchantmen with a last signal:

To Convoy J.W.55.B: from Commodore. I congratulate all Captains, deck and engineer officers and men on a fine feat of hard steaming, skill and endurance in what has been, under God's hand, a successful and historic voyage. Thank you for your cooperation. Good luck, and a quick turn round.

These were the thanks which the navy, and the whole nation, owed to the merchant navy.

## OPERATION NEPTUNE

By 1944 the 'hinge of fate', again Churchill's words, had turned against the Germans. Naval plans for the invasion of Europe had been started in the darkest days of the Second World War, in May 1942, when a staff was set up to examine the problems of a major cross-Channel raid. When this staff was switched to planning landings in North Africa, others continued to examine options and to prepare specialist shipping, bases, hards, and slips.

Operation Neptune was the name eventually given to the assault phase of the plan for the liberation of north-west Europe, when, on 6 June 1944, five divisions of American, British, Canadian, and other Allied troops with all their weapons, transport and stores were landed across open beaches heavily defended with every possible artefact and device which a cunning enemy could devise. According to the naval staff history: 'The loading and berthing arrangements, co-ordination of movements, measures for security from both enemy interference and stress of weather, disembarkation and the continued flow of reinforcements and supplies, as well as direct support of the Army by bombardment . . . were naval responsibilities calling for the most intricate and careful planning . . .' The scale on which this was planned and achieved surpassed anything ever seen in the history of the world: over five thousand ships took part in the first days of the operation.

According to Admiral Ramsay, now the Allied naval commander-in-chief, no single question was more often discussed during the planning than that of H-Hour. It was decided that low tide was needed to expose the extensive German underwater obstacles and as many hours of daylight as possible with a rising tide were required to carry the Allies ashore. This indicated a dawn landing, restricting the choice of D-Day to just two or three days in the cycle of the tides every fortnight.

4 June 1944 was a typical English summer's day: overcast, with low cloud, the wind blowing south-west force 6, and conditions expected to deteriorate. It was so far from the settled weather and clear atmosphere that the Allies wanted that the landing was postponed and ships already at sea turned back. Some forces, like the miniature submarines which were to act a navigation beacons, were already in place off the beaches and could not be recalled. Nevertheless, bold men predicted that on the morning of 6 June there would be a temporary lull and so the Supreme Commander, General Eisenhower, 'faced with the alternatives of taking the risks involved in an assault during what was likely to be only a partial and temporary break in the weather or of putting off the operation for several weeks until tide and moon should again be favourable . . . took the final and irrevocable decision: the invasion of France would take place the following day . . .' The consequence was complete tactical surprise: the Germans' own experts having advised that landings would not be possible at all, the German land commander, Rommel, had been driven to Germany for his wife's birthday and his subordinate commanders were gathered for a meeting in Rouen. Six battleships, two dozen cruisers, and over a hundred smaller vessels joined the bombardment of the beaches and enemy positions inland. More than four thousand landing ships and craft took part, and one of the features of the landings were

prefabricated harbours, known as Mulberries, which were towed into position, and used until better and nearer harbours could be captured as the Allies advanced.

Naval staff histories, like naval commanders' reports, are not noted for their poetry or boasting, but the author of the staff history of Operation Neptune could not help allowing himself to conclude that the success of the assault on Normandy

> stands unparalleled in history ... certain it is that a great page of history turned on that summer day in June when H-hour struck, the guns of the Allies opened and
> 'There came Neptunus on his way
> That hath the sea in governance'.

The next great amphibious landings in Europe were Operation Dragoon in the South of France, and Operation Infatuate to seize the island of Walcheren and open up the port of Antwerp which had fallen, almost intact, into Allied possession. This was an appropriate place to start to bring British naval operations in Europe towards an end. One of the earliest battles had been fought in these waters six hundred years before, and the British had tried to land on Walcheren several times since. In 1809, when the navy had carried out its role well but cooperation with the army had broken down, and the aims were similar to 1944: to take the Dutch ports of Flushing and Antwerp and help throw off the yoke of a tyrant. In October 1944 there was little mistake: though there were heavy casualties, British and Canadian forces, including Royal Marines Commandos, took Walcheren, and the way to Antwerp was open.

## THE FORGOTTEN FLEET

With the fall of Germany the Royal Navy could give more assistance to the US Navy in the Far East, and British Pacific Fleet was created in November 1944. Since the Japanese attack on Pearl Harbor in December 1941 the US Navy had been waging war across the Pacific, across one-third of the world's surface. By the time that Admiral Sir Bruce Fraser hoisted his flag as Commander-in-Chief, British Pacific Fleet, the scale of this war was such that the Royal Navy could only be the junior partner. Even before Fraser's arrival, in Australia, the idea of creating a British Pacific Fleet had been surrounded with political controversy and, in certain quarters of the US Navy, some suspicion. Quiet simply, the Royal Navy's concept of operations and its reliance upon fixed bases had not prepared it for operations in the Pacific, and there were immense logistical difficulties. The difference between the two fleets was that the US Navy was, wrote Admiral Fraser,

> designed to enable it to keep the sea in a manner which has not previously been attempted since the advent of steam. This outlook differs greatly from our existing ideas whereby a fleet returns to a shore base for replenishment of stores, ammunition, etc. . . . I intend to operate the British Pacific Fleet to the best possible effect in the most advanced operations in the Pacific and Fleet Admiral Nimitz [C.-in.-C. US Pacific Fleet] has agreed that I should do so, but this will not be possible unless the Fleet has adequate logistic support. Without such support there is no doubt that I cannot carry out prolong[ed] operations and take part in the same manner as the Americans . . .

As Fraser described it, 'The distances involved are similar to those of a fleet based in Alexandria, and with advanced anchorages at Gibraltar and the Azores, attacking the North American coast between Labrador and Nova Scotia . . .'

Nevertheless by VJ-Day in 1945, when Admiral Sir Bruce Fraser signed the formal surrender of Japan on behalf of the United Kingdom, the British and Commonwealth naval contribution to the war with Japan amounted to more than six hundred ships and almost a quarter of a million men, mostly veterans from the war with Germany. Many still think that the contribution of this force has never received the recognition it deserves, either in Britain or in the USA.

In 1939 the strength of the navies of the British Empire had been 317 submarines and ships of destroyer size and above. By 1945, despite losses of some 431 ships, the British and Commonwealth navies had, besides battleships and cruisers, 52 aircraft carriers, hundreds of destroyers, sloops, frigates, corvettes, and similar small warships used on escort duties, thousands of minor warships, and thousands more landing craft. Together the Western navies had swept the fleets of Germany and Japan from the seas, the Germans alone losing 785 U-boats, while millions of troops had been convoyed across the Atlantic without loss.

Compared to the First World War, the Second had been fought on the principles of a maritime as opposed to a continental strategy. The rescue of the army at Dunkirk, the defeat of German invasion plans, the opportunity to rebuild British strength, the opening of new fronts in Africa and the Mediterranean, and a series of huge-scale but daring amphibious operations had all been made possible by sea power: sea power wielded in the traditional way by a British navy, and its allies, which had been honed by centuries of experience.

# Chapter Thirteen

# Prologue to the New Century

By June 1945 the Royal Navy had reached its maximum strength ever, having grown from 118,932 Royal Navy and 12,390 Royal Marines officers and men and 73,240 reservists of all categories in 1939, to 776,000 RN and RM officers and men, 72,000 Wrens and 13,000 personnel serving in the merchant navy. There was no adequate count of how many men of all nationalities served in the merchant navy, and these figures do not include the thousands more men and women who had served in the Royal Navies of the British Commonwealth. In the Royal Navy 50,758 men were killed, 820 missing, and 7,401 prisoners of war: 102 Wrens had also been killed. After VE-Day the rundown began immediately, although the Second World War was not truly over for some until the Forgotten Fleet had been brought home from the Pacific, and the last of these ships did not arrive until 1946.

## THE YANGTZE INCIDENT

In 1949 the Yangtze Incident held the world spellbound for three months. The frigate *Amethyst* was trapped more than a hundred miles up the River Yangtze, partway to Nanking (the temporary capital of China), when she came under fire from the guns of the Communist Chinese who were advancing upon the Nationalists. Many officers and men were killed or injured in the battle and her captain died later of his wounds. The cruiser *London*, the destroyer *Consort*, and the frigate *Black Swan* were forced back in their attempt to relieve the *Amethyst* and brave attempts to resupply her by Sunderland flying boat came under renewed shellfire. Commander John Kerans travelled overland from Nanking to assume command, where, as fuel ran low, he communicated by radio but in plain language (the codebooks had been destroyed to prevent them falling into the hands of the enemy) with Admiral Patrick Brind, whose squadron was lying at the mouth of the river, about what to do in the event of a typhoon. He was told that, 'the golden rule was to make an offing and taking [sic] plenty of sea room': the message needed no code. In London the politicians cavilled and diplomats counselled that she should stay where she was lest by moving she should prejudice future relations with the Communist government, but, as on many occasions before in the story of the Royal Navy, naval officers on the spot made policy and acted. On 30 July under cover of darkness the *Amethyst* made a dash for freedom, and despite coming under heavy gunfire and being hit, by dawn the next day Kerans signalled: 'Have rejoined the fleet south of Woosong. No damage or casualties. God save the King.'

His commander-in-chief replied: 'Welcome back ... we are all extremely proud of your most gallant and skilful escape and that endurance of and fortitude displayed by everyone had been rewarded with such success. Your bearing in adversity and your daring passage tonight will be epic in the history of the Navy.' It was a minor incident but one which epitomized the enduring spirit of the Royal Navy.

## THE COLD WAR

In 1950 Communist forces attacked and overran South Korea, leading to the Korean War. For the next three years there was bitter fighting, in which the Royal Navies of Australia, Britain, Canada, and New Zealand took a full part: seventy-six warships in all, including four aircraft carriers. The Royal Marines also fought with distinction alongside the US Army and Marine Corps.

In 1956 Israel invaded Egypt and Britain and France intervened, ostensibly to protect the Suez Canal. Again there was no suitable base and the Allied task force, which included six aircraft carriers, was wholly airborne and amphibious. For the first time a Royal Marines Commando landed by helicopter, while two other Commandos took the more usual route across the beaches. The success of a helicopter assault led to the conversion of existing aircraft carriers into Commando ships, which could put advanced troops ashore or even deal with small wars themselves. In 1961 the idea was proved when Kuwait was threatened by her more powerful neighbour, Iraq, and within days of a call for help a cordon of Royal Marines had occupied the border between the two states. From 1963 onwards the same forces were taken up by Indonesia's confrontation with Malaysia, and with confronting terrorism in Aden.

Gradually the strategic balance settled into a Cold War, in which the Soviet Union and the West each possessed its sphere of influence and it seemed that there would be no end to this new and more dangerous conflict fought with bluff and the threat of nuclear warfare.

The Royal Navy struggled to keep up with the cost of the Cold War, but recognized the value of the technology, not least nuclear propulsion, which had the potential to restore a degree of autonomy that warships had not enjoyed since the days of sail. The driving force behind the American acquisition of nuclear power was the eccentric and deliberately rude Rickover, but he was no match for the charms of the skilled and diplomatic Lord Mountbatten, who was First Sea Lord 1955–59 and then Chief of Defence Staff. When the British nuclear-power programme fell behind, Mountbatten personally intervened to persuade the Americans to sell a complete power plant from one of their *Skipjack* submarines. The Royal Navy was deeply self-conscious about the significance of its first nuclear submarine and she was named *Dreadnought*, to remind the world and perhaps the navy itself that she was every bit as revolutionary as Fisher's all-big-gun battleship had been in 1906, and she was launched on Trafalgar Day 1960.


## BATTLE OF THE FALKLANDS

Eventually the costs of the Cold War caught up with the Royal Navy, and in 1982 it was announced that as part of a defence review the navy would lose the carriers *Hermes* and *Invincible*, all the specialist amphibious shipping, nine destroyers and frigates, several auxiliary ships, and between eight thousand and ten thousand men, and that Chatham Dockyard would be closed. Gibraltar Dockyard, a focus for the navy for over 250 years, was already slated for closure. Amongst the ships to be taken out of service was the Antarctic patrol ship *Endurance*, and this was taken by Argentina as a signal that Britain had lost her way and her will. On 2 April the Falklands were invaded.

The invasion caught the British government unprepared. While politicians procrastinated, the First Sea Lord, Admiral Sir Henry Leach, went in full uniform to see the Prime Minister in the House of Commons, where he advised her that the fleet could sail within forty-eight hours, telling her, 'If we do not, or if we pussyfoot in our actions and do not achieve complete success, in another few months we shall be living in a different country whose words count for little.'

In Portsmouth two carriers were in maintenance following that spring's exercises, the amphibious ship, *Fearless*, had reverted to her role as a training ship, and *Intrepid* had been already been paid off and her ship's company dispersed. *Intrepid* was never expected to sail again. All available manpower was called up to help complete repairs and store the ships. In Gibraltar Rear Admiral 'Sandy' Woodward had a number of ships on a routine exercise, which suddenly became rather real. He divided his forces in two, to go south immediately and to return to UK for replenishment. In Devonport, 42 Commando, Royal Marines were marched off parade with the order from their commanding officer, Lieutenant Colonel Nick Vaux, '. . . to the South Atlantic, quick march!' They actually travelled south in some luxury on board the P&O liner *Canberra*, who quickly became known as 'The White Whale'. A banner waved as they left read 'FOUR TWO CDO IS MAGIC ARGIES ARE TRAGIC'.

The Task Force sent to the South Atlantic was a huge undertaking, which included nearly thirty thousand men and 110 ships, many of them merchant ships taken up from trade. Some, even among Britain's friends, thought the islands could not be retaken. However, while politicians parleyed the fleet steamed south, the destroyer *Antrim*, the frigate *Plymouth*, and the oiler *Tidespring* pressing ahead to join forces with the Antarctic patrol ship *Endurance* on 14 April for the task of retaking South Georgia. Plans nearly went awry when a helicopter carrying special forces crashed on the Fortuna Glacier, a rescue helicopter also crashed, and then strong winds blew raiding craft out to sea. However, luck changed when the weather improved, and *Endurance*'s tiny Wasp helicopter made history by being the first helicopter ever to engage and damage an enemy submarine, *Santa Fe*, which was hit by an air-to-surface missile. After a brief bombardment of Grytviken started, marines were landed by helicopter and the Argentines there soon surrendered.

On 30 April, the Argentine fleet sailed in two groups, the aircraft carrier *25 de Mayo* to the north of the islands and the cruiser *General Belgrano*, armed with Exocet missiles, to the south. The Argentine navy was at sea on a suicide mission, and Admiral Leach told the Prime Minister that while it 'could take out some of the British ships, the Royal Navy would sink their entire Navy'. On 1 May Royal Navy and RAF Harrier jump jets, flying from the carriers *Invincible* and *Hermes*, struck the Argentine invasion forces in three raids, using a toss-bomb technique designed for nuclear warfare and dropping cluster bombs. A new aspect of modern war was the almost simultaneous reporting, and famously a BBC reporter told the world about the Harriers, that he 'had counted them all out and counted them all in'. While the frigates *Brilliant* and *Yarmouth* hunted a reported submarine, the destroyer *Glamorgan* and the frigates *Alacrity* and *Arrow* closed to within gun range of Stanley and opened a bombardment with 4.5in shells on the invader's depots and defences. The navy had arrived.

Admiral Woodward had wanted to provoke a response, and later that day the Argentine air force mounted several waves of attack against the fleet, which was now steaming eastwards, drawing the Argentine aircraft out to their extreme range, where Sea Harriers armed with air-to-air missiles shot down at least four aircraft. Under cover of darkness the bombardment ships returned to shell the Argentine army ashore in Stanley.

Next day the Argentine carrier intended to attack British warships, but was unable to find enough wind over the deck for the heavily loaded Skyhawks to take off. To the south, the *Belgrano* group still threatened and Woodward asked for revised rules of engagement, and when these were granted, the nuclear-powered

*Conqueror* attacked without further orders. Two out of three of her Mark 8 torpedoes, a weapon which had first seen service in the Second World War, struck the *Belgrano* and she sank with the loss of 300 lives. The entire Argentine navy retired to the west and took no further part in the war. However, the Argentines launched air-to-surface missiles against the destroyer *Sheffield* and, with very little warning, one slammed into the British destroyer, the unburned fuel starting a fierce and uncontrollable fire. *Sheffield* became the first British warship to be lost to enemy action since 1945. The sinking persuaded Woodward to operate even further to the eastward, at the cost of less time-on-task over the Falklands for subsequent Harrier operations.

Meanwhile, the main body of the fleet had rendezvoused at Ascension Island, where the ships were restowed and troops zeroed their weapons and practised landings. San Carlos, on the west coast of East Falkland, an inlet sheltered by high hills which would also deny enemy aircraft time to run in against the ships moored there, was chosen for an amphibious assault. The drawback was that San Carlos was nearly sixty miles from Stanley, the centre of gravity of the enemy's invasion forces and the political objective of the landing.

The landing took place on the night of 20/21 May: before dawn the Royal Marines' Special Boat Service had overwhelmed an Argentine observation post on Fanning Head, and another Argentine patrol seeing the landings withdrew hurriedly. Attacking aircraft concentrated on the warships rather than the high-value targets like the large amphibious ships, including the cruise liner *Canberra*, still in her white paint scheme. Five ships were hit, and one was sinking, but Sea Harriers patrolling outside San Carlos shot down ten aircraft. As anticipated, the raiding aircraft had had to come in low to avoid anti-aircraft fire, the surrounding hills had indeed prevented them from lining up their bombsights, and many of the bombs had failed to fuse. These were lessons both sides might have learned had they studied the campaign in Norway in 1940.

Bad weather now helped the British, restricting flying hours for the Argentines and enabling the disembarkation to proceed more or less unhindered. By 25 May eight defending ships had been sunk or damaged, but none of the amphibious ships, and the Argentine air force was running out of planes and pilots. By the end of May twelve Sea Harriers had shot down twenty-one aircraft during some ninety raids: the victory was both material and moral. Unfortunately, further out to sea the *Atlantic Conveyor* had been hit by an Exocet missile, burning ferociously and destroying ten helicopters. The marines who were now firmly ashore would have to march on Stanley and were about to give the world a new verb: 'to yomp'.

The Falklands War lasted only a few weeks. War had never been officially declared and in some minds it had amounted to no more than a little post-colonial scrap. Nevertheless, many lessons were learned or relearned. The Royal Navy had reasserted itself as the leading navy of the world, and one with recent fighting experience, which other navies were anxious to benefit from. Practical improvements included better damage control such as permanently rigged fire curtains, improved battledress, larger ammunition stocks, and closer cooperation between the navy, army, and air force.

More fundamentally, prior to the Falklands War divorce between the Royal Navy and its Royal Marines was looming. The marines were confined to tours of duty in Northern Ireland and practising for the defence of Norway against the Soviet Union. Neither of these roles contributed to the Royal Navy's concept of fighting a decisive battle in the North Atlantic against the Soviet fleet, and naval planners had even suggested the sacrifice of the Royal Marines on the altar of budgetary necessity. After the Falklands the Royal Navy and the Royal Marines realized that they needed each other, and since then have grown ever closer together so that today the commander of the surface flotilla and the commander of the amphibious group are equals.

Another immediate effect of the war was a reversal of many aspects of the 1982 defence review. Under this review British ministers had decided that, when pressed to reduce the defence budget, the central front in Europe should be maintained while the navy should be cut. There was now a growing realization in the navy itself that it had stated its case badly during the review, and out of this sense of guilt grew the need to develop the necessary doctrine to justify a navy in the conditions of modern war. This doctrine was successfully used to make the case for the navy and for expeditionary warfare in the defence review of 1997. The war also gave a boost to the development of joint warfare throughout British armed forces.

There were other consequences of world scale. A cover picture of the *Economist* magazine had carried the caption, 'The Empire Strikes Back': it was a message, telling the Soviet Union that the West was no toothless tiger but, when national interest was at stake, even in the remote Falkland Islands, would fight. Undoubtedly this had an effect on Soviet thinking: if Britain would fight under such circumstances then war in Europe would be no pushover, and neither the Cold War nor any subsequent hot war could be won. The Falklands War, by showing such resolve, marked the beginning of the end of the Cold War and so of the Soviet Union.

One of the ships which was hit, and survived, was the frigate *Plymouth*, and the archives of the National Maritime Museum hold a dramatic account of the day she was attacked:

Another clear sunny day ... mostly quiet for most of the day ... We slipped anchor and proceeded, getting just out of the sound when an Arg[entine] air raid was sounded off, and almost immediately we were bounced by 5 Mirage aircraft. These dropped at least 10 bombs, and fired their cannon, at us as we manoeuvred to dodge the raid. One of the Mirage aircraft was shot down by Seacat and a second by 20 mm cannon, with possible damage to a third.

*Plymouth* was hit by 4 bombs, which are guessed to be roughly 1000-lb ones none of which went off, and by a number of cannon shells, several of which did go off – probably between 20 and 30 shells actually hit the ship. Two of the bombs hit the sea, and bouncing upwards, passed through the mortar handling room. The port after quarterdeck ladder disappeared, with a corner of the handling room, taking off about 40 square feet of corner metal work. The second split a mortar bomb in half, and then passed through the handling room bulkhead, and overside. One of the three mortar barrel tubes was bent totally out of true. The third bomb hit the funnel, and passed through, perhaps partially exploding as it went through: the entry point is small, but the exit point is a large ragged hole, at least 30 square feet. Fortunately not much damage was done to the pipes etc in the funnel.

The fourth bomb hit a depth charge stowed with a second depth charge on the starboard edge of the flight deck. The bomb probably did not go off, but the depth charge did partially, before flying through the air, leaving its tail burning on the deck behind. A 20–30 foot square hole in the deck edge was made, and the Aft Petty Officers' Mess below immediately caught very severely on fire. Sheets of flame with thick oily smoke poured through the hole. The mess was eventually totally gutted, the dining halls forward were also gutted, and very severe smoke and fire damage was done to the after flat, especially the wiring.

The cannon shells hit all over the ship, with shots, all from the port side, hitting the hangar, upperworks, foremast, and gun turret, as well as two or three shots in the hull – including one beside the PO Caterer's chair which he normally occupies at Action Stations.

The ship's fire fighters very quickly attacked the fire. The flight deck party got 2 hoses going immediately, then a third, pouring water and foam into the gaping fire filled hole, and eventually, after about 15 minutes, combined with attacks from below, the fire was extinguished. It was necessary to cut loose the remaining depth charge, immediately beside the fire, because depth charges have a 'cook off' time of 45 seconds, and also to ditch 2 AS 12 missiles, stowed also on the starboard flight deck, as they might have gone off as well. This was done by the flight deck party.

Having assisted with this fire fighting, I then went forward to the foc's'le where assisting Wessex and Sea King Helicopters brought in several medical officers and men, plus breathing apparatus men in their fire suits. These were particularly important because the smoke aft made fighting the fire very difficult below decks. 5 casualties were also disembarked from the foc's'le to go to the sickbay ashore at Ajax Bay, two with broken arms, one with smoke in his lungs, one with a shell splinter in his forehead, and one with splinters elsewhere. None were serious, but the head case will require neurosurgery eventually, which is fairly serious.

The ship was still under way after the attack, and we returned to San Carlos, trailing a large plume of smoke, to anchor in our normal position close to the west shore of San Carlos water. HMS *Avenger* stood by us, offering to come alongside, but this was not necessary.

Once the fire was under control, we were boarded by Fleet Maintenance Group personnel to survey the damage and by Fleet Clearance Diving Team who were to survey the damaged mortar bomb. The bomb was eventually defused and ditched over the side after dark, the ship's company having been mustered on the foc's'le, the other end of the ship, where, having been addressed by the Captain, they sang songs.

The description of battle could have come from almost any period of the Royal Navy: the war had been remarkably effective and influential, and once more other navies wanted to learn the lessons of war.

## THE LESSONS OF THE PLATE AND *BISMARCK*

While Admiral Kenneth Dewar was working as a historian during the Second World War he mused on the nature of command at sea. He drew his lessons from the Battle the River Plate and the hunt of the *Bismarck*, observing that:

> successful tactics primarily depends upon an efficient method of command. That fact cannot be too frequently reiterated. Conversely, tactical failures can usually be traced to inefficient method of command. After four centuries of fighting, a great volume of experience has been accumulated on this subject but owing to neglect of research, it has not been utilised in this Country. Broadly speaking, there are three methods to choose from:
> Command by written instruction
> Centralised command by signals
> Command by general directives
> Examples of (a) are the Fighting Instructions (XVIIth and XVIIIth centuries) and the Grand Fleet Battle Orders (XXth century). They aimed at co-operation by laying down before hand what every ship was to do whilst ignoring what the enemy

might do. They required neither intelligence nor initiative from subordinate commanders who had merely to follow passively in the wake or the next ahead. This faulty conception has been responsible for numerous failures and missed opportunities.

Command by signal ... has never achieved a satisfactory degree of co-operation. No single authority can visualise the rapidly changing conditions in different parts of the battle and in any case dependence upon signals suppresses initiative and the fighting spirit of subordinate leaders. Like marionettes, they only come to life when someone pulls the string. It may also be the wrong string for signals are very liable to misunderstandings ...

Command by directives, which give full scope to subordinates, was the technique used by Ruyter, Nelson, Togo, Scheer and other successful leaders. It is the only system that has stood the test of experience. The Battle of the Nile provides a good example of this method. The directive was – attack the enemy's van and centre – the rest Nelson left to his captains. No other system of command could have obtained such remarkable results under such difficult conditions. In the words of Captain Berry of the *Vanguard*: 'Signals became almost unnecessary, much time was saved and the attention of every Captain could be almost undistractedly paid to the conduct of his own particular ship.'

It was this latter style in which the Falklands War had been fought, and which has become one of the hallmarks of the Royal Navy. Its officers are recipients of a common heritage, understanding almost instinctively what is required of them and what they can expect their subordinates to do for them, in very much the same spirit in which Barham gave his orders to Nelson in 1805: this is the true tradition of Nelson.

However, there is strong tendency to revert to the written word and to follow this blindly, or as Dewar lamented, 'the truth is that the techniques of command by written instructions and centralised command by signal are so deeply rooted in naval administration and training and that the majority of officers either do not understand or are opposed to other methods'. He had a sovereign remedy to overcome this weakness. 'Experience proves,' he wrote, 'that no permanent progress ... is possible without the active and sustained support of the Admiralty ... Officers whose experience is limited to technical and executive work seldom realise that history has any bearing on future operations...' There are plenty of examples in this brief story of the Royal Navy of the lessons of history.

## THE ROYAL NAVY IN THE NEW CENTURY

Today the Royal Navy can look back at the previous millennium with some satisfaction, but it can also look forward to a new century with some assurance, with new ships and equipment, and excellent people.

In the twentieth century, the navy survived both technical and physical changes. The Royal Navy in particular had survived the rise and fall of other major navies, such as the German, which threatened Britain's survival in two world wars, and the navy of the former Soviet Union, which menaced the free world during the Cold War. It had survived the advent of the submarine, the aeroplane, nuclear weapons, and long-range missiles, and even played a major role in the development and adaptation of these systems to naval uses. Undoubtedly navies in general will also survive future revolutions in military affairs and might even be the main beneficiaries of any innovations.

But even at the height of its power, and the Royal Navy was the largest in the world until the 1930s, Britain realized that she needed friends and allies. She sought help in exotic alliances and the idea of an Empire Navy. In their day the Anglo-Japanese treaties and the Anglo-French Entente Cordiale were unlikely but effective. The alternative idea of an Empire Navy, along the principle of one ocean, one fleet, was short-lived, a sacrifice to the natural desire for statehood by the dominions. About the same time, however, Alfred Mahan was proposing a naval consortium of the English-speaking nations: he would, presumably, be surprised and pleased to know the form in which de facto his naval consortium exists, primarily through alliances such as NATO and such strange sounding acronyms as AUSCANUKUS, and especially through the many other expressions of a very special relationship between the Royal Navy and the United States Navy. A very tangible expression of that relationship was that during the 1991 Gulf War only the ships of the Royal Navy and the Royal Australian Navy were trusted to be stationed up-threat of the main force of the United States Navy.

Looking to the future, the prospects for the Royal Navy are clouded. The British government's defence review in 1997–98 seemed to catch the grand strategic rhythm of the times with a pronounced shift from a continental strategy, in which NATO stared at the enemy across the northern plains of Germany and the grey swell of the Norwegian Sea, to an expeditionary strategy in which maritime forces play a significant role. The change in form is backed by a change in substance. The navy already has a new 20,000-ton helicopter carrier, *Ocean*, and two new landing dock platforms, *Bulwark* and *Albion*, and new roll-on-roll-off ferries have been ordered. The announcement has been made that the navy will be re-equipped with a new generation of fixed-wing aircraft, and two new aircraft carriers, as large as any warships the navy has ever operated, have been ordered. Some things never change: just like Trinity House's criticism of the *Sovereign of the Seas* in the seventeenth century, critics are wondering where the new ships will be built.

Equipment is not everything. Admiral Cunningham, it will be remembered, said that it takes three years to build a ship but three hundred years to build a tradition. The Royal Navy and Royal Marines of today are fewer than at any time since the 1850s, but the same traditions and the same quality remain. The people are as highly motivated, trained, and skilled as ever.

Moreover, sea-based forces, especially when integrated with the army and air force into joint forces, have a unique utility, in providing access to crises at a time and place of political choice, and can often be decisive on their own. Today's world of changing geopolitics and geostrategy, including the war on terrorism, might well have been designed for maritime forces which can deliver sea, land, and air power to the scene of action and can provide transport, mounting bases, airfields, stores depots, barracks, fire support, and hospitals and refugee havens.

History does indeed judge the Royal Navy as an institution of world class, which in the course of the several hundred years of its existence has played a prominent role at every level of strategy and operations, and amassed a rich heritage. And at the end of the twentieth century the Royal Navy was still regarded as one of the best, and not surprisingly a recently published naval plan concluded with the message that the Royal Navy intends to be 'A world class Navy, ready to fight and win'.

# Sources

There are no endnotes to distract the reader while reading this book, but all the manuscripts and books used as sources can be searched for by visiting the National Maritime Museum's excellent Web-based catalogue at http://www.nmm.ac.uk. The primary quoted sources are listed here, in order of appearance in the text (the call numbers can be browsed for by searching within the shelving scheme NLM).

## One Our owne Navie of Shippes

*The Libelle of Englyshe Polycye* A poem on the use of seapower, 1436. Sir George Warner, who edited this poem, complained that it was known by repute but insufficiently studied. He was right: the pages of the copy which he presented to Geoffrey Callendar in 1926 were still uncut seventy-five years later.

REC/1 Collection of naval documents, 1583–1778.

ADL/B/7 Warrant for payment to Benjamin Gonson, treasurer of marine affairs of 2000 li, signed R. Jones, 29 Dec 1558.

WEL/3 Report on an expedition against England by Spain, Spanish with English translation, 1587, 'Dictamen sobre la jornade de Inglaterra'.

HSR/HF/2–6 Five letters of Philip II of Spain with Instructions to Andrés de Alva for supplying the Spanish Armada.

UPC/5 Letters relating to adventures in an expedition of Sir Francis Drake and Sir John Norreys, 1588.

## Two Under Crown and Commonwealth

AGC/B/7 Adm Robert Blake: report to the Council of State about the battle of Terel on 3 Jun 1653, dated RESOLUTION, 16 Jun 1653.

**AGC/8/31**  George Monck, 1st Duke of Albermarle [sic]: autograph
letter to S Pepys, dated 9 Oct 1665 authorising issuing of ships
[sic] etc to seamen.

**HSR/A/3**  Report to King Charles II of an action fought against the
Dutch, Jun 1666, by Prince Rupert and the Duke of Albermarle
[sic].

**AGC/L/5**  John Lloyd, Surgeon of the STIRLING CASTLE: letter
dated 26 May 1692 describing the Battle of La Hogue, addressed
to Mr Searacord (?).

**GOS/9**  Discourse by Edward Randolph, English agent in Boston,
about Pirates with proper remedies to suppress them, 1696.


### *Three*  The Wonderful Year


**VER/1/2**  Admiral Edward Vernon: papers relating to the capitulation
of Porto Bello and to Cartagena, 1739–42.

**HWK/14**  Admiral of the Fleet Edward Hawke, 1st Baron Hawke:
letter from the *Royal George* off Penvins Point, 1759.


### *Four*  Exploration in the Age of Sail


**JOD/36**  Account of Anson's voyage round the world with inscription
by Lawrence Millechamp. [This file is 'restricted access', and this
transcript is taken from *Documents Relating to Anson's Voyage
Round the World 1740–1744*, edited by Glyndwr Williams,
Lecturer in history at Queen Mary College, and printed for the
Navy Records Society, 1967.]

**JOD/56**  Richard Pickersgill, narrative account of the voyage of the
RESOLUTION, Capt Cook, 1772–73. [Pickersgill's 'favourite
author' has not been identified.]

**BND/1/2/3**  Autograph letter of William Bligh to John Bond dated
Cape of Good Hope 23 October 1776.

## *Five* War with America

**KEI/2/1–4** North America 1775–82: letters received ROMNEY 1775–77, WARWICK 1780–82, letters and orders received PERSEUS 1777–80, prize papers 1774–83.

**BGR/28** Memorial of the services of Cdre Sir George Collier (1738–95) in America, 1776–79, compiled from original journals and papers by G J Rainier with corrections in Collier's own hand.

**REC/8** Collection of early nineteenth century transcripts of dispatches, 1780–98, with index, entitled 'Naval Actions'.

**AGC/12/11** Rodney, George Brydges, 1st Baron. Rodney to Whitshed Keene Esq., 1780–81, three holograph letters.

## *Six* Revolution, Mutiny, and War at Sea

**AGC/12/10** Rodney, George Brydges, 1st Baron (1719–92). Holograph to his wife, 1777–80.

**REC/8** Collection of early nineteenth century transcripts of dispatches, 1780–98, with index, entitled 'Naval Actions'.

**TRN/38** John Stradley. Memoirs covering his life at sea during the American War of Independence on HMS GRAFTON mainly in the West Indies, his return to England and his impressment back into the Navy, 1757–1825.

**BRK/14** Logbook of the ORION, Capt Duckworth, Apr–Jun 1794, with account of the Battle of the Glorious First of June, kept by Edward Baker.

**AGC/8/33** James Maxwell, Royal Marines: letter to his mother from LEVIATHAN, 2 Jun 1794, describing the Glorious First of June.

**AGC/1/1** F Aime: holograph letter to a friend about the Glorious First of June, dated from the Pegasus frigate, 13 Jun 1794.

**HSR/Z/26** Collection of miscellaneous naval documents, 15 Feb 1645–3 Oct 1825 and undated.

**HSR/Z/21** Printed petitions from seamen and marines, n.d.

**NEP/4** Letters from Sir John Jervis (Later Earl St Vincent) to [Sir Evan] Nepean, 1797–98.

**BGR/12** Statement of service 1789–1839 of Lt David O'Brien Casey

(1779–1853) including an account of the mutiny in the
HERMIONE, 1797.

AGC/24/6 Samain, Joseph. An account of the battle of Camperdown,
sent home by Joseph Samain of HMS VENABLE [sic] (Flagship of
Adm Duncan) to his father and mother, dated Nore, 18 Oct 1797.

AGC/J/9 [provisional reference] John Jup, ordinary seaman, to his
parents, HMS *Orion*, 26 November 1798.

AGC/22/3 Nairne, Alexander. Holograph to his brother, HMS
POLYPHEMUS, Jul 1801.

AGC/14/27 Stewart, Col William (1774–1827). Holograph to Sir
William Clinton. Written from HMS LONDON on 6 Apr 1801
describing the battle of Copenhagen.

AGC/H/2 Cdr Archibald Hamilton, H.E.I.C: letter to Charles Forbes
describing an action between Cdre Dance and Rear-Adm Linois,
14 Feb 1804, dated 17 Mar 1804.


## *Seven* The Campaign of Trafalgar

JOD/48 Lt William Pringle Green, notebook and pamphlets;
instructions on training ship's crews to the use of arms; journal of
HMS CONQUEROR chasing the French Fleet, 1805–8.

TRA/13 Holograph from Nelson to Lady Hamilton, VICTORY,
16 Mar 1805.

AGC/8/14 Thomas Mackinrey: holograph to his mother dated from
HMS VICTORY, May 1805.

MID/1/21 Folder containing loose In letters from Adm Sir Robert
Calder, 1805.

AGC/4/19 Adm Gravina: translation of a letter describing the action
with Sir Robert Calder, 22 Jul 1805.

BGR/8 Autobiography of Lt William Clarke, Royal Marines
(1784–1862) covering the years 1803–16 and written in 1839.

GIR/3 Twelve copies of orders, official papers and letters of Admiral
Lord Nelson, 1799–1805; the order of battle and sailing; and
Nelson's secret memorandum of 9 October 1805.

WEL/30 Lt William Rivers notes on Lord Nelson and the Battle of
Trafalgar, 1805, at which he was present, also anecdotes of Nelson
etc.

**JOD/41** Minutes of the battle of Trafalgar kept by W Thorp, seaman on HMS MINOTAUR, 1805.

**MSS/80/180.1** Letter from James Bayley on board HMS *Victory*, 1805.

**AGC/M/9** John Mason, Quartermaster of HMS AFRICA, to his family, describing the battle of Trafalgar, 23 Jan 1805 [sic].

**AGC/N/11** Paul Harris Nicholas, 2-Lt, Royal Marines: letter to his brother J Toup Nicholas, giving an account of the battle of Trafalgar, HMS BELLEISLE, Dec 1805, with a plan of the battle.

**JOD/41** A Journal Kept by one of the *Minotaur's* Ships Company on board the *Neptuno* Spanish Ship of 84 Guns taken 21st October 1805.

**AGC/M/5** Adm Sir Robert Moorsom: letters giving descriptions of the battle of Trafalgar, Oct–Dec 1805.

**AGC/23/5** Ross, Alexander. Original of letter from Ross written on board HMS EURYALUS to John Cruikshank, Rector of Banff Academy, giving instructions of the battle of Trafalgar, 21 Oct 1805, together with a copy of the letter in the handwriting of Rev. James Cruikshank, Minister of Fyvie.

## *Eight* Britannia Rules

**DUC/12** [Admiral Sir Thomas Duckworth] European Waters 1806: defeats it [the French fleet] off San Domingo, UK, Cadiz.

**BGR/8** Autobiography of Lt William Clarke, Royal Marines (1784–1862) covering the years 1803–16 and written in 1839.

**DUC/13** European Waters 1807: Dardanelles mission, UK, Channel Fleet.

**JOD/43** Journal written by Rear-Adm Robert Deans when he was Lt in HMS VENERABLE off the coast of Spain during the Peninsular War, 1812.

**HIS/24** Narrative of the capture of the Banda Islands, by Capt Christopher Cole, 1810.

**AGC/4/24** Sir Thomas Francis Fremantle, Vice-Adm: holograph to Viscount Melville, dated from [HMS] Milford Fiume, 10 Sep 1813, enclosing Chart of the Ships Position etc in the Adriatic.

**AGC/12/22** Rowley, Sir Charles, Adm (1770–1845). Copies of Sir

Charles Rowley's letter of resignation of the West Indian command, to Viscount Melville and of the latter's reply, 30 Sep and 10 Dec 1822. Autograph despatch signed to Viscount Melville, dated from the EAGLE, 2 feb [sic] 1814.

BGY/A/1 James Atkins, Sergeant of Marines: letters written to his uncle James Atkins, ironmonger at Windsor, 1804–9, includes letter written by W.A. Green on behalf of Atkins to his uncle, one letter of importance describing the action between the CHESAPEAKE and HMS LEOPARD, other letters concerned with pity, forgiveness and money.

MEL/102(B) [Robert Saunders Dundas, 2nd Viscount Melville] Letters received 1813–25.

AGC/23/7 Hillyar, James. Fifteen letters, 21 Jun 1811–6 Apr 1814.

## *Nine* The Long Peace

BGY/G/1 Robert Griffin, Colour Sergeant, Royal Marines: statement of service; list of ships on which he served; account of the expedition against Algiers, 1816; note on the surrender and death of Bonaparte; Greenwich out-pensioner's certificate.

AGC/7/31 Letter from Lieutenant Alexander Anderson, Royal Marines dated Navarino 23 October 1823 on board HMS *Albion*.

AGC/24/24 Adm Lord Frederick Herbert Kerr: copy of a letter from Lt Frederick Kerr to his brother Lord Henry Kerr, HM Frigate GORGON 16 Oct 1840, giving an account of the bombardment of Acre.

BGR/17 Autobiography of Lt John Blackmore 1815–1844.

MRY/6 Marryat's logbook and record of services, n.d.

AGC/7/31 Capt Edmund Moubray Lyons: autograph report, signed E.M.L., dated 28 Jul 1854, 3 a.m. to Capt E. O'Marney during operations in the White Sea, 1854–55.

TRN/65 Typed transcript of a letter from B.J. Sulivan (1810–90) Sep 1855, discussing Sir Charles Napier and the Baltic Operations in the Russian War, but the material you quote is Beaufort to Sulivan 1854 [Also transcripts of letters to and from B J Sulivan discussing Baltic Operations during the Russian War 1854–1856]

MRK/37 Official, unofficial and private correspondence relating to the voyage of the ROSARIO, 1871–72 in the South Seas, mainly relating to the kidnapping of islanders for the labour trade and to the affairs of the missionaries, including the death of Bishop Patterson on Nukapu.

SGN/D/4 'A System of Fleet Manoeuvres with and without Signals' n.d., by Adm Sir George Tryon and notes on orders and tactics written by Tryon, 1 Jan 1893.

MRK/21 Telegram book kept by Rear-Adm Markham while commanding detached squadrons, Mediterranean, Mar 1892–Jan 1894.

COW/17/1–6 Typescript of 'The Wheel of Fortune', Cowan's autobiography with many additional transcripts of documents and other papers concerned with the book n.d.

### *Ten* The First World War

DEY/41 D'Eyncourt's involvement in Tank Construction 1914–40: papers relating to the Admiralty Landship Committee 1914–15.

DEY/42 D'Eyncourt's involvement in Tank Construction 1914–40: correspondence and memoranda 1916 including a 'Report on Design and Construction of First Landship (Tank)'

NOT/31 Notes on the Royal Naval Air Service by Group Capt C. R. J. Randall, together with some biographical information, 1914–18.

COW/17/1–6 Typescript of 'The Wheel of Fortune', Cowan's autobiography with many additional transcripts of documents and other papers concerned with the book n.d.

AGC/4/38 Cdr Frederick Giffard: narrative letter describing the battle of the Falkland Islands, written to his mother from HMS INFLEXIBLE, 17 Dec 1914.

MSS/80/041.0 DARDANELLES Campaign, Letters from E Jordan to his Sister dated 1915.

MS84/152 KIMBELL, George T W, Account of the sinking of HM Submarine K17, 1918.

DFF/2 Duff's notes on the dismissal of Jellicoe 1917–18 with some copies of correspondence inside the Admiralty.

BLE/2 Papers relating to service in the Grand Fleet IRON DUKE

and QUEEN ELIZABETH 1914–18 including record of service,
certificates and photographs.

### *Eleven* The Interwar Years

COW/17/1–6  Typescript of 'The Wheel of Fortune', Cowan's
autobiography with many additional transcripts of documents and
other papers concerned with the book n.d.

COW/6  Album of letters received, commissions, signals and
memoranda 1889–1931 entitled 'Admiral Sir Walter Cowan, Bt
1884–1931'.

DEY/7  Papers relating to his [D'Eyncourt's] time at Armstrong
Whitworth (Elswick) 1902–12: concerning Royal Naval Ship
Design including plans, weights and trial results, of ships
unsuccessfully tendered for, HMS SWIFTSHORE, INVINCIBLE,
ADVENTURE, AFRIDI and floating cranes, report on underwater
torpedo experiment 1905–6 and of Palma's proposed 30 knot
destroyer.

BTY/13/2  British Naval Officers and Officials: Bellairs, R.M.
(1884–1959), letters 23 Dec 1922, 22 Nov 1929–6 May 1930.

BTY/8/2  [Admiral of the Fleet Earl Beatty] First Sea Lord, 1919–27:
Capital ship versus submarine, papers on the building policy of the
navy, 6 Dec 1920–20 Jan 1921.

ELK/2  Reports and notes on the Invergordon incident (mutiny) 1931
and letters 1966–67 from Capt Stephen Roskill who used the
material for reference.

ELK/11  'Aftermath of the Invergordon Mutiny', a report with a copy
and a covering letter written by Elkins to Cdr H Pursey in 1975.

CHT/1/2  [Admiral of the Fleet Alfred Ernle Motacute Chatfield]
Early life: autobiographical manuscript account of early life n.d.

### *Twelve* The Second World War

DEW/24  [Vice-Admiral Kenneth Gilbert Balamin Dewar] Second
World War: Historical Section monograph entitled 'The Conjunct
Expeditions to Norway Apr–Jun 1940. Preliminary Narrative'.

**GTN/7/5** File of academic correspondence between Gretton and Captain Stephen W Roskill, DSC, RN (Retd), including notes relating to Gretton's article for the Naval Review, 1980.

**TEN/21** [Admiral Sir William George Tennant] Papers relating to Dunkirk, 1940.

**MSS/82/061.0** BATTLE of Matapan, Account of, and Service Documents 1941.

**MSS/81/004** TOVEY, Admiral Lord (1885–1971) Papers, 6 Albums, and Diaries [Letter from 'ABC' Cunningham].

**COW/17/1–6** Typescript of *The Wheel of Fortune*, Cowan's autobiography. Admiral Sir Walter Henry Cowan, 1871–1956 with additional transcripts of documents and other papers concerned with the book.

**MSS/88/026.5** WATERS, Lieutenant Commander D W, Papers re Convoys, 1953 & 1954.

**MSS/90/002.0** ARCTIC Convoys, Memoirs of Rear Admiral M W S Boucher (1888–1963)

**MSS/90/002.1** BOUCHER, Rear Admiral M W (1888–1963) Memoirs re SCHARNHORST 1943.

**MSS/90/002.2** MURMANSK, Memoirs of Rear Admiral Boucher (1886–1967) re Convoys.

**MSS/90/002.3** SCHARNHORST, Memoirs of Rear Admiral Boucher (1888–1963) re Action of.

### *Thirteen* Prologue to the New Century

**MSS/88/058.2** FALKLANDS War, Diaries of Lt Commander K M Napier dated 1982.

**MSS/88/058.3** NAPIER, Lieutenant Commander K M, Dairy [sic] kept during the Falklands War, 1982.

**DEW/18** Second World War: Historical Section correspondence and memoranda on Norway 1940 and some notes written by Dewar at a later date.

# Bibliography

Aspinall-Oglander, Cecil: *Admiral's Wife: the Life and Letters of Mrs Edward Boscawen, 1719–1761*, Longmans, Green and Co., London, 1940.

Bush, Captain Eric: *The Flowers of the Sea: an Anthology of Quotations, Poems and Prose*, George Allen & Unwin, London, 1962.

Capp, Bernard: *Cromwell's Navy: the Fleet and the English Revolution 1648–1660*, Clarendon Press, Oxford, 1989.

Corbett, Julian S.: *Some Principles of Maritime Strategy. Classics of Sea Power*, ed. Naval Institute Press, Annapolis, 1988.

Cordingley, David: *Heroines and Harlots: Women at Sea in the Great Age of Sail*, Macmillan, London, 2001.

Delgado, James P.: *Across the Top of the World: the Quest for the Northwest Passage*, Douglas and McIntyre, Vancouver, 1999.

Duffy, Michael (ed.): *Parameters of British Naval Power 1650–1850*, University of Exeter Press, Exeter, 1992.

Gardiner, Robert (ed.): *History of the Ship*, Conway Maritime Press, London, 1996. A twelve-volume series whose titles include *The Line of Battle* and *Steam, Steel and Shellfire*.

——: *The Campaign of Trafalgar*, Chatham Publishing, London, 1997.

——: *The Naval War of 1812*, Chatham Publishing, London, 1998.

Gordon, Andrew: *The Rules of the Game: Jutland and British Naval Command*, John Murray, London, 1996.

Grove, Eric (ed.): *Great Battles of the Royal Navy: as commemorated in the Gunroom, Britannia Royal Naval College, Dartmouth*, Arms and Armour, London, 1994.

Hill, Richard: *The Prizes of War: the Naval Prize System in the Napoleonic Wars 1793–1815*, Royal Naval Museum Publications, Portsmouth, 1998.

Holmes, Michael R. J.: *Augustus Hervey: a Naval Casanova*, The Pentland Press, Bishop Auckland, Co Durham, 1996.

Hore, Peter (ed.): *Seapower Ashore: 200 Years of Royal Navy Operations on Land*, Chatham Publishing, London, 2001.

James, W. M.; Chamier, Frederick: *The Naval History of Great Britain during the French Revolutionary and Napoleonic Wars*, Conway Maritime Press, London, 2002, with a new introduction by Andrew Lambert. First published 1837.

Knighton, C. S.; Loades, D. M.: *The Anthony Roll of Henry VIII's Navy*, Ashgate Publishing for The Navy Records Society, Aldershot, Hants, 2000. In association with British Library and Magdalene College, Cambridge.

Laird Clowes, William: *The Royal Navy: a History from the Earliest Times to the Present*, Chatham Publishing, London, 1996. In seven volumes to 1900.

le Fevre, Peter; Harding, Richard (eds.): *Precursors of Nelson: British Admirals of the Nineteenth Century*, Chatham Publishing, London, 2000.

Mahan, Alfred Thayer: *Mahan on Naval Strategy: Selections from the Writings of Rear Admiral Alfred Thayer Mahan*, Classics of Sea Power, ed. Naval Institute Press, Annapolis, Maryland, 1991. With an introduction by John B. Hattendorf.

Parry, Ann: *The Admirals Fremantle 1788–1920*, Chatto & Windus, London, 1971.

Pocock, Tom: *Horatio Nelson*, The Bodley Head, London, 1987.

——: *A Thirst for Glory: the Life of Admiral Sir Sidney Smith*, Aurum Press, London, 1996.

——: *Battle for Empire: the Very First World War 1756–63*, Michael O'Mara Books, London, 1998.

Ritchie, G. S.: *The Admiralty Chart: British Naval Hydrography in the Nineteenth Century*, The Pentland Press, Edinburgh, 1967.

Rodger, N. A. M.: *The Wooden World: an Anatomy of the Georgian Navy*, Collins, London, 1986.

——: *The Safeguard of the Sea: a Naval History of Britain 660–1649*, HarperCollins, London, 1997.

Semmel, Bernard: *Liberalism, Interest, and Sea Power during the Pax Britannica*, Allen & Unwin, Boston, 1986.

Tracy, Nicholas: *Manila Ransomed: the British Assault on Manila in the Seven Years War*, University of Exeter Press, Exeter, 1995.

——: (ed.) *The Naval Chronicle: the Contemporary Record of the Royal*

　　*Navy at War*, Consolidated edition in five volumes with index, Chatham Publishing, London, 1998.

Tunstall, Brian; Tracy, Nicholas: *Naval Warfare in the Age of Sail: the Evolution of Fighting Tactics*, Naval Institute Press, Annapolis, Maryland, 1990.

White, Colin: *The Nelson Companion*, Royal Naval Museum, Portsmouth, 1995.

Woodman, Richard: *Arctic Convoys 1941–1945*, John Murray, London, 1994.

——: *The Victory of Seapower: winning the Napoleonic War 1806–1814*, Chatham Publishing, London, 1998.

——: *Malta Convoys 1940–43*, John Murray, London, 2000.

# Index

# JULIAN THOMPSON

## The Royal Marines

### From Sea Soldiers to a Special Force

PAN BOOKS

**A complete and authoritative history of one of Britain's
elite forces**

The Royal Marines' achievement, toughness, professionalism and
enterprise puts them in the same league as such other elites as the
SAS and the Paras. This is the stirring story of their rise from a
poorly regarded regiment in the eighteenth century to a special
force, brilliantly and authoritatively told.

The role of the Royal Marines in many central military campaigns, including Northern Ireland and a decisive contribution to
the recovery of the Falklands, is recorded in detail and brought
to life with previously unpublished material from the Imperial War
Museum and the Royal Marines Museum.

Major-General Julian Thompson joined the Royal Marines at the
age of eighteen, serving for thirty-four years. He led the 3rd Commando Brigade in the Falklands and was in the thick of the fighting.
He is now Visiting Professor in the Department of War Studies
at King's College, London, and is the author of nine other books
and editor of *The Imperial War Museum Book of Modern Warfare*.

'Major-General Thompson did more than most men to save
the Marines' very existence, and no one could have made
a better job of telling their stirring story'
**Max Hastings, *Evening Standard***

# MAX HASTINGS

## Armageddon

### The Battle for Germany 1944–45

PAN BOOKS

Max Hastings has researched archives in four countries and interviewed 170 witnesses to piece together the fascinating story of the climatic final months of the Second World War and the destruction of Hitler's Germany.

In this compelling study, the author addresses the big military and human questions and succeeds in offering a vivid account of what life was like in the battlefields, east and west, during the last eight months of the war.

'As a military historian Max Hastings has few equals'
***Times Literary Supplement***

'Max Hastings now stands in the first rank of
writers on modern war'
***Financial Times***

# MALCOLM BROWN

### The Imperial War Museum Book of

## The Somme

PAN BOOKS

The shadow of the Somme has lain across the twentieth century. For many it is the ultimate symbol of the folly and futility of war. Others see it as a hallmark of heroic endeavour and achievement.

This book offers a remarkably fresh perspective on the bitterly fought 1916 campaign; it also describes the later battles of the Somme in the Great War's final year, 1918. Using hitherto unpublished evidence from the archives of the Imperial War Museum, it tells its powerful and dramatic story through the letters and diaries of those who were there.

Distinguished military historian Malcolm Brown has woven the many and varied accounts by well over a hundred participants – mainly British, but with not a few Germans – into a rich tapestry of experience.

'Admirable . . . If you can buy only one book on the Somme, it should be Malcolm Brown's powerful and scholarly account'
**Richard Holmes, *Times Educational Supplement***

## OTHER PAN BOOKS

## AVAILABLE FROM PAN MACMILLAN

**JULIAN THOMPSON**
THE ROYAL MARINES                     0 330 37702 7    £10.99

**MAX HASTINGS**
ARMAGEDDON                            0 330 49062 1    £9.99

**MALCOLM BROWN**
The Imperial War Museum Book of
   THE SOMME                          0 330 49206 3    £8.99
The Imperial War Museum Book of
   THE WESTERN FRONT                  0 330 48475 3    £7.99

---

All Pan Macmillan titles can be ordered from our website,
www.panmacmillan.com, or from your local bookshop
and are also available by post from:

**Bookpost, PO Box 29, Douglas, Isle of Man IM99 1BQ**
Credit cards accepted. For details:
Telephone: +44 (0)1624 677237
Fax: +44 (0)1624 670923
E-mail: bookshop@enterprise.net
www.bookpost.co.uk

*Free postage and packing in the United Kingdom*

Prices shown above were correct at the time of going to press.
Pan Macmillan reserve the right to show new retail prices on covers
which may differ from those previously advertised in the text
or elsewhere.